*f*P

Every *Breath* You *Take*

A True Story of Obsession, Revenge, and Murder

Ann Rule

The Free Press

New York · London
Toronto · Sydney · Singapore

THE FREE PRESS
A Division of Simon & Schuster, Inc.
1230 Avenue of the Americas
New York, NY 10020

Photo Credits:
Author's collection: 1–22, 28, 34, 35, 38, 45
John Davenport: 39, 46
Police photo: 23, 24, 25, 26, 27, 29, 30, 31, 32, 33, 44
Leslie Rule: 36, 37, 40, 41, 42, 43

THE FREE PRESS and colophon are trademarks
of Simon & Schuster, Inc.

For information regarding special discounts for bulk purchases,
please contact Simon & Schuster Special Sales:
1-800-456-6798 or business@simonandschuster.com

Manufactured in the United States of America

10   9   8   7   6   5   4   3   2   1

Library of Congress Cataloging-in-Publication Data Is Available

ISBN 0-7432-0296-1

FOR SHEILA AND HER CHILDREN, WHO MEANT
MORE TO HER THAN LIFE ITSELF:

Stevie, Daryl, Frankie, Joey, Timmy, and Courtney
With the hope and belief that their lives will be
Happy and successful and forever influenced
By the memory of her love.

____Acknowledgments____

As I researched this book, I ventured into cities where I had never been before. Were it not for the graciousness and cooperation of so many representatives of law enforcement and the justice system, I could never have unearthed the details that follow. A trial reveals only part of any case. After the trial is over, I always try to learn more about the personalities involved and the back stories that make the case complete. My sincere thanks go to the Texas Rangers; the Sarasota County, Florida, Sheriff's Office; the Florida State Attorney's Office; the FBI (San Antonio Office); the San Antonio Police Department; the U.S. Attorney's Office, Western District of Texas; the Bexar County District Attorney's Office; the U.S. Marshal's Office (San Antonio); and the Honorable Edward Prado, U.S. District Judge, Western District of Texas.

Dozens of private citizens' lives were touched by Sheila Bellush or Allen Blackthorne. Somehow they found me—or I found them—often through the Internet. Their memories added dimension to Sheila's story. I cannot thank them enough: Lisa and Carl Glenn, Sheldon "Guy" Van Houte, Bruce, Randy, and Nick Van Houte, Rick and Kerry Bladorn, Gene and Don Smith, Stevie and Daryl Bellush, Debbie and Tom Oliver, Mary Fenlon, "MariMargaret," "Mysterybabyluv," Effie Woods, Jim Bingham, Susan Glenny, Susan Hedding, Pam Harrell, Kelly McGonigal, Mary Jeffus, Barbara Lilly, Wayne Cannon, Tracy Ray, Glyn Poage, D'Ann Wernick, and "Dr. Susie."

As I often say, my readers choose the subjects for my books. My mailbox was full of suggestions and help postmarked from Florida to Texas: Irene Lewis, Jolie Green, Carla Sue Baker, Dori Donovan, Alice "Bonnie" Bonbright, Susan Brandenburg, Judy McDonald, Patsy Asher, Sherry and Mike Shefman, Joanne Cotter, Julie Reynolds, Barbara Koch, Anne Meyer, Glenna Austin, Angie Semple, Courtney Semple, Kim Ferguson, Rita Herron, and Mary Wehmeyer.

And more thanks to my fellow media bench warmers at Allen Blackthorne's San Antonio trial: Kim Dean, WWSB-TV, Sarasota, Carey Codd, SSN6, Sarasota, Leanora Minai, St. Petersburg Times, Isabel Mascarenas, WTSP-TV, St. Petersburg, Paul Venema, KSAT-TV, San Antonio, Mike Zientek, KENS-TV, San Antonio, Brandy Ralston, KENS-TV, Jose Luis Alverdi, Jr., KVTV-TV San Antonio, Shari St. Clair, KTSA-TV, San Antonio, Tom Spaulding, Sarasota Herald-Tribune, Maro Robbins, San Antonio Express-News, Jackie Barron, WFLA-TV, Bob Stewart, *People* magazine, Loydean Thomas, Associated Press and Brigitte Woosley, sketch artist, Dallas.

To my longtime "first reader:" Gerry Brittingham Hay, and my good friends Shirley Hickman, Donna Anders, Tamra Corlis, Ethel Mickelson and Marni Campbell. They all helped me leap across the finish line with a very large manuscript in my arms.

My core team, my constant supporters, advisers and gentle critics have seen me through for many years. With gratitude and love, I salute my editors Fred Hills and Burton Beals, editoral assistant Frances Tsay, and my agents—Joan and Joe Foley in New York City, and Ron Bernstein in Beverly Hills. I'm also happy to have a wonderful new publisher at The Free Press: Martha Levin, and a great publicity team: Carisa Hays and Jenny Dworkin.

EVERY BREATH YOU TAKE

Every move you make . . .
I'll be watching you

—SONG LYRIC, STING

Cast of Characters

SHEILA'S FAMILY

Verma Gene Smith: Sheila's mother, born to Clennis Pearl and Charles A. Williams in Biloxi, Mississippi. Clennis later married Julius Pettus.

Gene's half sisters: Julie, Betty, and Teresa. Brother: Charles, Jr.

Gene's three husbands: Duane Anderson, Francis Anthony Walsh, Jr., and Don Smith.

Gene's children: Donny and Danny Anderson, Mary Catherine, Sheila Leigh, Kelly Anne and Kerry Brigit Walsh.

Sheila Leigh Walsh: Married to Allen Van Houte (later Blackthorne), two children: Stevie Leigh and Daryl Leigh.

Married to Jamie Bellush, four children: Timmy, Joey, Frankie, and Courtney.

Kerry Brigit Walsh: Married to Rick Bladorn, four children: Kelly, Ryan, Christopher, and Patrick.

SHEILA'S ASSOCIATES

Sue Tuffiash, Lisa and Carl Glenn, Effie Woods, Luke Soules.

ALLEN'S FAMILY

Karen Higley*, Allen's mother, born to Elva and the Reverend Zachariah Higley* near Pendleton, Oregon. Stepfather, Austin Alford.

Karen's sister: Violet. Half siblings: Debbie Alford Oliver and Leroy Alford.

Karen's husbands: Sheldon Van Houte, Melvin Schafer, Bill Cook, and Jim Freeman. Her children: Allen, Gregory, Peggy, Randy, Brian, and Linda.

Sheldon "Guy" Van Houte, Allen's father.

Allen's paternal grandfather: Robert Van Houte, Stanfield, Oregon.

Guy's sisters: Carol, Lydia, Gladys, Joan, Susan.

Guy's wives: Karen, Jeannette, Suzanne, and Chris.

Guy had nine children, including: Allen, Bruce, Randy, Nick, Michael, and Sheldon Junior.

Allen Van Houte Blackthorne's wives: Ellen, Mary, Sheila, and Maureen. Children with Sheila: Stevie Leigh and Daryl Leigh. Children with Maureen: Brandon and Jacob.

ALLEN'S ASSOCIATES

Daniel Rocha, former golf champion, sometime bookie, living in San Antonio, Texas. Wife Eva, three sons.

Sammy Gonzales, employed in a pro shop at a driving range in San Antonio, Texas.

Joey Del Toro, a football star in high school, college dropout, and fitness trainer, living in Corpus Christi and Austin, Texas.

Patricia Aday, housewife and mother, close family friend.

Ray Cevallos, golfing buddy, San Antonio businessman.

Rick Speights, golfing buddy, Danny Rocha's neighbor.

Tom Oliver, uncle and occasional business partner.

INVESTIGATORS

In Sarasota, Florida: Captain Jerry Eggleston, Lt. Ron Albritton and Detective Chris Iorio, Detective Chris Hallisey, Sarasota County Sheriff's Office. Forensic Technicians Lisa Lanham, Lt. Bruce Whitehead, Corporal William Kuchar, and Bob Creager. Serologist Peter Tsingalles, Ballistics Expert Terrance LaVoy. Patrol Officers Todd Thurow and Chris Laster. Paramedic Brian Balance. Sarasota Fire Department: Hoyt Williams, Jr., and Brian Balance.

In San Antonio, Texas: Texas Ranger Lt. Gary De Los Santos, Texas Ranger Lt. Ray Cano, Texas Ranger Sgt. John Martin, Texas Ranger Sal Abreo, and Texas Ranger Analyst Melanie Schramm. FBI Special Agent Michael Appleby, and San Antonio Police Detectives Richard Urbanek and Jesse Salazar. Bexar County District Attorney's investigator Buster Birch.

In Eagle Pass, Texas: Texas Ranger Brooks Long, and Texas Ranger Israel Pacheco.

In Austin, Texas: Austin Police detective Manny Fuentes, Texas Ranger Sgt. Joe Hutson, and Texas Ranger James Denman.

PROSECUTORS

In Sarasota, Florida: Florida: State Attorneys Charlie Roberts and Henry Lee, Sarasota County District Attorney Earl Mooreland.

In San Antonio, Texas: U.S. Attorney Bill Blagg, First Assistant U.S. Attorney John Murphy, and Assistant U.S. Attorney Richard Durbin. Bexar County District Attorney Susan Reed, and Chief Criminal Deputy Prosecutor Michael Bernard.

DEFENSE ATTORNEYS

Richard Lubin, Kurt Volker, David Botsford, Jack Pytel, Roy Barrera, Jr., Lori Bendseil, Roy Perez, Pat Stollmeier, Clint Glenny, John Curney, Jack McGill, Anthony Nicholas, and Gerald Goldstein.

JUDGES

Frank Montalvo, Pat Boone, Nancy Donellan, Edward Prado, and Judy Goldman.

Author's Note

IN MY THREE DECADES of writing about actual crimes, only once have I been personally involved in a case before I wrote about it. That, of course, was the story of Ted Bundy, who had been my partner at Seattle's Crisis Clinic a few years before he was exposed as a merciless serial killer. During the years I knew him, I had no more knowledge of the man behind the "mask" than anyone else who interacted with him. Indeed, I had a contract to write a book about an unknown killer—my first book contract—only to find out I would be writing about my friend.

Now, twenty years after that almost incomprehensible coincidence, another singular circumstance has touched me, making this book much more than the recounting of a tragedy that echoes and re-echoes in the lives of so many people. In a sense, I was chosen by the victim herself to tell her story, even though we never spoke, never met, and when I read about her fate, I had no reason to believe that we had any connection at all.

Her name was Sheila Bellush, and she was the age of my daughters. The premonition that haunted her for the last ten years of her life finally found her in Florida. Before that, she lived in San Antonio, Texas, and in Hawaii. I had never been to those places. My home territory has been the northwest since the mid-'50s—Oregon and then Washington.

My father's lifelong wish was to have a homestead in Oregon, a house high on a hill that overlooked trees, fields, and rivers. He found his beloved forty acres south of Salem, Oregon. For the last thirty years of their lives, my parents lived there on a ranch where the only sounds beyond the wind in the fir trees were the cries of hawks and eagles and the occasional cougar. It was such an obscure part of Oregon that few people had ever heard of it. I never lived there myself; I had long since moved up to Seattle.

Years after my parents were gone, but only two miles away from that ranch, a young couple found their perfect section of earth to build on. They were patching together their lives after three years of horror and bereavement, and a decade of dread before that. The wife had a number of missions to accomplish, and one of them was to find me.

She was Sheila Bellush's sister. When we finally met, she told me that she had tried many avenues to locate me, unaware of how easy it really was. Had she only called information in Seattle, she could have obtained my office phone number. In January 2000 I received an e-mail signed with her name; I learned later it was really her husband who wrote to me because his wife had grown discouraged when her efforts brought only dead ends.

Sheila's sister told me they were determined to try one last time, and then give up because they didn't know where else to go. Fortunately, she found me on the Internet, and I wrote back to her immediately.

"Ten years ago," she said, "when Sheila ended her marriage, she told me, 'If anything ever happens to me, promise me that you will see that there is an investigation.'"

Her sister promised.

There was more: seemingly a throwaway remark said half in jest. It happened that Sheila Bellush was watching the miniseries of my book Dead by Sunset *in the fall of 1995. Recognizing something in the character of a man accused of murder, she called her sister Kerry Bladorn and asked her to turn on her television set. "Remember what I told you about what to do if anything happened to me?" Sheila asked, and Kerry said she did. "And now promise me one more thing," Sheila said. "That if I'm not here, you will find Ann Rule and have her write my story."*

Again Sheila's sister promised. I learned later that Sheila had asked a number of her friends to find me if anything happened to her. And so I face an awesome project; I have been given a huge responsibility by a young woman who once read my books. After so many years this is the first time a victim has chosen me to tell the story of her life—and death—long before her premonition of disaster came true. I owe her the truth and the compassion of those who read this book. I owe her a voice when she no longer has one.

For a long time I have felt a kind of "presence" of the people I write about, much in the way homicide detectives come to know the murder victims they strive to avenge. But never, never have I honored a commitment urgently foisted upon me by a woman who was a complete stranger, and who has become as familiar to me as someone in my own family.

So this is for Sheila. I hope I get it right.

PART ONE

November 1997

_____ *Chapter One* _____

FRIDAY, NOVEMBER 7, 1997, was an ordinary day in Sarasota, Florida—or so it seemed. It was a weekday, and the morning began with the sun burning golden in an azure sky, but as one enthusiastic resident remarked, "The sun is always shining, and every day is beautiful in Sarasota. It took me a while to realize that I didn't have to take advantage of the days the sun shone the way I used to do in Connecticut; I could stay inside and read because there would always be another perfect day . . . and another . . . and another."

But later on this November day, clouds moved in over Sarasota. They were a peculiar leaden gray-purple shading to black, full of unpredictable electrical impulses that made one's hair stand on end. It was going to rain, but it wouldn't be a soft rain; it would surely be rain that thudded against the earth with a vengeance, forcing trees and bushes to the ground with the sheer weight of water, pounding the grass flat.

The entrance to the Gulf Gate subdivision was flanked by sweeping buff-colored brick walls bearing its name, but that was the limit of Gulf Gate's ostentation. In November the jacaranda trees planted there four decades ago were a froth of peach-colored blossoms, so lovely that they could not be real. Many of the summer flowers were faded, save some bougainvillea, and residents planted petunias and

The names of some individuals in this book have been changed. Such names are indicated by an (*) the first time each appears in the narrative.

impatiens to carry them through the winter until the late summer sun's molten heat fried them.

Once a family neighborhood where children played, Gulf Gate was home now to many older couples and widows, who kept their shades drawn and hired yardmen to mow their lawns and prune their glossy-leafed trees into round orbs that looked like green plastic. Gulf Gate was close enough to Bee Ridge Road and I-75 for easy shopping and access to downtown Sarasota, but it was quiet, the streets hushed and almost free of traffic in the middle of a weekday. More often than not, there was no one walking a dog, or even peering out at the street from behind jalousie windows, those windows whose very name originates in the French word for jealousy—"to see without being seen." But few of the residents watched from their cool rooms, because there was nothing to see outside.

One woman who lived in Gulf Gate *was* watchful, almost unconsciously moving often to the front windows of her home to scan the street for a strange vehicle or for someone she didn't recognize approaching her house. She had good reason to be leery, although she and her husband had taken every precaution to keep their address secret.

Most of the homes in Gulf Gate were owner-occupied, not lavish but very comfortable L-shaped ramblers, painted in the soft pastels of the Florida gulf coast, peach and pink and even lavender—sunrise and sunset colors. Many had Florida rooms and swimming pools to make up for Gulf Gate's distance from Sarasota Bay. Although the neighborhood was far away from the beach, the November air was usually drenched with the salty-clean smell caught in the wind as it raced east toward the Atlantic Ocean.

MUCH like the rest of Gulf Gate, Markridge Road was a wide, tree-lined street with single-story houses set on small, perfectly groomed lots. The white rambler with the yellow door and matching shutters in the 3100 block had once been the cherished home of an elderly couple. By 1997 they were both dead, leaving their house and its furnishings to their son. Most of the time he lived in a northern state and rented out the Markridge house. He had changed nothing; the place was frozen in a time warp with furnishings that were modern three decades earlier. "All the furniture, even the knickknacks, dated back to the sixties," one former renter recalled. "But there was a warmth about that house. Everything was still there, even their old sheet music and books, just the way they left it. We enjoyed that when we lived there."

The couches and chairs reflected the tastes of another time, but they were comfortable. The appliances were decades old too. The refrigerator was avocado green and the stove bright yellow—but they worked. The phone bolted to the kitchen wall above the dishwasher had a rotary dial. It took a lot longer to make a call than a push-button phone, but until November 7 that was merely inconvenient and not disastrous.

THE young couple who moved into 3120 Markridge Road in September 1997 had the look of dependable tenants, and they seemed to be pleased with the house even though they had six children and would have to squeeze to fit everyone in. They said they'd moved from Texas when the husband got a big promotion and they needed someplace to live in a hurry. Looking at their adorable bunch of toddlers, the landlord couldn't say no to them. He decided he could forgo occupying his parents' house for one winter.

The new renters had an excellent credit history, and they were attractive. Jamie Bellush was big and burly with the wide grin and the innate charm of a seasoned salesman. His wife, Sheila, was delicately pretty, very tiny and blond. Jamie did most of the talking, while Sheila seemed a little nervous. Well, the landlord figured, she had reason to be, with all those children to care for. The toddlers were winsome and totally captivating, and it was obvious that their parents adored them. The older girls' names didn't seem to fit them. The older sister, thirteen, was called Stevie, and she hovered over the babies as if she was a second mother to them. The other sister was a year younger, and her name was Daryl. Odd. Why would anyone give boys names to two very pretty girls?

Jamie Bellush explained that they were in the process of building a much larger home in Sarasota, so they could make do in cramped quarters until their house was finished in the spring.

No one in Sarasota knew that the couple had left a dream house 1200 miles behind them in San Antonio. It had been their ideal house in a wonderful neighborhood, so large that the Markridge rental would fit inside three times over. They had barely had a chance to live in it when they felt a desperate urgency to move. And move they had, under cover of darkness.

Only a handful of people in San Antonio knew where Jamie and Sheila and their six children were. They agreed it was best to tell no one except for their closest friends and relatives, including the couple who helped them move out of Texas in the dead of night. Sheila's family knew where they were in Sarasota and had their phone number, but not their street address. Maybe in time they could come out of hiding. It hurt Jamie and Sheila not to be in contact with so many people they loved, to contemplate holidays without those who were so important to them. Cutting off her life so abruptly was akin to cutting off her arm. Sheila only hoped that everyone understood that she had no choice.

Sarasota was a beautiful place to live, and thousands of people had chosen it because of that.

There was a magical blending of sea and land, merging so easily that it was difficult to see where Sarasota Bay ended and the sandy shoreline began. All the way south from Tampa, little lakes and rivers were mirrors reflecting the blue sky, and the soaring Sunshine Bridge rose like a giant roller-coaster over Tampa Bay. But it was dark when the Bellush convoy crossed it and they hadn't realized how high they were.

Had her circumstances been different Sheila would have loved the colorful history of Sarasota and the way the city embraced the arts. She still looked forward to exploring it with her girls and the babies when things were better. Although Ringling Brothers no longer wintered there, seventeen other circuses did and many circus folk lived there permanently. Ringling Brothers had thanked Sarasota with a wonderful art museum and a college.

There were sand castle contests, blues and jazz festivals, book fairs, local dramatic productions and Broadway plays on tour and the venerable Sarasota Opera House where the great Pavarotti once performed. Every season in Sarasota was packed with all manner of celebrations. Sheila loved to read and the new Sarasota library was huge and airy and filled with sculptures and soaring mobiles.

Marina Jack's in downtown Sarasota just off Route 41—also known as the Tamiami Trail—was the kind of restaurant Sheila would enjoy, with its circling staircase and magnificent water views. Someday, perhaps. For now, she and her younger children were entranced with simpler things like the tiny, tiny dust-colored lizards that darted from leaf to leaf and scuttled under bushes so quickly that they almost seemed to be figments of their imaginations. The cost of living was higher than in San Antonio; the rent on their house was a rather shocking $2300 a month. But Jamie and Sheila had chosen Sarasota because it might be a safe place to hide and, eventually, to start over.

One day they hoped to be able to be in contact with the people they loved, but for the moment they couldn't do that. They could give their address to very few people, and even *that* was a commercial mailing service, a "suite" that was really a locked mailbox in a mall.

They might as well have been in a witness relocation program. Although both Sheila and Jamie came from loving, extended families, they were essentially alone.

James Joseph Bellush was an ex-marine, still saddled with his childhood nickname in his mid-thirties, although he no longer looked like a "Jamie." He looked more like a football linebacker. Jamie was a detail man—a pharmaceutical salesman for Pfizer, and he was very good at it, an asset to the company. The very nature of his career meant that he often had to travel away from home to call on physicians in their offices along the west coast of Florida. It wasn't hard to sell Pfizer products, especially with the emergence of Viagra, but he still had to make his rounds. Jamie had been with Pfizer for a long time, and when he asked for a transfer out of San Antonio, the company accommodated him and gave him the Florida territory, a promotion. They even arranged to buy his house in Boerne, Texas, for the man who would replace him.

Sheila Bellush was thirty-five. She had worked in attorneys' offices since she was eighteen and had held an extremely responsible position in the law offices of Soules and Wallace in San Antonio for years. But now she was a full-time mom; there was no question at all of her going to work outside the home. She had more than enough to do. If she was discouraged at the prospect of fitting everyone into the Markridge house and being alone with their children while Jamie was on the road, she didn't complain. She did what she had to do, hoping always that their lives would become safer and calmer as time passed.

Sheila had no friends in Sarasota when they arrived in September, but she was working on that. She had always had friends, and it saddened her to have to leave so many behind without an explanation, although she suspected most of them knew why she had fled. Deeply religious, Sheila and Jamie were attending services at the Sarasota Baptist Church. It was a huge church with an active outreach program, and they were made welcome there. It was a start. They were rebuilding their lives, and she knew she could make new friends.

AND so November 7 *was* an ordinary day, but only in the context of Sheila Bellush's life. In truth there were no ordinary days for Sheila; she had lived with fear so long that it seeped like acid into any fleeting serenity she might attain, corroding her thoughts, sending jets of adrenaline through her veins. No matter how the sun shone or how balmy the winds wafting off the bay, Sheila never really felt safe unless she was inside the house with the doors and windows tightly locked against the world. Those who didn't know her well wondered if she might be just a little paranoid. Those who knew her story understood, but they were far away and didn't know how to find her. It was safer that way—safer for them and safer for Sheila, Jamie, and their six children.

Just two months earlier Jamie and Sheila had lived in Boerne, Texas, a countrylike suburb northwest of San Antonio, where they owned their wonderful new home. Now it seemed as though they had never lived there at all. Maybe it had been too perfect to last.

But Sheila still had Jamie, and he loved her and protected her and their babies. He had begun the paperwork to adopt Stevie Leigh and Daryl Leigh, Sheila's teenage daughters by her former husband, Allen. They had their difficulties trying to get naturally rebellious teenagers and a longtime bachelor on the same wavelength, but Sheila believed things would work out.

On November 7, 1997, Jamie was on the road south of Sarasota, planning to visit several doctors' offices for Pfizer. It was important that he familiarize himself with his new territory and potential clients in west Florida. But it was Friday, and he had promised to be home long before it was dark. They would have the weekend together. Sheila had no doubt that they would spend the rest of their lives together.

She was half right.

STEVIE Bellush, thirteen, was petite and small-boned like her mother, although she had her father's facial features and his dark hair. It was not difficult to say where she got her superior intelligence, because both Sheila and Allen, her father, were very smart. Stevie and Daryl, who was blond like Sheila, had always excelled in school and in sports. But they had been through a lot for anyone as young as they were; their childhoods hadn't been easy.

Now Stevie was in a wonderful mood as she hurried home from junior high school shortly before 4:00 P.M. that Friday. "I heard that a boy I liked was going to ask me out," she remembered. "And I wanted to tell my mom."

The front door was unlocked, and that was strange; her mother was adamant that they all lock the doors when they left, and even when they came back in after taking the garbage out. She didn't have a lot of rules, but that was one she insisted on. So it was unusual for the front door to be unlocked.

Afterward Stevie would remember that she couldn't make sense out of the first thing she saw when she walked into the front room. All of the babies were standing in the hallway crying as if their hearts would break. Her mother never let them cry; she always picked them up and soothed them. For some reason they had no clothes on—nothing but the little life vests they wore when they were in the swimming pool in the Florida room. Their faces were swollen from sobbing. Stevie thought they must have been crying for a long time.

What made the least sense to Stevie were the funny patterns of dark red specks on the babies' skin, some in their hair and on their feet. Some of them had swaths of the same color, as if someone had dipped a brush in red paint and then daubed at their flesh.

Shock and disbelief often block the mind from accepting what the eyes perceive. Even so, Stevie's dread was so great that there was a thunderous pounding in her ears. She patted the wailing toddlers absently and went looking for her mother, calling out for her as she moved through room after room.

Her own voice seemed to echo and bounce back from the walls. Stevie went out in the backyard and found no one there. She skirted the swimming pool in the Florida room and saw the babies' diapers inside their plastic pants on the table beside the pool, still shaped like their bodies. That wasn't strange; her half brothers and sister swam naked. If their diapers were still dry, her mom just put them back on after they swam. But she hadn't done that. All of their little bottoms were bare under their life jackets. Stevie couldn't figure out what was going on. She kept calling for her mother, and no one answered.

There was a funny smell in the house too—a hard, sweet iodiney-metallic odor, a smell Stevie could not recognize. . . .

_____Chapter Two _____

IT WAS ONLY by the purest luck, a perfect synchronicity, that Sheila Blackthorne and Jamie Bellush met in the first place. But the same could have been said about the way Sheila met Allen, and her first marriage had nothing pure or perfect about it. Maybe it was all a crapshoot, and if a marriage worked, it was probably because both partners tried hard to make it work. Sheila Walsh Van Houte Blackthorne Bellush had been blessed with a quick mind, beauty, and a personality that drew people to her. But she shared with her mother a curse that seemed to dictate she would not find happiness in love.

Sheila was Verma Gene's fourth child. Verma Gene Williams, called Gene, was raised in Biloxi, Mississippi, in the Great Depression and, like the majority of children of her generation, learned early to dread poverty. Clennis Pearl Underwood Williams and Charles A. Williams were not to be together long. Gene's father was murdered when she was only a little girl, stabbed to death, although she never really learned the circumstances of his murder. Later Clennis Pearl married Julius Pettus. Gene had a brother, Charles, Jr., and three half sisters: Julie, Betty, and Teresa. During the 1930s and the Second World War the Pettuses operated a trailer park. That was long before trailers were called mobile homes.

Gene grew up to be a pretty blue-eyed teenager with perfect features and fair, delicate skin that seemed almost transparent. She married Duane Anderson in the late '40's when she was only fifteen. Duane was in the army, and the Korean War loomed. Gene gave birth to two boys: Danny when she was seventeen, and then Donny. The marriage died partially of its own weight, but mostly because Gene was too young when she married Duane, and neither of them could deal with the responsibilities of real life. Everday probelems smothered any magic there might have been.

But Gene was a worker, and she took care of her boys. She grew up in Biloxi and Gulfport, twelve miles west along the gulf coast, and she felt at home there. She worked for years as a waitress and, after she was of age, as a bartender.

Gene's second husband was exciting and their courtship very romantic. She met Francis Anthony Walsh, Jr., when he was stationed at Keesler Air Force Base in Biloxi, and she was a young divorcée with two little boys. Francis —"Frank"—was very handsome, a short muscular man, which made him ideally suited to his assignment as an air force fighter pilot. Born on Valentine's Day, 1940, Frank was from Westport, Connecticut, a different world from Verma Gene's life in Mississippi. At twenty he was a few years younger than Gene, but she was so attractive that it didn't matter to him, nor did he mind that she came with two little sons. Frank was often away, and when the Vietnam War came along, he went overseas and Gene prayed that he would come back to her. She kept working as a waitress. It was hard work, and her muscles ached and her feet hurt from long shifts.

Gene gave birth to four daughters while she was married to Frank Walsh. Mary Catherine was born first, in July 1961. Sheila Leigh was Gene's next baby. She was born on October 19, 1962, while Frank was stationed in Topeka. Sheila was such a tiny thing. Gene fussed over her, worried about her, and watched her sleep to be sure she was breathing. But Sheila had a feistiness even then. Gene thanked God that both her little blond daughters were healthy.

But when Gene's next baby, Kelly Anne, was born in November 1963, she had a serious valve defect in her heart and lived only nineteen days. "We buried her on the day that President Kennedy was shot," Gene would remember.

Gene cried for weeks and asked God why he had taken her baby away. She had always been somewhat histrionic, acting out her emotions when she was heartbroken or grief-stricken. Heaven knows, she sometimes thought she had more to bear than any three women. Gene's tragic losses kept anyone from criticizing her dramatic outbursts. That was just the way she was. Her first son, Donny, seemed to be as sensitive as she was.

As Frank worked his way up through the air force ranks to major, he remained as exciting as always, but he drank a great deal, and half the time he was flying somewhere far away. His service obligations meant he was gone most of the time, and he never seemed to be there when Gene needed comfort. And when he *was* around, she got pregnant, despite birth-control pills *and* an IUD. As time passed, Gene had to accept the fact that Frank was an alcoholic. She had seen enough drinkers when she tended bar to recognize the signs, but she avoided facing it until she had to. Even so, she still loved him.

Sometimes the Walshes traveled from base to base, leaving Mississippi behind for assignments in Kansas and South Dakota. Gene dealt with the rigors of government housing at Forbes Air Force Base, a SAC base for B-52s and tankers in South Dakota, and with raising four children alone when she found she was pregnant once again. She had taken precautions and thought that couldn't be possible, but the obstetrician on the base said it was true. In order for the baby to have a chance to survive, he removed her IUD, warning Gene that she would probably abort the baby, or, worse, it might be born blind or developmentally disabled.

Gene flew home to Mississippi to deliver her sixth child. Kerry Brigit was born in June 1967, another baby girl when Frank had hoped for a boy. But she was alive and perfectly normal. "She was the most beautiful baby I ever saw," Gene recalled.

Frank insisted on spelling her name the male way—Kerry instead of Carrie. Gene was just relieved that Kerry was healthy. She finally allowed herself to believe that *this* little girl was going to survive. Kerry had fiery red hair, and sometimes a temper to match. She could be stubborn too, but Kerry was never as relentlessly strong-willed as Sheila was.

Her big brother Danny refused even to hold Kerry for months. "She's gonna die too," he said, "and I don't want to get to know her."

Kerry didn't die. She had very little memory of living in South Dakota, but her mother told her she had fallen down the steps in her walker when she was six months old. "I just grabbed her up and headed for the infirmary," Gene said "And I ran in shouting, 'My baby . . . my baby!' It turned out she wasn't hurt at all."

Although Gene's younger daughters were five years apart in age, they would bond for life. Kerry would grow to be taller than Sheila, but they looked a great deal alike, one blond, one redheaded. Sheila had bobbed hair and a swath of freckles across her nose. She looked at the world with the same clear blue eyes her mother did, but as small as she was, Sheila was the one among all the kids with a backbone of steel.

Gene had a tough time disciplining Sheila. "One time she ran away—or made a big show of leaving home. She ran into the woods and hid," Gene remembered. "I had just worked two shifts, and I was exhausted. I knew she was in there, and I called to her to come out and all she would get was a scolding and not a whipping. She didn't budge. I told her that if I had to come in and get her, it would be worse, and she'd get a switching *and* three weeks' grounding. She finally came out, and I switched her legs with a branch switch all the way home. It didn't really hurt her—it didn't leave a mark or anything. She wouldn't cry, though. She just put her chin up."

That was Sheila. Where most girls cried, she just set her chin and kept going, refusing to let anyone know that she was sad or scared or intimidated. Even as a grown woman, when she barely reached five feet and weighed ninety-eight pounds, she had plans and dreams and refused to give up when almost anyone else in her position would have quit.

Sheila and Kerry were always into something, sometimes driving their mother to distraction but often making her smile. One time when Kerry was only about three, Donny, their older brother, came to her "laughing and laughing. That was before he got 'sick,' " Gene said. "He said, 'Come look at what these little girls are doing.' Well, they had stuffed the bras of their bathing suits with toilet paper to grow 'breasts.' "

Gene caught them parading down the street on their way to the corner store. She had to laugh in spite of herself. Kerry had the most imposing paper bosom, although she wasn't more than a little bit of a thing at the time.

Kerry idolized Sheila. "Whatever she touched, it turned out okay," she recalled. "We both had piano lessons, and Sheila played the piano beautifully, but I hid when the teacher came over. She used to watch the boys at football practice and say she was faster than they were. And she was. She could beat them all in a foot race—even when they had a head start. And she was a wonderful softball player, even though she was so tiny."

"I tried to see that my girls had everything basic they needed," Gene said. "I could remember how good it felt to have money to go up to the corner store and get a Moon Pie and an RC cola, and my girls had that too."

Gene had the two boys by her first marriage, and then the three girls by Frank, before she had any idea that he was having an affair with an Asian woman on Okinawa. Possibly he married too young and he was escaping the responsibility of being the father to five children before he was twenty-seven. Maybe he simply could not be true to one woman. From time to time Gene left him, but she came back. What else could she do? She loved him.

Gene left Frank twice more, vowing that she could not live with a man who drank. The third time, she didn't come back. Part of her still loved Frank Walsh, but she finally had to accept that he would always be a drinker. She divorced him. Nothing really changed. He stayed in touch almost as much as he had when they were married, and his little girls adored him.

Their father was an almost mythic figure who came flying in from some far-off place they could only imagine and doted on them completely while he was with them. He took them fishing and hiking and for fun trips. And then he was gone again, leaving Gene to administer discipline and take care of their more prosaic needs. Gene was only in her early thirties herself. It must have been difficult for her to see her ex-husband with their little girls and wonder if she had made the right choice in divorcing him.

GENE returned to Gulfport and worked at the Ramada Inn and the Round-Towner/Down-Towner. "I worked the breakfast and lunch shifts," she recalled, "until two p.m. Then I went home and fixed dinner for the kids, did some laundry, took a nap. After that, I went back in the evening to work banquets."

Gene kept up that grueling routine for years, but she didn't remember it as being that hard. "The cops used to toot their horns at me and wave," she said with a laugh. "I just knew everybody there. All of us girls who worked at the Round-Towner called ourselves Hank Schrader's Raiders after the man who owned the restaurant."

Down at the Broadwater Beach, the piano player always stopped whatever he was playing when she walked in. "He'd change over to

'Jean, Jean, you're young and alive, come out in the meadow, Jean' when he saw me," she remembered, smiling.

She met Don Smith at Keesler Air Force Base. Gene had never really dated anyone except military men, and the third man in her life was no exception. Like Frank Walsh, Don was an air force fighter pilot. He flew 254 missions in Vietnam in his navy Sky Raider. But Don Smith was about as opposite as a man could be from Frank Walsh. All the two men had in common was their short statures and their service careers. Don had raised two stepdaughters, and he had a son and a daughter of his own. He was as steady as a rock.

He was always there when Gene needed him, and that meant a lot to her. He loved her absolutely. Despite five children and the struggle to raise them, Gene was a very lovely young woman. She was still slender then and as pretty as her daughters were.

Don Smith welcomed Danny, Donny, Cathy, Sheila, and Kerry too, and he took on the role of a father happily. He was a little tougher on discipline than Frank was, but his conservative approach made the kids mind better.

Gene dated Don Smith for two and a half years, always warning him that she would never again marry a serviceman. If he wanted to marry her, he would have to retire from the air force.

"Don agreed," Kerry said later. "He was in the midst of retiring, and she was planning to marry him. I think she had gotten used to being taken care of and cherished. I call Don 'my dad' and my biological father 'my father.' Don is the one who raised me and the one I depended on."

Don took Kerry with him to get the marriage license in Pascagoula, and he and Gene were married on the base at Keesler on February 4, 1972.

Frank remarried, a woman named Barbara, but he still kept in touch with his girls. To Gene's chagrin—when she found out—he took Kerry to be baptized a Catholic without her mother's permission.

Gene and Don Smith, now retired from the air force, moved with their combined family to Chandler, Arizona, where Don realized his longtime dream of having a peach orchard. Don had grown up in Arizona, and his parents were there. Gene hated the Southwest and the baking heat. She often said, "I know I'll never go to hell because I've already lived through hell right here in Arizona!"

They went to the Mormon church, but Kerry ignored her runaway Catholic baptism and got on a bus gathering up youngsters for day camp at the Baptist church. "I loved it!" she said, laughing. "I hated the Mormon church."

Despite her fretting about the Arizona weather, Gene had made a wise decision when she married Don—for many reasons. She loved Don, of course, but even if she had stayed with Frank, she would not have been with him long. He started his last tour of duty in Vietnam on July 21, 1972. Five months later his fighter plane was shot down. It was two days before Christmas.

"Sheila probably would remember more about when our father was missing in action," Kerry said. "All I remember is that some men in uniform came to our house after dark and that my mother was crying. I wet the bed that night, and I hadn't wet the bed for a long time."

There were already a number of casualties in his unit when Frank Walsh was shot down as he banked low to wipe out an enemy anti-aircraft site. All they ever found of him were two teeth and his scorched flight card, and that was a long time later. His service number was 049303910, and his status became "Killed in Hostile Action—Died While Missing" long before that. He was only thirty-two when he died.

Both Sheila and Kerry took his death hard. Gene was distraught; it was something she had always feared, of course. In a sense she felt "widowed" rather than divorced from Frank Walsh. That feeling vanished when she received a letter from the Asian woman on Okinawa who told Gene that she had been Frank's mistress for many years—since long before their divorce. It was a cruel thing for the woman to do; it could not have eased her own sense of loss, and it hurt Gene.

Even so, when there was a memorial service for Francis Anthony Walsh, Gene sewed identical long pink dresses for Cathy, Sheila, and Kerry to wear with white shoes for the service. They posed for Don Smith's camera, their faces solemn, next to the white house the Smiths were renting in Chandler, shadows from rosebushes and trees dappling their dresses.

Gene's marriage to Don thrived. He was seven years older than she was, and he doted on her. No matter how down she got or how anxious, Don took it in stride. He was a good provider; he was a skilled architectural draftsman, working for an Arizona construction company, as well as tending his flourishing orchard. Now Gene finally had a chance to do her sewing and work on the crafts she enjoyed so much and for which she had such talent. A few years later the Smiths moved north, to Salem, Oregon. Don's boss had moved up to head Forest Homes out of Woodburn. The building business was booming in the Northwest, and his boss persuaded Don to transfer with him. With Gene so unhappy in Arizona, it didn't take much to get Don to accept the new job.

Even though Don and Gene were both used to the peripatetic service life, moving from the dry heat of Arizona to the soft gray rain that suffuses Oregon for much of the year was a tremendous change. Still, they liked Oregon, and the construction future there looked bright. Don had his air force pension to add to his salary, and they were doing fine. In 1997, he started his own construction business: Alpha Bravo Construction.

Salem is the capital of Oregon, watched over by a towering gold statue of a pioneer on the top of the Capitol Building. Set in the heart of the fertile Willamette Valley, Salem and Marion County produce bumper crops of cherries, strawberries, green beans, and roses. Roses line the parking strips, blooming from April until Christmas, but the skies are predominantly cloudy, and the rainy season is long and dreary.

Cathy, Sheila, and Kerry acclimated quickly. They attended school in Salem. Aside from visits to their Mississippi relatives, they never expected to leave Oregon.

A few years later, in the dark days of autumn 1978, Gene was to lose another child in November. As Donny moved through his teen years, his behavior changed imperceptibly. When he was sixteen, he went camping alone in the Arizona hills and came home deathly sick from something doctors could diagnose only as "similar to Lyme disease." Maybe his illness was causative or maybe it was only coincidental, but he was different somehow after that—moody and distant. More likely, he had inherited his father's manic depression. When Donny ran away from home, Don and one of Donny's paternal uncles agreed that it would be a good idea for him to go into the army, so Donny enlisted and was sent to boot camp at Fort Lewis, south of Tacoma, Washington.

The men in the family were sure that the service would make a man of Donny, but instead, it did terrible things to his psyche. Donny was already "weak," and Gene would refer to "before he got sick" and "after he got sick." Relatives recalled that he had a chemical imbalance, "just like his father."

When he was emotionally and physically abused by one of his commanding officers, Donny began to crack. He self-medicated with drugs and, unknown to anyone, built a homemade bomb. Donny was suicidal. He was stopped while driving erratically, and the bomb was found in his truck. His uncle, Jack Smith, who worked at Boeing in Seattle, went down to Fort Lewis to see what he could do to help Donny, and it was obvious to everyone that the boy didn't belong in the army. He was released on a Section Eight and declared unsuitable for service. He headed back to Arizona far more disturbed than he had been before he enlisted.

"It was the day before Thanksgiving, 1978," Kerry said. "Donny rode his bicycle more than twenty miles to the VA hospital closest to Scottsdale. They said they had no resources to treat him, and they sent him away."

Donny Anderson was twenty-one years old, depressed, and anxious. The day after Thanksgiving his brother, Danny, came home to the apartment they shared in Scottsdale and found Donny dead of a gunshot wound.

Gene had now lost two children during the month of November. She began to dread the eleventh month. First her baby girl and now her beloved dark-haired, brown-eyed son. Both gone just as winter began.

"My mother just kind of shut down, somehow, after Donny died," Kerry said.

SHEILA Walsh went to Sprague High School in Salem, taking college prep courses. She had seen her mother work double shifts as a waitress, and she vowed to get an education so that she would always have something she could count on.

Sheila asked a good-looking student to be her science partner, and he accepted readily. "Science happened to be my worst subject," Rick Bladorn said, "and Sheila was smart. I was relieved when she chose me."

Sheila got excellent grades, and she was named to the National Honor Society. She and Rick had known each other for three years before her little sister, Kerry, met him. They had already graduated when Kerry met Rick. She didn't approve of the man Sheila was dating at the time and set about playing Cupid, a role she was ill suited for. Never subtle, Kerry's intent was transparent, and Sheila realized what she was up to right away.

Rick was tall and handsome, but, most important, he was a really nice guy—not goody-goody nice but basically decent. When Kerry chose him for Sheila, she was sure she could convince her sister, with enough hints and carefully choreographed meetings, that Rick was the perfect man for her. Although they were good friends, there never was any spark between Rick and Sheila. Unfortunately for Kerry's plan, Sheila wasn't the least bit interested in Rick. She preferred to date men who had a bit of danger about them. Rick didn't feel any particular attraction to Sheila either. Both of them thought it was humorous that thirteen-year-old Kerry was so determined to look after her big sister that she tried to select her future husband.

A few years later it was Kerry who went to a party at the house where Rick lived with a couple of other young men. She was initially attracted to Rick's roommates; she would have wagered good money that *she* would never fall in love with Rick.

GENE Smith had married for the first time in her mid-teens and had teenage girls of her own before she knew it. Sometimes she clashed with Cathy, Sheila, and Kerry—especially Kerry. Gene had incipient diabetes, a disease that would have more and more impact on her life. She had been married to three different men over more than three decades, and finally she had found the right one. Endlessly raising children wore her down. She wanted time to live peacefully with Don and work on her handicraft hobbies—making her exquisite dolls and ceramics.

The Smiths bought a big old house in Salem at 1515 Liberty N.E., and Gene opened a doll shop in the detached garage. She made them herself, starting with the molds, and they were delicate works of art. She taught doll classes too, and attracted eager students. Working with fine fabrics, lace, paint, and wigs, Gene created dolls that were much sought-after. She and Don hoped someday to be able to travel as well.

By the time Sheila was a senior in high school, Gene was ready for her older daughters to be on their own. And the more they defied her, as all teenage girls defy their mothers, the more ready she was. As for Don, he wanted whatever Gene wanted; she was the one who always spoke her mind vehemently, and Don was the placator. His calmness was the reverse of her emotional intensity, and their marriage worked despite that or, more likely, *because* of that.

Cathy moved out first, married, and had two children. Sheila took a business course after high school at Chemeketa Community College in Salem and found a job with one of the top law firms with the best criminal defense attorneys in town: Brown, Burt, Swanson, Lathan, Alexander, and McCann. She still intended to go back to college and get a four-year degree, even though she loved her job. She might even go to law school herself.

Sheila's firm was deeply involved in a case that had national coverage in 1978 because of its landmark implications: Could a husband rape his own wife? The *Greta Rideout v. John Rideout* case sought to prove that a man could indeed be held criminally responsible for forcing himself on his legal wife against her will. John Rideout was acquitted, but the story spawned an intense movie starring Linda Hamilton, and when Sheila read the files, she found the question compelling.

Sheila proved very adept at handling the details in a law firm, and her bosses liked her. Kerry sometimes visited Sheila at work and was so impressed by the way Sheila answered the phone that she, too, memorized the firm name, just the way Sheila said it: "Brown-BurtSwansonLathanAlexanderandMcCann." Almost two decades later she could rattle the names off at will.

Sheila always had interesting stories to tell about things that happened at work. Of course, a lot of cases were run of the mill, but there were other clients besides John Rideout whose faces were familiar because of blanket coverage in the newspapers and television.

One day a muscular and handsome former star athlete named Randy Woodfield was brought through the waiting room at the law firm where Sheila worked. Kerry recalled that he made Sheila's skin crawl. "Randy Woodfield was the I-5 Killer* and he was arrested for shooting two women in Salem and a whole bunch of rapes in California, Oregon and Washington. Sheila said he was very nice-looking, but he gave her the creeps."

Although she wanted to get her four-year degree, Sheila had long had dreams of finding the love of her life, just as her mother had. She was fascinated with the law for its own sake, but she also thought it might pave the way for the kind of life she envisioned. She didn't mind working hard, but she longed for romantic love and wanted to have a husband someday who made more than just a comfortable living. But she was young and in no tearing hurry, because she had college in her future.

"Sheila always loved *glamour*," Kerry said. "She wanted to be glamorous and live a glamorous life, but she wasn't really very sophisticated. Every once in a while, she'd get us both dolled up and have us pose for a professional photographer as if we were models. But that wasn't the real Sheila. It's hard to describe, but there was always something about Sheila that just drew people to her. It didn't matter if she was all fixed up or if her hair was a mess and she didn't have any makeup on. People noticed her and wanted to be around her. It was almost as if she was a magnet. She was happy and sparkling and fun to be with.

---

* *The I-5 Killer* by Ann Rule, pub. 1984, the case of a serial killer and rapist along Interstate 5 in the Northwest.

"Sheila always wanted a home and children. When she met Allen, she was only eighteen and he seemed like the ideal man."

He did indeed. Only the timing was wrong. If Sheila let herself fall in love with him, it would mean she would have to forgo college. But Allen Van Houte had worked hard to create an image that almost any young woman would find appealing, and he was still a work in progress. When Sheila met Allen in the law office where she worked, she was instantly attracted to him.

It was the fall of 1982, and Sheila had been out of high school only a year. She was as small as a child, but her figure was perfect, and she had long blond hair and a beautiful face with gentian-blue eyes and a leftover sprinkling of freckles on her nose. She looked up at the man that her boss was introducing to her and felt her heart lose its rhythm for an instant.

Allen Van Houte was a client. Her boss had handled his divorce. Allen didn't mention *which* divorce, and Sheila assumed he had been married only once. He was six feet two and as handsome as a movie star, at least to Sheila. He had a thick mop of almost black hair and compelling brown eyes. Allen dressed impeccably, and Sheila had the distinct impression that he was a very successful businessman, even though he was only twenty-seven. Of course she said yes when he asked her out.

Allen knew all the best places to go in Salem, and he dropped names of exclusive country clubs and upscale restaurants where she had never been. He showed her his stereo store, and Sheila was impressed. He explained that he'd been forced to go through bankruptcy because his ex-wife Mary had "taken him to the cleaners." But he was really only reorganizing, and she shouldn't worry about it.

His divorce appeared to have been devastating to Allen. He was very sad when he spoke of his failed marriage. Mary had two children by a former husband when she wed Allen, and he told Sheila that he had tried so hard to be a good father to them, but his efforts were never enough for Mary. She took everything they had in the divorce, "even our house."

Sheila knew very little about Allen. He said that he was a native Oregonian, but revealed almost nothing about his early life. She assumed she would learn more when he began to feel totally comfortable and trusting with her. Now, on his own, he seemed to be a man who lived in the moment. After what he had been through, she could understand that he was hurt and hesitant to confide in anyone.

He was rebounding from the pain; Allen didn't want to dwell on the past, and he seemed to make his life up as he went along. He wanted to have fun, and he could be hilarious with his wit. Sheila found in Allen all the glamour she had longed for.

She was madly in love. Despite what he had been through, Allen was charming and funny and loving. By their third date Sheila knew she was going to marry him. He didn't even need to propose; it was a given that they would be together. She could hardly wait to be Mrs. William Allen Van Houte.

GENE was in her late forties and Don Smith in his mid-fifties when Sheila met Allen. They were very impressed with him too. He seemed to be everything they could hope for in a possible son-in-law. He was full of plans, and he was more than willing to include them as he expanded his business options. Yes, he told them frankly, he had just filed for bankruptcy, but he hadn't lost his stereo store in his divorce, and he knew he could make it work. When Allen spoke about big business and franchises and making millions of dollars, Gene and Don had no doubt he was going to do it.

Allen explained that Capitol Hi-Fi and Video Rental was really very successful. He had a great location in Pringle Park Plaza, the small mall next to the Salem Public Library and the Salem police headquarters. And that was only his flagship store. If he moved ahead with his plans for expansion, he promised the Smiths that he would offer them a share of the business.

Since Allen had lost his home in the Ironwood area of South Salem when Mary took it in the divorce, Don and Gene suggested that he might as well move into their home. He and Sheila were planning their wedding, and there was no reason he should be paying rent somewhere when they had plenty of room.

Don and Gene were doing well financially, and their credit was excellent. Don had a good job at Furrows, a building-supply company, as well as his pension from the air force. They could well afford to invest in Allen's store.

"He told my folks that he wanted a mom and dad, something he'd never really had," Kerry said. "He said he loved his grandparents on his mother's side, but that wasn't the same. He wanted to be my parents' son. He would give them a forty-nine percent share in his renamed Stereo World and he would keep fifty-one percent."

That would protect them, Allen pointed out, as he would be the one taking on all the risk. As the major stockholder, *he* would be responsible for all debts. Gene and Don eagerly agreed to invest in Stereo World. They used the substantial equity they had in their home to open a line of credit for themselves and for Allen at the Commercial Bank in Salem. Any of the three of them could use that line of credit.

The building boom had hit a slump, and Don's new job didn't have quite the opportunities that he'd had in his own business, but he was doing all right. Still, the chance to join in Allen's enterprises had come at just the right time.

Allen *was* like another son to Gene and Don. Gene looked at him and saw a resemblance to her lost boy, Donny. He was dark and handsome the way Donny had been, and she felt motherly toward him. "But Allen couldn't handle you loving him," Gene said. "He got nervous if I showed him any affection."

Allen told Don that he had been a serviceman too, and that gave them a bond. "He said he was a second lieutenant in the army," Don recalled, "after his being in the ROTC at Stanford. That's where he said his college degree was from."

The Smiths gave Allen carte blanche to use their vehicles and Don's boats. He was practically a member of the family, and Sheila was so happy about marrying him. She was making plans for a beautiful ceremony in the Methodist church in Salem.

Kerry tried to be happy for Sheila, but she was the one member of the family who didn't think Allen was such a great catch. There was something about him that frightened her, something more than how mean he was when he teased her. But she didn't say anything; she knew that nobody was going to listen to a teenage girl's opinion.

_____Chapter Three_____

IT WAS TRUE that Allen didn't like to talk about the "bad times" behind him, and he had his own reasons for relegating his past to his past. William Allen Van Houte's birth, in June 1955, was not a particularly happy occasion for anyone, although he was a beautiful baby with a nascent brilliance that was apparent early on. His father, Sheldon "Guy" Van Houte, was only nineteen when Allen was born; his mother, Karen, was three years younger. Allen's intelligence was not a genetic surprise; on his father's side he came from a family of highly educated people. His great-grandfather came to America from Holland and both he and Allen's paternal great-grandmother were teachers in California.

Allen's father, Guy, was born in California on February 28, 1936.

His father, Robert Van Houte, took up the family career and was also a much admired educator. He eventually settled in tiny Stanfield, Oregon, after leaving Berkeley, California, with several stops in other Oregon cities and Alaska. Along the way Robert's first wife abandoned him and their two children. Guy was three years old when his mother left the family in 1939, and his sister, Carol, who was born in 1934, only a couple of years older.

Guy recalled that he was an ugly kid. He was wall-eyed in his right eye, and he had polio when he was a year old, which left one foot turned at right angles to his leg. "My foot was turned completely sideways, and I had a brace I had to drag around on my left. I also had buckteeth, and I had all kinds of cosmetic oral surgery later. I was often in the Shriners' Hospital in Portland, and boy, the other kids were mean to me—really cruel. I was kind of an ugly duckling. I had no mama—and no daddy, not really. I would be riding my tricycle down Eighty-second Avenue in Portland along a four-lane street when I was three, *miles* from our house, and nobody cared. I wanted people to like me. I wanted to be *loved*. If you patted me on the head, I'd follow you and do anything for you. I really think that's why I went from one marriage to another to another when I grew up."

When Allen's paternal grandfather, Robert Van Houte, moved his family to Klamath Falls and Coos Bay, Oregon, where he taught in high schools, and finally to Stanfield, he was far from the family roots in Berkeley. Stanfield was just a smudge on the map between Hermiston and Pendleton, Oregon, some eighteen miles south of the Washington border. Along with all the other border towns, it was downwind of the Hanford Energy Site and Richland, Pasco, and Kennewick, the tri-cities that sprang up along the mighty Columbia River in the 1940s. It would be fifty years before whistle-blowers noted the remarkably high incidence of various malignancies among residents who breathed in the particles and dust carried on that wind.

Like everyone else, Robert Van Houte and his children swam in the rivers and streams of eastern Oregon. Robert married Iris, his second wife, during his time in Klamath Falls when Guy was about seven. He soon fathered four more daughters: Lydia, Gladys, Joan, and Susan. By the time Susan came along, late in her parents' marriage, her older half brother Guy was fathering children of his own.

With five sisters, it fell to Guy to carry on the family name and the heavy mantle his father laid on his shoulders. "Spoiled by all those sisters?" Guy asked. "No, not at all. I was a survivor."

Robert Van Houte was a formidable role model. He was a teacher first, teaching social economics and history in high school in

Stanfield. Guy was in the unenviable position of having his own father as a teacher. He was as bright as the rest of the family, but always felt maladept socially. He had inherited his father's protruding teeth, weak chin, and pigeon chest but none of his confidence.

"My dad wasn't very nice to me," Guy recalled. "He always dictated to me what I should do and who I should be. He was Jesus Christ, and I had it a little bit rough and was very defiant. If he told me I couldn't do something, I did it, and when he told me I was incapable of doing something, that really got me."

When Robert Van Houte headed for a goal, he always achieved it. He was superintendent of schools in Alaska, he knew the Kennedy family, and he was one of the founders of the Gray Panther movement, which supported the brain power and effectiveness of senior citizens. His biggest failure and disappointment may have been that he could never mold his only son in his own image.

Robert died of leukemia at the age of seventy-five. Although he apologized to Guy in the last year of his life, saying simply, "I never knew how to show love, and so I failed you," Guy never felt truly adequate, nor did he completely forgive his father for what he considered to be a miserable youth.

The one thing that fascinated Guy was electronics. "I took a course through the National Radio Institute, by correspondence, when I was ten or eleven, and I was a natural at it. My grandfather helped me get started at it."

It was Guy's grandfather who was his hands-on "parent." "My grandfather raised me," he said, "because my dad was building his career and he was gone constantly. My grandma died of diabetes when I was five, but my grandpa put me under his wing. He had his own trailer house on the same property where we had our houses, and I camped out there. I could relate to him, and he didn't put me down."

Guy's sister Carol Van Houte wasn't as lucky. She was put into a Catholic orphanage until her father and stepmother brought the family together. "She hated being in that place," Guy said. "And she resented me because I got to stay with Grandpa."

Guy got better-looking as he matured. His dark brown eyes were almost hypnotic, and he had dramatic arched eyebrows and an unruly thatch of dark hair. His face grew to match his features, and his crippled leg straightened out. Still, he was always amazed when girls were attracted to him.

Guy met Karen in 1954, when he was a senior in high school and she was two grades behind him. She was short, with ash-blond hair, and she was a wild one. Although Karen was a farm girl, her family relationships were as tangled up as Guy's were. Karen and her sister, Violet, were born to Elva and Zachariah Higley* during Elva's first marriage. Zachariah was a Pentecostal preacher who had chosen Elva to be his wife when she was barely fourteen or fifteen. Unfortunately, he was a man of aberrant sexual proclivities who didn't let his calling to the church distract him.

"He picked up young male waifs," a relative said, "for his own reasons. He taught children 'how to have sex.' "

Elva divorced Zachariah, and he moved to Oklahoma. Her second husband was Austin Alford, who was the father of Elva's son, Leroy, and of her youngest daughter, Debbie. Elva, Allen's maternal grandmother, was hardly the domestic or motherly type, and Zachariah had had to teach her how to cook. She was far more interested in horseback riding and bowling than she was in running a home.

Karen's stepfather, Austin, had lived through the Depression and swore he was going to have a self-sustaining farm so that his family would never go hungry. They bought an eleven-acre spread in Stanfield and raised their own beef, had a half-acre garden, and grew alfalfa in the pastures. The farm, however, was easier to handle than Elva's daughters by the Reverend Zachariah Higley.

It was Karen who drove her mother to despair and terrorized her half sister, Debbie. "She used to sneak out at night when she was in high school," Debbie—who was in grade school then—recalled. "I was afraid to tell my mother because it would mean such a hassle, and Karen got so mad at me when she got back and found out I'd told. So mostly I just lay there and hoped she'd come back before morning."

Karen had a terrible temper as well as periods of melancholy, and she sometimes threatened to commit suicide if things went wrong in her life. One night she decided to go for a joyride with a boy in her parents' pickup truck. "She made me go with her," Debbie said, "because she was supposed to be baby-sitting for me. But she went too fast and landed in a ditch, and I fell and hit my head. She said she'd kill me if I told."

So Debbie didn't tell. She believed that Karen had it in her to retaliate. She had a streak of cruelty that made Debbie wary. "She used to put frogs on the electric fence and watch them wiggle until they died."

It was Karen, reckless and headstrong, who attracted Guy Van Houte. Compared to what they had been through with her, Elva and

Austin Alford were a little relieved, perhaps, when she started to date the teacher's son.

"They didn't seem to mind my dating Karen," Guy said, "but for me it was ninety-nine percent sex."

On the other hand, Robert Van Houte disapproved of Guy's infatuation with Karen. He ordered Guy to stay away from her, and of course, his disapproval made her that much more attractive to his son. "We were madly in love when I graduated," Guy said. "Dad had taken off for vacation for the summer, after telling me to stay away from 'that girl' and that he would deal with me when he got back. So Karen and I went up to the Tri-Cities and got married that summer while he was gone. It was 'Screw you, Pop. I've already married her' when he got back."

But it was Guy who had messed up his life—and Karen's. He was nowhere near ready to be married, and even less prepared to be a father. The only thing his father was relieved about was that Karen was *not* pregnant when his son married her. Guy got a job in a sawmill in Pilot Rock, Oregon, south of Pendleton, and dashed his father's hopes that he would carry on the family tradition of teaching. He wasn't very good in a sawmill or at the cannery where he got his next job. Guy agreed to start college in the fall.

By this time Robert Van Houte had moved on to school superintendent, and he became more and more active in politics. He was president of the Oregon Education Association and a powerful member of the National Education Association.

"Of course, *I* was supposed to be a teacher also," Guy recalled, "but I just couldn't handle it. I went to Oregon College of Education in Monmouth—now it's Western Oregon State College—and was convinced that I wasn't suited for teaching."

Karen conceived their first child in early October 1954, as their hasty, ill-planned marriage was already beginning to wind down. It was, of course, a totally unplanned pregnancy. Guy, who would long continue his pattern of precipitous marriages and desertion when things became difficult, could not remember just when he left Karen for good. "I just block those kinds of memories out," he admitted. "It might have been the end of that year—1954—or it might have been after Christmas. I think it was sometime early in 1955. It was months before she had the baby anyway. It was such an asinine, stupid thing on my part."

He left Karen with the full responsibility for the baby to come. She would blame Guy, but she also blamed her baby: Allen. Karen always felt that Allen had destroyed her life by being born, and she was very vocal about it. If ever a woman was on a path to destruction, it was Karen Van Houte.

Guy kept going to college in Monmouth, taking courses that didn't even count for a degree in education. "I was barely hanging on with a 2.4 grade point average. None of it interested me. I still wanted to do something in radio or electronics, but I was doing what my father dictated."

And so William Allen Van Houte was born on June 5, 1955, in Eugene, Oregon. His mother, Karen, was sixteen and alone in her labor. His father was nineteen and already out of his life for all intents and purposes. As Karen was driven to the hospital, car radios were playing Bill Haley's "Rock Around the Clock" and Chuck Berry's "Maybelline." The mid-50's were a carefree, almost innocent time to be a teenager, but not for Karen Van Houte. She may have wondered why those years had disappeared so quickly for her. She could not have known that the pangs of labor that seized her body were going to be the easiest part of raising her boy child.

No one yet knew that the Hanford Project had probably sent poison into the land and the Columbia River, as well as the air. That June, when Allen was born, the Atomic Energy Commission announced its ability to build a cheap hydrogen bomb of limitless size. The Korean War had been over for a few years, and Vietnam was a far-off place few had heard of. Disneyland had just opened in Orange County, California. Jonas Salk had perfected the anti-polio vaccine. Allen would never have to fear being crippled by polio, but that was about the only head start he had on his father.

Karen Van Houte continued to live in the more metropolitan setting of Eugene, not anxious to return to Stanfield. But she needed help raising her baby boy, and she turned to her family. When she got her figure back, she was even more attractive than she had been when Guy Van Houte fell "madly in love" with her. She was very pretty, and she lightened her hair until it was quite blond. But she was still a nervous, impetuous girl, given to temper tantrums, frustrated by the turn her life had taken.

Much later Allen would blame his mother for all the negative aspects of his life, either recalling or creating incidents of almost unbelievable abuse. Odd, because she blamed *him* for everything.

Guy recalled that he saw his first baby once, and that was all. Even though Allen Van Houte looked so much like him that there was no question about who his biological father was, there was no connection between them as far as love or accountability went. Just as his father had had no time for him, Guy had no time for Allen. It was as if there was something missing in Guy; he had never learned what it meant to be a father.

Guy took more and more radio courses after he dropped out of college. He had great aptitude for electronics, technology, and engineering. "That's really what I did," he explained as he recalled his life's work. He *fixed* radios and television sets and, later, computers. He fixed computers; he never could understand how to use them.

Guy's talent at electronics was not something that he passed down to his first child. "Allen has no ability at all in electronics," he said with a laugh. "He doesn't know a transistor from a resistor, but he could always lie and B.S. his way through, and no one could tell."

It would be many years, however, before Guy Van Houte knew anything about what Allen could and couldn't do. After he saw him that one time when he was an infant, Allen's living conditions, problems, strengths, and weaknesses were as foreign to Guy as those of any other little boy in Oregon. Allen was living with Karen and her side of the family.

His aunt Debbie was a child when Allen was born, only eight years older than he was. She loved him immediately. She remembered the toddler Allen as "a fun little kid." He liked to dance to his favorite song "Wake Up, Little Susie," recorded by the Everly Brothers in 1958. Guy never knew *that* Allen; he was far away and busy with other things.

Allen seemed to be a fairly average little boy, smarter than most, with a stubborn cowlick and big ears that jutted out from his head, genetic hand-me-downs from his father. Karen continued to run away from her life, and Allen lived with his maternal grandparents, Elva and Austin, as much as he did with his mother. Although she had never been a demonstrative mother with her own children, Elva absolutely doted on the little boy, sometimes to Austin's disgust. She let Allen do anything he wanted. They argued over whether she was spoiling him. She probably was, but young Allen described his life with Karen as so bleak and miserable that both his grandmother and his aunt Debbie tried to make up for that.

Early on in his life, Allen learned how to come between happy couples, and he smirked at Austin when his grandmother let him have his way. He liked the sense of power he got when he disrupted others' relationships.

A child with a weaker sense of self than Allen would have been completely buried by the numbers of half siblings born to his father and mother, who were both remarkably fecund. As soon as his divorce from Karen was final, Guy married again. He and his second bride, Jeannette, who was also just sixteen at the time of her marriage, went to Walla Walla and got married. Heedless of the struggles of children with no fathers, Guy impregnated Jeannette, and she eventually gave birth to four children. Although he was loath to admit it decades later, he agreed that he had opted out of that marriage too, and just as he had with Allen, he took no financial responsibility for the children. They were adopted by Jeannette's second husband.

His desolate childhood had made Guy long for love, but it also left him skittish when anyone demanded more of him than he was able to give. He was not an admirable father. Before he was twenty-five, Guy Van Houte had abandoned five children, stubbornly shutting out any memory of them. "I woke up in the early sixties and felt that that was all a bad dream," he said. "That wasn't really *me*. I just denied my past and blocked it out."

It was a pity; he had come from good, solid stock, and he had passed down genes for high intelligence, but his first five children grew up in sparse and gritty emotional soil.

GUY's third wife was Suzanne. He met her in 1961 when he went to her home to fix her television set. Their attraction was mutual, and he was so taken with her and, by now, so ashamed of his past that he didn't tell Suzanne about his first two marriages or the children he had left behind. He must have known that the secrets in his past would surface at some point, but he chose to remain silent about his earlier life.

His third marriage lasted a long time—more than fifteen years—and Guy stayed around to raise the children that were born to him and Suzanne. They were all boys—Bruce, Randy, and Nick—and they lived in McMinnville, Oregon, during those years. Guy had matured enough to be an adequate father to his third family. He and Bruce and Randy were close, but not close enough for him to tell them about any of their older half siblings. The Van Houte family flourished for the first eight or nine years of Guy and Suzanne's marriage. But there finally came a time in 1970 when Guy had no choice but to tell Suzanne some of the truth about his past. He was forced to reveal that he had fathered a son fifteen years earlier, a son who was about to descend on them.

KAREN remarried as often as Guy did, and men moved in and out of her life constantly. Allen had no father figure he could count on, except for Austin Alford, his stepgrandfather. He would live with his mother, Karen, for a while and then with Elva and Austin. Karen's mother was in *her* second marriage, with children who were both siblings and half siblings. Her biological father may have been the source of Karen's erratic behavior.

While Allen lived with his grandmother and stepgrandfather, his mother sometimes joined them. And there were times when he lived alone with her, although those were not good times. More often than not, Karen was off somewhere and Allen lived with his grandparents. Theirs was the most stable household he knew. And so, like his father before him, Allen was principally raised by grandparents rather than by a mother and a father, and by his aunt Debbie, who loved him fiercely.

Karen was married three times after she divorced Guy. Her second husband was Melvin Schafer, and they eked out a hardscrabble living. Melvin was a sometime mechanic, and he and Karen drove pea-vine trucks in season. They often fought physically. Karen hit Mel with a frying pan, and he had to be hospitalized. She had black eyes, and he broke her nose with a baseball bat. Despite surgery, her nose resembled a boxer's after that.

Karen gave birth to a second son, Gregory, and then she had a baby girl, whom she named Peggy.

When Peggy was only an infant, Karen and Melvin parked at the bottom of a long grade, waiting for a friend who drove a logging truck. Peggy was sound asleep, so they left her in their car as they got out to watch for the truck. In a horrifying, almost slow-motion accident, they realized that the logger's brakes were gone, and they could do nothing but watch as the massive truck hurtled over the car where their baby girl slept. Peggy died in a jumble of crushed metal.

Karen had two more boys, Brian and Randy, and a girl named Linda. Linda was a tough tomboy like her grandma Elva, and a pretty little thing. For many of Karen's childbearing years Allen was all but forgotten and lived with the Alfords, where his grandmother always welcomed him with open arms.

"Allen ran away sometimes," his aunt Debbie recalled. "But he didn't go very far. One time, I knew he was hiding in the shed, so I went out there and stood a few feet away. I said in a loud voice, 'Oh, I'm so worried about Allen. He's run away and I'm so afraid of what he's going to do. Where will he go?' He came strolling out, grinning, thinking that *he'd* fooled *me.*"

But Debbie did worry about Allen. Once, when she was about eighteen and Allen was nine or ten, he was living with Karen in an old trailer over by Pendleton, Oregon. She was building a lean-to for the trailer, and she had Allen sawing wood. "It was a terribly hot summer's day," Debbie said. "And he was a kid. As I got close to him, I could see his eyes, but they were so dark brown that I couldn't even see his pupils. And even the whites were all yellow. I said, 'Allen, how long have you been sick?' "

"Several days," he answered weakly.

Debbie realized the boy was very sick, and she was in a quandary. She didn't have the authority to take him to a doctor, nor the money to pay for it. "I took him to the health department," she remembered, "and his urine sample was as dark as chocolate. He had infectious hepatitis. They put him in the hospital, and he had an intravenous drip for a week. All he could eat was baby food and Werther's butterscotch drops."

Debbie was relieved that the authorities had at least temporary charge of Allen. Karen was drinking a lot, and with a different man every time Debbie saw her. The only visitors the state allowed while Allen was in the hospital were Debbie and her mother—his grandmother Elva.

Allen survived, but it was touch and go for a while. He would live with permanent liver damage ever after.

During this time Karen's drinking exacerbated her tendency toward depression. On one occasion she came home late at night and headed straight to the bathroom, locking the door behind her. Debbie got suspicious when she stayed in there too long. "I just opened the door, and sure enough, Karen was there with a razor blade held against the skin of her wrist."

"I'm no good. I'm no good for my kids," she wailed. "I don't want to live."

"Sure you do," Debbie said. "Do you want them to wake up and see you lying dead in a pool of blood? Do you think *that* would be good for them?"

Debbie had little doubt that Karen and possibly her other half sister, Violet, had suffered abuse at the hands of their biological father, the Pentecostal preacher. Karen once told her a garbled story of being locked in the trunk of their father's car with Violet when they were very small. And then there had been one "reunion" visit to see their father in Oklahoma when all the children returned pale and jumpy. Those who knew of the traveling preacher's history of pedophilia suspected that he had molested his grandchildren during the visit. Indeed, Allen would one day say that he had been sexually violated as a youngster by "a church deacon."

Karen's third husband, Bill Cook, was a good-hearted man, although the two often had roaring fights. She and Bill did manage to tie up their broken marriages neatly, though. Melvin Schafer, her ex-husband, married Bill Cook's ex-wife. But Karen was a frantic and troubled woman, and her emotions grew more brittle, her temper more chaotic. Debbie's husband, Tom Oliver, recalled that "she never spoke below a scream. She screamed at her children constantly. I guess they got used to it after a while, because they barely paid her any attention."

Still, the screaming may have echoed in their heads. The time Allen spent in Karen's care might have had a devastating effect on the intelligent little boy, more than enough to offset the relative calm indulgence of his grandma Elva's home. Karen's concept of discipline could be violent. According to Allen, she once hit him on the head with a board when he left his tricycle behind her car and it was crushed. That was probably true; she often struck her children with whatever was handy, and her other sons recalled being hit with boards or firewood.

But in truth Karen was never as violent or as abusive to her offspring as Allen would later claim. He made her out to be a monstrous mother who beat him often. He said that more than once he woke up in the hospital after coming out of a coma because she had beaten him so badly. *That* wasn't true. He went to the hospital only once during his childhood, and that was when he had hepatitis.

He also claimed that his mother set him on fire. "Allen had a habit of leaving the stove burners on," Tom Oliver explained as he tried to straighten out that story. "Karen was *not* a good housekeeper, and her house was a garbage dump, full of paper and junk. She was always afraid the house would catch fire because those burners would get red-hot. She *did* hold Allen's hand over the stove burner so he would remember to turn it off, but she didn't set fire to him."

Not actually—but one time Karen poured lighter fluid on Allen's hand and threatened to light a match. She didn't follow through, but it didn't make her mother of the year.

"She had lots of problems," Allen said when he was in his mid-forties and had long since learned to couch his words to suit the situation. "There were abuse issues. She tried real hard in life, but she just could never get a handle on it."

Karen's violent temper was the aspect of her personality that got her into trouble the most, and her oldest son was the catalyst that set her off. Her third husband, Bill Cook, was a buffer between Allen and Karen, and usually jumped to the boy's defense. Indeed, when Allen told his story of being set on fire, he always said Bill saved him by smothering the flames with a blanket.

Karen's jobs and avocations covered the entire spectrum. She worked as a barmaid in a tavern in the crossroads town of Reith, Oregon, and she commanded fearful respect after she sent three rowdy males packing with the broken end of a beer bottle. She was as thin as a rail, but when she was angered, she was fearsome.

And then again, Karen sought religious surcease by joining a cult and was once a Pentecostal minister in Hermiston. Her church was a Quonset hut, and her congregation of ten included Indians from the Cold Springs Reservation.

Of all those around her, Bill Cook probably suffered the most serious injuries because of Karen's rage. Allen had been out of her home for years when Karen took a gun to Bill. Jealous, she shot him six times in the groin with a .22, but though his injuries were painful, she apparently didn't hurt him in any permanent way.

"She knew just where to shoot," Tom Oliver said laconically. "She hit what she was aiming for."

Still furious after that attack on Bill, Karen put down the .22 and grabbed a shotgun by the barrel, dragging it behind her as she moved through the house to do more damage. But the trigger caught on something, and the gun roared. Karen was hit in the shoulder, arm, breast, and stomach. She lost her arm and suffered other wounds that would haunt her throughout the rest of her life.

The shootout naturally drew the attention of the Umatilla County Sheriff's Office. Karen said she had been trying to commit suicide. Whether that was true or she had shot herself accidentally, no one ever figured out. The house was a bloody mess, and Karen was far more seriously injured than Bill.

"She never intended to shoot herself," Tom Oliver recalled. "But she needed the suicide story to keep from going to jail for shooting Bill. She couldn't have killed herself with that shotgun anyway, because her toe wouldn't have reached the trigger. The gun just hit something and went off. In spite of all her surgeries, she still has buckshot in her from that."

Allen went to see his mother in the hospital. "She spat at me," he recalled, "and said, 'You are the reason for my life's entire problem.' "

Karen Van Houte Schafer Cook's life vacillated between her indomitable spirit and her Job-like bad luck. Even with only one arm, she was an accomplished artist. She painted beautiful landscapes of buffalo on the Western Plains, and she was a cartoonist. There was little she couldn't train a horse to do, although she once lost several teeth when a pony bolted as she held the reins in her mouth.

Three of Karen's sons would eventually go to prison: Greg, Brian, and Allen. When Greg was released, he could not deal with the outside world. He snuck into a convenience store after hours, not to rob it but to get police attention when he shot out the store's window from the inside. He got what he wanted; he went back behind bars at the Oregon State Prison, where he felt more secure.

Brian was always viewed as the "bad luck kid" among Karen's children. When he was still in his teens, he lived with an older woman who had children. He too was incarcerated for a few years on lesser charges than Gregory and was released in 1986.

Karen's daughter Marilyn grew to be an absolutely beautiful girl. When she was in high school, a much older man—who was married—fell in love with her and worshipped her. She dropped out of high school to be with him. It was to be a loving, if somewhat bizarre, relationship that lasted for decades.

Karen's last marriage, to a man named Jim Freeman, was the most peaceful. He was good to her, and when he died, he left her a nice mobile home. By then her gunshot injuries had made her health precarious and she needed a safe place to live. Her half sister, Debbie and her husband, Tom, tried to care for Karen, but they wouldn't take responsibility for the mobile home, because one of her recently paroled sons moved in.

In her early sixties, Karen looked closer to seventy-five, and she characterized herself as having been a "very good" mother. But that was a stretch too. She was not a good mother—far from it—but she wasn't as cruel as Allen later portrayed her.

_____Chapter Four_____

AS HIS GRANDPARENTS grew older, Allen was harder to deal with. He had never had consistent discipline, and he was manipulative and unpredictable. Grandmother Elva still doted on him, but her husband was less entranced. Allen was always the golden child, and he was adept at getting other children into trouble. With his big brown eyes and his guileless ways, he could tell whoppers and adults believed him. Inevitably there were consequences, and Allen's lies caused disruption. His grandparents came close to divorce a few times—all because of him.

Nearing fifty, Elva had been raising children for more than thirty-five years. She liked to travel and bowl, and it was difficult to do that when she was raising a teenager who sometimes mirrored his mother's rage. But she would never have asked him to leave; she idolized Allen. She hoped that maybe someday he could take over the farm along with her son, Leroy, and her daughters Debbie and Violet.

In those years Allen's mother, Karen, was taking care of her fourth husband, Jim Freeman, and was in as stable a situation as she had ever been in her life. But Elva didn't delude herself into believing that Karen would ever come back to the farm.

In 1970 Debbie and Tom Oliver paid a visit to her parents' farm in eastern Oregon. Allen told his aunt Debbie he wasn't that happy on the farm and asked if he could come live with them. A little taken aback, Debbie and Tom said they didn't have time to decide what to do at the moment, but maybe they could talk about it the next time they came to visit. It would depend on how Elva and Austin felt about it too, since they had raised Allen for most of his life.

The Olivers were a young couple just starting out, and they lived in a big old house in Siletz, Oregon, on the Pacific Ocean. Siletz is a small village near the popular beach resort town of Newport. They owned a sewing-machine and vacuum-cleaner store. Debbie was only twenty-three and Tom six years older, and they often welcomed strangers into their home when someone needed a place to stay. They were active in their church, sponsoring "Christian coffeehouses," where Tom preached some, and he baptized people in the Siletz River.

It was an era where peace and love abounded and hippies counted on the kindness of strangers. "We had all manner of guests," Debbie recalled. "There was one woman and her little boy who stayed for a while. We heard her come downstairs to the bathroom near our bedroom on her first night, and she brushed her teeth. I nudged Tom and said, 'Wait a minute, she didn't *have* a toothbrush in her things.' We found out she was using Tom's toothbrush!" Debbie laughed, remembering a different and easier way of life.

Back in Siletz after their trip to the Alfords' farm, Tom and Debbie were sleeping early the next morning when they heard someone banging at their door. It was Allen. He said he had been trying to sleep outside between their place and the nightclub next door, but drunks kept urinating on him. "I've come to live with you," he announced.

They realized that he must have left the farm near Hermiston shortly after they did, and he admitted that he had started hitchhiking as soon as they left. It was a long trip, at least three hundred miles. "He was cold, and he had blisters on his heels because he wore cowboy boots with no socks," Debbie said. "He wanted us to take him back along the road someplace where he'd hidden some arrows that went with his bow in a ditch. That's about all he had—his bow and arrows."

Tom and Debbie exchanged glances and shrugged. They took in people they didn't know who needed help, and Allen was a relative. They drove him back to pick up his few possessions, and agreed to let him stay with them for a while and see how things worked out. Allen told them he was sixteen, but Debbie did some figuring; he was only fifteen. And he had simply walked away from the grandmother who had taken him in and cherished him over the years without so much as a good-bye.

Debbie had always had a soft spot in her heart for her nephew, sorry for the boy who was shuttled from one home to another for most of his life, alternately deprived and indulged. He seemed so eager to see the world and to learn about things. It was dangerous for him to be hitchhiking, and the Olivers suspected he would just run away again if they made him go back to his grandparents.

In some ways he had never been exposed to the world. "It was just little things," Debbie recalled. "He had never heard of a strawberry soda. I sent him down to buy himself one, and he came back with pop. So I said, 'No, go ask for a *strawberry ice-cream soda*,' and he thought that was delicious.

"Allen got some of his vocabulary mixed up in those days. He would cry, 'You don't have any symphony for me,' and I'd try to explain the difference between *sympathy* and *symphony*."

At fifteen Allen was gullible. When Tom kiddingly told him to roll down the window on their Subaru station wagon as they went through the carwash, he obeyed—and got a faceful of suds and water. He seemed malleable still, and Tom and Debbie hoped to set him on the right path before he was grown and his emotions were set in stone.

Allen loved the beach, and he spent hours there playing with the black Lab pup the Olivers got him, and fishing and crabbing. He was so proud of his first two crabs, but Debbie was horrified; they were both illegal. One was a female crab and the other a Japanese crab. "I told him to take them back, but he was determined to keep them, and he shouted, 'No!' so we cooked them."

Allen seemed to enjoy the Olivers' Christian activities and went to church with them three or four times a week. When school started, he even taught a Bible-study class to other high school students. He didn't have friends, though. He was a loner for a long time, and his aunt Debbie still worried about the lost boy who fit in nowhere.

"Allen was a very sweet little kid as a small child," she recalled, "but even then he wanted control, and he wanted more as he grew older." He could not lose, whether it was chess or checkers or something more important. Once, Tom tried to show Allen who was boss as the two wrestled. Tom, who had learned self-defense when he was in the navy, demonstrated how he could hit a pressure point near Allen's thumb. Allen fell to his knees instantly, shocked by the immobilizing pain. Then, after Tom let go, he closed his eyes and remained silent, as if programming himself.

"Now do it," he told his uncle. When Tom repeated the pressure-point trick, Allen didn't react at all. Tom was dumbfounded that a teenage boy could deactivate his response to pain with his mind.

"He took his emotions under control," his aunt Debbie said. "That's what he learned as a kid. He had to."

And he still did. The Olivers understood that; he had never had any control over his life or his future. They knew what Karen's moods could be like. She intimidated adults, not to mention her adolescent son. It was natural that Allen would strive for some mastery of his own fate.

Debbie knew a lot of the bad things that had happened to Allen from her personal observation, and she had heard the furtive rumors about the unfortunate visit Karen and her children made to see her father in Oklahoma. Apparently the "Reverend" Zachariah had managed to sexually abuse all his grandchildren while they were there. She shuddered to think of what he might have done to Allen.

Allen was a smart kid, and at first the Olivers found him prickly but lovable. Trying to make up for his early years, they cut him quite a bit of slack. Tom Oliver was a big man with a soft voice, and a solid Christian. But he would always be conflicted in his feelings about Allen. In one breath he insisted that he knew Allen in a way no one else ever had, because he was the only person Allen ever really confided in. He called him "a wonderful kid." But a few minutes later Tom recalled that Allen and his friend Steve Thurmond had stolen from him and Debbie. The boys took their car and anything else they wanted.

In Steve, Allen had finally found a friend. He was a boy the Olivers had taken in along with the rest of the displaced souls who came their way. In giving shelter to Steve, they truly turned the other cheek. When Steve stole from their store, his own parents washed their hands of him. "They didn't care if he went to jail," Debbie said. "But we felt sorry for him, and we told him he could live with us and work off the debt. He and Allen got to be friends. Of course, he ended up stealing from us again—the car and a sleeping bag too."

Tom and Debbie kept trying. Steve had a beautiful voice, and he liked to sing "Bridge Over Troubled Water." They sensed he was a very unhappy boy who was looking for something to hold on to. The Olivers were saving to take Allen and Steve to Disneyland by putting all their spare change in a big glass jar. But when they pulled it out to count it one day, they saw that all the silver money was gone and there were only pennies left.

"Allen and Steve stole it," Tom recalled, "so we took the pennies, and Debbie and I went to the movies. That's all we had left." Steve moved away, and the Olivers heard belatedly that he had committed suicide. No one knew why.

Allen wasn't good at doing chores. Tom asked him to build a pig-pen one day, and he did a halfhearted job of it. To make a point, Tom and Debbie went to Allen's school and asked that he be dismissed for the afternoon because he had left his chore unfinished. He was furious, but he came home with them and rebuilt the pen.

"There," he said "They won't get out of that. They'd have to have cork boots to get out."

The three piglets burst from the pen almost before he uttered the words, and Allen chased after them in his hip waders, stumbling through an outbuilding full of manure. "Let me kill them," he screamed in frustration. "Just let me kill them!"

The baby pigs darted away from him when he made a triumphant dive to grab them—and fell headfirst into the manure, filling his waders with the pungent stuff.

He had neither the knack nor the desire for farming; he never had. At sixteen Allen Van Houte was an impatient teenager who knew what he wanted and was already searching for shortcuts to get there. Some of them taught him painful lessons. He was hiking once on the sandstone cliffs above the ocean and didn't feel like retracing his steps to get back to sea level.

"Before I could stop him," Debbie said, "he slid right down those cliffs to the beach. He burned his bottom good on that rough rock, and he raced across the beach when he landed to douse it in the ocean."

Debbie understood that it was difficult for Allen to show affection. "He couldn't say 'I love you,' but I think he knew we loved him," she said. "Finally, one time, we were riding in the car and Allen was in the back seat. He put a hand on each of our shoulders and said, 'I love you guys,' and we were really touched."

As vehemently as Tom Oliver described Allen as "a great kid to have around," there came a time when he began to talk about moving on. He was curious about his father, Guy. After staying with the Olivers for over a year, he told Tom he wanted to meet his dad.

"I warned him," Tom recalled. "I said his dad might not be what he was expecting."

Tom knew there was no point in dissuading him. Allen never overtly defied Tom; he just went ahead and did what he wanted. There was a kind of invisible wall around him that nothing could penetrate, and now he was adamant that he wanted to meet his father. Tom checked around and found that Guy was living with his latest family up in McMinnville, about seventy miles away. He finally agreed to arrange a meeting.

Tom and Debbie didn't think Allen would ever want to *live* with his father or that Guy would want him.

Guy and Tom would differ about whether Tom took Allen to McMinnville or Guy came to Siletz, but the father and son did meet. "He decided to go live with his father," Tom said. "I told him right out that he might as well hold a gun to his head."

Guy Van Houte had a different version. "Tom called me and said they couldn't keep Allen any longer," he said. "They wanted me to take him."

Tom and Debbie Oliver had tried their best, but Allen was a puzzle they could not figure out. He *was* fun to have around, but then again, he was often moody, angry, and inscrutable. They were stunned when they realized that he was ready to walk away from them as casually as he had walked away from his grandparents; it was as if the human beings in his life were expendable and interchangeable. They hoped that being with his natural father might give him some feeling of permanence, but they doubted it.

By this time Guy Van Houte was thirty-five years old and in a much more stable marriage than ever before. He said he was finding it hard to press down the guilty memories of the children he had abandoned. Now he regretted the times he had shrugged off the responsibility of caring for them. He was amenable to Allen's moving in with him and Suzanne and their three boys.

The problem was telling Suzanne. Bruce was twelve, Randy was ten, and Nick was three when Guy broke the news to his wife. "I was so ashamed of my prior life that I never told Suzanne anything about it," Guy admitted. "I finally told her about Allen the night before I was to go and get him."

Suzanne didn't argue with him; she may have been too shocked to realize that a teenager she never knew existed was coming to live with her family with virtually no prior warning.

Guy took Bruce and Randy with him when he went to Siletz to pick up Allen. They were immensely curious about this older boy who was related to them. While Guy was inside talking to Tom and Debbie Oliver, Allen walked toward his half brothers along the rutted driveway of the farm where he had been living. They could see at once that he looked more like their father than either of them did, except that Allen didn't have Guy's overbite. Both Guy and Allen had dark hair so thick that it looked almost like a wig, the same arching eyebrows, the same penetrating eyes. Guy's ears stuck out, and so did Allen's, and they had identical oddly shaped heads, large for their bodies and kind of squared off flat in the back.

It seemed strange to his half brothers that Allen had been living on the Olivers' farm in Siletz while they lived in McMinnville; throughout their lives they had often been less than seventy miles apart geographically, and yet they never even knew about Allen.

He approached them now, cradling a duck in his arms, petting it and cooing to it, saying, "This is Quacky." Allen introduced them to the duck, explaining it was his pet, and the younger boys leaned forward to stroke it.

"He's my favorite," Allen said with a grin. Suddenly his words tumbled out rapidly. "But I can't take him with me, because I'm going to live with you guys."

Before they could react, Allen tossed the hapless duck into the hog pen next to him. He laughed as the pigs leaped upon the duck, tearing it to pieces instantly, feathers and blood spraying grotesquely. Bruce and Randy stared at him, shocked.

Neither of them would ever forget that first moment when they met Allen, or the shredded remains of the duck in the mud of the hog wallow.

Allen never looked back.

Chapter Five

SUZANNE VAN HOUTE was dismayed by the changes Allen made in her household. Guy told her the boy had had a hard time, being shuttled back and forth between his mother, his grandparents, and his aunt and uncle, and she tried to understand. She was a sweet-tempered woman, and she made an effort to be, if not Allen's mother, his friend, who welcomed him into her home. But to be truthful, she was a little afraid of him, more for her boys than for herself. Although he had the gawky, unfinished look that most teenage boys have, he sometimes looked at her as if he were older than time. His eyes were penetrating and speculative, and she wondered what he was really thinking behind his bland mask. And Suzanne kept remembering the phone call she received from Debbie Oliver.

Randy recalled that Debbie had called his mother shortly after Allen came to live with the Van Houtes in McMinnville. "She said, 'I'm sorry. We're scared for you. Be careful. He's dangerous—he's not like other people.' "

Debbie would deny that she ever made that call. It was typical of Allen's story; his life would be described by revisionists on all sides, including himself, and no one could ever be sure which versions were the absolute truth.

Allen's oft-repeated stories of life with his mother were hair-raising to Guy and his younger half brothers. He insisted that his mother had poured lighter fluid on him and then lit a match. He vividly recalled his terror as he was engulfed in flames. He also told them that Karen punished him by hitting him with two-by-fours.

Tom Oliver had verified that story. She used a two-by-four on all her kids. Karen had to have been a virago to treat her children that way. Guy was glad Allen had escaped her early on.

Allen attributed his mother's behavior to the fact that she was often suicidal and usually took out her depression and fury on him. And no one—not her supporters and certainly not her detractors—ever disputed that part of his story.

Guy had not seen Allen since he was a tiny infant, so he had no idea how many of his son's complaints were true. But he knew that Karen was high-strung and temperamental. That had been one of the problems between them during their very brief marriage. Still, Guy's response to Allen's tales of horror from his childhood was oddly flat. Guy always felt he had suffered as a child too, and viewed Allen's alleged abuse as having little to do with him. After all, he'd been treated almost as badly; *his* mother had also abandoned him.

Guy viewed Karen as a deranged woman who, not surprisingly, had failed to be the sweet wife he expected or a good mother to Allen. Now he and Allen were together, both survivors. For all the guilt he took upon himself—virtually none—they could have been brothers; they were separated by less than two decades in age. Guy would always speak of Allen as if he were only another man and not the son he rejected before his birth. If even a fraction of what Allen was telling them was true, it was understandable that he was a bitter young man. With his big head and ears, he seemed at first to be just a nerdy, needy, kid.

Suzanne and Guy gave Allen his own room in the back of their house, a room that Randy and Bruce came to call the chamber of horrors. Allen invented "games" there to play with his younger brothers and their playmates. In one game he tied his brothers' hands behind their backs and gave them a tennis racket to hold in the other. And then he whipped at them with a fishing line baited with salmon lures with big hooks. Their challenge was to fend off the hooks before they dug into flesh.

"We didn't really get hurt," Bruce recalled. "Allen snagged one neighbor kid, though. But he was interesting too, kind of like our new big 'thug brother.' Most of the things he did our mother didn't even know about."

Allen pounded black powder into brass shells and lit it. The only injuries were to a neighbor's Saint Bernard. Somehow the younger boys were able to keep Allen's sadistic games secret from both their parents. They were intrigued by him and at the same time afraid of him. Years later they still grinned as they recalled some of Allen's outrageous stunts and his dark games, seeming not to resent his insinuation into their lives. In a way they continued to admire his ability to "slide" on everything. For most of his life he never got caught or punished; he always came out a winner, and Bruce and Randy clearly envied him a little.

One time, though, Allen's predatory side did get him in trouble. Randy and Bruce had an eleven-year-old friend who lived five miles outside McMinnville. His father was influential in McMinnville, and Suzanne and Guy approved of his friendship with Bruce and Randy. The boy sometimes rode the bus home with them. Later his sister, who was a high school student, would drive by to pick him up. She was a very pretty girl. Allen was attracted to her and finally asked her out to a drive-in movie.

"Their date was okay at first," Randy remembered, "but then Allen started getting pretty 'friendly' with her. She fought him, and he ended up choking her and almost raping her. She was scared to death of Allen after that. Her dad didn't want to press charges, but we saw the bruises on her neck, and our friend wasn't allowed to come to our house anymore. And then they moved to the Midwest shortly after."

Bruce and Randy also remembered an incident where Allen took a butcher knife to a neighbor kid, although the boy managed to get away. "Allen had a terrible temper," Randy said.

It was a long time later when Guy found out what was happening between his sons. "He took Bruce and Randy and tied them up," Guy said, "and he would hold knives to their throats. Of course, they reported that to their mother, and she told me to get him out of there. By then she was starting to really go to pieces on me."

Guy always seemed faintly surprised that Allen was causing trouble in his home, and even a little annoyed that he was called upon to deal with it. He had expected that things would go more smoothly, since he was putting himself out to give Allen a home, albeit sixteen years late.

Suzanne Van Houte had good reason to disintegrate emotionally. She felt she had unknowingly invited a viper into her nest. When she noticed that her underwear was disappearing from the laundry, she asked Allen about it. He looked at her as if she were crazy. She knew he wanted her to be crazy so he could go to Guy and complain about her. He was never happier than when she and Guy argued. She didn't know it, but Allen had been the same with Tom and Debbie. Since he was not part of any family, he did his best to put a wedge between couples who seemed to share something that he could not fathom.

Whenever the family went for a ride, Allen insisted on sitting in the front between Suzanne and Guy. His brothers described a time when Guy had to go back to the house for something while the rest of them waited in the car. "Allen just turned around," Randy said, "and told our mother, 'I'm going to break you guys up. And I don't care what it takes.' Just out of the blue, he said that."

Bruce and Randy were only junior high school age, but they understood that Allen felt rejected. They even sympathized a little. Sure, he stretched a lot of rules and did openly malicious things, but they had lived with his father their whole lives and he hadn't. "And then there was the person he said he had for a mother," Randy said.

Bruce and Randy believed all the things Allen told them about his mother, and they often felt sorry for him. Their own mother was soft and loving, and they could not even imagine that she would ever pour lighter fluid or gasoline on them and light it.

"Allen's mother had this live-in boyfriend named Bill," Bruce said, "and I guess he put the fire out with a blanket right away. Bill stuck up for Allen, until his mother got mad and shot Bill—but he didn't die."

"I guess that's why Allen didn't have any burn scars on him," Bruce continued, "because Bill put the fire out so quick."

Allen repeated the same stories, subtly changed, to any number of people. He always would. He told Bruce and Randy about the time when he and Karen lived upstairs over the bar in Reith. "He said she took on three guys in the bar once with a broken beer bottle—and put them all in the hospital," Randy said. That was another of Allen's favorite anecdotes.

SUZANNE was not inclined to be as lenient with Allen or give him more tender treatment because of his alleged horrible childhood. Allen frightened her. She didn't doubt that he meant it when he said he was going to destroy her relationship with Guy. He was always churning things up.

"He almost cost me my marriage," Guy said. "Still, I kept him around for more than a year. I finally got rid of him."

Not completely. Allen was living on his own at seventeen, but he was still in McMinnville. He was working in the Hamblin Wheeler men's clothing store after school. He learned how to dress there and bought himself a basic wardrobe at a discount. He began to dress "business casual," according to Randy. It made him look older than he was, and successful. He was a far cry now from the boy who had run away from the farm in Pendleton with bare feet stuffed in old cowboy boots. His façade was growing smoother all the time, and he became better and better looking as he moved through his teens. He looked like a male model. Now all he needed was a pipe and an ascot and he could pose for an ad in *GQ*.

Although Allen no longer lived in Guy's home, "He was always around," Guy said. "He graduated from McMinnville High School. He did fine on his own."

Indeed, Allen seemed remarkably self-sufficient, although he would sometimes call Guy when he was in trouble, a practice that would continue long after he was a grown man. Invariably he began each new tale of woe with "Daddy . . ."

By the time he finished procreating with his four wives and one girlfriend, Sheldon "Guy" Van Houte would father seven sons and two daughters. Allen was his oldest. His second son and namesake— Sheldon, Junior, by Jeannette—died in a police chase out of Walla Walla, Washington, when he was only fourteen or fifteen. That tragedy may have made it difficult for Guy to cut his ties with Allen completely. Conversely, there was always a kind of rivalry between Guy and Allen.

"Dad and Allen have always been head to head against each other," Nick Van Houte said. "My dad is very controlling and competitive with his children. I think that hit a nerve with Allen because Allen has always been very bright and intelligent, and he and my dad really tried to outdo each other. It's like a game of chess with them. In fact, that's the game they always played. And they took it 'off the board' quite a bit."

Despite his professional look, Allen hardly seemed headed for success. The next phase of his life remains murky and vague. According to Guy, Allen joined a "Moonie cult" in California in 1973 right after he graduated from high school in McMinnville.

"It wasn't the real Moonies," Guy added, "but it was some kind of religious cult tied to an outfit in Salem that was trying to recruit all the young people they could. Allen was completely into it. When he came back to me, he was totally brainwashed, unsure of himself. Allen didn't know who he was—he was heavily religious. It didn't last long. He popped out of it in about a month, and then he went to work for me."

Allen had seen his mother as a Pentecostal minister in Hermiston. He himself went through periods where he allegedly turned to religion and became extremely devout, but only for a while.

Allen's brothers explained that his connection with the California cult was about more than religion, although they remembered a period when he seemed terribly pious. Their recall was that Allen was "washing money," serving as a courier for a group known as the The True Answer and the large corporation allegedly connected with it.

Allen had a way of plunging totally into different lifestyles, but he had no staying power. Sometimes it was religion. Sometimes it was alcohol or drugs, and occasionally he alluded to an important role he was playing in secret criminal conspiracies.

"He told us he came into JFK Airport in New York from Switzerland with money taped all over his body," Bruce Van Houte said. [The cult] wanted him back, and he was afraid of them. He said the FBI grabbed him at JFK and interrogated him for thirty-six hours. They went all through his luggage, but they never searched him. *That* was the brainwashing he told our dad about; he was scared."

Was any of it true? How would an eighteen-year-old kid in a little town in Oregon hook up with a group laundering millions of dollars? More likely, it was all an elaborate lie. Allen's alleged detention and interrogation by special agents would never appear in any rap sheet connected to him. (In fact, the FBI denies that anything like that ever happened. "We wouldn't interrogate *anyone* for thirty-six hours," Mike Appleby, an FBI special agent assigned to San Antonio, said. "There's nothing to that.")

But Guy apparently believed that story. Father and son, they were both connected and estranged. Guy Van Houte had spent his life defying *his* father, turning away from the pattern cut out for him by a cold father who was rarely there for him when he was child, even if the turning away meant that he would end up repairing television sets rather than teaching engineering.

Allen, denied a father totally during *his* early years, set out as a young teenager to redesign himself into the very image of success. Both he and Guy railed against the desertion of their male—and female—parents, but neither had the empathy to see his own reflection in the other's eyes.

"They were—*are*—very much alike," Kerry Walsh Bladorn commented once. "They were both good at conning you. The difference was that Guy had a heart."

After Allen left their house to live with his father's family, Tom and Debbie Oliver accepted a call from their church to travel to Mexico to build an orphanage there, and they left Siletz for almost a year. Along their travels they sharpened scissors "to support God's work."

They didn't see Allen for a long time. "He had no one to oversee him," Debbie said regretfully. "He had too much freedom, I think, and he changed. He was different when we came back. He looked bad the next time we saw him," she added with a shudder. "He had moved to the 'dark side.' " Allen's eyes were hooded, and he didn't seem the same person as the teenager they had taken into their home.

Allen's recklessness and daredevil tendencies had only accelerated since they had last seen him. "He had this Datsun 240Z, and he drove off the Santiam Pass and hit a tree," Tom said. "He had head injuries, and it left him with blood clots in his brain. They're still there, I guess, because the doctors said it was too dangerous to operate. I suppose they could cause him trouble at any time—I'm not sure."

_____Chapter Six_____

ALLEN VAN HOUTE was obsessed with females from the time he hit puberty. He came by it naturally; his father was never without a woman. After Suzanne divorced him, Guy went on to marry his fourth wife, Chris, thirty-five. It was to be the only union that produced no children, although Chris had a child from an earlier relationship. When he was well into his fifties, Guy lived with a twenty-six-year-old woman, Susan, by whom he had his ninth child, Michael.

Allen had always regaled his younger half brothers with bizarre sex lore, schooling them with scenarios worthy of Krafft-Ebing. Although they were avid listeners, they weren't converts. "I made up my mind I was *never* going to do *that* when I grew up," Randy said. "Some of Allen's stuff was just too weird."

After the incident with the frightened girl in McMinnville, Allen realized how close he had come to being arrested for attempted rape. He learned to suppress his lust and hide it behind a charming façade. He was so handsome by the time he was a senior in high school that he could pretty much pick and choose the girls he wanted, at least *outside* McMinnville. In town, however, rumors still painted him as a little odd and perhaps more than a little dangerous.

Allen always returned to the one girl he had dated consistently from the time he lived with Tom and Debbie Oliver. He met Ellen Langley* in Bible school in Siletz. She was a very nice girl, a religious girl who had been adopted by the devout Langley family. They went steady, or rather *Ellen* went steady with Allen, while they were still in high school.

"Ellen was a bighearted girl," Tom Oliver said. "She had long blond hair and skin like porcelain. But she was insecure. Allen's women have always been insecure."

Because Allen tended to tell everyone a slightly different story about his activities and they all had variations in time lines, it is impossible to pinpoint exactly where he was, and with whom, at any given time. Nineteen seventy-three appears to have more activities packed into it than would be humanly possible. He probably graduated from McMinnville High School at least a semester early, in January or February 1973. He did not, however, go on to Stanford University as he liked to tell people. Anyone bothering to check up on his résumé would find that Stanford had no record of his ever being registered there. Indeed, he didn't attend any college. It was his native intelligence and ability with words that allowed him to fool people.

Nineteen seventy-three was probably the time when Allen was involved in his Moonie money-laundering venture, whatever that really was. He was only a few months out of high school, so he could not have been very deeply involved in cult activities; he was away from McMinnville for less than a month.

And then Allen decided to join the army. He and Ellen reportedly found an army recruiting program where husbands and wives could enlist together. They were married on April 12, 1973, and joined the army on June 4. They went first to Fort Dix, New Jersey, for basic training and were then sent to an army base in the South.

Allen told his uncle Tom that he was terrified of the alligators there. Perhaps. He was let out of the service a few months later with an honorable discharge, but just barely. Apparently Ellen was released at the same time. After their stint in the army, the couple went to Mexico for a while on Allen's Gold Wing motorcycle.

"Allen treated Ellen terribly," Guy Van Houte said. Randy and Bruce Van Houte also remembered seeing Allen beating Ellen. "He would just go off," Bruce said. "He had a psychotic temper."

Ellen was no match for Allen; her dreams of a romantic marriage were rapidly draining away. It didn't matter who or what was in Allen's way when he lost it. He and Ellen had a young German shepherd, and Allen told her that it would be okay locked in their apartment for two days while they took a short trip.

Bruce was with them when they returned home. The dog had soiled the carpet and chewed up a lot of woodwork. While Bruce watched, horrified, Allen beat the dog with a two-by-four. There was nothing Bruce or Ellen could do to stop him, and she ran crying out of the apartment.

When Ellen came back, the dog was lying still on the floor. She said, "Honey, we need to get Lady to the vet," but Allen didn't even glance at her. He was smiling, watching television. The dog was dead.

One story said that Ellen gave birth to Allen's first child, but he would not allow her to keep the baby. He insisted that she place it out for adoption. In their five-year marriage Ellen suffered a great deal of physical abuse; he choked her and hit her. When she became pregnant for the second time, Allen deliberately kicked her in the stomach. Fearful that the fetus was severely damaged, Ellen had an abortion the next day.

They lived in Salem in an apartment and occasionally invited Bruce and Randy over for the weekend. Allen was an exhibitionist and preferred an audience when he had sex, but the boys were embarrassed and refused to watch. Nevertheless, he flaunted his grotesque sexual tastes in front of his younger half brothers. He deliberately left "letters" where they would be sure to find them, letters describing his sexual encounters.

Allen was not only a sadist who enjoyed playing cruel jokes on others, he was a masochist who took sexual pleasure himself from tiptoeing just on the edge of death. He demanded that Ellen tie his hands and then hold his head underwater in the bathtub until he passed out.

Only then was she allowed to let him up. When she sometimes panicked and pulled his head out of the water too soon, he was enraged that she had spoiled his orgasm.

As far back as anyone remembered, Allen was also a crossdresser. He had stolen Suzanne Van Houte's underwear when he lived with Guy's family in McMinnville, and his obsession with dressing as a woman increased over the years. All of his sexual perversions grew in intensity and had many variations. Just as he orchestrated neardrowning experiences in order to reach a shattering climax, he liked to take chances when he dressed as a female. He would have Ellen, and other women in his life, drop him off in full female regalia a long way from home. The exciting challenge for him was to make his way along public streets back to his apartment without being caught.

Ellen hated all of it, but fear kept her from trying to get away from Allen. After five years she finally found the courage to leave him. Their divorce decree was granted on January 30, 1978. Thereafter Allen always denied that he had ever been married to her but the written records of their marriage are contained in Oregon vital statistics files.

He was never without a girlfriend. Some knew of his kinky tastes and accepted his cross-dressing and masochism with equanimity; he kept his preferences hidden from others when he suspected they would be shocked. Some of his women were much younger than he, and others were older. There was one slightly older woman named Lisa, a psychologist from Independence, Oregon, who was fascinated with Allen both as a subject and as a lover. On one occasion she slipped him some Thorazine, which rendered him unable to move but released his latent hatred for her and all women. Temporily paralyzed, he breathed hoarsely that he wanted to kill her, and he would— if only he could move.

"When he was with Lisa," Randy said, "that was the only time in his whole life I really liked him, and that's when he was a pothead. He was really mellow then. Lisa was cool too, but it didn't last."

"She *knew* who Allen was," Bruce said. "He had problems, and she understood them. She was very good-looking and older, almost a mother figure to him. He hit her a couple of times, though, and that was it. He had been mellowing out, and I think he was trying to change, but Lisa had two boys, and she had him figured out. I think Allen was actually trying to do some self-examination then—that's the only time I ever saw that side of him—but they broke up, and he was back to being Allen."

His father and others who knew him well differed on whether

Allen ever drank to excess. "We talked about that often," Guy said, "because I drank a lot. But Allen was like me. He hated to be out of control, and alcohol made him lose control. He was a total control freak."

Tom Oliver disagreed; he insisted that Allen did drink. He saw Allen drunk on many occasions. "One time we were in Vancouver, Washington," he said, "and we went to Elmer's to watch a Portland Trail Blazers game, and we heard these two drunks arguing. And I recognized Allen's voice. 'That's Allen,' I said. He was with a business associate for a company he was going to start in Vancouver."

It was in the early '90s, and Tom and Debbie had lost track of Allen for some time, but they recognized his voice instantly. He came over and sat in their booth, catching up. Coldly he asked about his grandparents Elva and Austin. For the first fifteen years of his life they had treated him like a son and given him a home, and yet he asked Debbie flatly, "Are they dead yet? They must be dead by now."

"They would love to hear from you, Allen," Debbie said.

"I don't have time for that," he answered, swiveling his head toward the basketball game on the television screen and signaling for another drink.

With a few more drinks, however, Allen grew sentimental. He began to cry and told Debbie, "I've always loved you. You're really my mom."

"Allen and this guy he worked with wanted to go to Tony Roma's," Tom said, "and his friend and I picked Allen up—he was too drunk to stand by then. Since he was wearing a long cowboy raincoat, we just laid him down in the back of a pickup. He stayed there, passed out in the rain, while his friend went into Tony Roma's. He was so drunk that he didn't even wake up when the rain pelted down on him."

Apparently Allen was able to turn any excessive drinking on and off. The only addiction that stayed with him was the sexual addiction that revolved around his transvestite/masochistic fantasies. He didn't keep diaries or journals of his strange activities—nothing beyond the letters he left for his brothers. But *they* never forgot. Curious as they were as adolescents, Allen's sex life repelled them.

By the mid-'70s, with his marriage to Suzanne over, Guy Van Houte moved to the Tacoma, Washington, area. "I designed the *Saturday Night Fever* dance floor," he said, but then he retracted his sweeping claim a moment later. "Actually, I designed the *concept*," he explained, "and then half my design was stolen from me."

Guy named major celebrities in the music business whom he blamed for the loss of a patent.

If he missed making millions with his disco dance floors, Guy Van Houte did have a thriving business in the late '70s when he built and lit dance floors as flashy as those that John Travolta pranced on in the hit movie. "We lit up the Rain-Tree clubs and all the spots along the Pacific Highway strip by the Seattle-Tacoma Airport, *and* all the service bases in Washington State," he recalled. "All the NCO clubs at Fort Lewis and McChord Air, and the Evergreen Inn out of Olympia where the Washington politicians stayed. We were busy."

Although they were both highly intelligent, Allen had not inherited Guy's aptitude for electronics. But he had another talent; he was a consummate salesman. He became the advance man for his father's company and was very skilled at that. He covered a good portion of the West Coast for Discotheque Systems, Inc., signing up almost every club he visited. They clamored for the lighted dance floors Guy designed.

Guy marveled at Allen's ability to close a deal. "He could bring home *anything,* and I mean absolutely anything," he said. "He made the deals. I was living in an apartment in Spanaway, Washington, then, and I had a huge dining-room table. I remember how Allen came in once and said he'd sold a big club." Guy started asking him about the details.

"Did you get a check from them for the down payment?"

"Nope."

"You know you have to get a down payment for a job as big as this."

Allen responded by pulling out a large paper shopping bag, upending it, and pouring the contents into a punch bowl on the table. There were $10,000 banded packages of bills in the bag. They filled Guy's punch bowl and tumbled over the sides.

"There was fifty thousand dollars there," Guy marveled. "He came back with that much cash, and they didn't know him from Adam. But Allen could convince anybody of anything. People trusted him. He was *the* flim-flam man supreme."

Tom Oliver said that as an adult Allen always had a lot of cash. He would loan it to family and friends, but he charged a high interest rate. Once, he opened the trunk of his sports car to show Tom that it was full of money. He also had three guns hidden there. Tom had no idea where Allen got all that money, and he didn't particularly want to know the details. He, too, had heard the money-laundering story when Allen was supposedly working for a cult. Lord knows what he had gotten into lately. It might well have been some of the legitimate cash Allen collected as advances against the dance floors. Wherever he got it, money was certainly of vital importance to him. He had known poverty as a child, living in squalor at times. Now, Allen's façade was all success; what he might have felt inside was safely hidden from the world.

Guy and Allen worked together well in the boom of the disco era—there had been an endless demand for the ornate dance floors with undulating colored lights. Guy was very skilled at the intricacies of varnished wood laid down in mosaic patterns next to strips of brilliant light displays, and Allen's salesmanship was unparalleled. But by 1981 disco was no longer in. It had been so hot when everyone was into synchronized dancing that it seemed as if it would go on forever. But suddenly nobody was interested in their product any longer. The bonanza was over, but they both took it philosophically. They had lived well while it lasted, and Guy had been able to employ Randy and Bruce too. Now they regrouped. Guy went to Bend, Oregon, and opened up a television store, and Allen talked about his concept of bringing the ultimate stereo store to Salem, Oregon.

It was to be just a start for him. He never thought small, although no one could have even imagined the scope of his ambition. Allen opened Capitol Hi-Fi and Stereo in the Pringle Park Plaza in Salem, sure that his first store would soon become a franchise blanketing America.

And then he would be rich.

ALLEN met Mary Kelley, who became his second wife, in Tacoma, Washington, when he was working with Guy on the disco dance floors. They were married, possibly in Oklahoma, on November 13, 1979. Like all of his domestic alliances, there were many versions of the specifics. Allen claimed that Mary was his *first* wife, and said they had been very happy while they were dating, but the marriage itself never quite worked. "I left for Taipei on our wedding night on a business trip," he later told a reporter. "I was supposed to be gone three weeks, but I was away for nine months." He thought that his long absence got their marriage off to a bad start.

Perhaps it did. Or perhaps the whole story of a nine-month trip to Asia was made up. But there were other reasons. Although Allen certainly didn't bring it up in interviews, Mary, too, suffered from violent domestic abuse, and she had brought two small children to the marriage. She believed that Allen would be a wonderful stepfather but soon found that her charming suitor had become a husband with a maniacal temper. Allen was much taller and heavier than she was, and he pushed her, slapped her, and pulled her hair when she did something that irritated him.

When they were first married, Allen and Mary lived in Gig Harbor, Washington, a picturesque little town just across the Narrows Bridge from Tacoma. He was still working for Guy in the dance-floor business then and planning to start his stereo chain. But it wasn't long before Mary, like Ellen, was desperate to leave Allen. She tried in vain to find a way to escape.

It would take her three years.

Mary grew to be absolutely terrified of Allen. She knew that he had guns, and he frightened her more by threatening to kill her children if she ever tried to leave him.

Allen's sexual preferences revolted Mary, but she went along with him to keep peace in the house. She was mortified once when he insisted on handcuffing them together and then couldn't get the cuffs to open with the key. They had to call the fire department to free them. Allen laughed about it when he told his brother Randy, but Mary was humiliated.

Allen's abuse finally became so bad that she chose the lesser of two evils. Surreptitiously she managed to pack her things and the children's and slip away from him in the summer of 1981. Mary filed for divorce in Oregon and then headed for her mother's house in Yreka, California.

Tom and Debbie Oliver were living in Sutherlin, Oregon at that time, and Mary dropped in on them. "She had her two children and her pet bird with her," Tom recalled. "She stayed two days with us." They could see that Mary was as frightened of Allen as Ellen had been, and they felt sorry for her. Since she had run to them for protection, they sheltered her. When she pulled herself together, she left, heading south. Then she completely disappeared.

Sometime later the Olivers stopped in a restaurant in Mount Shasta, California, and were surprised to look up and see that their waitress was Mary. Her face turned pale, and she started to run away. But they had seen her, and Tom hurried after her, explaining gently that they were no threat to her. Mary was so afraid they would tell Allen where she was. She begged them not to. "Allen said he'd kill my children if I left," she said.

"We told her not to worry, that we would never tell Allen that we'd seen her or where she was," Tom said.

_____Chapter Seven_____

BEHIND THE PERFECT MASK he wore, *this* was the man that Sheila Walsh met in November 1982, the man she fell completely in love with and agreed to marry on their third date. They could not actually be married until February 1983, when Allen's divorce from Mary would be final. But Sheila was willing to wait. At least Allen would be living with her family, and they could be together.

Allen knew his way around Salem. He often hung out at the Battle Creek Golf Club or in the cocktail lounge of the Golden Dragon, a Chinese restaurant. He liked the Black Angus too, and frequented another very nice restaurant that was a favorite with transvestite customers—sophisticated-looking "women" whom Sheila in her innocence didn't recognize as men in drag. Allen was also enthusiastic about the Barter Exchange Club, with offices in the Reed Opera House, where he said that he could get almost anything he or the Smiths should want simply by exchanging goods or services.

He was the definitive man about town, and yet he seemed delighted to move in with Sheila's mother and stepfather and her sister Kerry. Gene thought he must have been lonesome, and she liked him because he wasn't afraid to quote the Holy Bible when he expressed himself. He was sophisticated, but he had a good heart—she was sure of that.

Kerry had found Allen entertaining and amusing at first. When he wanted to, he could be a lot of fun and self-deprecating. Talking about his long list of half brothers and sisters, he was hilarious. Speaking of his brother Brian's conviction for sodomy with a minor, Allen laughed and said, "He got arrested for following too close." But in reality, Allen appeared to have no more connection to his half siblings than to any stranger he met on the street. They meant nothing at all to him. His intelligence allowed him to be witty; his lack of empathy let him make fun of any target.

Kerry soon learned that Allen was not the faithful, tender lover her sister Sheila thought he was. "Allen took over my bedroom when he moved in with us in 1983," she remembered. "He brought a very expensive stereo with him, and he set it up in my room. One day I went in there to listen to it while he wasn't home, and I fell asleep on what used to be my bed."

Kerry was fifteen, and Allen was twenty-seven. She woke up, horrified, to find him lying on top of her. When she struggled to get away from him, Allen said in his quiet, persuasive voice, "Hey, this is okay. We're just keeping it in the family; there's nothing wrong with that."

Kerry was able to escape, and she avoided being alone with Allen after that. "But I didn't tell anyone," she said. "I didn't want to hurt Sheila. But the truth was that I knew she wouldn't have believed me anyway. She thought he was wonderful."

At fifteen, in a family where everyone else doted on Allen, Kerry knew it was hopeless to warn her parents or her sister. She tried to tell herself that his attempt to force intercourse on her had been only a momentary impulse on his part and that he would be good to her sister.

But she didn't really believe it. In many ways Kerry was a keener judge of human nature than any of them. She knew almost from the beginning that there were *two* Allens; one was perfectly groomed, handsome, and utterly lovable and charming. The Smiths and Sheila had yet to see the other side of him.

SHEILA had no idea that she wasn't going to be Allen's second wife, that she would actually be his *third* wife. Neither Ellen nor Mary would have envied her; they were still trying to put time and distance between themselves and Allen. Even if they had been in touch and knew about Allen's engagement, neither would have been brave enough to warn Sheila of the dangers ahead. Just as Kerry knew it would do no good to tell her sister that Allen had tried to rape her, the women who had fallen in love with him years before Sheila met him knew she would be blinded with love. Telling her the truth would be an exercise in futility. Allen was a wonderful salesman, or—as his father characterized him—"a superior con man." He could make anyone believe anything, and he seemed to be the most trustworthy of men.

And he was so handsome.

But there were a lot of things that Sheila didn't know about Allen. At the age of twenty-seven he had already been arrested a number of times, but even if she *had* reason to check out her fiancé's background, there was nothing on file that would have raised bright red flags. Records had been purged, and there were no longer any details on his early arrests.

If Sheila *had* been able to access them, she would have seen that on December 19, 1975, Allen Van Houte, twenty-one, was arrested in Salem for second-degree theft. The details and disposition on that case had been erased. On January 24, 1977, he was arrested in

McMinnville for driving while his license was suspended. The fine was fifty-three dollars; there was no record of whether he paid it. The records of the Oregon State Police for docket number T76518 were shredded. However, he would have to have had several traffic violations to have his license suspended.

A lot of young men in their early twenties have run-ins with the law, and it scares them enough to change their ways. Nothing scared Allen enough to alter his attitude about laws and rules and ethics and morals. He learned only that he was smarter than almost anyone, and that he never had to pay the price for what he chose to do.

AT Allen's insistence all the dresses for Sheila and her attendants came from Nordstroms'. The ceremony was on February 4, 1983, in the old Methodist church on State Street in Salem. In a way the choice of the church fit Allen. In 1848 Jason Lee, a Methodist circuit rider and pioneer, founded Salem and Willamette University. Lee himself was something of a pragmatist. When his first wife died while he was back east recruiting followers to join him in far-off Oregon Territory, the devout preacher immediately found a second, sturdier, woman to marry and bring back to Oregon so he wouldn't have to make an extra trip. Today he lies buried in an old cemetery near Bush's Pasture in Salem, a wife on either side of his grave.

Although Allen Van Houte appeared to fit *his* wives interchangeably into his life and he, too, had vision, his resemblance to Jason Lee stopped there. Although he frequently quoted the Bible, he had no intention of serving mankind and the Lord. He intended to become a captain of industry, a multimillionaire, and it mattered a great deal to him that he have a wife who befit that image. He needed a partner who was absolutely committed to him and his goals, a woman who adored him. And Sheila did. She was going to be the ideal wife for him; she was blond and beautiful, intelligent and socially desirable.

Allen and Sheila had a lovely reception at the Elks Club, just down the street from the Methodist church, and Allen appeared to be delighted with his beautiful new bride. "I thought Sheila was bright, ambitious, and wanted to achieve something with her life, and I wanted to share it," he said later. Sheila *was* bright and ambitious, and she had high hopes for their future. She felt lucky to have found a man who was so right for her when she was only twenty.

Funded principally by Gene and Don Smith's open line of credit at the Commercial Bank of Salem, Allen had re-established his stereo store in Salem and opened a second Stereo World in Corvallis, Oregon, some forty miles from Salem and the site of Oregon State University. The showrooms were full of expensive equipment, and music of the era played while shoppers deliberated. Michael Jackson's "Beat It," Irene Cara's "Flashdance," and Sting's "Every Breath You Take" were among the most popular records of the year. Music was a big part of Allen and Sheila's life.

While popular music was hot and sexy and sometimes even a little violent, it was ironic that the movies people flocked to see in the mid-'80s were romantic and sentimental, in keeping with the way Sheila was feeling. *Tender Mercies* and *Terms of Endearment* were the films that everyone remembered in 1983, and they were both three-handkerchief tearjerkers.

By midsummer Sheila was pregnant and thrilled about it. Allen seemed to feel the same way she did. The business was going well, and her world was as wonderful as she had always dreamed it might be. It didn't matter whether the baby was a girl or a boy. Allen had picked out two names that would work for either one. They were both names of women in the entertainment industry: Stevie Nicks Van Houte and Daryl Hannah Van Houte.

Allen had his own good reason for selecting those names. In case he should ever need additional Social Security numbers, he could use those of his children and no one would be the wiser. Sheila didn't know that. She just thought the names Allen chose were cute and unique.

Kerry almost convinced herself that what seemed like Allen's sexual moves toward her had really been only his warped sense of humor. She tried to get along with him because Sheila loved him so much. When Allen asked her to take a ride on his motorcycle, she agreed to go. But before she knew it, they weren't just racing around Salem. Allen hit the freeway and then the winding road through the Van Duzer Corridor toward the Pacific coast. He rode his motorcycle the way he drove his cars, way over the speed limit, and he took suicidal chances. Kerry was terrified as she clung to him and begged him to pull over.

"The way he went around those curves," she recalled, "I was sure we were both going to be killed. I pleaded with him to slow down, but he just laughed and went faster."

He brought her home unharmed, and Kerry vowed never to get on a motorcycle with him again. But there were still times when he tricked her into riding in his Porsche convertible; she would have had to make a huge scene to avoid riding with him, and she was still only fifteen and wondering if she was being a fraidy cat. But Allen's driving was as aggressive and confident as his personality. Even with a patrol car behind him, he passed six cars ahead of him, and he darted in and out of lanes. One trip to Corvallis just about reduced Kerry to tears. Allen loved that; she realized that he enjoyed frightening her. In the front seat, pregnant Sheila said nothing.

Sheila's family had little contact with Allen's. They didn't know his mother, Karen, but they met his grandparents Elva and Austin Alford. Elva sometimes came to Salem for bowling tournaments. During the first year of their marriage, Allen and Sheila saw little of his father, Guy, and his stepbrothers. After their marriage they moved to a high-rise apartment building in Portland. The commute to Salem wasn't that difficult, only about forty miles. Allen wasn't spending that much time in his stereo stores anyway.

SHEILA had seen flashes of Allen's temper, but she was completely unprepared for a shocking encounter they had on September 8, 1983, six months after their wedding. That night her world tilted and began to edge off-balance.

Allen loved sports cars, and even though he drove way too fast, he was a skilled driver. On that Thursday night Sheila and Allen were driving south on I-205, the interstate freeway that runs north and south along a low bridge over the Columbia River between Washington and Oregon. They were headed toward Portland and were a tenth of a mile north of the Eighty-second Avenue off-ramp when a motorcyclist on a Harley-Davidson with a woman hugging his waist passed Allen. That irritated him, and his foot hit the accelerator.

Sheila begged him to just let it go, but Allen sped up to overtake the cyclist. The car and the motorcycle kept apace, weaving and changing lanes as Allen pursued the biker. When the biker swerved a little as if he was going to cut in front of their car, Allen hit the accelerator and deliberately smashed into the Harley. The cyclist, David Keith Taylor, died instantly.

In front of a horrified Sheila, the female passenger, Nancy Jane Kirk, was thrown over the top of Allen's car, landing on its trunk. She clung there as Sheila begged Allen to stop, but he only drove faster, swerving sharply until the critically injured young woman finally slipped off his car and rolled down a bank.

Allen never slowed down, not until he got to a pay phone in Oregon City. He dialed Guy Van Houte's number. "Daddy," he pleaded, "what'll I do?"

Allen told Guy what had happened, and, to what he said was his everlasting regret, Guy advised his son, "You tell the police that you were just driving along with your pregnant wife when this Hell's

Angel came up and started playing games with you. Say he tried to force you off the road. You were in a panic. You honked at him to warn him, but he just kept cutting closer and closer. You felt terrible when he misjudged, and he slid under your wheels. Say you didn't even realize there was a woman with him. You had to think about Sheila—you were afraid something would happen to her and she'd lose the baby."

That was what Allen did, and his father backed him up.

When he was arrested by Clackamas County sheriff's deputies, he repeated what Guy told him. He had done the only thing he could to protect his wife against some wild biker who wanted to race, and who was cutting in and out and harassing him, taking chances. The crazy fool had miscalculated, Allen said, and laid his bike down right under his tires. There was nothing he could have done to avoid him. Nevertheless, Allen was cited for leaving the scene of an accident without exchanging information or rendering any assistance to either of the people on the motorcycle.

Sheila knew what had really happened—that Allen had deliberately hit the motorcycle and then driven in a way that would make the injured woman lose her tenuous perch on the back of his car. But they had only been married six months, Sheila loved Allen, and she was carrying his baby. She listened to him explain that he had had no choice so many times that she began to believe it. She *wanted* to believe it.

Allen pleaded not guilty, and his trial was scheduled to start on April 19, 1984. He was represented by counsel who repeated the scenario of a man with a pregnant wife terrified that she would be injured—or killed—by a crazy biker on a Harley. On April 26 a mistrial was declared when the jury could not render a verdict. On June 4 docket number 83–654, the case against Allen, was dismissed.

Once more Allen sailed away free. For more than fifteen years Guy told no one that Allen had run over the motorcyclist deliberately. But Sheila *knew* what had happened. She was now more bound to Allen than ever, trapped by a lie that she had participated in if only by an error of omission. Their first baby was born in Corvallis while they waited for Allen to go to trial. Stevie Nicks Leigh Van Houte was only a month old when her father's case was presented to a jury.

Stevie was a pretty little baby with dark brown hair like her father's. Allen posed for early family snapshots, cradling Stevie in his arms and smiling for the camera. In the background the camera caught Gene's doll-making table. It was covered with disembodied heads with empty eye sockets giving what should have been a sweet picture a grotesque air. Allen smiled with only half his face; the corners of his mouth tilted up, but his eyes had a certain flat, distrusting stare.

BUSINESS seemed to be booming at Capitol Hi-Fi, and Gene and Don were pleased with their investment. They had no idea that bills were not being paid and that the business was teetering on the edge of failure. Someone had sued the store in Salem for selling defective equipment, but Allen told them not to be concerned—it was only a nuisance suit.

Don Smith cosigned a loan so that Allen could buy a 911 Porsche, and Allen often drove Don's van and his green Chevy pickup truck. Don had a boat too, a hydroplane with a 454 Chevy motor. The Smiths were so close to Allen that he had access to their vehicles and whatever papers went with them. They were family now.

Allen and Sheila moved to Corvallis, and Kerry visited quite often. She was amazed once when Allen took a vase off the shelf and showed her that it was stuffed with large bills. "He told me he always wanted to have cash around in case he needed it in a hurry," Kerry said.

In the summer of 1984 the Smiths began to see the tiny stray threads of a business starting to unravel. They weren't too worried, because Allen said he had collateral to back up the loans they were making. He told them that his storage warehouse outside Salem was full of new television sets. Don was stunned to find that the locked warehouse was filled with junky old TVs that didn't work. There *was* no collateral beyond what was in the showrooms of the two stores.

Don was more shocked when he was notified that his driver's license had been taken away because of his failure to pay traffic fines. He had no tickets; Allen had duplicated his license, and *his* infractions were being entered into Don's driving record. It took a long time for Don to convince the Oregon State Police that he was not the driver with the violations.

It only grew worse. Allen had the title to Don's van and sold it. Don learned to his dismay that all his cars and boats were listed in Allen's name. He had no idea how Allen had managed to get the titles and have himself listed as the legal owner. Allen sold the hydroplane, but Don got that back. He tried to sell the pickup truck, but Don put a stop to that by telling the buyer that Allen didn't own the truck. Although they didn't want to believe it, it seemed that Allen had come into Gene and Don's life and immediately started converting their assets to himself, ruining their credit and their good records.

Compared to that, their realization that Allen had never graduated from Stanford or any other college, and that he had never been a second lieutenant either, hardly surprised them. Allen clearly had some problems with the truth. Even so, when he told them that they had no choice but to file bankruptcy, they were stunned. All their money was gone, their credit rating was destroyed, and their only assets were the stock in the stores and their heavily mortgaged home. Dunned for bills that Allen had run up, they were completely bewildered.

By August 1984 their high expectations on Allen and Sheila's wedding day had crumbled. He was not the man they thought he was; he looked at them mockingly and brushed aside their concerns. And then Sheila got sick. When Stevie was only five and a half months old, she was diagnosed with spinal meningitis. She was very ill, and yet Allen would not take responsibility for caring for his baby daughter.

"He went golfing," Kerry said, "and he didn't even visit Sheila in the hospital. I took care of Stevie, and I lost all respect for Allen when he refused to let my mother visit Sheila in the hospital."

Allen was doing his best to separate Sheila from her parents. He would have kept her away from Kerry too, but he needed Kerry to baby-sit Stevie. He didn't want to be tied down changing diapers and walking the floor with a baby.

There were times, however, when Allen did want Stevie with him. Fighting in bankruptcy court, taking Gene and Don down with him, he had to attend hearings in the federal courthouse to determine who was responsible for the bills that were piling up. "Allen brought Stevie to those meetings," Don said. "He explained that he had to baby-sit because there was no one to care for her. Gene would have taken care of her, but he had shut her out. Kerry would have too, but he wanted to look like a caring father to the bankruptcy judge."

Allen was already planning his escape from the messiness in Oregon. He had made arrangements to move to Hawaii, and, once there, Gene and Don Smith would never get a backward glance. Allen blamed the stereo-business failure on them, saying they had mismanaged money and had no heads for business. It was a terrible blow for them. At a stage in life where they had looked forward to retiring, they were left holding the bag and the bills. Although he had his pensions, Don was past the years when he could command a large salary. He and Gene still hoped to save their home, counting on some income from the radios, stereos, and speakers still in the closed Stereo World stores.

They were not to get even that. Randy Van Houte admitted years later that Allen had hired him to help strip the stores of all the stock. In the dark of night, television sets and stereos were crated in containers to be loaded onto ships bound for Hawaii before the Smiths even knew they was gone. (Later Allen's brothers would say that the FBI came looking for the merchandise in Hawaii and failed to find it. But again the FBI has no record of that. More likely, the searchers were from local law-enforcement agencies.)

"In the end we got *nothing* from the stores," Gene said. "The Christmas before, Allen was very generous with everyone else, giving people boom boxes and television sets. He didn't give us anything that Christmas—or ever. He cleaned everything out and shipped it to Hawaii."

Sheila was forced now to choose between her parents and her husband. Barely recovered from her meningitis, she listened as Allen told her flatly they were moving to Honolulu. He was adept at quoting the Bible when it suited his purposes, and he harked back to the days when he lived with Tom and Debbie Oliver and taught a Bible-study class.

"Sheila," Allen said, "the Bible says that when you marry, you must leave your parents and cleave unto your husband. You know that is your Christian duty."

Sheila was torn. Although she wasn't aware of how it had happened, she knew Don Smith was no dummy at business and that Allen had to have cheated him and her mother to fool them so completely. The blinders were partially off her eyes, and she realized that her husband was not the knight in shining armor she had once believed him to be. But she still hoped that they could salvage their marriage. She had Stevie, who wasn't a year old yet. How would they live if she left Allen? And Allen was right that the Bible said she should cleave to him.

Besides, Sheila still loved Allen. How could she give up when they were only beginning their marriage? He was a man who could weave such a spell with the right words. He told her that it was just bad luck that the stereo stores had closed, and that he had never promised her parents a sure thing. Sheila knew that Allen liked to travel and have fun when he should have concentrated more on the business. It had been his fault more than anyone's that they were bankrupt; he was the one who wasn't tending to business, but she couldn't bring herself to leave him. So much was already gone, and she was trying to save what she could. Allen promised her that they would make a new start in Honolulu, and she believed him. She *had* to believe him.

And so Sheila chose Allen. It was to be the beginning of a long estrangement from her mother and stepfather. Allen assured her that he was going to make a fortune in Hawaii. Someday they would come back to the mainland and make it up to her family.

Allen cut a number of ties as he flew off to Hawaii. Tom Oliver had stayed close to him, an uncle/father figure for years, but he shook his head, remembering how completely Allen vanished. "I lost Allen when he went to Hawaii, and then when he brought his father over there to go into business with him," he said. Tom had never believed that Guy was a good influence on Allen. By this time he wasn't sure which of them—father or son—was the bad influence.

Sheila, Allen, and Stevie moved to Hawaii in October 1985. They rented a big house in Honolulu, and Allen started to look for another business endeavor, convinced that he was overdue to hit the mother lode. He liked Hawaii, and he liked the Far East even more. He felt an affinity with Taipei, Taiwan, and Eastern culture, particularly after he read James Clavell's *Shogun*. Leaving Sheila behind in Hawaii, he headed off again to Taipei to look for the right product around which he could build his empire. In the meantime, they could survive by selling the stock from his stereo stores in Oregon.

_____Chapter Eight_____

ALLEN VAN HOUTE was a hurricane who had ripped his in-laws' lives off their foundations and then moved on. Back in Salem, Oregon, Gene and Don Smith were going through hard times. Don was almost fifty-three and had lost a lot; it wouldn't be easy to recoup. Under their bankruptcy they were allowed to keep their house at 1515 N.E. Liberty. But there was a mortgage on that. And then they learned that Gene's parents were in failing health back in Biloxi and needed the Smiths to take care of them. They had no choice but to leave Salem, and they arranged for one of Gene's sons to move into the Liberty Street house. He promised to make the mortgage payments.

Gene's last child living at home was Kerry, who was seventeen. Cathy had moved out a few years earlier, and Sheila had broken her mother's heart by running off to Hawaii with the man who had betrayed them. When her brother's family took over the house, Kerry moved her things out to the detached garage where Gene had her doll shop.

In the aftermath of her parents' bankruptcy, home, as Kerry had known it, had evaporated. She could have gone to Mississippi with Gene and Don, but she was a junior in high school in Salem. At first she lived in a cheap apartment with two friends, and then she moved in with a friend's mother—Bev Moreland, who was a high school counselor. "She gave me a place to stay and someone to listen to me until I graduated," Kerry recalled. "It really helped."

She figured she could graduate a year early from Sprague High School by taking extra classes. She had a very important goal; she was going to go to Hawaii and see Sheila. She needed to reassure herself that her big sister was all right. In order to do that, Kerry worked at three jobs: at the Keizer Retirement Center as a nursing aide, in the office at the high school, and selling a photographer's services over the phone. She saved her money, and when she graduated in January, 1985, she bought a plane ticket and flew to be with Sheila.

Kerry loved Hawaii, and she stayed a month, but it was an uneasy month. She could not believe how bad Sheila looked, worse somehow than she had the previous summer when she was hospitalized with meningitis. "She was four months pregnant with Daryl then," Kerry remembered. "But she looked like one of those starving people in Africa. She was so thin that her arms were like sticks, and she had a little tiny belly sticking out from her pregnancy."

Kerry had long been concerned about Sheila. "Allen could be so much fun to be with, and he had a great sense of humor," Kerry recalled, "but that was only one side of him. I was worried about Sheila because I knew she didn't tell me about most of the bad things in her marriage."

Indeed she didn't.

When Kerry arrived in Honolulu, she joined a very crowded household. Also, in January 1985, Allen had summoned Guy and Randy Van Houte to Hawaii to join his new business. Suddenly he was in touch with a number of relatives he hadn't seen in years. They apparently believed that he was going to succeed this time in his plan to make millions. His half sister, Linda, had even convinced her wealthy boyfriend that Allen was on to something and obtained $20,000 to help him start his latest venture.

With his slate wiped clean of debts after the Oregon bankruptcy, Allen was well on his way. He told Kerry that he had discovered a fascinating product during his trip to Asia. He believed it had everything American consumers would want. He reckoned that even more than music, people needed something that would improve their health, build their bodies, and most of all, take away their pain. In Taiwan he had seen a device that could stimulate muscles with an electric pulse that made them contract involuntarily. He predicted that it would seem like magic to customers if they could build their muscles without exercising.

Allen saw the potential in these devices, even though it would take a little fine-tuning by someone who understood electronics. And that, of course, was his father, Guy. And so Guy, his fourth wife, Chris, her two children, and Allen's half brother Randy had moved into the house Allen had rented. Allen also had a golden macaw named "Beth-the-Bird." It was a multilevel home with a formal living room at the top of the front steps, and then up another level to the family room and kitchen. There were four bedrooms arranged in different wings.

Kerry was relieved to meet Jonda Pinter, who had been hired to be Stevie's nanny. Jonda was a warm woman who had five children of her own. She was wonderful with Stevie and seemed to care a lot about her sister. Sheila told Kerry that Allen had insisted on their going on a luxury cruise, without Stevie, and she had no choice but to go, but at least she knew that Jonda would take good care of her baby.

The first name Allen gave to his miraculous device was the Health-Tronic. Beyond the money his sister got for him, Allen needed a big stake to start his new venture. He went to the Bank of Hawaii and applied for a loan. How he did it only he could say, but somehow he managed to convince the bank he was a good risk. Either he didn't tell them about his bankruptcy in Oregon or it didn't affect their decision. No one ever argued that Allen was not a genius at selling himself, and he had a most viable product.

The $160,000 he borrowed from the Bank of Hawaii went to buy the more than three thousand muscle stimulators he planned to import from the Far East. He explained that his company, Pacific International Electronic Supply, would sell these miraculous devices to both physicians and patients to rehabilitate injured muscles. The market was endless, Allen said. Not only would his stimulators regenerate weakened and damaged muscles, they would undoubtedly appeal to athletes everywhere. They would also sell to customers who didn't want to go to the effort of doing exercises to become perfect specimens.

As Guy was fond of saying, Allen knew "nothing about electronics," but he was a salesman. Allen wasn't a particularly good businessman either, but he had vision. Guy had run businesses, albeit small television and stereo repair shops, but he knew more about the basics than Allen did.

When Allen summoned his father to Hawaii to join him in his new enterprise, it seemed initially be a meeting of the minds and a chance for them to reconcile. But Guy was not as naïve as he liked to claim, and he knew his first son's patterns of behavior. Still, he and Randy had gone off to Honolulu with great expectations.

Neither they nor Allen would ever agree on *who* actually changed the "wave pattern" on the electric stimulators so that they performed as advertised. Guy insisted that he was the one who understood the concept; Allen would one day testify that he was the guiding force behind the muscle stimulators. At any rate, when Allen brought back the three thousand stimulators manufactured by the Taiwanese, Guy and Randy stood by to modify them. "We did the internal operations," Guy said.

"Originally, the idea was to sell it to 'jocks' to build up their muscles while they were sitting in their chairs, drinking their drinks," Guy said. Randy tested the stimulator and found that it really would take an inch off a waistline in a few days—all without exercise—although it couldn't be used indefinitely. Muscles could only get so tight.

KERRY was impressed with Allen's office. "It was very nice, very plush, with salespeople and staff in suits and dresses. There were booths where people could get hooked up to the EMS's for an hour. Allen told them that they would lose weight and get muscles, and they *did*."

Allen even had one of his electro-muscular stimulators packed into an expensive leather briefcase in a package designed for businessmen. His pitch for them was that they could build their muscles while they traveled on planes. He used the device himself, and Kerry could see that his stomach muscles were very defined and impressive. This time, she thought, Allen might just be on to something.

Although she was persuaded that Allen was headed for success, Kerry was taken aback when he continued to talk about his ambitions. He had only begun, he said, to realize his goals.

"Allen told me that he wanted to control the world's food production," Kerry recalled. "He said that whoever controlled food would control the whole world, and he intended to become President of the United States! He said he knew how to grow a hundred acres' worth of food on only one acre of land by using hydroponic gardening."

Kerry looked at her brother-in-law closely to see if he was kidding her, and saw that he was dead serious about seizing more power than any living man. "Later I saw *The Omen*," Kerry said, "and I thought, Oh, my God, Allen is the devil."

Allen's ambition, of course, bordered on megalomania, but he said it with a straight face, and he actually seemed to believe that one day he would indeed control the entire world.

Allen bought TV commercial time in Hawaii for the stimulators using the Health-Tronic name. His ads were ubiquitous. Now he suggested that the Health-Tronic would cure illness and restore paralyzed limbs. That was not entirely true, and illegal to boot, but it didn't bother him. Guy claimed that Allen said "The hell with the FDA."

Allen did, however, add a microchip that he bought at Radio Shack in an attempt to make the Health-Tronic meet Food and Drug Administration codes. It made little difference. He didn't really know what he was doing, and the FDA viewed his expanded operation as a scam.

DESPITE the apparent success of Allen's business and the presence of Jonda, Kerry saw that her fears about Sheila had a basis in reality. Sheila had been delighted to see her and seemed happy about her second pregnancy, but she was clearly troubled in her marriage.

Kerry was only seventeen, and Sheila was twenty-two, but Kerry wasn't fooled. She saw bruises, and she heard the way Allen talked down to Sheila. Her sister was somehow diminished, and she had lost a lot of her feistiness. Pregnant, caring for a small daughter, she was also working outside the home for attorney Roy Anderson and sharing her house with Guy Van Houte, his wife, Chris, and Guy's son Randy. Kerry was relieved to see that Chris was a calming factor whenever things got tense in the house. "She loved Sheila," Kerry said, "so that made me feel better."

Randy liked Sheila too. And Guy frowned when he saw how Allen manhandled her. He watched, disapproving, when Allen grabbed Sheila by her blouse collar and held her up against the wall, her feet dangling, as he lectured her. However, neither Guy nor Randy stood up to him. It was his marriage.

Allen was smart enough not to pin Sheila to the wall while Kerry was in the house. But she had seen Sheila's bruises and the haunted look in her eyes. Kerry set her jaw and went to Allen and warned him what she intended to do if he hurt Sheila. Despite her age, no one ever doubted Kerry when she was serious, and she was very serious when she realized that her sister was being beaten.

"I told Allen," Kerry recalled, "that if he continued to beat my sister, I would get a gun and I would shoot him. I think he saw that I meant it. I would have done it too."

It was so hard for her to see Sheila the way she was in Hawaii. She had been deliriously happy only two years before when she was Allen's bride in their fairytale wedding. It was worse than Kerry had thought. When Randy confided to her some of the horrific details of Allen's first marriage—to Ellen—Kerry's heart sank.

But there was nothing she could do to substantiate her fears. Sheila shut down when Kerry questioned her, and it was clear she didn't want to leave Allen. She still hoped that their marriage would get better. Maybe if Allen's dreams of being a dominant force in industry came true, he wouldn't be so angry. Kerry tried not to think of Allen's plans to take over the whole world. He had to be exaggerating.

KERRY flew back to Oregon. She could have lived in her folks' house with her stepbrother's family, but she enjoyed having her own place. It wasn't really like living in a garage, because Gene had fixed it up nicely, and she could use the kitchen and the bathrooms in the house.

Kerry broke off with a longtime boyfriend that spring of 1985. She was visiting with Margie Barger, her best friend's mother, whom she called "Mom," when they heard a knock on the door. "Margie always had food out for anyone who might be hungry," Kerry said. "I went to the door, and there stood Rick Bladorn. I slammed the door in his face, half-teasing him. But he knocked again."

Rick was the man Kerry had chosen for Sheila. He was twenty-three, and at first Kerry thought he was too old for her. Four-and-a-half years is a big gap when you're seventeen. But Rick was persistent. He was such a nice guy, and good-looking, and he was determined that Kerry was the girl for him. She knew he was right, and before long they moved in together; they would stay together ever after.

That June of 1985 Kerry and a girlfriend drove to Biloxi to see her grandmother Clennis Pearl, who was undergoing treatment for failing kidneys. It was quite a summer. Kerry was sick in the hospital for a week, Sheila's daughter Daryl was born, and, in Vietnam, they found Francis Walsh's remains. Just before Daryl was born, a very pregnant Sheila met a plane in Hawaii to accept the remains. Kerry went to Biloxi for the burial services. Her father was put to rest at last between Kelly Ann and Donny.

_____*Chapter Nine*_____

IN HAWAII, Allen had pushed too fast and too far afield of his original business concept. It was one thing to sell a product that appealed to the vanity of consumers, and quite another to advertise it as a cure-all. In late May 1985, at the instigation of the FDA, U.S. marshals and customs officials arrested Allen and seized his warehouse full of 2700 muscle stimulators, the bulk of his stock. It was a major scandal in Honolulu, and stories ran on television and in the Honolulu *Star-Bulletin* for weeks. Both Allen and Guy were castigated in the media. The Bank of Hawaii was not pleased. It put a lien on the muscle stimulators, demanding payment.

It was a terrible time for Sheila. Kerry had gone back to Oregon, and Sheila was hugely pregnant. As irrational as it sounded, Allen accused her of being pregnant by a lover. It wasn't true, but it hurt her. Daryl Hannah Leigh Van Houte was born in Honolulu in July 1985, and now Sheila had two little girls under sixteen months to take care of. She was thankful for Jonda, who assured her that she would help Sheila look after both the baby girls.

No one will ever know if Sheila was aware of the full extent of Allen's perverse sexual appetites. But with more pressure on him from the FDA and the prospect of his business failing, he turned more often to cross-dressing. He was using prostitutes to help him dress up as a woman and to engage in complicated and arcane sex games. Sheila was too ashamed to tell anyone, especially Kerry. There were aspects of Allen's true personality that she could never have imagined. On top of his other raunchy eccentricities, he was a voyeur who "liked to watch."

Allen's own half sister, Linda, who had done her best to help him, was very concerned about Sheila. She tried to protect her from the fast-approaching implosion of Allen's business and from Allen himself. But as the FDA put a lid on his Health-Tronics in the fall of 1985, he did what he always did—he walked away. In early 1986, he slipped out of Hawaii and left his father and half brother behind with a faltering business. He and Sheila and their two baby girls headed for Texas. Allen made no pretense of staying with a sinking ship, and he felt no loyalty to his father. Guy was a big boy, and he had taken his chances, right along with Allen.

WITH Allen gone, Guy stayed with the project in Honolulu, convinced that he could modify the muscle stimulators so they would become medical devices that did what Allen claimed they did. Guy and Randy managed to retrieve them legally from the closed warehouse, relabeled them, and set about getting FDA approval for them. The bank waited to see. It had nothing to lose by waiting; unless the stimulators worked, they weren't worth much.

Guy and Randy were determined to get FDA approval to make the muscle stimulators legal medical devices. That was the only way, Guy figured, they could make a go of the business Allen had started. "It was a viable product," Randy said. "But it wouldn't have mattered to Allen. It could have been total hokum, and if Allen could fool the public and make a quick buck, he wouldn't have cared."

Guy made some electronic modifications. The concept of the stimulator had been around since the '60s. It was similar to a TENS unit, a device worn by patients who suffered constant pain from injuries and illnesses. The TENS unit provided stimulus that overrode the sensation of pain—not a cure, certainly, but a workable alternative to heavy-duty and addictive pain medication. Guy's EMS unit was designed to do more than "buzz" or "tingle" the affected area; it could actually make muscles contract. When it did, it would encourage blood flow in the area and could reasonably be expected to enhance healing.

Guy formed a new company, calling it WestPac Electronics, and he ultimately received approval from the FDA that allowed him to relabel the stimulators as health devices rather than exercise devices.

Allen had run out too soon, and now his father, his chief competitor, was reaping rewards from *his* brainchild. He had meant to leave Guy holding the bag. Now he realized the bag was full of gold and he was slowly being forced out. The only contact Allen had with Guy and Randy was about the business.

For all intents and purposes Allen and Guy were estranged. For the rest of their days they would speak ill of one another and would one day stop communicating entirely. It was probably inevitable. Guy had ignored Allen for the first fifteen years of his life, and now Allen had no use for Guy. He set about a plan to wrest the business from his father. Guy had little doubt that Allen could do it if he chose. As long as the EMS business was on the rocks and the government agencies were closing in, Allen wanted no part of it. But when Guy managed to get FDA approval, he dreaded Allen's reappearance.

Later Guy would say, "It was like the classic tale of a Roman warrior who realized the man lying on the ground beneath his sword was his own father, and, even so, he plunged the sword through his heart."

Guy liked to recall a conversation he once had with Allen about eternity. "You may go to heaven," Allen told his father flatly. "I won't. Because I have sold my soul to the devil."

_____Chapter Ten_____

As THE AFTERMATH of Allen's betrayal of her parents rolled on, Kerry had no one to count on in Oregon but Rick Bladorn. Rick recalled how he worried about her, and tried to make sure she had enough to eat and didn't freeze living in the garage, but Kerry insisted her situation was never that desperate. "I could eat at Marge's and I could go in the house any time I wanted. I kind of *liked* the garage; it was my own space."

But there was no doubt that Rick gave her emotional support at a time when her family had scattered to the four winds and she was gripped with a premonition about her sister Sheila, a dark shadow she could not shake.

After they had arranged for Gene's mother, Clennis Pearl, to have the kidney dialysis she needed to stay alive, Don and Gene Smith decided to settle in San Antonio, Texas. Coincidentally, Sheila and Allen were headed for San Antonio too. Kerry knew Sheila was disenchanted with her marriage and struggling to find a way out. She also knew it wasn't going to be an easy way for her to go. There was nothing Kerry could do but keep in touch with Sheila and hope for the best.

KERRY and Rick stayed together, a very young couple who had amazingly level heads. They lived for a time in Turner, Oregon, a little town between Salem and Albany. Rick knew everything there was to know about cars and metal fabricating, and they made plans to start their own business from the ground up, even though it meant they would have to live in a camper on the back of Rick's truck.

For Christmas 1985 Sheila and Allen and the two baby girls had come to Oregon. It was the first time that Kerry had seen Daryl, who was five months old, and Kerry was pregnant with her first baby. Sheila clearly adored both her baby girls, but Kerry could see that her concern about Sheila wasn't without justification. Sheila seemed even more unhappy with Allen than she had been in Hawaii. It was very important for the two sisters to be together, although Kerry felt helpless to do anything for Sheila. Allen set the tone of the Christmas visit early on. "What do you think of your sister?" he asked Kerry.

"She looks half dead," Kerry shot back, referring to all the weight Sheila had lost.

Allen chuckled and said, "I know. She's probably going to kill herself."

It was almost as if Allen was programming that thought into Sheila's head, and then again, it might have only been his bizarre and acidic sense of humor.

Allen's mien was hardly that of a man who had left Hawaii after a rout. He seemed very confident and carried a briefcase stuffed with big bills. He showed its contents to Rick, saying he planned to buy a Mercedes.

Cars were a common ground for Rick and Allen to talk about. Although the two men could not have been more different, at least they were both interested in cars. Allen wanted Rick to find him a Mercedes on the gray market.

"I knew a man who imported Mercedes through the gray market," Rick said. "But he did it legitimately. There were so many restrictions in the United States, and any buyer had six months to make the modifications on the cars so that they complied with American standards. If they didn't, the Mercedes could be seized and never returned. I explained that to Allen.

"He laughed," Rick continued, "and told me that he knew a way to bring a Mercedes in without following any of those rules. He said that he could hide the car in such a way that no one would ever know where it came from. He had no intention of making the modifications. Allen always had a way to get around laws."

But Rick wanted no part of such a transaction. Allen shrugged and closed his briefcase.

The two couples were playing cards one night at the home of a woman Allen knew. Allen kept sniping at Sheila, and that angered Kerry. She hated it when he made her sister seem a dumbbell. Trying to keep it light, Kerry said, "You better be nicer to her, Allen, or she might leave you."

Allen's response had no humor in it at all. "If she leaves me," he said carefully, "I'll kill her, and I'll take the girls."

SHEILA and Allen began the new year, 1986, in Texas. They moved first to Helotes, a small suburb northwest of San Antonio, and later rented a condo a little closer to the city.

Furious that Guy was apparently making money from his invention, Allen decided to sever himself completely from his birth parents. He hadn't spoken to his mother, Karen, for a year, and now he simply shut her out of his life. He didn't want to carry the name Van Houte any longer either; his solution was simplistic, but it was the way he did things. He would simply change his name legally and become a different man.

Despite the faltering of his EMS enterprises, Allen still felt more at home with the culture of the Far East than he ever had in America. He continued to be fascinated with James Clavell's hero, even more so since he had seen the television miniseries of *Shogun*. Richard Chamberlain played Englishman John Blackthorne, an explorer and plunderer whose fortunes left him and his crew stranded in Japan in the fifteenth century. Allen saw his own reflection in John Blackthorne, a survivor at all costs—but more than that, an opportunist who could build his own world even though the sands beneath him shifted. The fictional Blackthorne had become a clever observer of Japanese politics and inveigled his way into a power position. To Allen he was more than a character in Clavell's imagination. Blackthorne was *real,* a model to emulate.

And so on March 14, 1986, William Allen Van Houte became Allen Blackthorne. Sheila knew why Allen had picked Blackthorne, but Allen denied the *Shogun* connection. He insisted that he changed his name because he had discovered that Guy Van Houte was not his biological father. Although he didn't say how he had learned this, he announced that he now knew that his real father was a man named James Blackthorne. A minute examination of Allen's family tree has never revealed a James Blackthorne. Furthermore, anyone who observed Allen and Guy Van Houte side by side would see that they were father and son; save for Guy's white hair, the two men looked almost exactly alike.

But Allen was going to be sure that no one saw them side by side. If he had his way, no one in Texas would ever connect Allen to the name Van Houte or to Guy.

With his new name Allen arranged to get a new Social Security number. He also had the use of two other Social Security numbers with male names: Stevie Van Houte and Daryl Van Houte. The girls were so young, they weren't using them.

With his surname changed, Allen cut off all contact with his family in Oregon, saying, "I have divorced my past." Only grudgingly did he stay in touch with Guy and the business in Hawaii, and that was because he intended to take it back when the moment was right.

He bided his time, waiting to pounce.

PART TWO

San Antonio

_____ *Chapter Eleven*_____

A HALF HOUR before dawn in San Antonio, Texas, the birds begin singing, filling the last soft dark with trills, calls, and cheeps. Turtledoves, mockingbirds, and grackles alike combine their chorus until it sounds as if every inch of every tree branch is filled with them. As the sun breaks the horizon, their songs fade quickly to silence. And then, like clockwork, they begin again precisely a half hour before sunset. During the heat of the day the turtledoves huddle together on the coolest earth in the shade of low bushes, and the grackles annoy tourists by dive-bombing their tables on the famed Riverwalk or outside the Mexican restaurants in the Market Square to boldly steal packets of sugar.

San Antonio is revered as the friendliest city in America, and rightly so. Warmth and courtesy are embedded in the psyches of San Antonians, and even road rage is rare on the freeways that encircle the city in ever widening rings as it constantly grows too big to contain itself and sprouts new suburbs.

The sun is brilliantly hot most months, and the earth so arid that nightly television weather reports include the aquifer level, to monitor the threat of drought. But when it rains in San Antonio, it rains; the huge drops form heavy curtains of water. Six to ten inches can fall in less than an hour, torrential rain that defies windshield wipers and washes across the freeways even though they are banked steeply so that the water will dissipate rapidly. Teenage boys rush to plunge their rigs into the challenge of the soupy mud alongside the freeway, until they are invariably trapped. Chagrined police have to haul them out with tow trucks.

San Antonio is the seat of Bexar County, and the pronunciation of Bexar gives a newcomer away. Natives say "Bear County," because the X is said to have once been the center of a cattle brand and is not a letter at all. Strangers say "Bex-ar."

Half of San Antonio's citizens are Hispanic, but there are a surprising number of descendants of early German settlers. The city has a diverse mixture of cultures, and it is both historic and modern. Jones-Maltsberger Road runs parallel to Nacogdoches, and Toepperwein intersects with Seguin. Visitors flock to the town of New Braunfels, northeast of San Antonio.

The venerable Alamo, site of a terrible siege in the winter of 1836 by General Santa Anna against Texans and Mexican colonists, still stands in the middle of San Antonio, steps from weathered brick streets. In reality the stone-and-mortar structure is shockingly small, almost a miniature of the towering fort it seems in paintings and photos. If one were to superimpose John Wayne's image over the Alamo, he would be a Gulliver, looming over its limestone walls.

There is great respect for history in San Antonio, from the Alamo Plaza to the crumbling missions south of the city. They are as strong as the God they honor, however, and only their corners are slipping away. Their weedy grounds have a patient dignity that transcends time and tragedy.

There are also soaring new buildings, but they have never been allowed to dwarf the city's heart and history. The Riverwalk—Paseo Del Rio—with its carefully channeled two and a half miles of river snaking between flagstone and cobblestoned paths, allows runners and walkers access to fine hotels and little restaurants along its shore. It is an unabashed tourist attraction, but it is a classy site that saves San Antonio the way Central Park saves New York City from being smothered by cement and steel.

A lesser known San Antonio attraction is a railroad crossing south of town, out past the old missions. It is a single working track surrounded by underbrush and spindly trees marred by crushed beer cans, hamburger wrappers, and other debris. Locals acknowledge cheerfully that it's haunted, and the tracks are a popular weekend spot, especially near Halloween. According to legend, a school bus full of children stalled on the track as a train barreled down on them. All the students perished. Several nearby streets bear children's names, which only solidifies the myth. Believers, and doubters too, sprinkle talcum powder on the trunks of their cars and park a hundred feet from the tracks. Even with their engines turned off, their cars drift toward the railroad crossing, gathering a burst of speed as the tires rumble over the ties. On the other side everyone jumps out to study the rear of their vehicles. Sure enough, there are tiny handprints there. Ghosts of dead children trying to save others—or imagination?

Both the very rich and the very poor live in San Antonio. Most of the boomers and generation Xers who are doctors, lawyers, young Turks, and entrepreneurs build or buy sprawling homes in the north end in neighborhoods and suburbs with large lots: Boerne, Castle Hills, Stone Oak, Hunters Creek, Shavano Creek, and Shavano Park. A disproportionate number of the streets in these areas have "Oak" in their names, which isn't surprising, because Bexar County has more oak trees than any other living tree, bush, or plant.

The very, *very* rich live in the King William district (named for Kaiser Wilhelm I of Prussia), below Durango Street and Hemisfair Park. The homes in the King William district are just as large, but more than a century old and carefully restored to their former grandeur.

H.E.B. has many supermarkets in San Antonio, but its Central Market on Broadway has no rival anywhere in America for groceries and gourmet food, with at least fifty kinds of *anything* from cheese to salami to breads. And kitty-corner down the street a block, across from the University of the Incarnate Word, Earl Abel's restaurant serves meals at the same location where it's been since its hostesses were in their twenties. Most are now over eighty. Fried chicken, catfish, biscuits, and homemade cream pie, and no trace of radicchio or sushi. Earl's patrons are older than the hostesses, and the decor was last changed in the 1960s: red carpet, heavy dark oak, and artificial flowers. It is a fine place to eat.

San Antonio is synonymous with fiesta, and almost any event is cause for celebration. Market Square has Mexican food and mariachi, although locals tend to patronize smaller, family-style restaurants. The benign air of the city prevails on Market Square too; a sixtyish man, frayed and sunburned, sleeps undisturbed on a bench, his bare toes peeking from his sneakers.

IN 1986 San Antonio was a perfect city for an entrepreneur who wanted to begin his life anew. In terms of population it was on its way to becoming the eighth-largest city in America. Long the site of military bases (Lackland Air Force Base, Kelly Air Force Base, Brooks Air

Force Base, Fort Sam Houston), San Antonio had also attracted major medical research facilities, including the South Texas Medical Center complex and the University of Texas Health Sciences Center. For anyone wanting to tap into the endless opportunities in medical research and related fields, San Antonio was an optimum choice.

The fact that San Antonio had at least twenty-five golf courses also pleased Allen; he had always intended to become more proficient in the sport. The rest of the city's charm had no effect on him. He focused only on his next goal; he was akin to a color-blind man exposed to a rainbow. He never saw *anything* unless he needed it for his machinations, or if it could demonstrate to the world that he was a success. The most beautiful women, the fastest cars, the biggest houses, and—eventually—the greenest lawns mattered to him only as advertisements for himself.

Sheila was a beautiful woman when Allen married her, but the strain of their roller-coaster life had worn her down. She liked San Antonio. What she hated was her marriage. After three years with Allen her eyes were open to the bizarre secrets he no longer bothered to keep from her. She was mortified when Allen came home late one night and told her that the police had stopped him as he drove through Castle Hills. He'd been dressed in drag. It wasn't against the law, but it was awful to think that her husband was still doing things like that.

Even though Sheila had always had a job, working for one attorney or another, Allen began to call her a gold digger while they were still in Hawaii. He also accused her of cheating on him. Perhaps it made him feel justified in his own infidelities, although he clearly didn't consider hiring prostitutes to act out his sado-masochistic fantasies as being unfaithful.

Jonda—Stevie and Daryl's nanny—had moved with the Blackthornes from Honolulu. That was a comfort for Sheila because she still had to work. With Jonda nearby, at least she didn't have to worry about her little girls. But, by now, Jonda could not deal with Allen. She moved to California in six months.

Sheila soon found a job with the law firm of Soules and Wallace. She was an excellent personal assistant who could handle every detail for a busy boss, and she had glowing references from the lawyers she had worked for in Oregon and Hawaii. That made finding a job easy for her, even though she didn't have the college degree she had coveted. Sheila became Luke Soules's assistant and planned his schedule and his travels. She was a stickler for decorum in the office and thought slacks and pantsuits were never meant to be worn in a law firm. In staff meetings she often reminded the other women of the dress code she had initiated at Soules and Wallace. Nobody took offense; Sheila was popular with the staff and, outside of work, a lot of fun.

If she held out for any hope of happiness and, perhaps, even for her very survival, Sheila knew that the time would come when she had to leave Allen. His machinations and lifestyle were chipping away at her self-respect. She also knew that it would be very, very dangerous to make the break. Allen didn't love her or even want her—that was obvious—but he was sadistic enough to keep her with him just because she wanted so much to go. And she was afraid of Allen, despite the brave front she put up.

Kerry knew it. She visited in San Antonio as often as she could, and saw that Sheila was teetering on the edge of asking Allen for a divorce in 1987. "She was miserable," Kerry said. "But she was afraid to leave. I remember her saying, 'If I stay, he'll kill me, and if I leave, he'll kill me, but at least I'll have a fighting chance. And maybe I can keep my girls safe.'"

There was something in the way she said it that indicated that Sheila didn't mean that Allen would beat her to death. She was talking about something far more deadly than a black eye or a broken arm. Because she was in no way histrionic, her somber acceptance of what she absolutely believed to be true was even more frightening.

IT didn't take long for Allen to be back in business, this time in San Antonio. He was promoting the same product he'd introduced in Hawaii, determined to advertise it as a *medical* product rather than merely a device to tone muscles. Guy had managed to make it legal, and Allen would take advantage of that. For the moment he *had* to deal with his father.

Allen's new Texas business was called EMS and featured the EMS 250. It was the same old Health-Tronic, renamed. Guy's West-Pac Electronics in Honolulu was now legally selling the devices, and Allen was buying them at a greatly reduced price. Guy bought the circuit boards that drove the device from a company in Taiwan that manufactured them in a garage. He paid $25 apiece for them. Allen bought the one-time Health-Tronic from WestPac for $125 apiece, and after some minor assembly in Oregon, he sold them for $1700. If he received a purchase order for more than five hundred, he would lower his price to $495 apiece, which meant he was clearing only $370 per unit instead of $1575, but in that volume it didn't matter.

Allen was such a good salesman that he could present a concept to men with far more social status and education than he had and mesmerize them. He was most pleased that he was able to gather a staff of highly educated men to work for EMS. They, of course, believed that he had an advanced degree from Stanford University. He knew the lingo, and he fielded every question they had. His pitch to them was that *he* had invented this "novel and unique" medical device, and then he had hired a man in Hawaii named Guy Van Houte to manufacture it. Since his surname was now Blackthorne, no one realized that he was related to Guy. Indeed, Allen never hinted that they were anything but business associates.

In his travels Allen often passed through Oregon and sometimes stopped in Sutherlin to visit Tom and Debbie Oliver. They had returned to the sewing-machine business after their missions to Mexico, and Tom could not help being impressed with Allen's claims for his new muscle stimulator. When Allen invited him to join EMS, Tom agreed. Allen was almost thirty-one now, and not the gangly kid who had lived with the Olivers fifteen years earlier. Although Tom disapproved of the way Allen treated the women in his life, and kept his promises never to tell Allen where his ex-wives were hiding, he admired his business sense, and the product seemed legitimate.

"I'm able to go out now and get *bankers* to work for me," Allen bragged. Tom saw no reason to doubt him.

One member of Allen's staff at EMS was a young businessman named Jim Bingham. Tall and blond, Jim knew San Antonio well, and he had an impressive circle of business friends in banking and real estate. Jim's ethics were unquestioned and Allen needed someone like that. He hired Jim to be EMS's director of finance. He made Bill Gregorich*, who was in his late forties, president and head of marketing. Bill was short and overweight, rapidly balding, with a florid face. He had exaggerated some of his résumé, claiming to have been the director of marketing at the Savin Corporation, which manufactured copy machines. His actual position was not that high at Savin. He also claimed to be a former marine fighter pilot, which was not true.

It was a case of a fooler fooling a fooler, and Allen believed Gregorich. Gregorich was an avid drinker and an equally avid golfer. Allen liked that; his own interest in golf was growing stronger all the time. They also had something else in common; the two men often tried to outdo each other in telling filthy jokes.

Cornelius Nau, Jr., M.D., a neurologist/psychiatrist, became director of medicine, and his credentials were legitimate. Nau was impressed with Allen's devil-may-care attitude, although he frowned on some office practices. Bill Gregorich began to give "personality pro-file tests" to EMS employees. "He was acting as some kind of lay psy-chologist," Jim Bingham said, "and that really ticked off Nau, who put a stop to Gregorich's testing everyone."

Terry Young was an earnest and dependable man in his twenties whom Allen appointed head of sales. As different as the men were in temperament, all of them were very enthusiastic about the prospects of EMS. The device would be either sold or rented to physicians, who would then provide it to their patients. Allen promised that it would enhance healing, strengthen muscles, improve blood circulation—and it *would*, indeed, do those things. The potential market was wide open. Allen might have been a charismatic preacher or a dynamic po-litical candidate, but he happened to be a business entrepreneur. Peo-ple liked him, wanted to believe him, and were caught up in his seemingly positive energy.

Allen's offices were even more impressive than his Honolulu setup. He rented twelve hundred square feet in a high-rise office building just off IH 10 West and Loop 410. There were four private offices as well as a large conference room that adjoined Allen's own huge office. He installed a very sophisticated phone system.

But some of the EMS office procedures—or lack of them—jarred Jim Bingham, who was accustomed to a business atmosphere. Jim re-alized early on that Allen and his supplier in Hawaii, Guy Van Houte, were frequently at odds. "Allen was always fearful of losing credibil-ity with Guy Van Houte and his ability to obtain 'the device,' " Jim said, recalling how puzzled he was by Allen's vehemence. "I over-heard several shouting matches he had on the phone with Guy. He said Guy was putting the pressure on him to order and pay for the device."

Without the muscle-stimulating devices, Allen would have no product to sell, so Bingham could understand why he would struggle to maintain his relationship with this Van Houte in Honolulu, but he wondered why he was so angry about it.

Allen's moods were hard to chart. He would be up one day and down the next. Benign or furious. One day he was cut off during a long-distance phone conversation and was so enraged that he ripped the phone lines out of the wall, causing almost $5000 in damages to the expensive Nickle Phone System.

Jim knew why he himself had been brought on board. EMS was looking for financial backing so that the company could expand as a major force in the health field, and it would be Jim Bingham's job to help find investors. He knew the movers and shakers in San Antonio, those businessmen who might be likely to invest in a legitimate innovative product in the medical field.

One man Jim approached was Dan Parman, the force behind one of the fastest-growing communities in America—and one of the most desirable. Stone Oak, bordered by U.S. Highway 281 North, Loop 1604, and Blanco Road. Stone Oak appealed to upper-middle-class Bexar County home buyers as it blossomed from what had once been rugged cattle-ranch country. In 1980 Parman had the vision to purchase the 4300 acres that became Stone Oak. He had predicted that San Antonio was about to burgeon toward the north, and he guessed right. He visualized Stone Oak as a community that would be self-contained, with homes, schools, churches, shopping areas, business complexes, and medical care—all built on the hilly, craggy landscape where trees would remain lush and the San Antonio River would nourish the earth.

Unlike Allen Blackthorne, Dan Parman was not only a businessman but a philanthropist who wanted San Antonians to live in good houses in communities that provided more than endless flat land with gridlike lots. As he realized his goals, he gave millions to the University of Texas Health Sciences Center, endowing the Dan F. Parman Chair in Medicine and the Parman House and Conference Center.

Two months after Allen hired him, Jim Bingham went to Dan Parman as an emissary from EMS. At that point Jim believed in the future of the company and was confident that it would be a good investment for Parman. Once introduced to Allen, Parman was impressed. Since he and Jim Bingham knew each other, and Jim was confident that Allen's business was a solid investment and vouched for it, Parman loaned EMS $200,000 on a handshake with Jim. The loan was peanuts to Dan Parman, but he had been around the block, and he wasn't totally dazzled by Allen's footwork.

"Jim," Parman said at the time, "this Blackthorne is either the slickest con man I've ever met—or he's for real."

Even though he, too, would begin to have some doubts about Allen, Jim felt comfortable about EMS borrowing the money from Parman. Bingham and Dr. Neil Nau were distantly related, and Neil's father, Cornelius Nau, Sr., was a highly regarded San Antonio pediatrician. Allen might be a new face in San Antonio, but the executives he had picked were longtime, respected residents. All in all, EMS seemed solid.

Indeed, business looked great for a while, despite the lavish way Allen spent money. However, some time after Bingham arranged for the $200,000 loan, he began to notice behavior that he characterized as Allen's "squirreliness." Allen seemed to concentrate more on having fun and living well than he did on following proper business protocol. Sometimes Bingham thought that Allen and some of his top executives acted as though they were a slightly older Billionaire Boys Club, delighting in off-color jokes, raucous humor, and tales of sexual conquests.

Forewarned, Dan Parman placed one of his own top CPAs, Bob Dorsey, onsite at the EMS office to be sure that the company operated in a strict, businesslike manner. "With that move," Bingham recalled, "Bob and I wanted to make sure Allen paid the employees on time, produced financial statements, et cetera." Allen was far too casual about maintaining records and paying his debts and obligations.

Of course, his new business associates didn't know that the Bank of Hawaii was looking for him about the $160,000 loan he'd skipped out on. He *was*, just as Dan Parman had suggested, "the slickest con man he'd ever met." In terms of scamming, Allen was a veritable genius, and he was getting better at it all the time. His operation in San Antonio made his Hawaii business look shabby.

After the $200,000 loan was injected into EMS, Allen grew so confident that he no longer tried to hide any of his less than savory habits. Bingham even wondered some mornings if Allen might be high on drugs when he came to work. "His mouth would be very dry, so dry that he had trouble pronouncing words. One of the salesmen told me that Allen was using Demerol."

One day Allen came to work in a laid-back and oddly jovial mood. He commented about how "great" he looked, Jim Bingham remembered. "He said he had just gotten out of bed and come in to work, and he kept exclaiming how great he looked without putting any effort into getting dressed or bathed. That was when I suspected he was doing drugs of some kind. He was slurring his words pretty good that morning."

Allen could not hold his liquor well and never drank much, although he often invited "the crew" to join him at TGIFridays after work for drinks. On the occasions that he did drink more than usual, Allen's inhibitions loosened rapidly, and he bragged about hiring prostitutes on out-of-town trips.

Allen, Neil Nau, and Terry Young drove identical cars leased by the company for its executives: black Toyota MR-2s. They sometimes raced in the hills around San Antonio. They entertained clients sumptuously or just joined up for dinner together. Allen's street smarts impressed Dr. Nau; he seemed to have been everywhere and done everything. There was no question at all that he was fascinating; the question was how much of what he said was the truth. None of them had ever known anyone like Allen Blackthorne.

Neither Sheila nor the other wives were invited along on company evenings. Sheila worked all day for Luke Soules and really preferred to be home with Stevie and Daryl in the evening anyway. Whether she knew that Allen was cheating on her with a pretty young saleswoman at EMS is unknown; she never mentioned it to her sister or her friends. But she found out soon enough when Allen insisted on moving the woman—who was very attractive, but slightly ditsy—into their Castle Hills home. Her name was Cori* and she stayed with them for only a few weeks. If Sheila knew for certain that Allen and Cori were intimate, she didn't tell anyone. Later she told her close women friends that she had known and been totally humiliated.

Allen joked with some of his executives about Cori's shock when he explained his sexual preferences. "She keeps saying 'You're *sick!*' " he said with a laugh.

Cori moved out of the Castle Hills house in disgust. She had no idea that such things as masochism and cross-dressing existed in the real world. Finally it was too much for Sheila. It was not a matter of *if* she would leave Allen for good; it was only a matter of *when.*

To Bingham's alarm, daily operations at the company were becoming more bizarre, and Allen soon made no pretense at all of being a reputable businessman. For a time he employed a young male Distributive Education student on a part-time basis. During a required evaluation meeting with the teenager's DE teacher, Allen commented that if he were seventeen, he would be "staying high on Demerol and chasing girls all day long" and not worrying about job training. The teacher stared at him, bemused.

Jim Bingham went on a business trip to Houston with the EMS president, Bill Gregorich. Bingham had never been particularly impressed with Gregorich. "He reminded me of the typical burned-out alcoholic salesman who bragged about what a great love life he had twenty-five years ago," Bingham said.

The two men were supposed to meet with a very prominent Houston physician to pitch the EMS devices to him, a man Gregorich said was a close friend of his. "He said we could wait in a bar near the guy's house until he came home from work. Well, it disintegrated into a disaster when we went by his house to see if he was home yet. Gregorich had been drinking for two hours, and the doctor's wife came home to find him urinating in their shrubbery. Turned out Gregorich wasn't a friend of the doctor's at all, and he was incoherent by then. I had to make the presentation."

Not surprisingly, it was a no-sale. Bingham was embarrassed.

Back in San Antonio, Jim Bingham told Neil Nau about the incident, and Nau told Allen. Allen told Gregorich that Jim had "informed" on him. "That was the start of my demise at EMS," Bingham said ironically.

For Jim Bingham, the whole EMS experience was daunting, if not outright grotesque. He had worked for the company for six months, but he'd been paid only $3000 total in salary. Allen explained that he had suffered "financial reverses" because of Guy Van Houte, a situation he claimed had occurred *after* he persuaded Jim to leave his previous job and come to EMS. Of course, he said he had never intended to deceive Jim and entice him to quit a good job to join EMS. Jim doubted that. Anxious now to escape from a company that apparently ran on the whims of the owner, he tendered his resignation.

"Allen stared at me with a funny look on his face," Jim said. "And then he came out from behind his desk, walked up to me, and kissed me on the lips."

Astounded, Jim stepped back and saw that Allen was smiling sardonically. Terry Young, who had seen Allen's strange response to Jim's resignation, told him, "Jim, be careful. You just got the kiss of death."

When Allen appeared to be sanguine about Jim's desire to leave the company, it only made him more wary. Allen suggested that Jim needed to relax and think about his decision, and offered him the company credit card. "He said to take my wife and kids on a vacation, all on the company. He said he wanted me to take time off to decide if I really *did* want to continue working for EMS. I suspected he was setting me up, and I didn't accept his offer. I could only imagine what he might do if I ran up charges on the company card. Afterward he told everyone that he had fired me because I wasn't an 'effective employee.' "

Accountant Bob Dorsey resigned a few weeks after Jim Bingham left, when he learned that Allen was no longer returning Dan Parman's phone calls.

Bingham felt responsible for the $200,000 he had obtained from Parman to give to Allen. Now he set about trying to see that it was repaid. He knew Parman didn't need it; Stone Oak was bringing in many millions to Parman's firm, but it was a debt of honor and $200,000 was a sizable sum, which Jim felt responsible for. With Parman's approval he began to trace the circuitous path of Allen Blackthorne. He had met Tom Oliver when he came to San Antonio for training, liked him, and called him.

"Oliver told me that Allen had changed his name, that it used to be Van Houte and that he was really Guy Van Houte's son!" Jim said. "He also knew that Allen had changed his Social Security number after he left the bank in Hawaii holding the bag for a large business loan."

Astounded at the relationship between Allen and Guy, Jim discovered that there were many more sides to Allen Blackthorne/Van Houte than he had realized. He would never know if his investigation was causative, but Allen *did* repay Dan Parman the $200,000 he had borrowed. He made arrangements for Parman's collateral—a certificate of deposit at the NBC Bank of San Antonio—to be released to Parman. Allen allegedly had a new investor, the Southwest owner of a medical equipment company, who had advanced him $600,000 for exclusive rights to the EMS device.

Wherever he got the money, Allen paid Dan Parman back. Jim Bingham was curious, however, and he did a little more checking into the background of his former boss. He called Stanford University and learned that Allen had not graduated in engineering from that college; indeed, there were no records that showed Allen Van Houte Blackthorne had ever been at Stanford at all.

"The way Allen could convince experts that he was a registered engineer was a truly remarkable achievement," Jim said. "He didn't have any formal training in engineering or the sciences."

Jim did nothing with the information he had gleaned, but it validated his concerns. He was grateful to be done with EMS and Allen Blackthorne. As it was, Allen was already spreading rumors that he had fired Jim because of his heavy drinking.

UP in Oregon, Tom Oliver was working hard because of his belief that the EMS *was* a valuable product. He met with the female head of a state of Oregon department that oversaw rehabilitation programs for workers injured on the job. If Oliver could convince the state of Oregon to validate the EMS-250 as a device to treat disabled workers, it would be a huge coup for the company and for him too.

"The lady had several questions about the muscle stimulator, and I placed a conference call to Allen's offices in San Antonio," Oliver remembered. "All that was required was that Allen and his fellow executives explain the way the EMS-250 worked and the positive results they had gathered. But they seemed impatient with her questions and gave shorter and shorter answers.

"She told them that she wasn't satisfied that the device would enable those on disability insurance to get back into the work force, and needed to ask a few more questions," Oliver said, and was horrified by the response from Allen's office. "Lady," a voice barked over the phone's speaker—maybe it was Allen; maybe it was Bill Gregorich— "you won't be satisfied until you lean over and pull up your skirt."

The woman, who had a high office in the Oregon State administration, hung up the phone as if it were a snake. The interview was over, and Oliver could not apologize enough that he had inadvertently subjected her to such crudeness. He was totally humiliated. Of course, there was no longer the possibility that EMS would have credibility with the state of Oregon.

"I went home in shock," Oliver recalled. "I was walking up the stairs, and I keeled over with a heart attack."

It was an incident similar to the disastrous visit Jim Bingham had made with Gregorich to the doctor in Houston. Allen had apparently no concerns about how he or his staff at EMS interacted with potential customers. The president of a company cannot urinate on the shrubbery in an exclusive neighborhood or insult the head of a state office and continue to expect goodwill. No business could survive with such an attitude, even if it had a superior product to sell.

And Allen's company was beginning to deflate like a balloon with a hole in it.

_____ *Chapter Twelve* _____

ALLEN WASN'T CONCERNED. More than ever he felt in charge of his own destiny. He had money, cars, women, and male friends who admired his style, and that was what mattered. He had a wife and two little girls at home, but one would hardly know it. Although Sheila didn't confide everything in Kerry, she had to have been living a life of quiet desperation as Allen carried on affairs with one woman after another, even bringing some of them into her own house.

As Cori moved out, and Sheila threatened to go, Allen had another woman waiting in the wings. She was Terry Young's fiancée, Shirley*, whom Allen employed as his personal secretary for a short time. Perhaps he only wanted to prove to his own top salesman that he could point his finger at any woman and break up whatever relationship she might be in.

Shirley was very pretty and wholesome-looking, and she had an infant son. According to Terry Young, Allen threw the baby boy across the room in a rage and broke his arm. Realizing that she had been fooled by a man who had no affection for her or her baby, Shirley didn't stay with Allen long.

SHEILA's family had done their best to keep in touch with her. Gene's feelings were still bruised over the way Sheila had sided with Allen when he sent her and Don into bankruptcy, but Kerry and Rick were determined to maintain contact with Sheila. She *needed* her family: Kerry had seen how overpowering Allen could be and how he could convince almost anyone that black was white. Sheila had never meant to hurt her parents. With a tiny baby to care for and still in love with Allen, she hadn't seen any way out but to follow him to Hawaii. Once there, things had only become worse. With more creditors hounding them, Sheila had then gone with Allen to San Antonio, only to realize that she was just as expendable to him as any other woman. The difference was that Sheila had a legal right to some of Allen's assets and her daughters deserved some financial support. She couldn't possibly take care of them on her salary alone.

Kerry had long sensed a desperation in her older sister. Sheila was not at all conflicted about wanting a divorce, but she was clearly afraid of Allen. She had lots of women friends in San Antonio, and that eased Kerry's mind, but Jonda Pinter had moved away to Santa Rosa, California, which was a major loss for Sheila. Kerry knew that Sheila's marriage was as good as over, and she had seen some of the reasons with her own eyes. Still, she understood that there were things Sheila had never told her. "She tried to protect me," Kerry said.

Sheila was frightened, and that was so unlike her; she had always been strong, and so stubborn. She had lost that part of herself. Although she never became inured to Allen's kinky sexual fetishes and to the pain of his introducing prostitutes to their intimate life, she had put up with these outrageous betrayals because she was afraid of him. She once confided to Jim Bingham and Terry Young that Allen liked to be tied up and whipped by male prostitutes. "He made me hire them for him," she said softly, embarrassed and humiliated but still needing to tell *someone* the details of why she had to leave.

Sheila never told any of her friends or her sisters the extent of Allen's brutality toward her; she was too mortified. But she did tell her girlfriends that he had tried to drown her by putting her head in the toilet and flushing continually. And she told them how diminished she felt when Allen had other women in his bedroom and deliberately left the door open so she would hear the sounds of sex games.

It took tremendous courage for Sheila to leave Allen for good.

They were still living together in Castle Hills, the suburb northwest of San Antonio, in the fall of 1987 when the last nail was hammered into the coffin of their marriage. On September 5 Allen became furious with her over some real or imagined thing she had done. He was convinced that she was doing something behind his back—cheating on him with other men—which would have been well-nigh impossible, as she spent her time either working or looking after Stevie and Daryl.

In the white heat of terrible quarrels, Allen always said that Daryl wasn't his—that her real father was Roy Anderson, the attorney Sheila had worked for in Hawaii. That was so bizarre and not true. But Stevie looked just like Allen, and Daryl was blond and resembled Sheila. That was enough for Allen to doubt her.

Roy Anderson had never had a romantic relationship with Sheila, and he did not care for Allen. He once told Kerry that he viewed Allen as a chess player, but one who played chess with people's lives—a man who seemed to relish holding the strings that made others dance.

Allen, who spent money for flash and pleasure, begrudged any that Sheila spent and said she wasted his money. She did like to shop and to take her friends out to lunch or treat them to a haircut and beauty makeover, but her expenditures were not even close to his.

They were in their bedroom that September night when Sheila saw the familiar dull red of rage suffuse Allen's face. There was nowhere for her to run, and by the time she managed to call the Castle Hills police, she was a mass of bruises. She told the responding officers that Allen had accused her of "screwing him over."

She said he began by beating her with his belt, promising her she would never walk again and that he was going to "mess up my face." Allen was more than a foot taller than Sheila and outweighed her by a hundred pounds; her efforts to protect herself were forlorn. Allen had progressed to hitting her with his closed fists. Sobbing, she showed the officers the purple marks on her left jaw, ear, and upper arm. Allen was charged with battery (a misdemeanor), and Sheila was given a Family Violence Card from the Bexar County district attorney's office.

Terrified at the thought of what he might do to her for calling the police, Sheila hid in a church basement and called Tom and Debbie Oliver to tell them that she had to leave Allen. They had heard the same terror in the voices of his first two wives, Ellen and Mary. It was inevitable, of course. Under the smooth guise of a successful businessman, Allen was still the angry boy who distrusted women and blamed them for all of his troubles. He had no trace of allegiance to anyone—

save, perhaps, his aunt Debbie—and he *did* move people in and out of his life like chess pieces. The only difference was that his rage burned hotter now and his need for revenge and reprisal was more entrenched.

The Olivers had always liked Sheila. They accepted her collect calls every night as she continued to hide in the church basement. "And Allen would call too, when Sheila and the children first left," Tom said. "He would keep me on the phone for five or six hours, until three a.m."

Allen's fury at being "abandoned" disturbed Tom because he was never quite sure what he might do. Once, when Tom complained that he had been ripped off by someone, Allen calmly told him that he would take care of it. "He said he could go into a Mexican restaurant in San Antonio, lay money on the bar, and pay someone to kill the guy," Tom remembered. "I told him I wasn't *that* upset."

FINALLY Sheila put her little girls in her old white Cadillac and headed toward Santa Rosa and Jonda. She knew that Jonda would hide her. All she could think of was flight. She drove straight through to California. Allen guessed where she was going, took a plane, and arrived at Jonda's house on Sebastopol Street at almost the same time Sheila did. It was as if he had a net over her and no matter where she ran, he was right behind her.

Sheila had Daryl, who was two, in her arms as Allen began to rant at her. They argued, and their shouting grew louder, until Allen grabbed Sheila around the neck and forced her roughly against a wall. Trying to protect Daryl, she lost her balance and fell hard. Allen leaped into the Cadillac and roared toward the rear gate of Jonda's property. A man who had seen Allen attack Sheila made the mistake of trying to stop him. He realized too late that Allen had no intention of stopping, and he couldn't get out of the way in time. Allen hit the man, knocking him onto the hood of the car. Then he slammed on the brakes just before he hit the fence, throwing the injured man to the ground. Allen smashed through the fence and raced away down the street.

Eventually he circled back to Jonda's house, where he found the Santa Rosa police waiting for him. They arrested him for assault and battery, and when they checked him through Wants and Warrants, they found that Allen Blackthorne was also Allen Van Houte, who had an outstanding warrant out of Corvallis, Oregon, for theft by deception that dated back to September 1985, a residual charge relating to the massive exodus of his stereo stores' stock.

While Allen was in jail in Santa Rosa, Sheila drove the white Cadillac north to Oregon, seeking some place where she and Daryl and Stevie would be safe. She was in such a state of panic that she had an accident on the way. Fortunately, neither she nor the girls were injured. Sheila was only twenty-three years old, but she looked as if she were in her mid-forties, her face almost skeletal and washed of color. She probably didn't weigh more than eighty-five pounds. When her family saw her, they barely recognized her; she looked like a concentration-camp victim. If Kerry thought Sheila looked emaciated in Hawaii, that image paled beside this haggard woman who glanced nervously over her shoulder whenever a car drove by the house.

The wonderfully happy bride of four years earlier was gone entirely. All Sheila wanted to do was to get away from Allen and raise her daughters. At the moment she needed a place to hide from Allen's reprisal when he got out of jail in Santa Rosa. She suspected he already *was* free and would be furious.

He was—both free and furious. Allen had called Neil Nau to send the $15,000 needed to bail him out of jail. Nau told Jim Bingham later that Allen said he had been arrested because he had inadvertently written a bad check for a sports car.

"We were all scared," Kerry recalled of the time when Sheila came to Keizer, Oregon, where she and Rick were living. Rick immediately hid the Cadillac so Allen wouldn't spot it. But apparently he hadn't followed Sheila. They were never sure, however, *where* he was, knowing it wouldn't have taken him long to bail out of jail in Santa Rosa.

"We had weird phone calls," Rick said. "There was someone on the line, but they never spoke."

Sheila stayed in Oregon as her bruises healed, and she put on a little weight. She had residency in Bexar County and needed to keep her good job in San Antonio with Luke Soules's law firm. If she got the courage to divorce Allen, she would need that job to raise Stevie and Daryl until she got child support. Safe with her family, Sheila began to believe she *could* go back to Texas, where her job waited and she had a solid group of friends.

When she arrived back in San Antonio with her little girls, she found what she had come to expect: Allen had not been punished in any real way for breaking the law or ignoring the moral codes other people adhered to. He was back in Texas without having served any jail time.

In May 1988 Allen pleaded no contest to the battery charges resulting from Sheila's beating in Castle Hills the prior September. He was fined $100 and given a year's deferred adjudication. On August 19 he was sentenced to eighteen months' probation and fined $425 for his assault and battery in Santa Rosa. No supervision was ordered.

Sheila never went back to live in the house she had shared with Allen in Castle Hills. She found an apartment she could afford and began a determined effort to fight Allen the only way she could—in court. Janet Littlejohn, an attorney in Luke Soules's firm, agreed to advise Sheila on the intricacies of divorce law. There was no way that Sheila could afford to pay a full-time attorney, but she was able to cut her costs by doing much of the paperwork herself. At first she and Janet knew each other only as co-workers. Later they became friends as Janet admired Sheila's bravery and resolution in the face of overwhelming odds.

Janet Littlejohn, now an elected Texas district court judge, had maintained a family-law practice for seven years, and with her help, Sheila filed divorce proceedings against Allen in October 1987. Now that she had known him for five years, she had a searing understanding of why his first two wives had divorced him and fled for their lives. She remembered who she was when she first met Allen and realized how painfully naïve she had been; she didn't know then that there *were* people like that.

There are relatively simple divorces, and there are those where every step along the way to a judgment is hard-fought. "This divorce was very hotly contested," Judge Littlejohn recalled. "It evolved over a period of time with property disputes, custody disputes. In discovery each [party] learns the other's side. There is information, documentation, interlocutories, depositions, and sometimes stipulations. There should be a timely progression."

Littlejohn advised Sheila to be very careful to document all contact and phone calls she had with Allen. "Everything should be in writing," she warned. "Communicate with him only in writing if you can." Sheila kept careful notes of every conversation she had with Allen.

Sheila, Allen, and Jim Higdon, his attorney, were present when Sheila gave a hundred-page deposition on October 15, 1987. With Allen looking on scornfully, Sheila spoke of the times he had threatened to kill her. "He told me he would kill me or have someone do it. [He said] that he was 'in a position to have it done.'

"Once [when Stevie fell into a pool] he was yelling at me, if I ever let something happen to the kids, he would kill me. 'You know what I've told you before,' he said. And I said, 'Yes, that you would have me taken care of.' He said he would make sure I never walked again and 'I'll have your face maimed.' " Sheila added that Allen threatened to have her "taken care of" if she ever left him or hurt his business.

Janet Littlejohn took notes herself during Sheila's divorce deposition and saved those handwritten notes in the growing file of the *Blackthorne v. Blackthorne* divorce.

Sheila's divorce was finally granted on September 22, 1988. She was awarded primary custody of Stevie and Daryl, while Allen had visitation rights. He got the house in Castle Hills, and Sheila got her Toyota, $1250 a month in child support, and medical insurance for the girls. Allen had fooled engineers and scientists into believing he had advanced degrees. Now he set out to learn the law. His business was finally crumbling due to his profligate spending and lack of organization. He claimed to be indigent and unable to afford an attorney: "I didn't have anything. I got the house in the divorce, but the problem was that there wasn't any equity in the house, and then on top of that the judge ordered another hundred thousand dollars. There was a dispute between Sheila and I as to what the equity was in the house. Real estate in San Antonio in 1988 wasn't booming."

Allen said he had given the chalet house back to the owners who had sold it to him.

Former colleagues of Allen's had formed their own company. Allen said he had been pushed out and left with nothing. Sheila believed that Allen said this to prevent her from getting the share of the company that was rightfully hers. Sheila attempted in vain to find some of Allen's share of EMS, but there was nothing there.

Since he could not afford an attorney, Allen set out to learn whatever he needed to know to represent himself. As his father once said, Allen could learn how to do anything. "Put him in a room with the textbooks on how to do brain surgery, and in three days he could do it."

"He could do whatever he wanted," his brother Randy added. "He wanted to learn scuba diving, and pretty soon he was better at it than anyone I know. If he wanted it, he got it."

One thing was apparent. Allen had no intention of giving Sheila anything. If he was forced by law to support Stevie and Daryl, he would—but grudgingly. There was no alimony in Texas, and Sheila would not have wanted it anyway. She wanted only her share of the businesses formed during her marriage, and support for her children.

Allen filed a Chapter Seven to rid himself of *all* debts. But he was forced to agree with Sheila that there were some nondischargeable debts on both their parts. Sheila had to sue EMS to separate her assets in her marriage to Allen from his bankruptcy. If she didn't do that, she would realize nothing at all, but Allen would have a fresh start. She was finally awarded approximately 22 percent of Allen's business worth—$275,000. That was only on paper. First Allen had to win a suit against his former business partners to get that. He would claim that he gave Sheila the major share of the settlement, while he took less than half of what she got. In truth she got nothing that she could put in the bank.

Given the initial success of EMS, Sheila's 22 percent was a relatively modest share of the income Allen had enjoyed, and it would be a long time, she knew, before she actually received any of that, if ever. She was fully aware of how good Allen was at hiding assets. Sheila figured she could get by on her salary and the child support, and she was grateful to be free. One day she might realize her settlement and be able to give Stevie and Daryl a better life.

It should have been over in 1988, but it was only the beginning of a very long, very ugly war where two children were pulled between parents as if they were rubber bands. All too soon it became obvious that Allen had no intention of letting Sheila walk away unscathed. She realized that he would hound her to the ends of the earth if he could.

He didn't want her, he didn't love her; she was only a pawn in a terrible game, but she had no idea how tenacious he could be.

Sheila looked for a small apartment, knowing that it wouldn't be anything like the huge chalet that Allen was stalling about vacating in Castle Hills. They had paid $160,000 for it, at least $25,000 more than most San Antonio homes cost then. It was a lovely place, but it didn't matter; the fact that she had escaped her bizarre and punishing marriage and could now make her own decisions made up for anything she might have lost.

To Allen, Sheila was the enemy. The more she fought him—and stubborn as she was, she continued to fight him—the more he was determined to freeze her out and force her into abject poverty.

But it was more than that. Allen wanted Sheila to be miserable. He had let Ellen and Mary go because in each of his earlier divorces he had someone better, at least in his eyes, to move on to. When he divorced them, he was not a wealthy man, but he resented their taking anything away from him. And he still burned over the fact that they had left him. With Sheila, Allen had experienced wealth, and he knew he would again. He was adamant about one thing; none of it was hers. None of it would ever be hers. And Sheila would live to be sorry she had defied him.

Like a phoenix rising from the ashes, Allen looked around for a new start. He took a job in a suburb of Dallas for a firm called Armstrong Medical, but worked for them only three or four months. He never told anyone why he was fired, although his trouble with a number of banks would surface later and offer a probable explanation. "They didn't want me working there anymore," he said vaguely. "Then, basically, I scratched by."

He went to Las Vegas once, hoping to win big, but lost everything and came back to Dallas flat broke.

His half brothers remember that Allen indulged his sexual appetites, along with his compulsion to gamble, during this period of his life. He had always been turned on by bondage, and he met a girl at a Black Angus restaurant and convinced her to accompany him to Dallas. "Her name was Debby something," his brother Randy said, "and he held her hostage in his apartment there. He had this apartment with wall-to-wall mirrors in it. I guess she finally got away from him."

Either the captive girl called the police or there was another reason that Allen had to flee. He had money in his freezer for emergencies. He pried that loose from the ice and escaped from Dallas.

_____Chapter Thirteen_____

CARL GLENN met Sheila in early 1989, when he moved into an apartment complex in the 800 block of Vista Valet Drive, north of San Antonio. Carl worked on an offshore oil rig, living and working on the floating drills that bounce like huge corks in the Gulf of Mexico. He was gone more than he was home, and his wife had divorced him. Brandon Oaks was the only apartment complex in the area that welcomed single parents, and Carl's friend Rod Bookout, who lived there, urged him to move in. The next time Carl came in from working offshore, he and Rod went out to the Brandon Oaks pool.

"Sheila was the first woman I met," Carl Glenn said in his deep Texas drawl. "She and a friend were sunbathing, and I struck up a conversation with them."

Carl was quiet, a little shy, but Sheila recognized that and drew him out into a friendly conversation. He asked her to have dinner with him the next time he came off the oil rigs, and she agreed. They were not slated to have a romance, but they would be close friends for years.

Brandon Oaks was a good place for young parents, and a num-

ber of them had been through bitter divorces that left them emotionally bruised. The apartment complex wasn't a "meat market," but it
was a place they could take the first tentative steps at rejoining the
world of men and women again. There were get-togethers, potluck
dinners, and picnics.

Rod Bookout was known for his chicken and dumplings, and he
usually brought that dish. Sheila and the women friends she met at
Brandon Oaks brought casseroles, salads, and cookies. Sometimes
they barbecued out by the pool. It was a nice way to get back into the
dating game without the awkwardness of blind dates. Sheila even
went out with Rod a few times, knowing he was a ladies' man and
that he wasn't someone to get deeply involved. She wasn't ready for
that anyway.

Sue Tuffiash, thirty-six, a dark-haired, dark-eyed friend of
Sheila's, lived in the apartment complex. Sheila's bedroom shared a
common wall with Sue's. They could serve as each other's alarm clock
in the morning just by knocking on the wall, and if they were ever
frightened by something in the night, it was nice to know that there
was a friend right next door. Sue became one of Sheila's special
friends, along with Effie Wood, who was an aerobics instructor and
fitness expert. They all had young daughters, whom they were trying
to raise on their own. Sue and Sheila particularly understood each
other because their ex-husbands weren't about to let go of them, not
without making their lives miserable. Still, they didn't want their children to suffer. They stayed up late sometimes, talking out problems
and sharing their fears and their hopes.

Sue and Carl Glenn began to date steadily in late 1989. Sue was
going through an nasty divorce from a San Antonio dentist, Dr.
Charles Tuffiash, forty-two. It wasn't long before Carl Glenn and Sue
Tuffiash became serious about their relationship. Like Sheila, Sue had
two little girls. They were nine and seven, and they played with Stevie
and Daryl. Sue and Sheila often traded baby-sitting. Carl and Sue
dated for six months, and in January 1990, they were engaged. They
hoped to marry on April 14, since Sue's divorce would become final
on February 20. Sheila was very happy for them.

But Sue had been through a year of hell with her ex-husband, and
Sheila watched as her friend struggled to be free. She knew now that
divorce didn't necessarily mean freedom. She was all too familiar with
the invisible cords ex-husbands could wind around the women who
had escaped them. Sue said that Chuck Tuffiash was playing sinister
games with her, just as Allen was with Sheila.

Of the two women Sheila put up the best façade. She hid her fear of Allen very well, trying not to let him put a cloud over her new life. Carl Glenn remembered her as a little bit of a thing with long blond hair who was almost always smiling. She had gained back the weight she lost after she fled Allen's beatings in Castle Hills and Santa Rosa, and her cheeks were pink again. Carl took photographs of Sheila out by the pool, laughing, wearing a one-piece black suit that would have fit a child. She was so small. She was still working for Luke Soules, scheduling all his appointments and making sure his practice ran smoothly, but she barely looked old enough to be in junior high when she was playing with her little girls.

Sheila had Stevie and Daryl living with her in her small two-bedroom apartment, except for the times when Allen claimed his visitation rights. On her own now, Sheila talked to Carl a lot about her biological father, Frank Walsh. "She had kept his coffee cup all those years," Carl remembered, "and it meant so much to her."

Sheila must have wished that her dad was still alive and that he could come back and protect her and her girls from Allen. Although she had tremendous responsibilities, she was still only twenty-five. Gene and Don Smith had moved back to Salem, but Sheila had apologized for what Allen had done to them and for staying with him after their bankruptcy. They were growing closer.

Sheila was beginning to date again and to rediscover her sense of humor. There was a man from Austin whom she called Mr. Awesome because he was so good-looking, and a man who lived in the apartment complex she dated for a while. Carl laughed as he recalled one of the few times Sheila had a man stay overnight in her apartment— on a weekend when the girls were with Allen.

"Some of Sheila's relatives showed up unexpectedly about eight in the morning. She shoved this guy in the bedroom closet, and he must have been standing there for about three hours while she had coffee with her relatives," Carl said. "When she finally told him he could come out, he told her he had to pee so bad that he almost peed into one of her shoes!"

Sheila wasn't a saint and didn't pretend to be. Her girls came first, though, and any man in her life had to accept that. She still hoped to meet someone and fall in love again, only the next time she would be smarter. She wasn't eighteen anymore.

"Sheila was driving an old junk heap of a car," Carl said, recalling the first time he met Allen Blackthorne. "It was in the summer of 1989, and Allen drove up in a brand-new Cadillac Alanti convertible. This was in the period during which Allen summed up his existence as 'scratching by.'"

It seemed so unfair to Carl. "Sheila was barely making it," he said, "and Allen was always giving her a hard time about the child support he was supposed to pay her. And here Allen came in his expensive car."

With his EMS-250 business in shambles, Allen claimed that his 1989 income was only $4500, and yet his style of living hadn't changed at all. Sheila was making $24,000 a year before taxes. She needed the child support the court had ordered Allen to pay, but she rarely got it.

IN 1988 Sheila put the girls in preschool and became friends with one of the teachers there: Minda Reece.* Minda was younger than Sheila, but they got along very well. Another of Sheila's best friends was a young woman named Kelly McGonigal, who did her hair. Kelly's daughter, Tiffany, was the same age as Stevie, and she sometimes spent the night at Sheila's apartment. What Stevie was afraid to tell adults, she told to Tiffany McGonigal, who told her mother. Kelly and Sheila believed that Allen was almost certainly touching three-year-old Stevie sexually, but Sheila knew she couldn't prove it to the police. All she could do was try to avoid visitations and monitor the times she had to let Allen take Stevie.

When Sheila told her friends that Allen refused to give her any of the furniture and other belongings that were awarded to her in their divorce, Minda and Kelly offered to go with her to the house Allen was clinging to in Castle Hills. That way Sheila would have some backup; she was quite sure that Allen wouldn't hit her if there were witnesses.

"Sheila was always afraid to go to Allen's house alone to pick up the things that she was supposed to get from his house," Minda recalled. "Sometimes the house was empty, and sometimes Allen was there with a date—he dated so many different women. But Sheila never found *any* of the furniture or household items that were supposed to be hers. He had hidden everything from her."

Both Minda and Kelly were impressed by the way Allen lived. His house was far nicer than the small apartment Sheila shared with her little girls. It was very large, with a lovely backyard. Kelly remembered that Allen had a huge aquarium with tropical fish in it. His furnishings were expensive, mostly leather. And there was a state-of-the-art Bang and Olafsen sound system. Allen explained that he had an ear that would detect flaws in a musical reproduction, since he had once owned a string of stereo stores. He had to have the best.

They saw the storage area full of "the devices that Allen sold at work," but there was nothing in Allen's home that was on Sheila's list of things she was awarded in the divorce. Either Allen had hidden the furniture that was hers, or he had disposed of it. As far as they could tell after comparing Allen's house and Sheila's apartment, she hadn't gotten *anything* in the divorce. Her car was held together with quick fixes and prayers, while Allen drove a succession of showy, expensive sports cars. He was always pleasant enough to Sheila's friends, but he claimed to know nothing at all about whatever it was she was looking for.

Most of Sheila's closest women friends knew that she was terribly concerned that Allen might be sexually abusing Stevie, but the signs were so subtle that she didn't have anything that she could prove. She was always nervous now when Stevie spent the night with Allen, but she was hesitant to defy the court orders. Minda sometimes helped Sheila hide Stevie and Daryl from Allen, although it wasn't something they could do too often, for fear he would go back to court with complaints.

"I helped her write petitions, went to court with her, and even to the police," Minda recalled. "I went with her to take Stevie to a psychologist, who confirmed that [Stevie] had been molested by her father."

In September 1988 Allen was charged with aggravated sexual assault involving three-and-a-half-year-old Stevie. The charges were eventually dismissed.

Four months later Allen wrote to a judge in the 225th District Court, claiming that he himself had been sexually abused by both his mother and a church deacon when he was eight. "Now after all this," he wrote, "I am accused of abusing my precious Stevie. What do I do? My life has defied my childhood. I am a good father. I have always attempted to do my very best for my family because I never had a family."

In retrospect it was only one more version of Allen Blackthorne's life—part reality, part fiction—and only he knew which was which.

Stevie began therapy with psychologist Dorothy Le Pere, who felt that she *did* display "classic symptoms" of a victim of sexual abuse.

In Brandon Oaks there were a number of about-to-be-divorced mothers whose lives were filled with dread. They seemed to recognize each other, and they provided what support they could to one another. Sue Tuffiash confided her suspicions that her ex-husband may have sexually abused one of her girls too. She had tried her best to get Chuck Tuffiash to go to counseling so her daughters would be safer with him, but he wouldn't go. In desperation Sue filed indecency with a child charges against Chuck on September 23, 1989. He was out-raged. Didn't she know what she was doing to his practice as a peri-odontist? Like Allen, Chuck could be very charming, and his new neighbors believed his story that it was Sue who was violent and who violated orders that allowed him to see his daughters. He told them that Sue's allegations were false and that she was trying to drive him insane. He seemed to them such "a great guy," according to one neighbor: "He would take my kid to the movies along with his two daughters."

Tuffiash complained that someone had vandalized his car, slash-ing his tires, pouring sugar into the gas tank, and throwing eggs at it. He suggested that it probably had something to do with his divorce. He never came right out and accused any particular person of trash-ing his car, but his silences were telling.

If Tuffiash maintained that Sue was trying to make him crazy, she was going through hell herself. Sheila did her best to counsel her. At the same time, she could not help seeing the events in Sue's divorce as a mirror image of her own. They both felt helpless and manipulated by men who were far richer and far more powerful than they.

Sue was afraid of Chuck; the dentist was six feet two and weighed 225 pounds, and she was five feet two and barely topped 130 pounds. In her divorce filing, she charged that Chuck had knocked her down, kicked her, and broken two of her ribs, leaving her with multiple bruises on her head, kidney trauma, and other injuries.

Indeed, after Sue complained about being beaten, she was sen-tenced to ten days in jail, suspended, on Chuck Tuffiash's counter-charges against her. Her troubles made Sheila realize that she was in for the fight of her life if she hoped to raise Stevie and Daryl without Allen haunting all three of them.

Since her child-support checks never came in with any pre-dictability, Sheila had to budget her salary very carefully. "She loved her girls more than life itself," Carl recalled, "and she would fight for them, but it was so hard for her. Allen gave them the things that money could buy when they were with him—expensive toys, things Sheila couldn't begin to afford."

Allen was officially on probation until March 19, 1991, for the beating he had given Sheila in their bedroom. Warrants were issued, a thirty-day jail sentence was suspended, but in the end nothing hap-pened to him, save the original fine and ninety-three dollars in court costs. For the record, Allen's probation was "terminated success-fully."

This, although Allen was ordered to pay child support—and didn't, ordered to pay his fines—and didn't, ordered to complete an Alternatives to Violent Emoting program at the Bexar County Women's Center—and didn't. He was eventually ordered to attend private counseling—and didn't. He had been allowed to move to Richardson, Texas, a suburb of Dallas, to take the job that lasted only a few months.

When Allen came back to San Antonio in 1989 after he lost his job in Richardson, he bought another house, this one off Northwest Military Highway on Cedar Canyon in Castle Hills Forest. It wasn't as impressive as the first home he'd lost in his bankruptcy, but it was very nice. He got a good deal on it because it belonged to a San Antonio Spurs basketball player, who had been traded.

Sheila's biggest fear was that Allen was going to take Stevie and Daryl away from her. Once, Daryl climbed up on the windowsill of their second-floor apartment and pushed the screen out. She fell into thick bark-dust below and was more frightened than hurt. But Allen rushed over and told anyone within earshot that Sheila was an unfit mother. Under his breath he threatened once again to kill her if she hurt his children.

Sheila had heard those threats so often that they had become only a steady thrum in her head. She was more afraid of losing her daughters to Allen than she was of dying violently.

Allen was the one who had the nicest house, the best car, and the ability to make anyone believe whatever image he wanted to project. Sometimes Stevie came home talking about how her daddy had prom-ised he would take her for a long airplane ride. That made Sheila's blood run cold. She was always relieved when the girls came back from visits to Allen.

Sheila's financial picture was growing gloomier. Allen had pored over lawbooks, seeking ways to win a reduction in child support. In the fall of 1989 he filed a motion to reduce the $1250 he paid Sheila to $350, and he also asked to take away all the girls' health insurance. He noted that he had served Sheila with notice of his intent; she had apparently chosen not to file an answer.

Allen won his motion by default.

Months later Sheila asked Mary Fenlon, an attorney at Soules and Wallace who was helping her with her legal paperwork, to check to see why her child-support payments were so low. She was stunned to find that Allen had managed to legally reduce his child-support payments to only $350 a month. Since he had rarely paid much of the $1250 either, claiming poverty, she had believed he was simply slow in paying. Of course, Allen had done it all without ever notifying her.

There was no way that Sheila could pay a lawyer; she stayed up late, laboriously filling out the forms that Mary Fenlon told her she needed to reverse the new child-support schedule.

CARL Glenn was injured in an offshore accident on the oil rig in December 1989 and had to have surgery to stabilize a ruptured disk in his neck. Sue Tuffiash took care of him while he was convalescing. They would be married within a few months, and they were happy.

Carl's voice was strained as he remembered a day a few weeks after his surgery. Sue had been trying to get some sentimental items back from Chuck, but Carl was convinced that she should not meet him alone. He couldn't go with her until his neck was healed, but he warned her to be sure to take someone with her if she had to meet with Chuck. He had never seen Chuck be violent with Sue, but he knew she was afraid of him when he was angry and she had told him about the times Chuck beat her.

Like Sheila, Sue was left with nothing—Tuffiash had kept everything when they separated. "The court ordered her ex to split their children's baby pictures with her. He'd promised to do that—give her the pictures," Carl said, "and she agreed to meet him in his dental office. She thought that would be safe, being in public and all. On February 28, 1990, I was still recuperating, and I was lying on the sofa when Sue got ready to leave."

Sue said that Tuffiash's receptionist, Kimberly Wenzel, would be there. Carl offered to go along, just in case, but Sue was afraid the sight of him might make Chuck angry and "set him off."

When Sue kissed Carl good-bye sometime early that morning in late February, she didn't know that Chuck had given Kimberly the day off to celebrate her wedding anniversary, that he might even have arranged the picture exchange on that day because of the anniversary. She expected to walk into the dental office with the staff there and with patients in the waiting room. But when she got to the office on Blanco Road and Chuck ushered her into the waiting room, Sue realized that her ex-husband had given his staff the day off. They were all alone in his office.

Since there were no witnesses, beyond Dr. Charles Tuffiash himself, no one can say exactly what transpired there that morning. Carl Glenn waited with growing apprehension for Sue to come back to their apartment. She never did. Instead, Chuck Tuffiash knocked frantically on his neighbors' door on Charlie Chan Street an hour and a half later. "We could not imagine what could have happened," Renna Burke said. "He was upset; he was crying—he was concerned about his little girls. I just had the idea he was afraid [Sue] was going to get them from school and do something nasty to them. When you have this big, big man crying on your floor— Well, I wanted to calm him down, get him help."

Tuffiash's hand was bleeding and wrapped in paper towels. He told Ron and Renna Burke that his ex-wife had cut him.

By the time Carl Glenn got to Chuck Tuffiash's dental office, police were there, warning him that he could not go in. Sue Tuffiash was lying dead in a cooling pool of her own blood. An autopsy would reveal that she had suffered multiple crushing blows to her skull and face, wounds that had undoubtedly been dealt with a claw hammer found in the examining room where she died.

Tuffiash himself had two small cuts on his left hand.

"He beat her to death with that claw hammer," Carl said in a carefully controlled voice. "And he claimed it was in self-defense."

With Bexar County deputy prosecutors Lindy Bordini and Catherine Babbitt presenting the case against him, Charles Tuffiash went on trial in September 1991. He testified to a number of bizarre "facts." Sobbing, he said that as he and Sue were getting ready to divide their pictures of their daughters, "Sue turned to me and said, 'You know, I molested the girls in their sleep,' and I said, 'I figured that.' And then she said, 'I'm going to molest them while they're awake,' and I said, 'I'm not going to allow you to do that.' She said, 'You won't be able to stop me, because I'm going to kill you!' "

It was a truly strange account, and it warred with the facts in evidence. Tuffiash testified that Sue had carried a bread knife in her purse and she lunged toward him. He said she began to stab his hands as he held them out in defensive gesture. But, although he said he had been cut six times in his left hand, doctors had found only two clean cuts.

It was highly unlikely that a woman as small as Sue Tuffiash would have attacked her hulking ex-husband with a knife. There *was* a knife at the scene, a knife Carl had never seen before. Bordini and Babbitt believed that it was a "drop knife," similar to a "drop gun," left at the murder scene to make it look as though Sue had gone to Chuck's office armed and ready to attack him. "He said she went after him with a bread knife," Carl Glenn recalled. "The knife he said Sue had with her had a serrated blade; he did it to himself with a scalpel."

Bordini described to the jury the scenario of how she believed Sue Tuffiash died. She had probably been bending over to retrieve photos of her children from a trash can in one of the defendant's examining rooms when he beat her over the head with the claw hammer.

"After he bashed her head in with the hammer," Bordini continued, "he placed the bread knife near her body and moved her hands to make it look as though she had used it to attack him." Only then, Bordini surmised, did Tuffiash use a scalpel to inflict the superficial wounds on his own hand.

Babbitt reminded the jurors that Dr. Charles Tuffiash had given eleven different versions of the way Sue Tuffiash died. He had claimed a blackout, temporary insanity, self-defense, and even tried to blame her murder on other people.

The jury deliberated for only three hours before they found Tuffiash guilty of his ex-wife's brutal murder. He was sentenced to thirty years in prison.

MANY years later it was clear that Carl Glenn would never really forgive himself for letting Sue go alone to retrieve her little girls' photographs.

One name stood out on the list of Chuck Tuffiash's personal references for his trial: it was Allen Blackthorne's. Allen had a way of insinuating himself into Sheila's life, befriending those who were against her or against her friends. Allen had told either Tuffiash or his attorneys that he had Sheila on tape talking to Sue, advising her that she had raised sexual abuse issues in her divorce from *him* and that it "had worked." But Allen never produced that tape, and so his value to Tuffiash's defense had been iffy at best. The consensus was that the conversation Allen alluded to had never taken place.

As her own court battles continued, Sheila fought as hard as ever. But something died in her when Sue died. They had become friends partly because they had so much in common. Their war stories were very much alike. They had always compared their situations and felt a kinship. Now Sue's two little girls were taken away from San Antonio to be raised by relatives back east; their mother was dead and their father was in prison.

Sheila was horrified that what Sue had secretly feared had come true. She knew it could just as easily have been her lying in a welter of blood. Chuck Tuffiash and Allen Blackthorne were eerily similar, charismatic and able to charm people into believing whatever stories they came up with. Sue had fought for her children too, and none of it had mattered. All the court judgments in the world hadn't made much of a difference.

Although Allen was never called to the witness stand in the Tuffiash trial, he was in the courthouse often. In fact, he went to lunch once at the Cadillac Arms, just down from the Bexar County Courthouse, in a group that included Carl Glenn and his mother. Carl was curious about Allen. He didn't like him much, but he wondered who this man was who could treat someone like Sheila so badly and was willing to stand up in court for the man who had killed the woman Carl had wanted so much to marry.

For some reason Allen decided to entertain those at his table with a bizarre confidence. He said he had been dating an interesting woman in Las Vegas. "Come to find out," Carl remembered, "this gal Allen Blackthorne was dating used to be a man."

Allen's brothers would verify his adventures in Las Vegas. He had bragged to them about sexual escapades there that went beyond anything in his real life, which was bizarre enough. When Allen went to Vegas, he invariably pulled out all the stops.

In one of the bleak ironies that mark human lives, Carl Glenn took a job as a prison guard. He had huge medical bills and wasn't well enough yet to go back out on the oil rigs. Still mourning Sue and missing the little girls he had planned to raise as his own, he helped open a brand-new maximum-security penitentiary, the John Connelly Prison. (In late 2000 this was the prison from which the Texas Seven—violent felons—escaped, staying free for months by pretending to be traveling evangelists.)

Carl was on duty one day as they began to bring prisoners into the chow hall to eat. Astounded, he watched as Charles Tuffiash shuffled in. "I don't know if Chuck recognized me or not," Carl said. "If he did, he didn't show it." Carl told his supervisor that he needed another assignment; he didn't want to be guarding the man who had savagely killed the woman he had loved.

Sheila tried to comfort Carl in his loss, making sure that he had a place to go on holidays—insisting that he come to her apartment for Thanksgiving. But she had her own ghosts after Sue was bludgeoned to death. Sheila knew that Allen was even more tenacious and angry than Chuck Tuffiash had been.

_____*Chapter Fourteen*_____

ALLEN'S EMS-250 PROJECT, long dead of its own weight and bad debts, had him looking around for another way to make money. His former partners said he had never bothered to divide up the company's assets in an equitable manner; he had simply "written himself a check and disappeared with everything that was left." Bill Gregorich suffered a fatal heart attack soon after.

In testimony some years later, Allen described his income during this period as having come from "some design stuff" on his prime product: the muscle stimulator. In truth he was engaged in another kind of design.

On December 14, 1989, Allen had failed to appear for a revocation of parole hearing, and a warrant was issued for his arrest—still on the 1987 Castle Hills domestic violence charges involving Sheila. It was a moot point; Allen was already in custody in Portland, Oregon, having been arrested a week before in his home state. Although he later insisted that he was barely able to scrape up enough to live on, he had many resources that allowed him to buy Cadillac convertibles and lay the groundwork for a new muscle-stimulator business.

One organization that funded Allen, albeit unknowingly, was the First Interstate Bank in Salem, Oregon. The Lancaster Mall branch sought restitution from Allen for $27,276.50, which he had acquired from the bank between September 21 and October 9, 1989. In another era Allen would have been deemed a flimflam man and a grifter, and he was good at it. He began his banking escapade by opening a checking account in the name of RS Medical, with an address on Dover Street in Salem. He opened the account with a $10,000 check from the American Express Centurion Bank. And because he had previously had an account at First Interstate and did not attempt to withdraw any cash from his new account, the bank did not verify the check with American Express Centurion. Two days later Allen deposited another American Express check, for $9500, into the new RS Medical account. And three days after that, still another check—this one for $8500—was deposited. Allen didn't write any checks on the account, so none of these checks was verified either. There was no indication anything was wrong until September 28, when the Salem Branch of First Interstate learned that Allen's first check for $10,000 had bounced because his account with American Express Centurion Bank was closed.

An immediate hold was placed on Allen's Salem account. Too late. A withdrawal of over $27,000 had already been made. An attempt to locate Allen Blackthorne at the Dover Street address proved that it was a nonexistent address.

Salem Police detectives were alerted and began to follow an interesting and circuitous trail back to Allen. First Interstate was not the only bank in Salem he had visited. The Security Pacific Bank said that he opened a personal checking account there on October 19, 1989. He presented his business card for RS Medical and gave an address of 13947 Cedar Canyon in San Antonio. Two days later he deposited a Texas unemployment-compensation check. Since Allen had represented himself as the head of a successful corporation, it struck the bank manager as odd that he should be receiving unemployment checks. He closed the account and sent a letter to the San Antonio address.

A disgruntled Allen showed up at Security Pacific, demanding to see the manager to ask why his account had been closed. He was given an appointment but failed to show up. He did come back six hours later, and so did the Salem police. He was arrested. Still smooth and persuasive, Allen insisted it was all a misunderstanding. When the Salem detectives asked him about his account with American Express, he was "shocked" that it was closed. As far as he knew, the account was in good shape. But when the investigators checked with American Express, the bank explained that both of Allen's accounts had been closed for ten months. "One had an overdue balance of fourteen thousand dollars," a bank official said, "and the other was overdrawn by three thousand dollars. If he has any of our credit cards on him, we'd appreciate it if you could seize them and cut them up."

On November 18, 1989, Allen posted $3000 bond and appeared in court three days later. He asked Judge Tornquist's permission to leave the state of Oregon, but the request was denied. Free on bond, Allen returned to Texas anyway.

Allen Blackthorne still owed money all over San Antonio and faced repaying what he had stolen from the Salem banks. December 1989 was probably the time when he planned to emulate his hero John Blackthorne and journey to Taipei, Taiwan, for a whole new start. In San Antonio he bought a ticket for Portland, Oregon, the first stop in his escape from America. He had ninety $100 bills on his person when he stepped off a Delta flight in Portland on December 7.

But someone had tipped off the Oregon authorities, warning them that Allen planned to leave the country. He was arrested at the airport. It seemed that he would finally have to face the consequences of his actions. Salem investigators had learned from one of his former in-laws that he was a con man of major proportions, with scams in Texas, Oregon, and Hawaii. They had contacted the Bank of Hawaii and learned about their eventual loss of almost $200,000 in Allen's failed EMS business. The Hawaiian bank was unaware of Allen's bank troubles in Salem.

On December 12, the Salem investigators talked with a bank official of the First Interstate Bank of Plano, Texas, and learned that the Texas bank had suffered a $17,000 loss in the same scam Allen had used in Salem.

Altogether the Salem detectives seized $15,246.42 from Allen, and the court ordered that his $3000 bond should go to the First Interstate Bank. On January 29, 1990, Allen paid an additional $9480 to finish his restitution to the bank.

Once again he received only probation. And once again Allen Blackthorne believed that he was invincible.

In March 1990 Rick and Kerry Bladorn made a trip to Biloxi to see Kerry's grandmother Clennis Pearl, realizing that it would probably be their last chance to visit her. She had been on kidney dialysis for years, and she was growing steadily weaker. Clennis had a bedroom set that she wanted Gene and Don Smith to have. It was a nice enough set, but it wasn't antique by any stretch of the imagination. It was the veneer-covered wood popular in Sears catalogues in the 1930s, but Rick promised Kerry's grandmother that he would rent a U-Haul trailer and move it back to Oregon. Rick was the antithesis of Allen; he was always willing to help anyone out. Sometimes he spread himself so thin, by promising too much to too many people, that Kerry got impatient with him, but mostly she was grateful that he had such a good heart.

Their plan was to stop in San Antonio on the return trip so that they could spend Easter with Sheila, Stevie, and Daryl. Rick and Kerry had two children of their own now: Ryan, who was as red-headed as his mother, and Kelly Ann, named for Kerry's dead sister.

They had a sad leave-taking when they drove out of Mississippi. Kerry knew she would never see her grandmother alive again. Their mood lightened as they drew close to Texas. Easter was early in 1990, on March 25, and Rick was going to have an Easter egg hunt for the four little cousins. As far-flung as the family had become, Rick and Kerry were determined to keep them together with traditions and visits. But when they arrived in San Antonio and visited Sheila at her apartment, she had disappointing news; it was Allen's weekend to have Stevie and Daryl, and she hadn't been able to get him to switch visitation.

"Let me talk to him," Kerry said, sure she could change his mind.

"Allen," Kerry pleaded, "we're only going to be here for two days, and we want the cousins to spend some time together. Couldn't you take your girls next weekend?"

He wouldn't budge. Finally, Allen got a half smile on his face and said, "Tell you what. You *can* spend Easter with the girls. If you want to see Stevie and Daryl this weekend, you guys can stay at my house."

Kerry knew it was a power play, but she had no choice if she wanted to see her nieces. Allen pointed out that there was no place to park the U-Haul at Sheila's apartment complex, and they could put it in his driveway.

He was in his new house in Castle Hills Forest. They saw that it was in a far more upscale section of town and twice as expensive as his previous house, but not nearly as charming. There was no pool, but other than that, it was a typical bachelor's pad. The rooms were large, and Allen now had his aquarium built into the headboard of the bed in the master bedroom. He had a huge television set.

Rick and Kerry agreed to sleep at Allen's house on Saturday night and spend part of Easter Sunday there. Sheila reluctantly said she would come over for Easter so she could share the holiday with her little girls. She was very uncomfortable, although she had to see Allen anyway when they exchanged the girls for visitation. With her sister and brother-in-law there, she wasn't afraid.

On Saturday evening Allen bragged to Rick that he had gone to court and been able to reduce his child support to a minimal amount of money. "He seemed very proud of his success," Rick recalled, "as if he had won a major victory."

Rick was surprised to hear that Allen intended to help Sheila buy a house in his neighborhood. That was a new idea and not one Rick figured Sheila would go for. He hoped it meant that Allen actually did feel some responsibility for Stevie and Daryl.

On Sunday morning Rick gathered the four cousins in Allen's backyard and supervised the Easter egg hunt. Sheila and Kerry sat in the kitchen, drinking coffee and watching the egg hunt through the window, while Allen sat in his leather recliner chair listening to the women talk. It might have been like old times—but it was only détente.

Sue Tuffiash had been murdered four weeks earlier, and Sheila was telling Kerry about it. She was clearly still very upset at the loss of her friend in such a terrible way.

"Sue deserved it," Allen cut in. "She pissed him off."

Shocked, Kerry and Sheila turned to look at Allen. He was staring at Sheila. "Don't *you* ever piss *me* off."

It was an overt threat. With her continual legal fight against Allen for equitable child support, Sheila *was* pissing him off.

It was the second time Kerry had heard Allen threaten to kill her sister. She had a clearer understanding now of the tightrope Sheila walked.

As they visited before Rick and Kerry headed north toward Oregon, Sheila told them not to worry. "One of these days," she said with a laugh, "I'm going to find a nice guy like Rick."

"Well, you could have had him when I was trying to fix you up in high school," Kerry joked. "Too late now. I've got him." Kerry was still a relentless matchmaker. She vowed to find someone who was worthy of Sheila.

On the drive home Rick told her what Allen had confided in him. "He told me you slept with Sheila's boss, Roy Anderson, when you visited in Hawaii, back when you were seventeen."

"What?"

"That's what he said." Rick was grinning. He knew better, and he also knew Allen was a liar. Allen's own predatory attitude about sex made him see wickedness wherever he looked.

Kerry sighed. Allen hated it when anyone else had a good relationship. He had always loved to plant seeds of doubt in people's minds. He just didn't understand that there was nothing that would come between herself and Rick.

That June, Clennis Pearl died, and Sheila and Kerry flew into New Orleans for the funeral. They went to Biloxi in a rented convertible and visited the gravesites of their father, Donny and Kelly Ann. They took pictures of each other—two pretty sisters, one blond, one titian-haired. Sheila was still very thin, and dark circles continued to smudge her eyes, but for the moment they were happy to be together. It seemed that they were always going to funerals or memorial services or to visit graves. Perhaps because they had lost so many people they loved, they were more able to appreciate the moment and the closeness they had always had.

When they visited their father's grave, Sheila broke down and sobbed for a long time. Both she and Kerry had always wanted a relationship with their grandpa Walsh, their father's father. They determined to get in touch with him, but it was too late. He died a few days after Clennis Pearl's funeral.

On the way home Kerry visited with Sheila in San Antonio before she headed to Oregon. Sue Tuffiash had been dead for only three months, although Kerry knew very little about her murder. They hadn't talked about it since that Easter morning in Allen's kitchen. Kerry and Sheila went to a popular cowboy bar one night to meet some of Sheila's girlfriends. They needed some lightness in their lives.

There was a *person* sitting at the bar, an obvious male dressed as a woman. "We spotted him first," Kerry said, "because he had such hairy legs, and they looked silly underneath a dress. I thought it was funny, but Sheila didn't. I didn't know then that Allen was a cross-dresser."

Sheila's attitude puzzled her, and Kerry said, "Oh, come on, it *is* funny! Anyone can see that it's a man."

And then Sheila looked out at the dance floor and froze. She whirled and told Kerry they were leaving. She was so determined—and angry too—that Kerry followed her without question.

"Sheila went up to the bouncer, and she was just screaming at him," Kerry said. " 'You let cross-dressers and murderers in this establishment! I'll *never* be back!' "

"What was that all about?" Kerry asked.

Sheila had never talked about Allen's fetish for dressing up in women's clothes. But she was more irate about the man she had seen on the dance floor. It was Chuck Tuffiash, out on bail before his trial. That he should be there, dancing with a woman, made her both sad and furious. Sue was dead and buried, and her killer was dancing in a cowboy bar and having a great time.

"That asshole killed her," Sheila told her sister, as angry as Kerry had ever seen her. "And he *planned* it."

As for Sheila's ire at seeing a transvestite at the bar, Kerry was older now, and Sheila was frank about some of Allen's sexual proclivities. She told Kerry that not only had Allen brought other women into their home, he had invited a male prostitute to live there for a while. She had been out of her marriage for almost three years, but certain incidents triggered both her pain and her wrath.

Kerry and Rick were very happy together, but Sheila was still alone. Mr. Awesome had not worked out, and Sheila had been dating a man named David, who also happened to be a dentist. She thought a lot of him and was hopeful that they might have a future together. But Sheila admitted to her girlfriends that she had a guilty secret. David disapproved of smoking, and Sheila was a closet smoker. She rinsed her mouth with mouthwash and brushed her teeth carefully before she went out with David, but he knew, and he scolded her. Like all smokers, Sheila failed to realize that nonsmokers can detect the odor of tobacco in hair and on clothing.

More than the smoking, David backed away from a long-term commitment. There were a lot of bachelors who were scared off at the thought of being a stepfather to two children another man had fathered. Stevie and Daryl came with Sheila as a package deal and that was that. Even so, Sheila still hoped her relationship with David would someday end in marriage.

In the meantime, she struggled to support Stevie and Daryl on what she made. There were big chunks of time when she didn't even know where Allen was, and then he would show up again, meddling in her life but doing virtually nothing to help her support their daughters. Even paying apartment rent was a struggle for Sheila. In spite of everything, she was usually upbeat and fun to be around. There were shadows in her life, but most people didn't see them.

Even though she lived with a fine sheen of fear over every contact she had with Allen, Sheila's inborn tenacity made her relentless in going after him for child support. Attorney Mary Fenlon filed a motion to modify support payments in May 1991 and also asked for back support from the days Allen was supposed to have paid $1250 a month.

Allen was held in contempt of court. Ultimately he didn't have to increase his payments, because he fought back by seeking a modification of child custody. That frightened Sheila, and she backed off on asking for more money. She was still afraid he would find a way to take Stevie and Daryl completely away from her.

Allen seemed to have an impenetrable shield around him; his charm and earnest affect worked for him again and again. Sheila and the little girls were barely getting by, but she felt helpless as she tried to force Allen to pay child support. She was sure he didn't want the nuisance of having them around all the time, but he might take them because he knew that was the worst thing he could do to her.

And then Allen's attitude seemed to change. He acknowledged that Sheila and the girls should have a house to live in and offered to help her swing it financially. He had told Rick he planned to do this, but Sheila was suspicious about his motives. She waited for the other shoe to drop—and it did. Allen's offer came with stipulations. He would help her buy a house, but *only* if she agreed to choose one in his neighborhood. In fact, he had found the perfect place; it was four houses up the street from his own home in Castle Hills Forest right at the midpoint of a cul-de-sac.

In retrospect, Sheila would be criticized for accepting Allen's offer; Allen always pointed to that as proof that they had been quite friendly for a few years after their divorce. They weren't, but Sheila was so tired of struggling to pay apartment rent, and the girls were getting older. They deserved to have a house and to live in a neighborhood where they had room to play. She accepted Allen's offer, but she invited Minda Reece to live with her and the girls.

Minda and her boyfriend moved Sheila's furniture into the new house. Sheila was still so sensitized to dealing with Allen on a one-to-one basis that she needed someone as a buffer and, to be truthful, a bodyguard. Minda was barely out of her teens, but she was wonderful with Stevie and Daryl. She agreed to move in with Sheila and be on hand when Sheila had to work late, as she often did. Since Minda had been with Sheila when she tried to get her furniture and household goods back from Allen, she understood the dynamics of their relationship and wasn't afraid of Allen.

The new house was very nice, and it felt wonderful to have enough space. For Sheila, however, the negative side of living four houses up the street from her ex-husband began to emerge almost at once. She had no privacy at all. Every time she left her house, she had to drive past Allen's house, and he could monitor her comings and goings. If she had a date, Allen knew it. If she came home late, he knew it. Although she didn't actually see him behind his shaded windows, she *felt* his eyes watching her.

Allen soon bought Stevie and Daryl little radio-controlled electric cars so they could pedal down the street to visit him. Rather than seeing him only during the court-ordered visitation, the little girls were at Allen's house frequently. He encouraged Stevie to come more often; she had always been his favorite. He still insisted that Daryl wasn't really his child. He had never held her when she was an infant, and he continued to treat her like an interloper. She was a bright little girl and knew her father didn't want her around. It hurt her, and living so close made Daryl's status with Allen more obvious than ever.

If Sheila had her choice, *neither* of her daughters would have to visit their father. Now if Stevie didn't get her way, she would run to Allen's house, and he would refuse to bring her back. Even when Sheila walked down the street and knocked on his door, he wouldn't let her take Stevie home.

Too late she realized she had played right into Allen's hands. He had her in a glass cage where he could spy on her, and he had Stevie available just down the street. All of Sheila's antennae were out, and she watched constantly to be sure Allen wasn't molesting Stevie. She couldn't be certain. She couldn't go to the police either.

Sheila had always believed in God. Despite her sometimes salty language and her raging against Allen, she was devoutly religious. When she could do nothing herself to change the way things were, she prayed. "God will take care of us," she often told Minda Reece and Kelly McGonigal. "I know he's going to take care of me and my girls and that everything will be all right."

IF Allen tried to insinuate himself and his venom between happy couples like Kerry and Rick, Debbie and Tom Oliver, and Guy and Suzanne Van Houte, one can only imagine how he hated to see Sheila in a relationship with another man. While she was living in her apartment in Brandon Oaks, he hadn't been able to keep close tabs on whom she dated. Now he saw David drive past his house to spend an evening with Sheila or to pick her up for a date, and it ate at him.

"Allen and David talked," Kerry remembered. "I don't know what Allen said, but after that Sheila and David broke up."

Sheila stayed only six months in the house up the street from Allen. As nice as it was, it wasn't worth the price she had to pay. She found a tiny, two-bedroom house for sale at 13115 Brook Garden Lane in a neighborhood that was not nearly as posh as Allen's, but she was overjoyed when she was able to finance it and buy it on her own. Stevie and Daryl looked at it with suspicion; it wasn't very nice. They didn't understand why they had to move into such a small house.

The girls were seven and almost nine now, and Sheila found it increasingly difficult to discipline them or to imbue them with her philosophies about morals and ethics. If she chastised them, they were as likely as not to say, "I don't have to do what you say. My daddy says we'll just go to the judge." Whatever she told them, Allen told them the opposite. He continued to give them presents that she could never afford, and to tell them that they didn't have to mind her. He taught them to disrespect other people's rights and property. Once, Stevie spilled her milkshake in a rental car, but as she grabbed tissues and started to wipe it up, Allen stopped her, saying, "Let it go. It's a *rental*. It doesn't matter."

Allen himself was a confirmed shoplifter, even when he was raking in hundreds of thousands of dollars a year. He enjoyed stealing little things from stores for the thrill of getting away with it. He began to encourage Stevie to shoplift, making it a conspiratorial game between the two of them.

In a way, it was better that Sheila didn't know the details of the way Allen manipulated Stevie's mind and the degree to which he ignored Daryl.

Despite Stevie's and Daryl's disappointment at the new house, they were all together, and they had a good time. Sheila knew her daughters loved her, and she counted on that as a shield against whatever Allen was doing to take them away from her.

"We were so poor," Daryl remembered a long time later. "All we had to eat was Top Ramen and beans and rice."

She wasn't exaggerating. It was all Sheila could afford after she made the house payment and paid utilities. She had to have a car to get to work, but even old cars cost money. She was physically worn down and fragile, but her determination never flagged. Allen was pushing to get total custody of the girls and she spent endless hours filing answers to his claims. The one thing she could not bring herself to reveal, however, was the extent of her ex-husband's perversions. The details were too humiliating to tell even her own sister.

_____Chapter Fifteen_____

STILL SEETHING over Sheila's successful suit to force him to pay her back child support, Allen fought her by seeking full custody of his daughters. He represented himself in hearings, and impressed the judge with his knowledge of the law. The case dragged on until trial on January 5, 1992, where Allen had an attorney represent him. He alleged that Sheila was mentally and physically abusive to Stevie and Daryl.

Allen claimed that Sheila had hired a baby-sitter who was abusive to the girls, discussing inappropriate sexual matters with them. It was true that Sheila had hired a woman named Maisie Hernandez* for housecleaning and occasional baby-sitting. Although she was forty-one, Maisie had been injured in an accident at sixteen, and her maturation had not kept up with her age. And she *had* taught one of the girls a "sex act" and been convicted of indecency. Finding baby-sitters wasn't easy for Sheila; like all single mothers, she worried about leaving the girls, but she had no choice. She was horrified when she learned of Maisie's behavior.

Allen was determined to beat Sheila any way he could; Sheila wanted only to protect the girls and have a life of her own. After eight days in court Sheila fought back. For the second time she accused Allen in public of sexually abusing Stevie.

Allen objected and contested her allegations. But he lost in his suit for custody and he was ordered to pay Sheila $6000 and $200 for health insurance. Allen filed for a new custody trial on February 28, 1992. His grounds were that the sexual abuse charges had not been "properly presented" in the January trial.

WHILE all the legal wrangling dragged on, Allen's business prospects and his social life were once more on the upswing. An acquaintance had introduced him to two wealthy Washington State brothers, Rick and Patrick Terrell, in 1990. They were looking for a business investment, and Allen was brilliant at making his pitch. Once more, he had presented himself as skillfully as he always had. He was smart, he was savvy, and his product—the EMS-250—was as viable as it had ever been. The Terrell brothers were impressed.

The EMS-250 would not aim for direct sales, Allen explained; rather, it was a mechanism that would be principally owned by the company, which Allen had already visualized as RS Medical. Physicians could rent it, or they could buy it if they liked, and then rent it to their patients. Most patients would show rapid improvement, Allen pointed out, making them loathe to give it up. It wasn't magic and it wasn't snake oil. The device stimulated muscles and also brought more blood to affected parts, enhancing healing. It was clearly a product whose rental would be by prescription only and where charges could be billed to insurance companies.

"It sends an electrical pulse into the motor neurons," Allen explained confidently to his potential partners, "causing muscles to depolarize—basically contract and relax. The various benefits of that is as a muscle pump or to increase blood flow. We have done work with a vascular foot—the diabetic foot."

Anyone in the medical field knew that diabetics were prone to amputations of the feet and lower limbs when sores on their feet didn't heal. Allen pointed out that his invention would overcome this. He also saw a huge market in selling to NFL and NBA teams to "treat sports injuries, particularly anterior cruciate ligament repair, and strengthen skeletal muscles."

It didn't matter that he'd never taken a college course. Allen Blackthorne was an intelligent chameleon, and he was a most convincing salesman. It was his claim that *he* had invented the EMS-250, and he certainly did not mention that it came originally from Asia or that his father had modified it. It was his, and his alone.

Rick and Pat Terrell saw a very confident, handsome man in the prime of his life, dressed well, driving a new car. He spoke well and he knew his product inside and out. And it was obviously an excellent product.

Of course, Allen didn't mention his debts, his bankruptcy, his ongoing legal haggling with Sheila—or anything negative at all. Like a reptile shedding its skin, he rid himself of the past and started over, bright and shiny new as ever. He had always had the capacity to begin again without feeling the slightest hindrance of conscience or regret.

Allen was not required to invest even a dollar in the new company that he formed with the Terrell brothers. They were strictly legitimate businessmen and mightily impressed by his experience. The new company would be located in Vancouver, Washington, although Allen would remain in San Antonio. The company name would be International Rehabilitative Sciences, doing business as RS Medical.

From the beginning, Allen earned $5000 a month and ten percent of the company's annual pre-tax profits. He also held 50 percent of RS Medical's stock. The privately held company sold other shares to investors. Allen regularly attended quarterly board meetings in Vancouver, which lies just across the Columbia River from Portland, Oregon, and he helped open and monitor the branch offices, which soon spread across America.

A decade before, Allen had deliberately run down and killed a motorcyclist on the I-205 bridge that was only a few miles from the offices of his company's headquarters. He drove that route back to his hotel without ever thinking of it.

The FDA, Allen's old nemesis, was still investigating him and his muscle stimulators, but he came up with an idea to best them. He suggested that RS Medical hire a "consultant" who would pose as a medical device manufacturer. Then RS and the other person would both file applications for FDA approval at the same time, to produce virtually the same stimulating device.

The consultant won approval in three months, while the FDA took a year to consider Allen's company's application, and then they turned it down. Allen used this disparate timing to show that the government was ganging up on a poor little company in Washington State. He was, as always, a convincing spokesman.

In June 1993 U.S. Magistrate John Primomo of San Antonio called the FDA "arbitrary and capricious" for ruling in an opposite manner on two identical products. Two years later U.S. Representative Joe Barton, a Texas Republican and chairman of the Department of Commerce's subcommittee on oversight and investigations, chided the FDA for causing RS Medical so much trouble. Shortly thereafter RS Medical and Allen Blackthorne were mentioned in the venerable *Wall Street Journal* as having devised a clever ploy to expose inequities in the FDA. Allen framed the article and hung it in his study.

Once more he had been validated. Was it any wonder that he considered himself someone who would never lose? Not in the final analysis. He might lose a skirmish or two, but he always won the important battles.

In the first seven years of operation, RS Medical went on to treat 50,000 patients. Its revenues in 1995 would be $8.7 million and almost double that a year later, at $14.2 million. By 1996 RS Medical ranked twentieth among the fastest-growing companies in the Vancouver-Portland area, and this included some rapidly burgeoning software companies. Allen not only got frequent raises in salary but he was collecting 10 percent of the profits right off the top. At last he had found the wealth he had always wanted.

ALLEN'S social life was not as successful as his business venture, and in 1993 he turned to a dating service, *Together,* to find women. An arrangement was made for him to meet a woman for drinks and dinner at La Scala, an upscale San Antonio restaurant. Hesitant about going out with a stranger, even one who came so well recommended by the matchmaking company, Allen's date, who was a tall, beautiful redhead, brought along her girlfriend Maureen Weingeist.

Maureen Karol Weingeist, thirty-two, was the daughter of a Houston oil executive who worked for Exxon, assigned to the company's office in Caracas, Venezuela. That was where Maureen was born on November 17, 1960, and she would always speak English with a slight Venezuelan accent. She had two sisters and a brother, but Maureen was the daddy's girl in the family. When her father died suddenly of a heart attack, she was devastated.

"Maureen was needy," a longtime friend explained, "but she was strong too. Does that make any sense? After her father died, she needed a man to cling to, but she was very smart and really good in business." Maureen had a college degree, and she had worked in Fort Lauderdale, Florida, for Kodak. She moved to San Antonio in the late '80s and took a job with Hewlett-Packard as a sales rep.

Maureen Weingeist was Jewish, a woman whose rather ordinary features changed completely when she wore a lot of skillfully applied

makeup. Friends described her as "very exotic-looking." She was petite, but she had a spectacular, full-breasted figure and long, thick
brown hair, which she teased until it was truly luxuriant. She dressed
in clothes that nipped her slim waist and accentuated her bustline,
and she wore high heels to show off her great legs. Maureen was a flirtatious woman, usually more comfortable around men than with
other women.

During the blind-date dinner where Maureen was supposed to be
the chaperon, it became embarrassingly clear that there was an intense attraction between her and Allen. He never asked her friend out
again, but Allen and Maureen began to date. The chemistry between
men and women has never been something to be charted or reduced
to a formula. But whatever it is, they had it.

Maureen was embarrassed by the way she and Allen met, so she
told her friend Pam Harrell that they'd met on a plane. "We talked for
hours and hours," she said.

"Bullshit, Maureen," Pam said. "You don't go on plane trips that
last for hours and hours. Where did you really meet him?"

Finally admitting the truth, Maureen went on and on about Allen
Blackthorne. He was handsome and wealthy and completely charming. She wasn't easily impressed; Maureen had come from money too,
and her family lived in Houston in a very posh neighborhood off
Memorial Drive. Moreover, she had a hefty bank account she'd
earned herself.

During her early days with Hewlett-Packard, Maureen earned a
base salary of $50,000 to $60,000 a year, but the company also paid
per diem and expenses during the training period. "They authorized
twenty-five dollars just for breakfast," an ex-employee recalled, "but
you didn't have to eat breakfast or any other meal out, and you could
still claim the money for meals. Lots of people did it, and it was a way
to build up your income quickly. It wasn't stealing; it was a choice,
and Maureen did that and she saved the money. She put it in different
bank accounts. After a few years with Hewlett-Packard, I'm sure
Maureen had saved a lot more than a hundred thousand dollars."

Maureen lived in the St. Tropez Apartments, off Fredericksburg
Road, and like a lot of single women in San Antonio, she enjoyed
going dancing and to clubs. "She was always madly in love," one
friend remembered. "Her romances never seemed to work out, but
she went from one to the next, hoping that the next man would be the
right one."

For a half-dozen years none of Maureen's romances ended in
marriage, although she dated some of the handsomest men in the city.

"San Antonio is a small town," a woman who worked with Maureen at Hewlett-Packard said. "When I date, I am very careful *not* to date local men. For a big city, this *is* a small town, and it's too easy to get a reputation. Maureen didn't understand that. She did flamboyant things that people remembered. One time, for instance, we were coming back from a sales meeting with a bunch of H-P employees, and we all had reserved seats together near the front of the plane.

"But Maureen found out that the San Antonio Gunslingers [a semi-pro football team] had already boarded and were sitting in the back. She walked right on by her reserved seat and went back to sit with them. That was just her."

After their once removed blind-date meeting, Maureen was soon "madly in love" with Allen and excited about marrying him. Her family in Houston was appalled because no one seemed to know anything about the man. One of Maureen's sisters was married to a bank president, and Maureen told Pam that he had hired a private investigator to check out Allen's background. Most of his life up to his arrival in San Antonio was—as he had planned—impossible to chart, but the PI reported back that Allen had never graduated from Stanford or any other university. He hadn't even *been* to Stanford.

When Maureen asked him about it, Allen explained, "Oh, I did graduate from Stanford, Maureen, but I attended the university under another name."

It was a laughable excuse, but Maureen believed Allen because she wanted to believe him. Her family didn't. They were so outraged and incredulous that she would seriously consider marrying a man who lied so blatantly that she was forced to choose between Allen Blackthorne and her mother and siblings.

She chose Allen.

"He was evil," her friend Pam Harrell said. "I don't know how to explain it, but when I went to his house in Hunter's Creek, there was some kind of karma there that was just evil."

According to her friends, Maureen was both obsessed with Allen and frightened by him. Still, her fear didn't stop her from wanting desperately to marry him. It didn't take long for her to discover that, sexually, Allen wasn't like other men she had known.

"She didn't like the things he did," a close friend said. "Maureen wasn't into all that kinky stuff, but she could live with it."

Maureen had worked for Hewlett-Packard for six years, but her career wasn't going well there. The company reorganized, and she was given a territory that was a long way from San Antonio, and difficult for a woman. She had to cover "the valley": Lubbock, San Angelo, Brownsville, Odessa. Sales reps were expected to drive, not fly, to their territories, and it was before the days of cell phones. Because it was four hundred miles from Lubbock to San Antonio, Maureen began to fly, and her expenses became too high for her sales perform- ance. She couldn't meet her sales quota, and she left Hewlett-Packard in 1993.

It didn't really matter to her. Allen proposed to Maureen on No- vember 7, 1993. That date, she would say later, meant more to her as a milestone to be celebrated than their actual wedding day.

PART THREE

Jamie

Chapter Sixteen

WHILE ALLEN WAS DATING Maureen Weingeist, Sheila had
met the man who would change her life in ways she could never have
imagined. For the first eight months of 1992 her world was very predictable. She had little time to date and a great deal of responsibility
between her job, her daughters, and her legal battles with Allen. As
the girls grew older, Allen's influence over them became ever more
worrisome. They could see that _his_ house in Castle Hills Forest was
plush and expensive, and then they came home to the plain little
house Sheila had bought. Their things were crowded into a tiny bedroom they shared; the whole house seemed boxy and confining. Stevie
and Daryl had more fun with their father, where they were allowed to
do anything they wanted. Their mother had rules and expected them
to do chores around the house.

Allen encouraged Stevie and Daryl to defy Sheila, sympathizing
with whatever complaints they had about her. Everything was an up-
hill battle for her, but skirmish by skirmish, she was beating Allen in
court. He had to pay back child support and see that the girls had
health insurance. Although she hadn't proved sexual abuse of a child
against him, he had not gained custody of the girls. And _he_ had to pay
the attorneys and court costs. In April 1992 a court order garnisheed
Allen's salary at RS Medical to pay child support. His life was finally

heading in the direction he wanted, and it made him angrier every time Sheila prevailed and put a pall over it.

In August, Sheila reluctantly agreed to go to a Garth Brooks concert on a blind date with a friend of Kerry's. But the evening failed to materialize, and when the date stood her up, Sheila was more disappointed than she expected to be. She had been looking forward to the concert and the possibility of spending an evening with an attractive man. Feeling rejected, she asked a friend to baby-sit with the girls and decided to fly to Santa Rosa for an overnight trip to see Jonda Pinter.

The return trip on Southwest Airlines had a stop in Phoenix. It was very warm in the plane with the air-conditioning off, and Sheila would later tell her friends she turned from looking out the window, where the desert heat made the tarmac shimmer, to glance down the aisle. A tall, solid-looking man was walking toward her and stopped next to the empty seat beside her. Southwest has no seat assignments, so he could have sat anywhere in the plane, but he was smiling down at her. He was square and burly, and he had a close crew cut. He wasn't handsome, but he had a good, dependable look about him. Sheila had had handsome men before. Allen was the best-looking man she ever knew, and he'd become ugly to her. She smiled now when the man in the aisle asked if the seat next to her was taken, and shook her head.

He told her his name was Jamie Bellush. They talked all the way to San Antonio, and she learned that Jamie was born in 1962, the same year as she had been, although he was four months older. He was a "detail man"—a pharmaceutical salesman—for Pfizer and an ex-marine who had seen action in the Gulf War. He said he had worked for Pfizer Pharmaceuticals for four years and had recently been assigned to San Antonio. At thirty he was still single.

Sheila was very glad to hear that. When the plane landed, Jamie Bellush insisted on giving her a ride home, and she accepted. For a weekend that had started out so badly, it suddenly had possibilities. She had been on her own for so long, standing up against Allen; she couldn't help looking at Jamie and thinking how strong and confident and *big* he was. He would be someone to have in her corner. Beyond that, she was attracted to him and sensed that he felt the same way.

Jamie was, indeed, interested in Sheila, although their backgrounds were very different. He came from what sounded like a very secure upper-middle-class family and what he described as a "loving, nurturing environment." Born in San Jose, California, where his father was a builder and real estate developer, Jamie was six when his father moved his family back to Newton, New Jersey. He had four brothers and sisters, his mother was a retired registered nurse, and his parents had been together for more than forty years. Jamie had done all the things Sheila had not—growing up during his school years in one town, living on a lake, and graduating from high school with the same group of friends. He played football, made the swim team, and worked as a lifeguard in the summer. He had a degree in chemistry from Ithaca College. At six feet one and 240 pounds, Jamie Bellush looked like a fullback or an Irish cop or a marine. He had a tough eye when someone annoyed him. But he looked at Sheila tenderly and they started dating.

To Sheila, Jamie must have represented security and normalcy, and he didn't seem at all put off when he learned that she had two daughters who were nine and seven. A lot of single men weren't interested in dating a woman with children, but Jamie liked the girls. Sheila's friends were delighted for her when they saw she was falling in love with Jamie. She deserved to have someone cherish her as much as he did. He seemed to see things in black and white, and he wasn't forever playing games with her head like Allen did.

One thing Sheila regretted mightily, now. After Daryl was born, she had vowed never to bear another child of Allen's and had her fallopian tubes tied to prevent any further pregnancies. As miserable as she was with Allen, she hadn't expected to be divorced. But she had known there mustn't be any more children. If the marriage didn't work out, she would have her hands full taking care of Stevie and Daryl. Sadly, she hadn't looked beyond that. The prospect of a second marriage had become dimmer and dimmer over the years.

And now there was Jamie. He wanted to marry her, and she was so happy about that. At first, he didn't seem upset that she could no longer have children. It was enough that they were in love. Jamie was Sheila's second chance at love, and he meant so much more to her because she never thought she would find him.

BUT even with her new happiness, there was more litigation with Allen, the charges continuing unabated from both sides. One would think that now that Allen had found Maureen and Sheila had found Jamie, their wars would sputter out. But it was as if their divorce had a life of its own and would continue to survive, fueled by hatred and acrimony.

It was possible that Sheila didn't even know how much Allen

hated her. In the fall of 1992 Mike McGraw, an executive with RS Medical, was in San Antonio for a business meeting with Allen, and he was shocked when Allen confided how much he hated his ex-wife. He said he had "contacts" who could take Sheila to Mexico and make sure she would never return. McGraw didn't take Allen seriously, although later he would have reason to remember the conversation. Allen had always liked to shock people and pretend that he played with the big boys.

It had now been four years since Sheila divorced Allen, but the penny-ante stuff continued. Sheila lost a support check, and Allen told the treasurer at RS Medical not to reissue it. If she was dumb enough to lose it, it was her own fault.

Long ago Sheila and Janet Littlejohn had been forced to file adversarial proceedings in Allen's bankruptcy to protect Sheila's assets. One of the judgments she had won gave her $75,000, all the arrears in child support, attorneys' fees, etc. Since Allen rarely paid the amount of child support in court orders, his debts to his daughters had only grown larger and larger. Some months he was $1000 behind, and some only $350. Although RS Medical was doing incredibly well, Allen still claimed poverty. Sheila was trying to preserve $120,500 for Stevie and Daryl. She believed Allen was hiding far more than that from her, either in offshore banks or with fancy bookkeeping. At the very least she wanted her girls to have money that would see them through college. Both Stevie and Daryl were very intelligent, and they deserved that education.

This time, Allen could not just walk away and start over—he had too much going for him with RS Medical—but Sheila didn't get all that Allen owed her. On November 11, 1992, another judgment was signed, and Allen agreed to sign a promissory note for $28,000. This was a trust to be built for Stevie and Daryl's college expenses someday. Allen was to deposit $500 a month into this trust, and if he would pay that, Sheila agreed to settle for $30,000. She got only $2000; the rest was for her little girls. However, she still owned 22 percent of the EMS business, at least on paper.

Sheila still hoped that the enmity between herself and Allen would eventually be defused and that they might one day treat each other with civility. "Allen," she wrote him that December of 1992, "I don't like the situation between us, and maybe someday it will change. However, in the meantime, the least amount of direct contact you and I have will be best. I think that what has happened in our lives has been a tragedy, but a situation with hope."

According to Allen, he did not speak to Sheila for the next three years.

SHEILA and Jamie met in August 1992, and their dating had rapidly become a courtship. Jamie found Sheila very beautiful and was proud to be seen with her. They just seemed to get along, and for the first time in years, Sheila was happy and optimistic. Jamie pressed her for marriage, and he was affectionate and kind to her two little girls. Stevie and Daryl were enthusiastic about Jamie too, despite Allen's negative remarks about him.

Sheila, Stevie, and Daryl became members of the Alamo Heights Baptist church, and the girls were baptized there in April 1993.

Sheila happily agreed to marry Jamie, and their official wedding date was set for June 26, 1993. However, when they went to their pastor at the Baptist church, he told them that Jamie should not live with Sheila and her daughters in his house on East Oakview Place unless they were married in the sight of God. Both of them were committed to their church, and they wanted to do the right thing. So, while they planned for a more formal wedding and a big celebration in June, Jamie and Sheila quietly went through a civil service in April 1993. Few people knew that they were married.

Sheila rented out the little house she had been so proud to buy. She and Jamie agreed she would sell it when the time came for them to buy their own house together. She continued to work for Luke Soules.

In preparation for her "wedding-wedding," several of Sheila's girlfriends gave her a hilarious bachelorette party. They had known her through so many years of sad and frightening times that it was wonderful to be able to celebrate her new life with her.

Sheila had arranged for a rehearsal dinner for the wedding party on June 25 at a Mexican restaurant along the Riverwalk. The mood at her house was ebullient until 6:00 P.M., when their celebration was interrupted by a knock on the front door. Stevie and Daryl were supposed to be home from a visit to Allen, but instead a process server asked for Sheila and handed her a summons. It informed her that Allen was suing to change child visitation and had asked for a restraining order. As she accepted the summons, she looked over the process server's shoulder and saw her little girls sitting with Allen in the car, parked in front of her house. He gloated as he finally allowed Stevie and Daryl to run to their mother. He was demanding an increase in his time with his daughters, a move that was clearly timed to mar Sheila's joy at marrying Jamie. The party was more subdued after that, but they still had a wonderful time along the Riverwalk, and Sheila and Jamie were determined to go through with their wedding the next day. They were so happy to be together that nothing Allen could do was going to spoil that.

Kerry and Rick and the rest of Sheila's family came down for the wedding, and Kerry recalled that Sheila was a "nervous wreck" as she got dressed. "She'd put yellow concealer under her eyes to hide the dark shadows," Kerry laughed, remembering, "and she was afraid it showed. She kept asking me, 'Can you see my yellow concealer?' "

Luke Soules, Sheila's longtime boss, was there, and their pastor arrived to perform the service, but the lovely backyard ceremony they had planned was impossible. The skies released a deluge of rain that flooded the backyard in torrents of water. The wedding party hurried over to the Baptist church and then came back to Sheila and Jamie's house for the reception. By that time the rain had let up a little, and their guests were able to move outside under an awning. It was to be one of many ceremonies in Sheila's life made memorable because of a violent rainstorm.

On June 28 Sheila was in court instead of being on her honeymoon. She knew Allen didn't really want more time with the girls; even when they went to his house, he didn't spend any more than token time with them. He played golf all day, and Stevie and Daryl watched television or went to the movies with Virginia L'Heureux, Allen's secretary. At first Virginia had held down the fort in the San Antonio office while Allen was traveling on behalf of RS Medical. During the time he was active in the company, he was at various times founder, CEO, and board chairman, and he traveled for the company and helped set up branch offices with sales representatives around the country.

Virginia began working for Allen in May 1991. She was a girl Friday, who packed his suitcases, took his dogs to the vet, paid his bills, made bank deposits and withdrawals, and even did his grocery shopping. After Maureen came along, Virginia's duties lessened and changed. Sometimes she spent her days with Stevie and Daryl, and sometimes she was just there, watching television, waiting for Allen to find something for her to do.

Allen's somewhat bizarre actions, particularly in his struggles with Sheila and his gambling binges, disturbed the executives at RS Medical. They knew more now about his background, although he hadn't lied to them about the potential for the EMS. Allen was the titular founder and CEO, but they wanted to remove themselves a few steps from him. In July 1993 Rick Terrell became president of RS

Medical and Allen was named vice-president of special projects. He would continue to travel for the company and come to the quarterly board meetings, but his main headquarters would be in San Antonio at his home on Hunter's Lark. Virginia L'Heureux and Allen continued to put in eight-hour days.

With Allen's latest legal maneuvering, Sheila was more resolute than ever. The only power she had over him was his sexual abuse of Stevie when she was a small girl. They had all had counseling to deal with the ongoing tug of war, and she felt it might be better for Stevie to tell the truth than to have to live with the threat of her father's continually seeking more visitation. The mention of bringing up his offenses against Stevie was akin to holding up a cross to ward off a vampire. Allen quickly dropped his motion, making it a non-suit.

Stevie and Daryl continued in counseling, their lives torn by parents who were figuratively at each other's throats. There was no question that Sheila and Allen hated each other, but there was also something more—as if they had each expected the other to make their lives complete and were still stung by the depth of the failure of their marriage. Their contact was through attorneys or a third party. They didn't speak any longer. When Sheila called Allen about the girls, he simply handed the phone to Virginia and said, "It's for you."

For a period of two or three years there were no overt confrontations between Allen and Sheila. Their rare conversations were by phone and uttered in short sentences, or by fax. Allen picked the girls up at school for his visitations, and usually Maureen drove them back to Sheila and Jamie's house. Sheila continued, however, to document everything in writing. She didn't trust him.

When she heard that Allen was getting ready to marry for the fourth time, Sheila was concerned for Maureen Weingeist; she had nothing against Maureen, but she thought she was making a huge mistake. That was like Sheila; she worried about other people a lot. She had often wished that Allen's first two wives had come to her and warned her that she was about to walk into a desperately dangerous marriage. Neither of them had; they had both gone underground to hide from Allen. Now, when Sheila learned that Allen was going to marry Maureen, her conscience tugged at her. She didn't know Maureen well, but she felt compelled to let her know the truth. They had exchanged brief conversations when Maureen delivered the girls after a visitation, she liked Maureen, and now Sheila called her and arranged a meeting.

Jamie and Sheila met Maureen at a San Antonio restaurant, the Blue Oyster Café, and Sheila tried to be tactful as she shared some of the worst of her own experiences as Mrs. Allen Van Houte/Blackthorne. But Sheila's warning was akin to shouting into the wind. As she began to relate some of the horror and brutality she had endured during her marriage to Allen, Maureen stared at her condescendingly as if she must be crazy. Maureen had no intention of walking away from Allen. She loved him, and he loved her, and if Sheila hadn't been able to stay married to him, that was surely because they weren't suited to each other. It had nothing to do with the relationship that Allen and Maureen had.

"Well," Sheila told Kerry later, exasperated. "I tried. I didn't talk to her out of spite. I wanted to warn her, the way I wasn't warned. But she's just stupid."

Predictably, Maureen told Allen everything Sheila had said about him, and although he was annoyed, he had an answer for it all. According to Allen, Sheila was a harridan, a money-hungry gold digger, unfaithful, and a bad mother. He just felt lucky that he had finally found someone like Maureen.

That was exactly what Maureen needed to hear. And soon she was pregnant and any thought of leaving Allen was ridiculous to her. She had managed to rationalize her doubts and anxieties about him. She *was* strong, but she needed and wanted Allen Blackthorne so much that she convinced herself that things would change after they were married.

They had one close call. Shortly before they were married, Maureen summoned the police to their home in Hunter's Creek. She and Allen had had a huge fight, which ended with Maureen running to her car and leaving. She had come into the relationship with a substantial nest egg of more than $100,000, and Allen wanted to pool their money in a joint account. When she balked, their arguing erupted into an open battle. By the time police arrived, Maureen had driven off, but she returned, and she and Allen worked things out.

Allen and Maureen were married on May 7, 1994. It was Maureen's first marriage, and she was four or five months pregnant with Allen's baby. She wanted to be a mother and thought she would be good at it.

Allen and Maureen had a home wedding at Allen's house in Hunter's Creek. It was white stucco and U-shaped. The wedding and reception took place on the tiled patio that was surrounded by banana trees. There was no pool, but a small fountain trickled in the background. Maureen's pregnancy did not show at her wedding. She wore an off-white, strapless gown with a tight bodice over a bouffant skirt. Allen wore a dark gray suit for his fourth wedding. There were fifty or sixty guests, many of them employees at various hospitals in the San Antonio area.

Like his three former wives, Maureen neither knew the depths of Allen's dark personality nor accepted what others told her. She seemed delighted to be marrying him and very much in love. But she soon saw aspects of Allen that she had not seen before. Their honeymoon wasn't at all what she had expected. They went to Las Vegas and spent the whole first evening at the gaming tables. At 2:00 A.M. Maureen excused herself and said she was going to bed. Allen stayed up all night gambling. At eleven the next morning, Maureen went looking for him and found him still gambling. He never slept, and she spent the nights alone in their luxury suite.

Maureen gave birth to their son, Brandon Lee, four months later, in September 1994. He was a beautiful baby and, like all of Allen's offspring, very bright. He was either Allen's third, fourth, or fifth child, depending upon which rumor about him was true. He was, certainly, the first son Allen was prepared to raise. Maureen was an extremely attentive mother and rarely left her baby.

A subtle shift in the balance of power took place in the first year of their marriage, and no one could know if it was orchestrated by Allen or by Maureen. Maureen had rules about marriage, and Allen happily acquiesced, although he said it took him a year to obey absolutely. Given his sexual predilection for being dominated, he had perhaps always searched for a woman who would call the shots. Maureen insisted that Allen be home for dinner on time, and whenever he was even a few minutes late, she simply threw his supper out on the lawn.

Maureen also expected to be feted on birthdays and anniversaries. She was apparently the first wife Allen had who demanded a great deal of *him.* Ellen and Mary and Sheila had all tried their best to please him, and the more they gave, the less respect he had for them. That was all changed now.

"After I learned the rules," Allen said, "I finally learned what love is."

He was not so happy in his new marriage, however, that he ceased his harassment of Sheila. The custody and divorce squabbles continued with growing ferocity.

_____Chapter Seventeen_____

JAMIE AND SHEILA were extremely happy in their marriage. Stevie and Daryl liked having a father figure living in the house, and they even argued sometimes about which of them would get to sit next to Jamie. Sheila began to put on a little weight, and her face filled out so that she looked like the healthy Sheila she'd been before her first marriage. They lived in Jamie's house in Alamo Heights, an older, well-established neighborhood near the central part of San Antonio. It wasn't far from Broadway, with its Central Market and Earl Abel's, and there was a great new mall nearby: Quarry Mall, where innovative builders had elected to save the old-time quarry and make it part of the shopping center, rather than destroy it. Stevie and Daryl liked Alamo Heights, and their friends were close by. It was the first time in years that Sheila and her girls hadn't lived in a state of anxiety and chaos.

Of course, there had been things to get used to. Jamie had never quite gotten over his time in the Marine Corps, and he tended to treat his stepdaughters like recruits. He woke them every morning by shouting "Reveille! Reveille! All hands on deck!" The novelty of that wore off quickly. He expected immediate obedience from them, and that was something they were not at all used to. Allen had always encouraged them not to obey their mother.

Although Jamie was gone a lot calling on doctors' offices for Pfizer, Sheila understood that travel was an essential part of his job. Physicians have discretion over which prescriptions they write, and it's important that they know and like their detail men. Jamie knew his stuff, and he explained new products, left samples, and was a familiar and welcome face in the clinics and offices in his territory.

Jamie and Sheila hoped to build or buy their own home one day, but for the moment they were quite content where they were.

IT was ironic—but pure chance—that Sheila had married *two* men who were closely connected to the medical field. She might have met a teacher or an engineer or anyone else on that day she waited for her plane to take off from Phoenix, but it was Jamie who walked down the aisle. Even Maureen's jobs had been at least peripherally connected to medicine. Since San Antonio was a mecca for health care in America, it wasn't that unusual that they would all be connected in some way with the field. All but Sheila; her world was the law.

While Sheila was alone when Jamie was on business trips, Maureen was on her own too. During the first six months of his marriage to Maureen, Allen was away most of the time, calling on RS Medical accounts and branch managers. His charismatic personality was a major factor in the success of setting the company up and establishing a network around the country. Even his own father, who had long since been squeezed out of the electromuscular stimulator business, admitted that he had never seen a better salesman or more brilliant entrepreneur than Allen.

But Maureen was lonesome and wanted Allen home more. He was usually gone all week, and she needed his help with Brandon. Beyond that, she was initially worried about how she would deal with visits from Stevie and Daryl.

"She asked me once," Pam Harrell said, "what she should do with them? I told her that all she needed to do was be their friend. She usually took them shopping and bought them things. Like Allen, she thought she could buy their affection. Sometimes I took my son, and Maureen and I would take them bowling, but they seemed standoffish.

"Allen's Hunter's Creek house had an open stairway that led up to a little nook near the roof. Whenever we brought Stevie and Daryl home, they would both run up there and hide. It almost seemed as if they were trying to get as far away from Allen as they could, as if they wanted to hide from him up there."

By 1995 Allen was phasing out his career as a working man; he had more than enough money to live on for the rest of his life. He wasn't quite forty, but he saw no reason to continue to work and spend so much time on planes every week. He agreed with Maureen that it was time for him to relax and enjoy some of the luxuries he could afford now. His active participation in RS Medical, at least as far as working a five-day week, was coming to an end. Even if he didn't work, he would be paid $28,000 a month, along with other perks, and he still owned a large share of RS Medical. His gravy train had no end in sight.

Allen had always been a gambler, and he traveled to Las Vegas often. Maureen went with him at first, but she soon gave up, realizing that he spent all his time at the gambling tables. She might as well stay home. "I thought I had my gambling under control," he remarked once, "but Maureen didn't think so. She thought I was addicted to gambling." It was one of the few things they argued seriously about.

Maureen always had a strong work ethic and a need to have her own money. She ran her own business out of their home, using her longtime connection with Hewlett-Packard. The company offered physicians the opportunity to try out some very expensive machines—imaging machines for echocardiography and sonography. If they decided to buy them at $85,000 apiece and up, that was fine. But for various reasons a number of the machines were returned to the company; they were virtually brand-new, but technically they were used, so they went into the pool to be resold. Various dealers were allowed to buy the machines on consignment *if* they had excellent credit. They had thirty to forty-five days to resell them at a profit before they had to pay Hewlett-Packard.

Always a careful money manager, Maureen did have enviable credit, and she became a dealer of refurbished medical imaging machines. She could buy a machine from Hewlett-Packard for something like $35,000 and sell it for as much as $65,000, with a full Hewlett-Packard warranty. Ironically, it was unlikely that the department she dealt with to obtain the imaging machines even connected her to a former employee who had sued the company.

It hadn't been that long since, at Allen's instigation, Maureen had filed a sexual harassment suit against Hewlett-Packard. For Allen there was *never* enough money; he was a multimillionaire, he never again had to work a day of his life, but he smelled money at Hewlett-Packard, and he carefully hatched a scheme where he could use Maureen. He was certain that she would be awarded substantial money for inappropriate behavior on the part of several managers she had worked for. Allen speculated that Hewlett-Packard would prefer to pay her off, rather than risk negative publicity.

But he guessed wrong, and Maureen's suit backfired. The huge company was not about to accept her allegations. Instead, they hired private investigators to check into her background and her reputation with the opposite sex. Had they found a timid virgin who was seriously damaged by the sometimes ribald office humor and sexual innuendo that is common in many companies, the end result might have been different, but the private investigators asked hundreds of questions of people who had known Maureen before she met Allen Blackthorne, and they heard her described as "very sophisticated," a confirmed flirt, and the kind of woman who would rather sit with the Gunslingers football team than with her fellow workers.

"Maureen told me later that Allen had put her up to filing the harassment suit," a former friend said. "She never understood that a woman has to be careful about her reputation in this town, and she lost the suit. We suspected that she had been taping all of our phone conversations with her, and that she had figured out how to break into our voice mail. So she didn't collect anything, and she also lost a lot of friends."

But apparently Hewlett-Packard didn't hold a grudge, if, indeed, one division knew what another was doing. Now most of Maureen's customers were from the valley region of Texas, which was once her territory. Her new profession allowed her to stay home with Brandon and, increasingly, with Allen.

In the mid-'90s, Allen and Maureen applied for membership in the Oak Hills Country Club and were accepted. Oak Hills was a luxurious and upscale club, and the initiation fee was $20,000 with monthly dues of $350. The Oak Hills golf course was one of the best in San Antonio. Even so, the Blackthornes were looked at a little askance by the old guard there.

Essentially retired, Allen could golf all day, every day, if he wanted. The game had always fascinated him, and he plunged into it with the same abandon he demonstrated in other activities. Soon he was totally obsessed with golf.

But Allen was also obsessed, *still,* with wreaking punishment on Sheila, partly because she would not give in to his having more access to their daughters, but mostly because she had bested him so many times in court.

NINETEEN ninety-five was to be a watershed year in so many lives. Verma Gene Smith thought she was going to lose Don when he had a heart attack while drilling a hole on the roof of their house in Salem to install a satellite dish. An aid car rushed him to the ER, where he underwent quadruple-bypass surgery. It was November, her worst month. Kerry, pregnant with her fourth child, Patrick, was devastated by Don's illness. Don was her "Dad"; she had already lost her biological father, and her stepfather was one of the rocks in her life. But Don came through surgery well, and they were all grateful.

Although Sheila and Jamie's marriage was proving to be a success, as the honeymoon bloom wore off a little, it was not without problems. Allen's insistence on visitations with the girls at his house was a constant reminder that he was still determined to be part of Sheila's life. Stevie had begun to pull away from her father, but Daryl was thrilled when he started treating *her* like the favored child.

Jamie was working hard and had also gone back to college to earn his master's degree in business administration. But the marine still lived and breathed in him, and he was a strict disciplinarian with the girls. He believed in spanking, and he often said that "one hand is for love and the other is for punishment." The laissez-faire treatment Stevie and Daryl were accustomed to with their father was diametrically opposed to the Marine Corps philosophy that Jamie lived by. Sometimes he made the girls stand in the corner, and occasionally he reached out with a huge hand and slapped them. Sheila tried to defer to him, but she was pulled in two directions. She didn't like the way Jamie meted out punishment, but most often, she allowed him to discipline the girls.

"We needed it, I guess," Stevie said some years later. "We were pretty out of control."

They were two exceptionally pretty, highly intelligent little girls about to become teenagers. Like their mother, they had lived for at least a decade with the erratic specter of Allen Blackthorne—sometimes overindulged, sometimes punished, and sometimes shoved aside when adult emotions demanded attention. Although counseling helped, their family life would never be anything remotely resembling *Leave It to Beaver*.

Soon there would be another phenomenon that made Stevie's and Daryl's lives far from average and force them ever so slightly out of the center of their mother's world. In early 1995 Sheila and Jamie had begun to wonder if there was any way they could have a child of their own. Sheila regretted that she had had her tubes tied back in the days she had stopped believing in love. Now, with modern fertility techniques, she hoped to give Jamie his own child. She was only thirty-two and healthy again.

They explored in vitro fertilization. First, Sheila would be given shots to encourage ovulation of a number of eggs each month, to increase the odds that one would be successfully fertilized. Then the eggs (or ova) taken from her ovaries would be mixed with Jamie's sperm. If conception occurred, the fertilized eggs could then be transferred to Sheila's uterus. There was, however, a greater than average chance that a multiple birth could occur, because more than one egg might be fertilized. Most of the quintuplets, sextuplets, and septuplets born in America *were* the result of in vitro fertilization.

It all seemed impossible, but physicians warned Jamie and Sheila that sometimes it took many tries before conception occurred. And sometimes, of course, it never occurred at all. It was a very expensive procedure; each attempt would cost around $10,000.

Jamie's parents in New Jersey agreed to help with the cost. In the late spring of 1995 Sheila and Jamie underwent their first in vitro process, held their breaths, and were surprised and elated when it worked on the very first try. Sheila was *pregnant*, and they were both ecstatic. After so much unhappiness, Sheila's joy was contagious. She didn't mind the morning sickness or the fatigue, but she was puzzled at how rapidly her abdomen was expanding. She was so small that she had shown quite soon with both Stevie and Daryl, but nothing like this. There was a good reason. An ultrasound showed not one, but *four,* babies.

She was carrying quadruplets.

Sheila and Jamie were excited, but cautious. Multiple pregnancies were prone to miscarriage. Obstetricians often advised selective abortion of some of the fetuses in a multiple pregnancy so that those remaining would have a better chance of survival, but that was something that Sheila wouldn't even consider. She was determined to carry all four babies and she knew they would live.

When her friends asked her what she intended to do with so many babies, Sheila grinned and said, "I'm just going to love them and take care of them and cuddle them." Sometimes, though, she was afraid that she was too happy and that something would come along to destroy the pure joy she felt. To Kerry she revealed a dark dread, a fear that had haunted her for a decade but had become very real when Nicole Simpson was slaughtered in June 1994. The reality of domestic violence and reprisal struck chilling chords in frightened women all over America, Sheila Bellush among them.

As the two sisters looked into a mirror, their faces side by side, Sheila said, "If O.J. gets away with killing Nicole, I know that Allen will think he can get away with it too. I'm afraid I won't be here to raise my babies. I'm afraid Allen will find a way to kill me."

Before Kerry could protest, Sheila shook her head and smiled. "No, it will be okay. God *wanted* me to have these babies, and He's going to take care of all of us."

From that point on in her pregnancy, Sheila was serene. She and Jamie were hoping to find a house big enough to hold all of them, someplace that was farther out of the center of San Antonio than Alamo Heights. They looked at places in Boerne, northwest of the city. The area was more country than simply suburban, ideal for raising children.

Sometimes now, Sheila felt that things could not be more perfect. Aside from the diminishing negative impact Allen had on their lives and the discomforts of her pregnancy, the only smudge on her world was that Stevie and Daryl were beginning to show signs of the rebelliousness of adolescence. But then she remembered how she and Cathy and Kerry had been; it was normal behavior. They had probably driven Verma Gene nuts too, and now it was just her turn.

Sheila was such a small woman that the task of carrying four babies at once was daunting. She would put on eighty pounds as her babies grew, nearly doubling her normal weight. The months passed, and she became, literally, almost as wide as she was tall, but she was still smiling.

In October 1995 her doctor ordered her into the Women's and Children's Hospital for bed rest. The weight of the babies against her cervix was tremendous and could send her into premature labor contractions if she didn't get off her feet. She still had four months to go before her due date, and her obstetrical team hoped to get the babies to seven months gestation. At that point they would be small, but they might have a fighting chance of survival. A mother carrying quadruplets had four times the chance of having high blood pressure, eclampsia (convulsions), or any of the other negative possibilities of pregnancy, but Sheila was steadfast in her determination to carry all four babies to delivery. With hope and prayer she willed them to be healthy.

When she had checkups, nurses in the ante-partum unit had to stand on either side of the doctors' examining table to support Sheila's belly, because the table couldn't hold all of her midsection. She didn't care. She was prepared to do whatever she needed to do to keep the babies safe and inside her womb as long as she could. The doctors kept reminding her that it was unlikely she would go to term, but every week counted. They knew she was doing everything she could to stay calm and quiet.

The Bellushes were soon well known to the nursing staff, who sometimes found Jamie a little overbearing, as he insisted that Sheila have the best of everything. He loved her, and his way of showing it could be a little demanding of the staff that cared for her. He didn't want anything to go wrong with "his" babies.

Kerry was pregnant too, and their delivery dates were both around February 1996. Despite her own pregnancy, Kerry was far more concerned about Sheila. One baby seemed like a breeze when Sheila was carrying four. When she called to say that she was going to have a cesarean section on December 5, 1995, and said Jamie had bought her a ticket, Kerry made plane reservations. "I knew that I couldn't be with Sheila in the delivery room," Kerry remembered, "so I arranged to be there as soon as the babies were born. It was a terrible flight—but I got there!"

Sheila posed for Jamie's video camera just before she was moved to the operating room. Her abdomen was so large that it no longer seemed a part of her. "We're very excited," she said with a wide smile. "Hi, babies! Hi, kids!"

Touching her taut belly, Sheila patted the quadruplets, who still shared her circulatory system, tapping four different spots: "Joey, Timmy, Frankie, Courtney—if I'm right."

As surgery began, the delivery room was packed with a few dozen vital participants: obstetricians, anesthesiologists, neonatology pediatricians, and nurses, who still had to support Sheila's massive belly. Jamie was there too, cheering her on.

Sheila was delivered of four tiny, but healthy, babies. They were not identical; they were brothers and a sister who happened to come into the world at the same time. There were three boys—Frankie (named for Sheila's father), Joey (named for Jamie's father), Timmy (for Saint Timothy), and one tiny little girl, Courtney. Timmy was the heaviest, at four pounds fifteen ounces; Frankie and Joey weighed four pounds ten and four pounds eleven ounces; and Courtney weighed three pounds even. These were very respectable weights for quadruplets who were two months premature.

When the tiny foursome were all delivered, only a minute apart, Sheila looked once more at Jamie's camera. "I'm very happy," she said. "Everyone's doing good, and your dad's really happy, which makes *me* happy."

"The birth of the quads was a controlled circus," one nurse remembered.

Knowing that their newborns would be big news, Jamie had choreographed the publicity ahead of time. His philosophy appeared to be "get it over with," and let all of the media have access to the story, so he had lined up a number of interviews and photography sessions. He was a good interview subject and seemed to enjoy the celebrity that came with being on television.

Nearly seven months pregnant herself, Kerry arrived at the hospital just as Sheila was in the recovery room. "I was with Sheila that night," she said, "when she went down the hall to the nursery for her first view of her babies. It took her a long time, and she pushed a wheelchair ahead of her for support, but they wanted her to walk. Her muscles had atrophied from being in bed for two months."

Although the Bellush babies weighed more than most quadruplets, they were still tiny and had been rushed to the neonatal intensive care unit (NICU). There they looked quite large compared to some of the one- and two-pound babies struggling to survive. The boys were 3 pounds 15 ounces, 3 pounds 10 ounces, 3 pounds 7 ounces, and the girl just 3 pounds. But premature babies are always at risk for breathing problems, undeveloped lungs, and myriad other threats to their survival. Courtney was the smallest, and she was put into a respirator while Sheila expressed breast milk to feed her.

"Sheila did most of the care of the quads," one nurse remembered. "But Jamie kind of melted every time he held one of them. It made you smile to watch him. Our only problem was that their girls were allowed to run all over the place, and they drove the staff on ante-partum and NICU *crazy.*"

It was predictable that Stevie and Daryl would act out; they had been the center of their mother's world since they were born, and now they realized they weren't nearly as interesting as their four new half siblings. The television cameras weren't focused on them.

Sheila had to go home without any of the babies. That was difficult for her, but they all needed extra time in the NICU until they weighed five pounds apiece and were more ready to meet the outside world. Within a few weeks they were all home, and the Bellush house was turned upside down. Courtney was the last to leave the hospital, and Sheila would keep her baby girl with her constantly for the first months of her life.

Suddenly the Bellushes were major celebrities in San Antonio. Sheila was known as the Quad Mom, and the Bellush family appeared on television with every milestone. They were naturals for human-interest stories. The babies were adorable, Sheila was beautiful, and Jamie's gruff sentimentality was endearing. Sheila even appeared on the Maury Povich show with her four babies, although the producers had made a mistake and touted her for having "natural quads," when they had really been conceived through the in vitro process.

One can only wonder what Allen thought of the wife who got away. Now Sheila had a loving husband who stood up for her, made a good living, and bought her a fine house where she could live with four new babies—*and his daughters.* It seemed as though every time Allen turned on the television, there they all were smiling into the cameras.

When she was finally able to bring the babies home, Sheila had lots of help. Effie Wood, her good friend from their apartment days in Brandon Oaks, volunteered on a regular basis and spent many days with Sheila and the quads. People from the church helped, and Sheila's legion of friends were happy to pitch in. Stevie and Daryl helped too, becoming almost second mothers to their half siblings, whom they came to love without reservation. They grinned happily as they lugged the babies around like four sacks of sugar at the huge shower Sheila's friends threw for her once they knew the quadruplets would survive.

The jam-packed days of child care were never onerous for Sheila; she genuinely enjoyed being with the babies. Each of them had an individual personality, and she loved seeing their differences blossom. Timmy was the largest at birth, and he did everything first. When Frankie started walking, he walked on tiptoe and had to have casts on his legs for a while. Joey was very quiet and thoughtful, and Courtney, so delicate and feminine, was the most reserved. Watching them, Sheila was totally at peace with her world.

Jamie and Sheila had found the perfect house. It was in Country Bend, a development in Boerne, a rural area northwest of San Antonio—a big house with plenty of room for a family with six children. The lots in Country Bend ran from one to three acres, and the house they chose in the 2700 block of Boerne Glen had a huge lot and a swimming pool. Sheila sold her house, Jamie sold his, and they put the money from their equities down on the Boerne Glen house. They moved in June 1996.

Rick and Kerry came down from Oregon with their new baby, Patrick, when he was four months old, and with their older children, Kelly, Ryan, and Christopher. Rick took videos of the baby cousins wriggling around on the floor, too young to play yet, but all of them calm and contented.

Allen's annoyance because Sheila was so happy in spite of his efforts to upset her may have corroded his enjoyment of his life with Maureen. Kerry met Maureen in a Target store by accident during the Bladorns' visit in June. Maureen was there with Daryl, who was still visiting her father on weekends. Kerry found her pleasant, and her toddler, Brandon, was a very handsome little boy who seemed intelligent far beyond his age. Allen had it all now, and Kerry hoped that his money and leisure and another marriage and family were enough to make him leave Sheila alone.

_____*Chapter Eighteen*_____

SHEILA WANTED TO REGISTER Stevie and Daryl at school in Boerne using the last name they'd always used: Blackthorne. That was their legal name, but she discovered that she needed to do it formally and enter it on their birth certificates. For many reasons, some oblique, Allen wanted the girls to use "Van Houte." Perhaps he still needed that name on their Social Security cards if he ever chose to use them.

If Sheila had a choice, she would have given Stevie and Daryl "Bellush" for a last name, but she doubted very much that Allen would ever relinquish the girls to Jamie. She just didn't want them to have to change Blackthorne when they'd had so many changes.

Allen was incensed when he learned what she was trying to do. He wrote letters to the school in Boerne, insisting that Stevie and Daryl be addressed as Van Houte. It would take money to change their names on their birth certificates, and Allen refused to pay half the cost. It was one more skirmish in a continuing battle.

Allen went a step further to punish Sheila. In August 1996 he called RS Medical and told Mike McGraw to stop withholding money from his salary for Daryl or Stevie. Frustrated and enraged, he referred to Sheila in terrible gutter terms that shocked McGraw. Allen didn't want Sheila to have *anything* from him any longer. When McGraw told him that the company couldn't just stop sending child-support checks that were specified in a court order, Allen demanded that "something be accomplished."

McGraw went to the company president, Rick Terrell, who ultimately decided that Allen would have to bear the brunt of defying the court. If he agreed to send them a note releasing the company from harm for disobeying the court order, they would stop payments to Sheila. Allen faxed the release at once.

RS Medical did stop payment on Sheila's check, but officials from Bexar County called, and McGraw wrote a replacement check.

It was such a picayune thing; Allen had more money than even he could ever spend, and his daughters deserved the small fraction of his monthly income that was theirs. But Allen was beginning to lose again. Every time he told Mike McGraw to stop sending child-support checks to Sheila, the Bexar County Child Support Registry ordered them sent. And Bexar County had even more power than multimillionaire Allen Blackthorne.

In the spring of 1996 Gene and Don Smith were visiting Sheila and Jamie at the Boerne Glen house and Gene was talking with Sheila in her kitchen when the phone rang. "Someone on the other end was screaming so loud," Gene said, "that I could hear it across the kitchen. It was Maureen. Sheila spoke to her very calmly, and she said, 'I tried to warn you, Maureen, and now I have a life and a family, and I can't be involved in your problems with Allen.' And then Sheila just hung up very quietly."

WHEN Jamie and Sheila first moved into their new house in 1996, the neighbors, Pat and Wade Aday, were very friendly. Wade was a pilot for American Airlines, and they had two sons, nineteen and eleven, and a daughter, eight. Pat Aday home-schooled her children. Their daughter, Beth,* was a few years younger than Stevie and Daryl, but she and Daryl were friends. Beth was utterly fascinated with the Bellush's four babies, and she spent all day in Sheila's house. She was a sweet child, and Sheila let her stay, although she wasn't really old enough to handle tiny babies and sometimes she was a bit of a nuisance. Beth often stayed while Sheila served meals, but that was fine; Stevie and Daryl were often at the Adays' too.

The next-door neighbors had a friendly relationship throughout 1996 and for the first three months of 1997. Pat Aday was a large, motherly woman whose activities revolved around her children. Although she and Sheila had little in common, and Sheila had her hands full with year-old quadruplets, the two women visited occasionally. Pat was proud that she had never left her children to have a career.

With Wade's good position and salary at American, Pat had never *had* to leave her home to work. She didn't understand mothers who left their little ones with sitters. And she was very strict about young teenagers dating. Had someone remarked that she was very judgmental, she would probably have been shocked, but, in truth, she was. Pat Aday apparently thought of herself as the moral compass of her neighborhood.

Sheila and Jamie were settling into their new home in Boerne. They enjoyed the pool and the hot tub, and Sheila's body was getting back to normal, although she had to have plastic surgery to remove the extra skin on her abdomen where it had stretched as she expanded, carrying four babies. She secretly planned to have her breasts enlarged and lifted too, although she wouldn't admit it, not even to Kerry. Sheila had always had a perfect, slender figure. But her mother, Gene, had gained a lot of weight over the years, and Sheila was afraid she might gain weight too, so she was careful with her diet.

She also watched Jamie's food intake, because he had a tendency to put on weight. She worried about his health, and she confided to Kerry that he was far less attractive to her when his belly hung over his belt. She couldn't control what he ate on the road, but she could serve healthy meals at home.

Although Sheila had more energy all the time, the first year of the quadruplets' life was still a period where everyone in the family concentrated on them. But the initial period of mutual admiration between Stevie and Daryl and Jamie was over, as it could be expected to be. Real life took over. Everyone was exhausted with caring for the quads, and tempers sometimes grew short.

One night Jamie poked his head into Stevie's room to say good night and found her asleep with a candle still burning dangerously close to her curtains. He had warned her before about leaving candles burning, and he felt sick at the thought of what might have happened. Later Stevie told the Adays' older son that Jamie had awakened her by hitting her in the temple with his fist, knocking her head against the drywall next to her bed hard enough to make a dent. She exaggerated her version of the incident because she was angry with Jamie. He probably did hit her—the degree of force was questionable. He lectured Stevie, telling her that the whole house could have gone up in flames and they all might have died. She *knew* that was true, and she was sorry, but she resented Jamie for punishing her so harshly.

Stevie was boy crazy early on, and she was beginning to sneak out to meet junior high school boys. Jamie was furious about that. Sheila's girls were only eleven and twelve, and they were much too young to be dating or sneaking around with boys. It was hard to discipline them anyway, because Allen had no rules for them at all. He allowed the girls to go to the movies with boys when they were at his house. He seemed to have two motives for everything he did with the girls; he didn't like them interfering in *his* plans when he wanted to golf or had business phone calls, but he also took great pleasure in countermanding Sheila and Jamie's position on what the girls could or could not do.

Not surprisingly, Daryl had begun to talk back to Sheila and then ran to the Adays next door to complain when Sheila punished her. Pat Aday was always there with a sympathetic ear. In fact, Pat had begun to be highly suspicious of what went on at the Bellushes' house. She believed everything the girls told her and thought Stevie and Daryl were punished too harshly.

Subtly but inexorably, a neighbor-to-neighbor feud had begun. Few parents are perfect, and few would question that Jamie's corporal punishment was too strong by most standards. Sheila's nerves were often frayed as she tried to juggle her marriage, the care of the quads, and two sassy and disobedient pubescent daughters. With Pat Aday commiserating with them every time they ran to her house after they were disciplined, Stevie and Daryl only became more incorrigible. It was bad enough that they had always done whatever they wanted at their father's house; now they had next-door neighbors to tattle to. Stevie wasn't going to Allen and Maureen's any longer, but Daryl was, and she let Sheila know that Maureen was *much* nicer to her than her own mother was.

Furtively Allen began to explore his options in gaining complete custody of Stevie and Daryl, or, perhaps, just Daryl. According to Maureen, Daryl had pleaded to come and live with them, and she and Allen had many discussions about how they should handle this. The dynamics of Allen's relationship with his daughters had changed drastically. Now that Stevie no longer visited him, he seemed, at least for the moment, relieved.

"She and Maureen locked horns," Allen explained. That was certainly true. Maureen told one of her maids that Stevie was "a bitch," but that Daryl was "all right."

Stevie was adamant that she would not go to Allen and Maureen's house. She was old enough now to recognize his sexual abuse for what it was. Allen dealt with that by declaring Daryl the "golden child." Daryl was not sophisticated enough to question why the father who had virtually ignored her for most of her life was suddenly showing an interest in her. She was simply happy that he did. Since Allen had lost all control over Stevie, he clearly had decided to move on to Daryl, grooming her for whatever role he decided he wanted her to play in his life.

Maureen followed Allen's lead and went out of her way to treat Daryl as a most welcome guest in their home. The two got along well, and Daryl adored her little half brother Brandon. Maureen was pregnant with her second child—a boy, according to her amniocentesis results. She recalled that she felt Daryl would fit smoothly into their family, while she had her doubts about bringing Stevie into the mixture, especially when she would soon have a new baby.

In truth, Maureen wanted what Allen wanted, and despite her denials, she really didn't like Sheila very much.

WHO can say when watershed moments in lives occur—those human decisions that trigger landslides of emotion? Once begun, there is no going back. March 2, 1997, may well have been the day that the earth beneath Sheila Bellush's life shifted. It was a Sunday, and she had a bad time with Daryl. When Daryl talked back, Sheila gave her the age-old warning, "You're going to get a beating when your stepfather gets home."

According to Pat Aday, Jamie had come home and reached out to take one of the babies from Sheila's arms so that she could spank Daryl. In truth, Sheila hadn't touched Daryl, but she had alarmed her because Daryl expected to be physically punished. And Daryl could be very dramatic.

"Daryl ran to our house," Pat would recall. "She was whimpering, upset, nervous, and she started having an asthma attack. 'How can we help you?' I asked."

Since Stevie had defected from her father, Allen was most solicitous of Daryl. Now she sobbed that she wanted to call her daddy. Pat said that of course she could. Daryl was hysterical, and Pat agreed that her father should be summoned at once to give her emotional support. Next she called the Bexar County sheriff and reported that a child had been abused.

Allen rushed over, and with his visit to Sheila and Jamie's next-door neighbors, he had accomplished his goal. He was back in Sheila's life, as close as next door where he could watch her. Pat Aday was impressed by what a sensitive and concerned father Allen Blackthorne seemed to be. He was nothing at all like Sheila, who had bolted through Pat's door demanding to know why she was interfering in *her* family and *her* business and then stomped home before Allen arrived.

Harry Chamorro, a deputy from the Bexar County Family Crisis Unit, responded to Pat Aday's call. He spoke with Jamie and Sheila and quickly determined that Daryl had not been beaten at all. Jamie agreed that he had spanked the girls in the past, using a belt, and Chamorro warned him that he could not use "objects" to discipline his stepchildren. But the situation had all the earmarks of a neighborhood beef, something cops saw often. Sheila, however, was still furious with Pat Aday for calling the police and for poking her nose into the Bellush family.

"Why don't you just declare my daughter a runaway?" she asked Chamorro. "Then we can say that my neighbors are harboring a runaway!"

The deputy pointed out that wasn't going to happen. Daryl went home with Jamie and Sheila, and Pat kept her thoughts to herself. However, she certainly admired Allen Blackthorne. The man was a millionaire, and yet he had dropped everything to come to his daughter's rescue. He seemed very sad to Pat, and she wondered if both girls wouldn't be better off with their kind and considerate father than with the angry people who lived next door to her.

Allen attempted to have the San Antonio *Express-News* publish information about Sheila's unsuitability as a parent. He gave a reporter copies of taped phone conversations he had with his daughters and with Child Protective Services to show that he was a concerned father. On one tape Allen's voice was heard talking to Stevie.

"You have a right to be safe at home, honey," he told her.

"Dad," Stevie said, "I *am* safe at home. I'm not scared of being at home. If I was scared, I wouldn't be living here. I could have moved out last year."

"Well, honey," Allen cajoled, "you don't have the right to be hit. And you know what, it needs to stop."

Allen told a Child Protective Services caseworker that he had hired a private detective, who was watching the Bellush home. At that point he hadn't hired anyone; he didn't need to. Pat Aday was watching all the time.

MAUREEN had coined a name for Sheila. She called her the Black Cow. The "cow" part stemmed from Sheila's ability to carry and nurse so many babies at once. Only Maureen knew why she deemed her "black," since Sheila was as blonde and rosy as ever. Maybe it was because Sheila cast a shadow over Maureen's life with Allen.

Allen had now gained a major foothold in Sheila's neighborhood. No one could be more charming or more convincing than he was when he wanted to be, and he knew he had Pat Aday on his side. He thanked her profusely for being such a caring person that she would stick her neck out to protect his precious daughter. Very soon Pat considered herself a friend of the Blackthornes' and not just an informant about what went on in Sheila's house.

Predictably, the formerly amicable relationship between the Bellushes and the Adays was over. Now minor skirmishes began.

Sheila and Jamie built a dog run along the property line between their house and the Adays' yard. They had two pets: Chesty was a yellow Lab, and Jamie had brought home a stray Weimaraner they named Rudy after the restaurant where he found it. They were both good-sized dogs, and Sheila couldn't have them running through the house with the babies. They needed a safe spot outside for them.

The Adays measured their property line carefully and were convinced that one side of the dog run had slipped over onto their yard. Chesty and Rudy barked a lot, and the Adays complained. Then in May 1997 Pat discovered that someone had tampered with their pool equipment; she wasn't sure if it was deliberate vandalism or if perhaps some of the teenagers who hung around Stevie had simply been fooling with the valves and timers.

She installed four bright floodlights in the pool area so that she could keep an eye on her property. "It wasn't long before *three* of the lights were knocked out," she said. "I replaced them, of course."

Unfortunately, one of the high-beamed lights shone directly into Sheila and Jamie's bedroom window, and they complained. When the lights remained bright and focused on their window, Jamie called the police. It was a shame, really. The neighborhood in Boerne was to have been a haven for Sheila and Jamie, and the Adays had always enjoyed it there too. Now the brewing conflict was marked by frequent clashes.

At length, Sheila decided that it was ridiculous for them to be feuding. It blunted her joy in her wonderful home, and she suspected that it must be the same way for the Adays. She was determined to make peace. Yes, she had been upset when Pat Aday called not only the police but Allen too. But that had happened months ago, and Sheila felt that if she and Jamie and Pat and Wade just got together, they could talk it out. She swallowed her pride and called Pat. Sheila said she was sure they could be friends again if they worked out the misunderstandings they had.

She was met with a stone wall. The Adays refused to discuss it; they weren't interested in being friendly. Pat had heard from Allen what a monstrous mother Sheila was. And the Bellush dogs were still barking at night, making sleep impossible. Wade went out to see what was going on one night when the barking grew frantic and he flushed three boys from behind the Bellush house. When he asked them what they were doing there, they said they had come to see a friend. Before he could question them further, they took off running.

Once more the Adays called the Bellushes to complain. Did they know that their girls had boys sneaking around at night? Who knew what damage they might cause in the neighborhood as they laughed and horsed around under Stevie's window? As it was, Wade added, someone was smashing their floodlights and fooling with their pool, breaking the equipment.

Sheila and Jamie were not responsive to this latest complaint. What was the use? Sheila had tried to mend their differences and got nowhere. She had no idea at that point, however, how close the Adays were growing to Allen. Had she realized that, she would have been very upset.

"We weren't friends at first," Pat said of Allen and Maureen, "but we grew closer."

In truth, the Blackthornes had become Pat's instant best friends. Allen didn't seem at all like a multimillionaire. He was just an anxious father. He assured Pat that he was deeply concerned about his daughters, and he was terribly grateful that Pat was keeping an eye on Sheila and Jamie's house "for the girls' sake." It was hell for him, he sighed, to worry all the time if his children were all right.

Pat began to keep a journal about what went on at the Bellush house. "I kept notes after that first incident," she said. "I didn't figure it was going to get any better over there."

PAT Aday was *exactly* the kind of friend Allen had hoped for. She was in a position to watch everything that went on next door at Sheila's house, she was distressed about Stevie and Daryl, and she disapproved of Sheila. On the other hand, she liked both Allen and Maureen. Pat's journal grew to forty-three pages of notes. She typed some of them and tucked them neatly into the report she might have to refer to one day if Allen asked for solid information that would save his daughters.

Whenever anything went wrong between Stevie and Daryl and Jamie or Sheila, the girls complained to Pat. Sheila's efforts to deal with her own daughters were constantly undermined. Allen was delighted to hear all of the details. His divisive tactics were succeeding beyond even his expectations.

"I asked Allen if he would like me to take pictures of any injuries I might see on the girls," Pat said, "and he said no. I told him that if he changed his mind, to let me know. I did take a picture of Stevie's leg—there were two strap marks on the back of her right thigh, and they looked red and bruised."

Pat took a photograph of Daryl too, documenting red marks on her face and leg. Daryl had a naturally ruddy complexion, and the slightest slap to her skin tended to look like a welt.

Although he had at first demurred, Allen saved all the photographs. *Perfect.*

He was beginning to form new plans to best Sheila, even though it *was* satisfying for him just to know that she and Jamie had no privacy with the Adays watching them. That still wasn't enough. He wanted to wreak revenge in the most powerful way he could.

Odd, really, because Allen and Sheila had been divorced for nine years. Time seemed not to diminish his hatred of her but to exacerbate it.

Chapter Nineteen

MAUREEN AND ALLEN had moved into *their* new home in late March 1997, and it was a mansion that would have impressed almost anyone but royalty who lived in actual palaces. Their house on Box

Oak in the Shavano Creek complex had 9000 square feet of living space. It was built of pinkish sand stucco, a Moorish-style edifice with arched Palladian windows, a tower, balconies outside most rooms, and four columns at the three-story entry. There were six bedrooms and even more bathrooms, and the landscaping was professionally done. In San Antonio it was worth over $800,000; in Beverly Hills it would have sold for $3 million.

Although he could have hired gardeners to do it, Allen himself kept the grass like green velvet. He seeded and reseeded, and mowed it every few days with a commercial riding mower. He was obsessed with his lawn, just as he never approached anything he really wanted to do in a halfhearted way.

The Blackthorne home was a showplace in a neighborhood where *every* house was splendid. If it was a bit nouveau riche, anyone who knew about Allen's hardscrabble past in junked trailers and cramped, smoky apartments over taverns would have nodded understandingly. Little Billy/Allen Van Houte was on top of the world financially as Allen Blackthorne, and he needed this gargantuan house to show the world.

Although Maureen was pregnant again that spring of 1997, it seemed almost anticlimactic. She carried a single fetus; Sheila had produced four babies in one sweep. Maureen was excited about her pregnancy and insisted that Allen was too, but later Allen couldn't remember just when their second son, Jake, was born. He and Maureen were both chain-smokers, and even pregnancy didn't make Maureen quit.

Jim Bingham, Allen's one-time employee, ran into him that spring, and Allen invited him to his house, seeming to have completely forgotten the enmity between them when he fired Bingham with a kiss on the mouth. But Allen had walked away from many former business associates, and each phase of his life was a kind of rebirth for him. He may not even have remembered that much about Jim.

Bingham was suitably impressed by the Blackthornes' estate on Box Oak, but a bit bemused to see that, despite their immense living space, Allen and Maureen would not allow anyone to smoke in their mansion. Instead, they had moved recliner chairs down to their double garage along with a television set. There they permitted smoking.

"Maureen was pregnant," Bingham recalled, "but she was still smoking heavily. Both she and Allen chain-smoked. I remember how they tossed lighted cigarettes back and forth to each other."

Despite their wealth and the fact that they had the largest and most lavish home in Shavano Creek, Allen and Maureen did not fit in. They had a certain gaucheness about them that their neighbors found offputting. They were so anxious to make immediate close friends that many of those who lived along the wide street drew back, suspicious.

Maybe they detected a hidden agenda. Neither Allen nor Maureen made friends simply for friendship's sake. Allen had always had a reason to befriend the male buddies in his life, and he used them and discarded them when he no longer needed them. The closest male bonding he probably ever experienced was with his uncle, Tom Oliver, but Allen picked Tom up and let him down periodically, usually when he wanted Tom to help him with something. He seemed oblivious to the fact that Tom and Debbie were probably the only people in the world who had loved him unconditionally since he was a small boy. He had long ago lost touch with his half brothers and even denied that he was in any way related to most of them.

Maureen was almost pathetically eager to make friends. When she found that one neighbor shared her birthday, she insisted that meant they were going to be best friends. She also needed an audience. She was decorating her huge home and continually asked her neighbors to come over and show their approval of her choices. The house was sparsely furnished, but its expansiveness didn't necessarily mean it had the finishing touches that marked it as classic.

"There was no crown molding in any of the rooms," one neighbor commented, and that was de rigueur in the houses along Box Oak. Maureen had every room painted a different color, and she hung "hideous art," according to a woman who was summoned to compliment it.

Next Maureen ordered the painters to paint clouds on the domed ceiling, and in the family room there were rocks painted on the walls to make it look like a cave. Brandon's room was charming, though. "His room was decorated with a jungle theme that was perfect for a little boy, and the new baby's nursery had fish murals," the neighbor said. As each room was finished, Maureen begged the other wives in the neighborhood to come over and see it.

"It would have been attractive," one woman said, "if she had done the mural thing in only one or two rooms. But it got to be excessive. Every room had a theme, from the nursery to the master bedroom to the living room. It wasn't homey at all. It was a little bizarre."

The Blackthornes' pool was huge and square, and their breakfast room was larger than most dining rooms. But as much as Maureen tried to make their pink mansion perfect, she and Allen rarely *lived* in it, tending still to drift toward the garage and their office, which was next to it.

Allen had his flawless lawn, mowed, fertilized, and continually reseeded, and Maureen had her murals. "The joke along Box Oak was that Allen acted as though he'd get arrested if he didn't plant his winter rye grass," a husband less enthusiastic about lawns said.

Allen also had golf to fill his days, but Maureen was fairly housebound. She *wanted* to be with her boys and was nervous away from Brandon and, later, Jake. Even her business was conducted from her home office. Lonely, she made friends of her household staff, although she could be cruel to them too, her temper flaring unexpectedly. Basically, Allen and her children were Maureen's whole world, her link to what went on outside the confines of her home.

Allen was generous at loaning or giving things away, and Maureen always tended to give people things rather than to show them real affection or trust. And many of her former friends didn't trust her, especially around their men. Probably the longest friendship Maureen ever maintained was with Pam Harrell, the young woman she worked with for six years at Hewlett-Packard.

Pam and Maureen both wore a size two or four, and sometimes shared clothes. Maureen had often confided intimate details of her life to Pam throughout her various affairs. Pam was as close a friend as she ever had, but they grew apart after Maureen's lawsuit against Hewlett-Packard. During her single days Maureen had often flirted with her women friends' lovers or fiancés. Some women avoided introducing their boyfriends to Maureen because of her reputation for doing that.

In a sense Maureen and Allen were perfect for each other, but they didn't quite fit into Shavano Creek. And it wasn't snobbishness on the neighbors' part, because few residents there came from old money, and both Maureen and Allen were well dressed, presentable, and intelligent; it was more that they just didn't get it. They dropped in on people at remarkably inappropriate times and didn't understand why it *was* inappropriate—they might have been happier living in a trailer park or an apartment house where people visited back and forth all the time. Alone together, they were somehow unfinished. They seemed to need other people in which to see their own reflections and assure themselves they were real.

But they were living in one of the richest suburbs of San Antonio, where residents had chosen huge lots for privacy's sake, and where everyone else lived in their whole house and not just in their office, garage, and driveway.

Allen seemed never to sleep. If the weather was balmy, he moved his recliner out onto the driveway so he could see the street and the neighbors' comings and goings. Even in the wee hours of the morning, he sat there, his eyes fixed on the street. Susan Glenny, who lived directly across the street with her lawyer-husband, Clint, recalled the night she took some medication and had an allergic reaction that made her hands swell.

"I had to get my rings off because my fingers were turning black," she said. "It was really late, so I told my husband to just stay with the kids and I'd go down to the fire station to get my rings cut off. It was three a.m., but Allen was still sitting out there, watching. He raised his hand and waved.

"It got kind of creepy after a while. Whenever we came home after being gone for a few hours, Allen would call out to us and tell us everyone who might have come by our house."

A woman who lived alone next door to the Blackthorne mansion was horrified when she realized that Allen was not only watching her, he was filming her with a video camera. She had a high wall built to close off his view of her home, and Allen went to the homeowners' association and complained that the wall didn't fit the code. Truly spooked, the woman sold her house and moved away.

And yet Allen and Maureen were both generous with their neighbors. In some ways Allen was as dependable as Good Neighbor Sam. "If I knocked on his door at two a.m. or, more likely, found him in his driveway," one former neighbor recalled, "and said, 'Allen, I need a hundred thousand dollars,' he would have given it to me. It may have been a power thing. He seemed to want you to borrow things from him. His lawnmower cost over five thousand dollars, but he would have loaned it to you in a minute. When you were over there, they were so nice as long as you talked about *them*. They would never say, 'Oh, how are your girls doing?' because they didn't care about your life at all."

And there never seemed to be any secrets in the Blackthornes' lives. Much of their interaction took place in their front yard or in the sweeping circular driveway that swept between sections of Allen's lovingly tended lawn. Their marital disagreements and child rearing were on a stage for all to see and hear.

Maureen and Allen didn't seem to grasp that other people had worries and concerns too. They both saw themselves as the center of the world. Except for Pat Aday, they did not, however, seem to have any friends outside Shavano Creek. They found one reason after another to ask neighbors over to their home and then refused to let them leave, finding any excuse they could think of to extend short visits into hours. "They were always saying, 'Come over,'" one woman said. "And then when we were edging toward the door, Maureen would say, 'I've ordered pizza—you're *staying!*'"

Allen hadn't been to Las Vegas for a long time when he announced he was leaving for a three-day gambling trip. He was known at the Vegas hotels as a big enough spender that he got the red-carpet, door-to-door treatment. The casino sent a limo to pick him up at his mansion on Box Oak, flew him to Las Vegas, picked him up at the airport, and drove him to a huge luxury suite, as well as providing him with free tickets for any show in town.

"On this trip," one neighbor said, "the casino lost. Allen won fifty thousand dollars."

Allen played golf every weekday, all day long. Maureen set his golfing schedule. He was allowed to golf all day, but he had to be home for supper, and weekends were family time. The Blackthornes' neighbors learned that they had to be sure their children weren't riding bicycles along Box Oak at 6:24 in the evening because Maureen insisted that Allen *had* to be home by 6:25.

"He would come roaring around the corner with one minute to go," one nearby resident commented. "He actually seemed to be afraid of making Maureen mad. You could hear her yelling when he was late." And Maureen did have a temper; when her voice was raised in anger, it could be heard up and down the block. She still threw Allen's supper out on the lawn if he was even a minute late.

If he got home on time, Maureen would call out, "Was it a good day?" Some days Allen won more than $15,000, but more often he lost. It didn't matter. He could afford to lose. He had regular foursomes he played with, and his neighbors had no idea how much he bet on his golf game. He was still a gambler; he had only changed the game.

Allen's gambling seemed to be one of the few things about him that bothered Maureen, because he didn't always win. There was one time when he had to confess to her that he had lost $30,000 playing golf. This time, she didn't scream at him. She was silent, stunned that they had lost so much money in one day. Her silence was more threatening to him than any yelling or nagging could have been. He had grown up with a woman screaming at him; he had long since learned to shut that out.

Oddly, although Allen had to toe the line with Maureen and obey her rules—allowing her to be in charge of the money and forsaking credit cards in his name—Brandon, their toddler son, had no discipline at all. Maureen bragged that he slept in their bed until he was four. Her philosophy was that no one must ever say no to Brandon. He was a truly brilliant little boy, and he soon saw how the household was run. Brandon called Allen "Papa" and ordered him around, saying, "Papa . . . *Papa!* Do you hear me? I want . . ." And Brandon always got what he wanted.

Maureen hired Hispanics to care for the flowers, the house, and as nannies. They were told they must not discipline Brandon, no matter what. But once Brandon went too far. He spit on the maid, and the girl, outraged, walked right past Maureen and told Allen what had happened. Allen spanked Brandon, and Maureen "went nuts," according to the housewives who watched the aftermath.

Maureen adored her children, rarely left them, and cossetted them from a world that might demand *anything* from them. "In many ways," a nearby resident said, "she was a good mother. She really seemed to love her boys and want the best for them. She was always there for them."

Sometimes, however, Maureen seemed a little concerned about Allen's behavior. She confided to a neighbor that she had come home to see the electrician they'd hired coming out of one of their bathrooms. When she looked inside, Allen was there—stark naked. He told her he had been swimming in their pool and was just changing.

"Is that strange?" Maureen asked.

"Well," the woman mumbled, "it wouldn't happen in my house."

IN early 1997, in their old neighborhood, Hunter's Creek, Maureen and Allen had hired their neighbors, attorneys Lori Bendseil and her husband, Ray Perez, to represent them. Despite his millions, Allen was always looking for bargains when it came to legal representation. As he moved into upscale areas, many of his new neighbors were also lawyers, and he charmed them initially into representing him in his legal fights to gain more visitation. He felt that because the attorneys were his neighbors, they would charge him less than other lawyers would. He didn't even count the questions they answered in the casual setting of the neighborhood; he assumed that was free legal advice.

Allen's pet story was always that Stevie and Daryl were being abused and beaten and he was worried sick about them. The lawyers he hired naturally expected to be paid, and they were chagrined to find that Allen ignored their bills. In fact, he was so dilatory about paying his legal bills that he ran through any number of attorneys.

As for paying Sheila child support to help with the girls, Allen remained a frugal man. He did not like to pay for anything that did not give him pleasure. For instance, although he had lived in Texas for a decade and was worth millions, he still licensed his vehicles in Oregon, where the cost was much lower.

In Shavano Creek, Allen and Maureen cultivated their new neighbors, Clint and Susan Glenny, who lived directly across Box Oak from them. Glenny was a lawyer, and the minute he got home from work, Allen and Maureen hurried across the street ready to discuss the latest legal hurdle they faced. Allen's stance continued to be that when such conversations took place after business hours, they were not billable. Now, instead of spending time with his family, Glenny was captive in his own home, listening to endless reprises of Allen's travails with his ex-wife.

Glenny's firm agreed to represent Maureen for a short time in 1998. It was something he rapidly regretted. He and his wife, Susan, began to dread the sound of their doorbell; now that Allen was an official client, he and Maureen seemed to believe they were his most important clients and that he was on call twenty-four hours a day. Although Glenny's firm billed Allen, he never paid them.

On Susan's birthday the Glennys planned to have a quiet and romantic evening. "I even told the Blackthornes that Clint and I were looking forward to an evening alone," Susan said. "But, sure enough, Clint wasn't home ten minutes before the doorbell at our porte cochere rang. Maureen and Allen were standing there, grinning, with a birthday cake for me. They came in—and stayed and stayed while they proceeded to discuss their case against Sheila."

Although Allen didn't pay Clint's firm, he made a grand gesture when Susan went to the Methodist Hospital to give birth to her second child. She was returned from the delivery room to the most luxurious suite in the maternity unit: Ten South. She said that there had been a mistake, but was told, "No, the next three days have already been paid for by Mr. Blackthorne."

"Clint wanted me to move to a regular room," Susan said, laughing. "But I said, 'No way. I'm staying right here. If it's the only payment you ever get from him, I'm going to enjoy it.' "

Allen was a paradox. Despite the fact that he was extremely handsome, dressed impeccably and was a multimillionaire, many who knew him considered him an eccentric, pathetic, annoying, nerdy golf cheat with a domineering wife. Others viewed him as a callous and cutthroat businessman. The cops who had stopped his car in Castle Hills and found him dressed as a woman let him go with a warning, scratching their heads. He was a weirdo, but hadn't broken any laws beyond traffic laws.

Despite his idiosyncratic ways, few would argue that Allen was anything but brilliant, a man with a golden touch. And no one in Shavano Creek ever thought of him as dangerous. His persona changed like an anole lizard moving from leaf to tree to flower, its color and shade continually different. His façade never quite matched his real life, but his genius was that no one suspected that—except, perhaps, Sheila Bellush.

_____*Chapter Twenty*_____

ON JUNE 25, 1997, Allen filed yet another legal motion against Sheila. It had been eight years, nine months, and three days since their divorce was final, but the warfare continued. Allen sought to have Sheila held in contempt for allowing Stevie to avoid contact with him and asked for an order to enforce visitation. Sheila had been hiding her older daughters from Allen for most of their lives. When she became too frightened for the girls' emotional and physical safety, she couldn't bear forcing them to go to Allen's. But Stevie was old enough now that Sheila would have had to take her to Allen's kicking and screaming.

On July 7 Sheila responded to Allen's latest legal maneuver by seeking a protective order and asking for an increase in child support. Allen was using Lori Bendseil and Ray Perez as his lawyers.

Kerry Bladorn visited Sheila that week in July. On the twelfth, she was in San Antonio for a Mary Kay sales seminar, and she sensed right away that her older sister was not nearly as happy as she had been the year before. Sheila was frightened again. Allen was creeping back into her life, despite the fact that she was married to Jamie.

"Kerry," Sheila sighed, "will it ever end?" It was a rhetorical question; they had been through the same conversation so many times before. Sheila usually answered it herself, reassuring Kerry that God was still taking care of her and, now, of all her babies too. But there was a nervous tautness about her as if, finally, she was losing her resiliency.

Sheila, Kerry, and Rick, along with some of Kerry's fellow Mary Kay saleswomen, went out to lunch that week at San Antonio's Market Square. As they were enjoying their Mexican food, Sheila spoke of her fear of her former husband. The women she had just met stared at her, openmouthed. "My friends thought that Sheila was crazy," Kerry remembered. "They had no idea that she *really* was living in a kind of scary soap-opera life. They thought she had to be exaggerating, but I knew it was the truth."

Kerry witnessed the Adays' harassment for herself. "Sheila and I were out swimming in the pool about nine thirty," she recalled. "And then we sat in the hot tub, talking and laughing, but we weren't really loud. The next-door neighbors turned on these huge floodlights that shone right in our eyes. Sheila told me that was the way it always was."

On July 21, 1997, the legal tug-of-war over Daryl and Stevie began again in District Judge Frank Montalvo's courtroom. Montalvo had general jurisdiction over both civil and juvenile cases. His goal was always to "fashion a resolution that is in the best interest of the children."

Montalvo could see that each side was out to settle an old score, and he called all the parties into his chambers. He was desperately trying to figure out a plan to help Stevie and Daryl. He thought there had to be some way to set up counseling so that the girls could get the best from both their natural parents.

Sheila no longer believed in counseling as the answer. That had been the court order too many times before; the girls had been seeing therapists for years, and now she and Jamie went too. Allen had never followed through. Sheila said she was quite prepared to bring in the counselor Stevie had seen eight years before—the one who had heard her little girl discuss her father's sexual abuse and her feelings of fear and confusion.

For the first time Allen realized that Sheila meant it. He was going to be stripped of his charisma and revealed as a loathsome father. He could not, of course, allow that to happen.

On July 22, the next day, Allen and his attorney Ray Perez waited outside Judge Montalvo's chambers. Allen told Perez what he intended to do. He was not going through with his motion to hold Sheila in contempt and to enforce visitation. Nor was he prepared to face off with *her* on her motion seeking the protective order and the increase in child support. He was finished. "I'm going to give up my parental rights," he told Perez.

"*What?*" Perez asked, astounded.

"I'm not going to fight it anymore. I'm going to tell the judge that I'm giving up all parental rights to Stevie and Daryl."

Ray Perez tried to convey to Allen what that would mean. If he should take such a drastic action, it would be as though he had never been Stevie and Daryl's father at all. He would have no say in their upbringing, no more connection to them than some stranger would have. In the eyes of the law they would no longer be his daughters. Perez asked Allen if he realized that.

Allen nodded. He understood that. He said he and Maureen had discussed it, and he knew what he was doing.

Judge Montalvo looked at Allen with the same shock and consternation that Ray Perez had. Maureen perched on a chair next to Allen, nodding when he said he was giving up his parental rights. His voice broke with sobs, but the judge saw no tears.

"It shocked me," Montalvo recalled. "I tried to talk him out of it."

Judge Montalvo said that Allen had been adamant. He said he could no longer subject his new family to the constant battles with Sheila. He was simply going to walk away from his daughters. The judge didn't believe it would benefit the girls. "They won't be better off without their father in their life at all," he told Allen.

"He had a flat affect," Montalvo recalled. "For a moment there was some sobbing, and I asked myself why it didn't seem sincere."

Maureen put her arms around Allen and comforted him. His keening echoed in the judge's chambers, and Ray Perez also heard his sobs.

But Allen was determined. Odd that he had fought so hard to wrest Stevie and Daryl away from Sheila, even to the point of having the Adays spy on them. For nine years he had insisted he was desperately concerned about his daughters' safety, and yet now he was simply abandoning them. He certainly had adequate financial resources to wage a long-term battle, far more than Sheila and Jamie could muster.

But he undoubtedly realized that the charge of sexual abuse was going to come out in court and then, perhaps, in the newspapers and on television. Whether it would or not—since juvenile proceedings are usually sacrosanct—Allen believed it would. His secret life, his murky world of sexual aberrance, was something he protected at all costs. The Oak Hills Country Club wouldn't view that kind of publicity favorably. And he didn't want his golfing foursomes to look at him knowingly or with distaste.

When he realized that Allen was adamant, Judge Montalvo accepted his motion to give up all parental rights to his girls. But the judge didn't want Stevie and Daryl to learn that their father had given them up without someone experienced in emotional trauma close by to soften the blow. After all, Daryl believed that her father wanted her to live with him and Maureen and Brandon in the big pink palace on Box Oak. Openly, Stevie was rejecting Allen, but she might fare worse at the stunning news. A young teenager might be quick to believe that *she* had somehow driven her father away forever.

"I specifically told the parties that *no one* other than the counselor tell the children," Montalvo said.

Allen circumvented even that. A few days later Stevie and Daryl were in a hotel in Kerrville, Texas, on a family vacation. Daryl managed to find a phone booth and she dialed the 800 number Allen had given her so she could call him whenever she wanted.

"I called my dad," Daryl remembered. "And he said, 'Something happened, I just wanted the beatings to stop, honey. I didn't know how else to do that. So I gave up all my parental rights. Legally I'm not your father any longer.' "

Daryl couldn't really grasp that. Her father didn't say she wouldn't be seeing him, and he assured her she could still call him. "Stevie was in the hotel, too, that day," Daryl said, "but she wasn't seeing him at all—she didn't want to. So I didn't even tell her."

Allen had beaten the judge. *He* had told Daryl himself with what some might call vindictive relish. He was not their father anymore, and he implied it was their mother who had caused all the trouble that led to this finality. Criticized later for telling Daryl that he'd given her up, Allen said, "It was a proviso that I hadn't agreed to."

Predictably, things got worse at the Bellush home in Boerne. Stevie soon found out that Allen had abandoned her and Daryl. After learning that their father had cut all ties with them, both Stevie and Daryl acted out their pain.

Pat Aday continued to keep her journal, even though Allen had told her that he had been forced to give up all rights to his girls. She still watched the Bellush house avidly, waiting for something to happen.

For his forty-second birthday on June 5, 1997, Maureen had given Allen the best present she could think of: golf lessons at a posh resort in Sun River, Oregon. Since Allen had to be at a board meeting for RS Medical in Vancouver, Washington, the timing would be perfect. He could attend the meeting and then travel east of the mountains in Oregon to Bend.

Sun River was located about sixteen miles south of Bend, and it had a sumptuous main lodge and any number of condo-like structures with fireplaces and all the amenities. The air always smelled of sun-baked pine trees, and the golf course there was renowned, much sought-after by wealthy golfers. Allen, who had grown up in eastern Oregon, was no longer a poor boy; he would be going back a multi-millionaire. Maureen knew he would enjoy that.

Now, of course, he had given up his daughters. Maureen would recall that she felt terrible about that, especially losing Daryl. Whether Allen was still grieving, only he knew. Probably not, because he was maneuvering ways to get around the court order that was supposed to sever all ties. He had already managed a meeting with Daryl, getting a message to her to meet him at the Children's Museum in downtown San Antonio near the Alamo. That was against the rules, but Allen had never played by the rules.

When the time came for Allen to use his birthday gift from Maureen, he chose a rather unlikely companion for his trip to the Northwest on July 27, 1997. Of course, Maureen herself didn't want to go; she wasn't a golfer, and she was seven months pregnant. She had Brandon to care for and her business too. Allen had been playing golf for a year or more with a young Hispanic named Danny Rocha. One of the caddies at Oak Hills—a man dubbed "Smell Good Jerry" because he did—had introduced the two men, and they hit it off.

Danny was nearing thirty, although he looked older. He was a squat man with his head set almost on his shoulders. He wore thick glasses for his nearsightedness, and he didn't look at all like an athlete. But he had once been the amateur golf champion of San Antonio and had played on the varsity golf team of his junior college. Many San Antonio golf aficionados believed that Danny could have done well in the pro golf circuit, but instead, he dropped out of school, married, and became the father of three sons.

Danny Rocha was also a well-known bookie. He would take bets on anything from football to basketball to golf. Until he met Allen Blackthorne, however, Danny's profit from gambling wasn't exactly munificent. He and his family lived with Danny's aunt Otilia in the upstairs of her very small house.

That all changed when Danny and Allen started to play golf together. Danny quickly noted that Allen wasn't half the golfer he thought he was, but he was twice the gambler. Allen would bet on *anything*. Almost all golfers bet, but the wagers are usually five bucks a hole or less. If a golfer loses a hole, he can "press" on the next hole—kind of a double-or-nothing wager. Allen had been known to bet up to $8000 a hole!

Danny's slice of the bookie operation was minuscule at best. He counted on what he could make as a golf hustler, and Allen allowed him to enjoy a whole new level of wealth. Allen had the best clubs, the best bags, the best golf clothes, and he looked great on the course. And yet he was still a nerd in the sense that he didn't quite fit in on any of the numerous courses he played. Danny knew that the men he played with—mostly Hispanics—saw only dollar signs when they looked at him. Allen seemed totally oblivious to that.

Danny's income rose rapidly as he played regularly with Allen. It was a little like a patsy playing a patsy. Danny tended to believe everything Allen told him. Why wouldn't he? Allen lived in a house that was beyond anything Danny had ever dreamed of. He drove expensive cars and never had to work at all. When Allen spoke of his dream of building his own perfectly designed golf course one day, Danny believed that too.

On the other hand, Danny let Allen win the first few times they played, even though some of the regulars laughed behind their hands at Allen's clumsy stance and his braggadocio. Danny slowly reeled Allen in, and then he began to win. It was Danny Rocha who had won the big money from Allen, the $30,000 payoff that made Maureen turn pale.

With his winnings from Allen and some of his bookie profits, Danny was able to leave his aunt Otilia's cramped attic in July 1997 and buy a grand brick house in Stone Oak, a desirable new neighborhood. His good friend Rick Speights lived right next door and had, in fact, suggested that Danny could probably swing the house deal. Danny put $10,000 cash down and paid the owner, Randy Robertson, another $10,000 several weeks later. He was so naïve in legitimate business matters that he didn't even ask for any signed papers. He took over the owner's payments of $2000 a month, something that wasn't a burden for him as long as he was playing golf with Allen.

Danny loved his new house and the way his life was on the upswing. He and his wife had privacy, the boys had lots of room to play, and Danny particularly relished the long summer evenings when he and Rick Speights would drag lawn chairs to their mutual property line, where they had cut a hole in the fence, sip on beers, and talk about their lives. Allen was at most a golfing buddy—a pigeon, really—but Danny considered Rick a true friend. He and Rick often talked of going into business together, some legitimate business. Rick worked at an asphalt firm, laying down roads and parking lots in the hot Texas sun, and Danny knew his bookie business was only peanuts.

Truth be told, Danny wanted to emulate Allen Blackthorne's lifestyle, to be able to have more free time. "Rick mentioned that he knew somebody up in Dallas who had opened a sports bar," Danny would recall. "His idea was something similar to what they have up there. I liked the idea because I wanted to become legitimate, but I wanted a place where I could launder some of the money that I was making. Rick wanted to go into business because he was pretty much living paycheck to paycheck."

Oddly, Danny didn't seem to hear the disparity in his words— "legitimate" and "laundering money" don't really go together.

Rick and Danny visited ten locations where there were bars they might buy and turn into sports bar. Danny figured he could probably get Allen to help them finance such a venture. Allen didn't say yes, but he didn't say no either. He left Danny hanging.

Danny and Rick came up with all kinds of ideas during their late-night discussions. One was an invention—a mirror that would reflect a child or an animal standing behind the back bumper of an SUV. They figured it would probably save lives, and also make them a small fortune if they could interest the manufacturers. That was another venture they hoped Allen would finance.

Danny had numerous reasons to stay in Allen's good graces. Figuring his highest winnings in their almost daily golf games, he recalled, "I'd have to say over ten thousand dollars and under thirty thousand." To avoid problems with the IRS, Danny preferred to be paid in cash by gamblers who had bet wrong, although on occasion he did accept checks from Allen. Any regrets he may have had about dropping out of college, of failing to go on the pro circuit, diminished. Life was good for Danny Rocha.

So when Allen asked Danny to go with him to Sun River, he accepted eagerly. Ray Cevallos, another member of their frequent golf foursomes, evinced interest in going too, but Allen said he only wanted Danny. Maureen's brother, Phil Weingeist, flew with them from San Antonio to Houston, and then Allen and Danny flew on to Portland, Oregon. Danny had never flown first class in his life, and his eyes widened as he saw the flight attendants bringing one free drink after another. Then they had a meal that was nothing at all like food in coach class. It was Sunday, July 27. As they sat in the luxury of first class, Danny noted that Allen was drinking heavily.

Danny brought up the SUV mirror idea, but Allen dismissed that at once. "He said it was horrible," Danny said. "That there were too many models of SUVS, and it would cost an unbelievable amount of money."

Danny decided he had better not even try the sports-bar idea. He had never seen Allen drunk before, but now he was definitely slurring his words. And the more he drank, the more maudlin he became. Allen knew that Danny adored his own family, and according to Danny, his good golf buddy began to tell him how worried he was about his daughters, his little girls—Stevie and Daryl. Allen seemed miserable as he talked about what a cruel and vicious mother they had. His voice cracked when he said he was worried sick about them, that their mother was physically abusing them, beating them, not to mention their stepfather, Jamie Bellush.

"Somebody should beat Sheila up, so she'd know what it feels like," Allen said drunkenly. "Then maybe she'd treat them better."

Danny put it down to the alcohol. Allen had never confided anything personal to him before.

Allen's voice rose, carrying to other passengers in the first-class section, and Danny looked around nervously. Allen said he was tired of Sheila and wanted to "do something." Finally lowering his voice, he asked Danny if he knew anybody who would kill Sheila.

"Let's not talk about it right now. Let's talk about it later," Danny said. "I thought when he sobered up, it would go away and fizzle out."

When they landed in Portland, they rented a car and drove a mile down the road to the Shilo Inn, the motel where Allen usually stayed on his trips to board meetings. They shared a room. It was very late, and Allen was due at an RS Medical board meeting at eight the next morning.

After a short drive north across the Columbia River, Danny dropped Allen off at the RS Medical offices outside Vancouver, Washington. Allen introduced him to a few people, but Danny wasn't interested in attending the board meeting, nor did Allen ask him to. Some of the people at RS Medical wondered who the swarthy man with Allen was and what part he played in his life, but then Allen always walked a path that angled away from the average man's.

Danny drove off in the rental car to take in some tourist attractions. He spent his days sight-seeing and his nights playing cards with Allen, who always had to have a wager down on something. They wouldn't be going to the golf resort in Bend until Thursday, so Allen wanted to play gin rummy to while away the time. Danny was agreeable. He could take Allen's money that way, too, but he grew weary long before Allen did; Allen wanted to play cards all night.

Danny noticed that Allen's phone calls to Maureen were very long, more than an hour. He tried to leave the room during those calls and give them some privacy. He loved his wife, but he was past that honeymoon stage where you stayed on the phone endlessly. He would have thought Allen was past it too, and he wondered what they had to talk about that long.

Allen's apparent obsession with his ex-wife's treatment of his daughters continued, and Danny had to revise his first opinion that his tongue had been loosened by too many free drinks on the plane. Allen didn't drink for the rest of their trip, and yet he continued his theme that Sheila had to be punished—that nothing else would stop her from hurting his daughters. Allen said he'd spent $200,000 to get custody of his girls, and even that hadn't helped.

Hell, the guy seemed almost frantic about it. Stone-cold sober, Allen kept asking Danny if he could find someone to kill Sheila. Danny shook his head. "I told him I didn't know anybody that would kill her [but] that if he wanted to have her beat up, I could probably get someone to do that."

Despite his continual harangue about destroying Sheila, Allen still had time for gambling. He was in a gambling frenzy. If it wasn't cards, he and Danny bet "on anything that moved." They played golf games within golf games, putting on the greens while waiting to play through. They bet a dollar a hole, but Danny explained that in gambling, "a dollar means a hundred dollars." They hit golf balls into the Willamette River, trying to see who could get closest to a buoy. Allen could well afford to hit dozens of balls into the river.

On July 31 they drove to Bend, in central Oregon. There Allen went to golf school every morning, and then he and Danny teed off at noon and played until it was too dark to see the course.

Even on the golf course, Allen kept bringing up his problems with his ex-wife. "I remember coming off a green," Danny said. "He actually made a gun symbol with his hand, and he put it to his head, and he said that there's times that he wants to end his life because he can't stand not being able to protect his children, and having to watch them grow up under the abuse that they were growing up under. He said that he had tried to protect them legally through law enforcement, tried to convince Sheila to stop beating them, and apparently none of them were successful. He told me he'd thought about what I had said, and he thought that beating *her* would be a better way of going about stopping her and asked me if I would help him find someone to do it."

Danny promised that he would look into it when they got back to San Antonio. He was shocked when Allen "shifted gears on me." Danny's idea of a beating was a few blows, but Allen had a different concept. "He wanted her crippled in a wheelchair, with no tongue," Danny said.

Allen seemed sanguine after that. On the drive from Bend back to Portland, he brought up the golf course he planned to build. As Danny remembered it, "He said, 'Well, Danny, you know I'm going to invest twenty million dollars in the golf-course project, and if you handle the situation with Sheila, I'll give you twenty-five percent of that.'"

After another all-night session of gin rummy, the two men boarded a plane for San Antonio on Monday, August 4. Allen slipped Danny $700 "for cab fare," when it only cost $20 to go to Stone Oak from the San Antonio airport. Danny was relieved to be alone. Nine days with Allen was pretty intense. But a familiar refrain echoed in his head. Sheila Bellush was a witch, a terrible mother who endangered her daughters when she flew into a temper. Someone had to do something about her before she *really* hurt them.

Never once had Allen said anything to Danny Rocha about having given up his parental rights. Danny had his faults, but he considered himself a loving father to his three small sons; he could empathize with Allen's anxiety if his daughters were in that much danger from their own mother. But he still tried to tell himself that Allen wasn't really serious when he described what he actually wanted done to Sheila.

_____Chapter Twenty-one_____

THERE WERE MANY things about the summer of 1997 that were disquieting. At a time when Sheila and Jamie had expected their lives to move serenely, there was strife. Their good neighbors were now enemies. Sheila and Jamie had the girls, but nothing was getting better. Stevie and Daryl were veering out of control. Jamie's concept of discipline was physical, and that only made the girls more resentful. It didn't help that Allen had violated the Court's order and told them himself that he wasn't their father any longer. That had hurt them badly.

Sheila had further plastic surgery that summer, breast implants. She had never had much on top, and nursing the quads had diminished even that. Her surgeon was skilled, and he made two small incisions beneath the areolas of each breast and inserted the saline implants. Sheila now had the best figure she had ever had in her life. "She didn't even admit it to me," Kerry said. "But I know she had it done. She had gotten through so many problems, but when Allen gave up on the girls, she thought things were going to get better. She was still trying to start her new life."

But then an odd—frightening—thing happened. One night Sheila and Jamie noticed that a car was following them somewhere back in the dusk, turning when they turned, stopping when they stopped. They were less alarmed, but more disgusted, when they realized it was the Adays' eighteen-year-old son.

Jamie still had to travel a lot; that was part and parcel of his job. Effie Wood came over to spend time with Sheila, but more often she was alone in the big house, feeling that something about her world had shifted and would never right itself.

THE first part of August was rather quiet as the sun burned hot over San Antonio. Allen continued to play golf five days a week, and his usual partner, Danny Rocha, played in a number of tournaments, one in Corpus Christi. As Danny strode around the course or measured the putting shots in his head, one thought kept intruding: the proposal Allen had made to him. Allen brought it up all the time now. On one hand, Danny was horrified that he would even think of participating in a plot to harm a woman, no matter how hateful she was. On the other hand, Allen was offering him the chance to own a good chunk of a $20 million-dollar golf course. That was a tempting proposition. Allen even said he would make Danny the manager of his golf course. He and his family would be set for life.

All Danny had to do was find someone willing to beat Sheila Bellush up. He didn't even have to get his own hands dirty or bloody. Allen would provide the money to pay off the guy who actually did it. Danny would be the go-between, and Allen would trust him to pick the right guy. Although Danny was a golf hustler and a small-time bookie, he didn't really have any underworld contacts. But Allen seemed to think he was connected somehow to the Mexican mafia.

Having 25 percent of a $20 million-dollar golf course was too much for Danny even to comprehend. What was much more real to him was the sports bar he and Rick Speights wanted to operate. He'd be willing to settle for that. *That* might be incentive enough for him to get involved in the plot against Sheila. *That* was real.

Around August 10, Danny decided to confide Allen's offer to Rick. Rick was his best friend, almost like a brother. Sitting in their lawn chairs in the soft Texas night, Danny told his neighbor that he was pretty sure that they wouldn't actually have to torture Allen's ex-wife. They could probably "just have her beat, but not let Allen know that's all we're going to do." Danny figured they could then get Allen to finance their sports bar.

Later Rick and Danny wrote down what they would need on a long yellow legal pad. They came up with a total of $400,000—considerably less than the $5 million Allen was hinting at, the 25 percent interest in his state-of-the-art golf course.

Like Danny, Rick couldn't really conceive of a *murder* plot; he thought Danny was exaggerating. He told him that he should probably just ask Allen for a loan. The man had more money than he knew what to do with.

On August 11 Danny met Allen at the Precision Driving Range. Danny had once managed it, he knew most of the staff and the customers, and he felt comfortable there. It seemed like any other day. Allen brought his toddler son, Brandon, with him. As Allen chipped shots, Danny said that he was willing now to help him with his concerns about Sheila. But all he really wanted in payment was a loan for a sports bar. Danny handed over the sheet with the figures he and Rick had scribbled.

Allen began shaking his head. "He got upset," Danny said. "He said that was way too much money. He didn't want records leading back to me for that kind of money."

That didn't make any sense to Danny, but it sounded as though Allen had been talking pie in the sky about the golf course and was too cheap to loan them real money. The meeting ended with both men angry. It hadn't turned out the way Danny had expected at all. He felt he was being used and was ready to "end it all" with Allen.

But he didn't. Two days later Danny and Allen, along with Rick Speights, headed off to play golf on a new course, Colo Vista, in Bastrop, Texas. Allen paid the bill at Colo Vista, $760.13, and he was totally affable. Both Rick and Danny were happily surprised when he did a 360-degree turnaround on their sports-bar idea. Suddenly he was enthusiastic. It sounded as if he was going to lend them the money, and he was full of ideas they might use to make their bar a hit.

Sitting in the back seat of Allen's car, Danny shook his head in disbelief. He'd never known a man who changed his mind more than Allen. He'd been so mad the other day, and now it was almost as if he'd thought up the sports-bar project himself.

On August 18 Danny took his wife, his aunt Otilia, and his three little boys to Disney World for a week. He was still thinking about Allen's

6666666666666666666666666666666666666666
666666666666666666666666666666666666666666666

He just said he had a friend whose ex-wife was hurting his kids, and she needed to be beaten to get her to stop. But then he mentioned Allen Blackthorne, and Sammy was suitably impressed. He knew Blackthorne as a very rich man; he'd lifted his bags into the cart for him, and Blackthorne had only the best.

Still, Sammy was reluctant. He couldn't stomach beating a woman. He shook his head.

Danny looked into Sammy's eyes. "Sammy," he said, "it's just a simple *chingasos,* that's all."

It was a Spanish word for a minor scuffle—a couple of backhands or maybe slapping people around to get their attention without really hurting them.

"A simple *chingasos,*" Danny intoned. "Nothing more."

"Just a *chingasos*?" Sammy repeated, thinking hard.

"Yes."

"Okay, okay," Sammy muttered. "How much would this guy pay? Twenty thousand dollars maybe?"

"Allen is wealthy, but maybe ten. I don't know. I'll have to ask him."

At that moment something was set in motion, something that would be very difficult, if not impossible, to stop.

_____Chapter Twenty-two_____

ALLEN WASN'T DEPENDING totally on Danny Rocha; he always covered his bets, and he was working on a number of fronts to see that Sheila would never triumph over him again. He had Pat Aday, who was still observing everything that took place at the Bellush household. If Sheila made one misstep, he was certain he would know about it within minutes.

More than ever, punishing Sheila had become Allen's obsession, his avocation, his hobby, apparently his main goal in life. It didn't seem to matter that Maureen was only a few weeks away from delivering his second son. None of the riches he enjoyed mattered either. Sheila was still winning. He had been forced to back away from his child-custody suit one more time. Far worse than that, he realized now that he had made a huge tactical error by giving up all his parental rights to Stevie and Daryl. He had handed over his trump card.

• • •

In Bexar County, sworn officers of the law may also work as private investigators during their off-duty hours. Allen hired Bexar County Sheriff's detective Fred McDermott to keep an eye on Sheila. McDermott had warned Allen that it was "the dumbest thing you ever could have done" to give up his parental rights, and now Allen saw that he was right. Even so, McDermott continued the off-hours PI job he had taken on with a vengeance and, some might say, with tunnel vision.

Sheila had no idea how intensely Allen was focusing on her. She suspected that he and Maureen had been to the Adays, but she had never actually seen them there. Still, she felt a kind of pervasive dread, the same dread she had confided to Kerry and her friends from Mary Kay. She tried to put it down to the knowledge that Pat Aday was constantly watching her and the enmity she felt from the house next door. She and Jamie had come to the decision that they would never have peace unless they gave up their new home. They had to get far away from Allen, and the sooner the better. They couldn't stay in Boerne Glen, and she grieved over that loss.

But Sheila and Jamie continued to believe that their new family would flourish. Their lives together weren't over. They would just have to start fresh far, far away from San Antonio.

It wasn't going to be that easy.

It was Pat Aday's vigilance that came through for Allen first. August 31, 1997, was another bad Sunday at the house next door. On Saturday, Pat had noted that Sheila and Jamie Bellush were apparently out of town. The housekeeper, Amanda, was there and some young man, but she hadn't seen the Bellushes. Pat allowed Daryl to use her phone to call Allen. She prided herself on the fact that she never sent the girls home when they "came over wanting friendship." Allen rushed immediately to the Adays' house, still the concerned father that Pat had always perceived, and she did her best to keep him in touch with his girls.

On that last day of August, Pat sat out by her pool with her two younger children and saw Sheila Bellush come home. Shortly thereafter, Daryl ran out of her house looking very upset and plopped down at the fence line between the two properties. As Pat recalled it later, she saw Sheila come out of her house with Stevie and start to yell at Daryl to get back in the house.

Sheila had reason to be angry. She had just found out that Daryl was still sneaking out to meet Allen, even though he had legally given her away. After so many years of conflict and struggles with him to get help to support the girls, that would have been enough to make

Sheila—and most mothers, for that matter—lose their patience. And Sheila lost hers.

Pat kept her eye on the Bellush house, and sure enough, it wasn't long before Daryl appeared again and came running to the her house. "She said her mom had beat her with a belt," Pat recalled, "right through her jeans. She had a small deep cut on her right hand and five strap marks to her left side."

Pat quickly grabbed her camera and took pictures of Daryl's injuries to give to Allen, and then she called the police. In turn, they called the fire-department EMS crew to tell them they were en route to a call where a minor was reported to be injured.

When the officers arrived, they found a sobbing twelve-year-old girl with reddened skin on her face and leg. Daryl told them that her mother had found out from the sitter that she had been sneaking out to go to the Adays'. She said her mother had been unpacking her suitcase and had stopped to smack her every once in a while. Sheila had also called Daryl a few choice names and made her look in the mirror, saying, "That's the face of a liar."

And she probably had. Sheila never denied it. She had been pushed to the wall. Kerry, who loved her two nieces very much, recalled that she ran out of patience with them from time to time herself. "They could just look you in the eye and disobey," she recalled. "My kids never tried to get away with that. But one time Stevie kept jumping on the bed, defiantly, after I told her not to. I spanked her with a belt—not hard, but hard enough for her to know I meant business. I understand why Sheila was angry that day." Allen had taught his daughters to defy their mother from the time they were small.

Sheila was dealing with heartache too. Their weekend trip had been to Florida to find someplace to run to. Jamie's bosses at Pfizer had given him a promotion and transferred him to the Florida territory; they would even help him sell his house quickly. Pfizer could probably put the detail man who replaced Jamie into the Boerne Glen house and save him the financial loss that invariably comes from having to sell precipitously.

But after Jamie and Sheila had looked at the small Florida houses that were for rent, it was so hard for her to come back to her dream house that had held such endless promise only months ago. Jamie had stayed on in Florida for a few days, and Sheila was alone when she found out that Allen was *still* manipulating Daryl.

After checking Daryl's "wounds" and finding them not at all serious, the Bexar County investigators called Allen and asked him if he would take her—at least until things simmered down. Of course, he could not. He wasn't legally her father any longer, and he had to admit that to them.

The investigators were very serious as they talked to Pat Aday and Daryl. Daryl sobbed and sobbed. "It has to stop. It just has to stop," she wailed.

The Adays offered to take her for the night. But that was hardly a solution. Feelings between neighbors were running very high. Sheila couldn't take Daryl back home. And so the only solution under the law was to arrest her! She was booked into jail on suspicion of child abuse. Of necessity, Daryl was taken to the Bridge, a juvenile detention center.

It was all over a spanking.

Stevie was alone with the quadruplets. Sheilah had told her to call their good friends, the Janzes, and ask them for help with the babies. "They took Mom to jail," she sobbed. Stunned, the Janzes hurried over.

The headlines that ensued pleased Allen immensely: QUAD MOM ARRESTED FOR CHILD ABUSE! It was almost more than he could have hoped for.

On Monday morning Sheila appeared in court before a dozen video and newspaper cameras. She wore a print dress with a white collar and bent her head in humiliation as the judge continued her case and released her on bond. The story made headlines and all of the Monday-night television news coverage. Sheila had been a heroine such a short time ago, a heartwarming human-interest story, when she carried her four babies and posed so happily with them as newborns and on their first birthday. Now she felt like a pariah. A criminal hearing on the charges against her was scheduled for September 15. She promised that she would be there.

SHANNON Garcia worked for Child Protective Services as an investigator of child abuse and neglect. She checked out calls that came in to the Texas State Hotline in Austin and complaints from citizens, law enforcement, and other agencies. After thoroughly investigating the complaints, she made determinations as to their veracity. The incident involving Sheila and Daryl came to her as a Priority 1—meaning that immediate action was needed.

Shannon looked over the complaint and then met with Daryl in the Bridge. Wearing one of his "two hats," Deputy Fred McDermott was present during her interview, not as Allen's investigator but as a sheriff's officer. Daryl was in "good condition" as far as Shannon could see—well nourished, healthy. The day after the alleged beating, the only injury Shannon could detect was a scratch on Daryl's right hand. She certainly didn't look like a child who had been severely beaten, but a verbal order was in place ordering her into state custody.

One thing puzzled Shannon Garcia. Detective McDermott seemed to be intensely interested in this case, more so than other family beefs and abuse cases he had investigated. He seemed particularly intrigued by Sheila and her plans.

Shannon talked to Sheila and found that she chose not to answer questions about the brouhaha with Pat Aday and Daryl. Her attorney had advised her not to discuss it unless he was present. But Sheila did confide that her family would be moving to Florida on September 8. She would, of course, return for her criminal hearing.

The Bellush case was "staffed," and CPS caseworkers saw no validity in it as far as an abuse case was concerned. It sounded like a mother who was only trying to discipline her twelve-year-old, who had blatantly disobeyed her. Yes, Sheila had called Daryl some derogatory names and had used a belt, but they did not view her behavior as having the earmarks of a chronic abuser. They also noted that Jamie and Sheila Bellush were already being seen by Family Services at their own request and had asked for counseling sometime earlier so that they might deal with their children in a more productive way. This made an impression on the deciding board. "Their recommendation," Shannon recalled, "was that the case be non-suited."

That meant that the Bellush family would be allowed to continue counseling on their own and that the state of Texas saw no benefit in removing Daryl from her home. The plan was that Sheila and Jamie would proceed with their move on September 8. Sheila would return a week later to get Daryl and fly with her to Florida for placement in a YWCA shelter there—until the family could work out their difficulties.

Sheila told very few people that they were moving, and those were relatives and the friends she had trusted for years. Her sisters knew she was going to Sarasota, and her parents. Carl Glenn, who had been engaged to Sue Tuffiash when she was murdered, would worry about her, she knew, so she called him and his wife, Lisa, and said that she and Jamie would be moving. "She told us that they had to leave right now," Lisa said, "and that she couldn't explain. We didn't know what was wrong, but we figured she would get back in touch when she could. She did tell me that Stevie was finally ready to testify against Allen about the sexual abuse and that had forced him to give up his parental rights."

Sheila called her dentist's office and told the receptionist and the hygienist that she had to move to Florida on her psychologist's advice—that she had to go to protect her babies—and she wanted them to have a billing address. It was a Mail Boxes, Etc. address.

On Labor Day weekend, packing hurriedly, the Bellushes, the Janzes, and Mary Fenlon's brother Steve loaded up a caravan that would leave for Florida under cover of darkness. They couldn't take everything, but they took as much as they could in a rented U-Haul, a van, a truck, and a car. Their destination was Sarasota, where they had the small rental on Markridge waiting for them. Jamie had his new territory covering the southwest coastal towns of Florida, and he promised Sheila there would be another house, a new house they would build to be just what they wanted. "Better than before," he said.

Pat Aday watched covertly from her pool deck or from windows shaded by blinds. She noted the activity next door on September 6. There were a number of cars coming and going, and people were walking in and out carrying large trash bags. "I figured they were moving," she said, "leaving their house."

Pat called Maureen Blackthorne and said, "Something is going on over here!"

"They're moving," Maureen breathed.

Pat Aday also called Fred McDermott. She had given a written statement about what had happened on August 31, hoping that might be enough to stop the Bellushes from running. Allen would be so upset if Sheila got away after what she had done to Daryl, and if she managed to take Stevie away from him too.

It took McDermott two days to get back to her, and by that time, it was too late. After checking the house next door, he told Pat that the Bellushes were gone.

Sheila and Jamie coordinated their move with their friends like a military team synchronizing watches. It wasn't easy slipping out of Boerne without alerting the Adays, but somehow they managed to hide their actual leave-taking. It was a 1200-mile trip from San Antonio to Sarasota. The four-vehicle caravan left town with the sure sense that someone had to be following them, but they felt safer with every passing mile. Sheila was sad that she couldn't say good-bye to most of her friends.

They were going to leave Allen far behind and move into a world where he had no idea where they were, where he had no influence over them or the girls. They had to do it this way.

The babies whined and cried and then fell asleep from exhaustion. Stevie fidgeted, complaining that all of her friends were back in

Texas and that she would probably never have a friend again. The trip took almost three days, and they arrived in Sarasota at 2:00 A.M. Exhausted, they put the babies to bed and settled into their new house.

And Sheila's heart broke, knowing that Daryl was still locked up at the Bridge. Even though she knew she was going back for her as soon as she could, it was a terrible feeling to leave one of her children behind. And Daryl was disruptive and angry. She needed time and counseling.

She had no other choice.

They had to leave a lot behind. Effie Woods and other good friends volunteered to go to the Boerne Glen house and box up what was left—some for storage, some for Goodwill.

Pat Aday was worried about Daryl, so worried that she and her husband talked it over and decided they would offer to adopt her. She had her notes to support what she had seen, and she allowed Maureen's attorneys to videotape her as she recalled everything she knew about Sheila. She hired Pat Guerra—an attorney who had once represented Allen—to represent them in their petition to adopt Daryl. It was the least they could do for Daryl and for poor Allen.

STILL a little shell-shocked, the Bellushes settled into the house on Markridge in Sarasota. It was a cute little white house with yellow trim, but it was much smaller than the Boerne Glen house, much smaller even than their Alamo Heights house, and it was filled with other people's furniture. But it was far away from Allen Blackthorne, and that made it the most desirable house in the world.

On September 14, Sheila flew alone to San Antonio; she had to go to court the next day. The judge released Daryl into her custody, but Sheila was wary. She didn't know what frame of mind Daryl was in, and it didn't help to see the Adays in the courtroom watching the proceedings intently. Sheila was aghast that they thought they could come in and adopt *her* daughter.

To be on the safe side, Sheila asked Shannon Garcia, Daryl's caseworker, to accompany them on the plane back to Florida. "I went with Sheila and Daryl because Sheila didn't want to be alone with Daryl," Shannon said. "She was afraid other abuse allegations might be leveled against her, and she wanted me there to avoid any chance of that."

Sheila knew that Daryl was too angry and too much influenced by her father and the Adays to come back into the family home, at least for a few weeks. As it was, they were practically sleeping on top of each other. Stevie was in the dining room, and the four babies were in jammed-together beds in one bedroom. It wasn't the ideal situation to try to mend all the hurt feelings and misunderstandings. Daryl didn't know she was going to the YWCA shelter until they got there. Maybe it wasn't the best way to do it, but it seemed the only way to make the flight to Florida without her kicking and screaming and crying.

With Shannon along, they managed the trip with reasonable calm. Daryl wasn't happy about the Y, but Sheila promised her it was only for a little while and that she would come to see her as often as she could. She kept her promise. She wanted Daryl home even more than Daryl wanted to be there. Keeping her family together was all Sheila ever wanted, but they had a long way to go before that could happen.

Sheila registered Stevie in school, and she and Jamie joined the Sarasota Baptist Church. They needed to have a church home. They were welcomed, and for the time they were in church, their lives seemed serene. Everyone noticed the family with the four adorable toddlers and the two pretty preteen daughters. Daryl was with them on most weekends now, and she went to church with them too.

But when Mike Landry, one of the pastors, came to call on his new parishioners, he was puzzled. He waited at the front door for a long time and saw Sheila peeking out through the blinds at him. When she recognized him, she hurried to let him in. But he wondered if she might be just a little paranoid. He'd never made a visit where new members seemed so suspicious. There was a hesitancy about Sheila, and even though she was friendly, Landry left realizing that he actually knew very little about her or her family.

The Bellushes got a phone—unlisted, of course—and Jamie arranged for a box at the Mail Boxes, Etc. outlet over on the Tamiami Trail. There probably wouldn't be much mail, since few knew where they were beyond a few trusted friends in San Antonio and their families, but they needed some kind of address.

The counselors at the Y shelter assured Sheila that it wouldn't be long before Daryl could come home. They would all be together again. Workmen had broken ground and laid the footings for their new house in the East Lake subdivision. Everything they had to leave behind in San Antonio—at least in a house—could be replaced and even improved.

Jamie was gone during the week, familiarizing himself with his new territory. Outside of church activities, Sheila kept to herself. Her new neighbors barely knew her beyond watching her as she jogged down the Gulf Gate streets pushing her quadruplets in a four-seated stroller, her golden hair lifting in the wind. She smiled and said "Hi!" but she didn't stop to talk. She was lonesome and begged Kerry to come and visit in the first week of November, a late celebration of Sheila's birthday.

BACK in Boerne, Effie Woods spent as much time as she could cleaning up the Bellushes' vacated house. She had always been the kind of friend who went beyond what most good friends would do. But sometimes—and this was odd, because Effie wasn't the skittish type—she had a sense that there were eyes watching her through the windows of Sheila's house. She would hear the crunch of a twig outside or a car's brakes and she froze, wondering who was outside.

Not Allen, she was sure. That wasn't his style. Effie knew he had always relied on other people to carry out his less appealing chores. And it wasn't the woman next door who had always watched Sheila, although Effie saw Pat Aday staring from her property sometimes when she came and went. No, it was more the kind of feeling she might get if a stranger was just beyond the windows watching her.

In truth, someone was, but Effie wouldn't realize that for a long time.

PART FOUR

Sarasota, Florida

Chapter Twenty-three

IT WAS EARLY on the morning of November 7, 1997, when Jamie left the house on Markridge. He had a full day ahead. He planned to drive south along I-75 and call on doctors in the Fort Myers and Naples area. Later Sheila dropped Stevie off at Sarasota Middle School and then stopped on the way home at McDonald's to buy breakfast for the quadruplets.

She had a lot to do that day, but she always had a lot to do. The laundry piled up if she didn't keep on top of it. Frankie, Timmy, Joey, and Courtney alone could fill a couple of loads a day, and then there were Stevie's clothes and clean shirts for Jamie. It was like shoveling out the Augean stable—the more she washed, the more there was. She always had laundry just folded, laundry to fold, and dirty laundry. She tried to work out some kind of system with plastic bins for everyone, but the house was so small that it wasn't easy.

And Sheila believed that taking time to play with the babies, to give them a chance to paddle in the swimming pool and read stories to them before nap time was even more important than housework. She loved every minute she spent with them. They would be two in a month, and they had so much energy and so much curiosity.

Stevie did chores around the house too. It was her job to see that the trash was out on pickup days, the cans hidden behind the shrubbery that grew beside the garage. Her mom reminded her each time to lock the door leading into the garage from the side yard when she was done. If there was one cardinal rule in the household, it was to keep the door locked. Stevie wasn't sure why, but she knew that door was so hidden from the street by tall tropical shrubs and trees that no one could see who went in or out. When they were all home, they kept the jalousie windows open; there wasn't enough space for anyone to crawl between the slanted glass segments. And if Sheila was away when Stevie came home from school, she left the front door unlocked so Stevie could get in. But after dark it was always locked.

Stevie knew her mother was frightened and that Jamie was nervous. She knew they had left for Florida in darkness so that no one would see them leave, and she thought she knew who frightened her mother. It was her father; he had always been the one who made her mom miserable.

THAT Friday morning Sheila came home from dropping Stevie off and from McDonald's, and she backed her blue Ford van into the driveway. She couldn't put it in the garage; they already had their pickup truck parked there, along with a lot of their belongings. From the van to the front door was only a few steps.

She was going to let the quads swim. That tired them out and made them ready for a nap after they had a snack. The pool was screened by the walls of the Florida room, and there was no need to bother with bathing suits. She just took off their Pampers and, if they were still dry, popped them back on after their swim. But she *always* put their life jackets on. There was no way she could watch four toddlers at once in a pool, and their safety was her prime concern.

There was nothing particularly unusual about this Friday morning, nothing to make Sheila more afraid than she usually was. She had lived for so long with a steady thrum of repressed fear. Sometimes she felt as though she was always waiting for the other shoe to drop.

It was very quiet in the house, and she and the quads were alone. She hugged them and talked to them steadily as she always did. And then something was there. Maybe it was a noise. Maybe she smelled acrid perspiration. Maybe she caught a glimpse of something out of place.

Her heart thumping, she whirled with half a question on her lips . . .

BETTY Herman had lived in Gulf Gate on Blue Water Street for thirty years, and she recognized most of the residents and the vehicles they drove. Sometime between nine and ten on the morning of November 7, she had pulled out of her driveway and turned right on Goodwater Street when she saw a man she didn't recognize walking toward her street. He just didn't fit in the neighborhood. "He was wearing a Desert Storm–like uniform," she said, "which was not usual to see in Gulf Gate—a camouflage [uniform]."

The man Betty Herman saw was trim and seemed to be of medium height with short dark hair. He looked so out of place that she regretted that she hadn't locked her house and even considered turning around and going back. She watched him in her rearview mirror until she saw him veer off. He had turned south on Blue Water and was headed toward Markridge Road. Relieved that he was walking away from her house, Betty Herman went on about her errands.

Kathleen Wingate lived in the 3100 block of Regatta Circle in Gulf Gate, a block away from the white-and-yellow house on Markridge Road. She had to take her cat to the vet about seven, and then left again shortly after eight. She wasn't sure which errand she was on when she noticed a white car with Texas plates in front of her. She recognized it as a late-model Mitsubishi. "I thought it was odd because at that time of the year—early November—we didn't have snowbirds," she recalled. "And we don't have snowbirds from that state on my street anyway. That's why I remembered that car."

Jacob Mast was a lawn-care worker with contracts to work at many of the homes in Gulf Gate. It might have been snowing up north, but the grass was still growing in Sarasota, and Jake was mowing it in a yard on Blue Water, around the corner from the Bellushes' house. He tried to do several yards on the same street on the same day, and he'd already made a good start on this Friday morning when he saw a white car pass by. Even if he didn't always recognize the drivers, it was his habit to wave. The driver of the sleek white car ignored Jake and stared straight ahead. Jake watched curiously as he saw the car being parked in front of a corner house on Goodwater Street.

Jake Mast was a somewhat timid man who was slow to speak, but he didn't miss much. He was careful not to stare at the man who got out of the white car and headed down the street toward Markridge, but Jake monitored his progress. There was something about the man that frightened him, but he couldn't say exactly what it was. The guy was young and muscular and wore a uniform—a camouflage uniform and combat boots. *In Gulf Gate?*

Jake cut neat parallel strips of grass, moving from yard to yard. Every time he came up to the street, he glanced covertly at the license plate on the white car parked near the corner of Blue Water and

Goodwater. He was extremely careful not to be obvious about it. He was very frightened. For some reason the stranger had danger emanating from him. To remember the license number, YBR-62G, Jake made up a mnemonic clue: "Yes, Bob runs sixty-two girls." He kept repeating it silently to himself. He was so intent on remembering the letters and digits that he failed to note which state had issued the license plate.

An hour or so after he saw the stranger, Jake Mast heard a loud sound and looked up to see the white Eclipse burn rubber and race away.

It was more than six hours later when Stevie hurried home from school, bursting with the news that she was pretty sure she was going to be asked out by the boy she had a crush on. She was only thirteen, but she could hardly wait to have a real date. She was in a tearing hurry to grow up. Her mom always listened to her problems and to her happy news.

The front door was unlocked, and her mom's van was parked in the driveway. She hadn't told Stevie that she would be gone; she always told her if she had plans for the time Stevie came home. Stevie expected to find her just inside, cheerfully asking about her day.

Stevie walked through the front door and immediately heard the babies crying. They were huddled together in the hall, and they didn't have anything on but their life vests.

"I figured maybe my mom had left the room to go to the bathroom, or another room for something," Stevie said a long time later. "I opened one door and didn't see her in there. I went into her bedroom, walked in the bathroom—nobody in there, so I walked outside. Didn't see her."

With a roaring sound in her ears because something was making her afraid, Stevie searched the house and the backyard. At length she turned to the left, looking toward the utility room. But the kitchen was between Stevie and the utility room. It didn't look right. It was the same kitchen, small and narrow, but the floor was covered with piles of clothing.

Nothing was making any sense to Stevie. Her mother would never leave the babies alone, not even for a few minutes. But she couldn't find her anywhere as she walked through the house. The babies waited in the front hall, and they weren't acting as they usually did. They were always excited to see their big sister come home. Now they huddled together, their cries softened to hiccuping sighs.

Stevie stared at the scattered clothing trailing through the kitchen from the utility room as if someone had just thrown it there willy-nilly. In the kitchen doorway there was another mound of clothing. She looked more closely and saw that it was a person, a person crumpled on the floor in a sea of red . . . red. . . . red.

Then she realized that the person on the floor was her mother, lying motionless in the doorway, just in front of the dishwasher. Her face and her arms and her blue shirt were all covered with the same red. The wall phone over the dishwasher was off the hook, and the kitchen drawers were open.

Stevie just stood there, the enormity of what she saw so stunning that she could not believe it. She walked into the bedroom, where there was another phone, and dialed 911 with numb fingers. But then she hung up. Had she *really* seen her mother lying in the floor in all that blood? She thought that somehow she had imagined it.

She walked back to the kitchen. It wasn't a terrible dream. Her mother was still there. Stevie picked up the wall phone and couldn't understand why the 911 operator was on the line. (Once a call is placed to 911, the Sarasota County system locks onto the line even if the phone is hung up on the other end.)

Actual 911 Transcription

"Hi, this is 911 Center. What's the matter?"

"[Crying] My mom . . . my mom . . ."

"What's your address?"

"Ummmm . . . 3120 Markridge."

"Okay. What's going on?"

"My mom—"

"Your mom, *what?*"

"My mom is dead."

"Your mother and dad are fighting?"

"No. My mom is dead."

"Ma'am, I can't hear you."

"My mom is dead."

"Okay. What makes you think that?"

"There's blood all around the place, and she has a cut on her neck."

"Do you think that she did this on her own?"

"No."

"Is the person that did this to her still there?"

"I don't think so."

"Okay, calm down. Stay on the line with me. I need you to calm down. Okay, who else is in the house there?"

"I have my other brothers and sister."

"How old are you?"

"I'm thirteen. I just got home from school."

"Okay. Calm down. Do you know the person who did this?"

"No, I don't know who did it. I just got home."

"Okay. . . . We have help on the way. What's your last name?"

"Bellush. B-e-l-l-u-s-h."

"And your first name?

"Stevie."

"You still there, Stevie?"

"Yeah, I'm here. . . ."

"Okay, we have somebody on the way. You're at 3120 Markridge Road."

"Yes, and I need to call my stepdad."

"Okay. I want you to stay on the phone with me. Okay?"

"Oh, my God—there's blood."

"Until somebody gets there, then you can make your phone call. Where is your mom?"

"She's standing—she's *laying* by the kitchen door."

"Okay. You said it looks like she's—"

"Her throat has been cut."

"Been *cut*?"

"Yes."

"Okay. Stay on the line. Are your brothers and sisters younger than you?"

"Twenty-three months."

[Stevie had begun to cry hysterically, and the 911 operator urged her to try to calm down.]

"The kitchen door is open." [Stevie is sobbing.] "There's blood all over the phone. . . . My *mom* . . . "

"It's just you and your brothers and sisters there?"

"I don't know."

"Okay, Stevie, calm down. Do you see anything else around there?"

"The door is open."

"The doors are open?"

"No—the door is like the kitchen door is . . . Ummm—there's blood going through the laundry room all the way to the kitchen and . . . Oh, God, and my little brothers and sisters are in their life vests so I think she was probably outside."

"You think she was outside?"

"Yeah, and she came in, and oh, my God!"

"Okay, Stevie, we have help on the way."

[Stevie begins to sob again as the horror of what she saw cuts through her shock.] "Oh, God. She's dead."

"Stevie?"

"Frankie—"

"Stevie, I have three units on the way, okay? Can you see them from where you are?"

"No, I— There's someone here."

"Okay. Go to the door, Stevie. Go to the door and make sure it's the officers."

"They're here. Okay. Okay. Bye-bye."

The operator could hear male voices in the background. She could not begin to imagine the tragic shambles Stevie and her four tiny brothers and sister stood in.

____Chapter Twenty-four____

TODD THUROW was a Sarasota County deputy sheriff, working uniformed patrol, assigned to the second watch in Zone 9, the Gulf Gate area. He responded to the dispatcher's call and arrived at the Markridge address at approximately 4:25 P.M. on November 7. Thurow walked through the front door and saw a young girl standing next to the victim on the floor. He gently took the phone from her hand and hung it up.

No child should ever have to see the terrible injuries done to the woman who lay crumpled in the kitchen doorway. Thurow could detect no signs of life in the victim, and he immediately took Stevie out of the house. Deputy Chris Laster arrived a minute or two after Thurow. They saw the four toddlers, who all looked to be the same age, took them outside, and asked Stevie to watch them until more help arrived.

Chris Laster had been a paramedic for six years. He looked at the woman lying on the kitchen floor. She had been there a long time; the blood on her skin had dried, and the blood on the floor had coagulated and cracked into segments on the edges of the pools of red liquid like mud in a drying pond. She was not bleeding from any of her wounds. Laster knew that she had been dead for some time, that it was much too late to save her.

The dead woman had a massive wound to her neck, and Thurow

and Laster saw what looked to be defensive wounds on her hands and arms, but there was so much blood that it would be impossible to say how many injuries she had suffered. She was fully clothed in blue jeans and a blood-soaked blue shirt. One leg was bent beneath her body, and the other was extended. From the looks of the kitchen, it was clear she had put up a tremendous fight.

She was a small woman, pretty even in death, and fragile-looking. Even for experienced policemen, this was a terribly difficult sight. The thought that her daughter had seen her like this haunted them. The quadruplets—for surely they were quadruplets—might still be young enough that they didn't realize what had happened to their mother. The deputies hoped that was true.

Deputy Thurow talked to Stevie. She was crying and on the verge of hysteria, but she was holding herself together so that she could take care of the babies who clung to her.

"Do you know who might have done this?" Thurow asked her.

"Yes. I know who did it, but he didn't do it himself. He probably hired someone to do it."

"Who?"

"My father did it. My father—Allen Blackthorne."

SIRENS wailed throughout the usually quiet Gulf Gate neighborhood. Hoyt Williams, Jr., a firefighter/paramedic with the Sarasota County Fire Department and his partner, Brian Balance, arrived next. The deputies asked them for help on two matters: they needed someone to see to the quadruplets, and they needed a paramedic to confirm that the woman inside was dead.

Williams handed the first of the quadruplets to one of the EMTs on his rig and followed the deputies into the house. He saw the terribly injured blond woman and knelt to confirm that she was, indeed, dead. "There were no signs of recent life," he recalled. "She had no pulse. She was not breathing. We noted a large amount of blood around the patient, and noted that her pupils were fixed and dilated, and that her fingers were stiff and nonpliable."

Rigor mortis, the stiffness that occurs in the body after death, had already begun. No amount of resuscitation would bring her back. There was no need for haste. It was far too late to save Sheila Bellush. Now Sarasota County investigators had the awesome responsibility of doing a meticulous probe to find the killer or killers who had murdered the young mother who could no longer hear her four babies' frightened cries.

The fire-department crew checked the toddlers and found that they had dried blood on their skin, but since they had no wounds or scratches, the blood had apparently come from their mother. There was evidence that they had huddled next to her for some of the six hours they had waited alone in the house for someone to find them.

Frankie had blood inside his life vest where it had dripped or splashed from some height down onto his chest. The only logical conclusion was that he had clung to his mother's leg while she was still upright and moving across the kitchen to the phone. With her last breath of life and her blood rapidly draining from her body, Sheila had managed to get the phone off the hook, but then she collapsed and fell backward before she could make the rotary dial connect with 911.

Investigators took photographs of the little blond toddlers, wearing disposable diapers now, their eyes wide with loss or terror or shock—whatever emotion babies who have just lost the center of their world might feel.

Jamie Bellush wasn't far from home when his pager sounded. He had an urgent message from the Sarasota sheriff's office. When he called, he was told only that there was an emergency at home. He drove as fast as he could, worrying that something had happened to the babies.

When he pulled up in front of his house, he learned that it wasn't the babies; it was Sheila. Newspaper photographers caught the poignant scene of Jamie in his shirtsleeves and Stevie in the shorts she had worn to school. He was hugging her and trying to comfort her as they stood in front of the house. It was far too early to even try to come to terms with their loss.

Stephanie Hayes, who was head of the nursery at the Baptist church, appeared like an angel to care for Stevie and the quadruplets. She opened her home to them for as long as they needed a place to stay. None of them would ever go back to the house on Markridge.

Stevie was in shock, and the toddlers were very hungry and exhausted from crying. Still, Stevie worried about the little ones. Having to care for them immediately after her tragic discovery had saved her from falling apart. The five of them needed to be together.

Daryl didn't know yet that her mother was gone. She had been moved to the Eckerd Camp for children with emotional and discipline problems. There counselors protected her from hearing any news broadcasts until family members could tell her what had happened.

Stevie had been adamant that her father, Allen Blackthorne, was the only one who might want her mother dead. The Sarasota County sheriff's office put out a BOLO (Be on the Lookout For) on Allen

Blackthorne, but there were no reports of anyone seeing him in the Sarasota area.

TODD Thurow had already started a "contamination sheet" listing the people who had been in the house at the time of Stevie's hysterical call and shortly thereafter. Everyone who entered would be listed. He and Chris Laster reeled out yellow crime-scene tape and strung it around the perimeters of the yard on Markridge. Criminalists were on their way to process the scene and gather evidence.

Captain Jerry Eggleston of the Sarasota County sheriff's office dispatched Lieutenant Ron Albritton to be the command officer at the homicide scene. He had investigated innumerable murder cases, but this was unlike anything he had ever witnessed. A bachelor, Albritton was tall and solid, and he was able to put on at least a patina of calm at the terrible scene. He saw that it was important to get the toddlers away from the house where their mother lay dead, and for the moment, he left their father, Jamie Bellush, alone with Reverend Landry, who had rushed over the moment he heard the news.

Detective Chris Iorio received a call from Ron Albritton asking him to report to the scene of a homicide in Gulf Gate. The details of the situation on Markridge sounded like a horror story. Iorio had seen a lot of horror; he was the Sarasota sheriff's office's prime interrogator of child molesters, and he was a master at it. He was able to hide his disgust as he questioned adults who had savaged children for their own pleasure, and he had an enviable conviction record. But even he shuddered when he saw Sheila's body.

Ron Albritton walked a circumscribed path to where the victim lay. It was clear that she had fallen straight back without making any effort to break her fall; her left leg was jackknifed so completely beneath her that the sole of her foot rested against her left buttocks, and her right leg was caught in a throw rug. The top of her head projected into the living room, resting against the doorjamb, next to an organ on which was a picture of the Bellushes and their six children beaming at the camera.

There was so much blood leading from the utility room that the kitchen floor was awash with it, and the articles of clothing that the victim's feet must have tangled in were stained crimson. It was almost incredible that the dead woman had enough blood left in her body to give her the strength to reach above the dishwasher for the phone.

It would take an autopsy to say which of her wounds had killed her. There was a round bullet hole, rimmed with gunpowder, in the center of her right cheek, but there was also a bloodstained filleting knife, its tip bent, lying in the laundry room next to a woman's gold earring. Whoever the killer was, he or she had wanted to be certain that Sheila Bellush was dead.

The forensic team, led by crime-scene technician Lisa Lanham, moved in. They walked shoulder-to-shoulder back and forth across the yard and around the whole perimeter, looking for something that might be out of place. And they did it again with metal detectors. Only then did they move inside the house. Sheila's body still lay undisturbed. It was vital that they find some clue, however infinitesimal, to the person who had done this to her before she was moved.

Outside the kitchen and the utility room, there was little sign that a violent crime had occurred in the house. The furnishings were nice, if a little dated. At one time the original owners had apparently bought a whole houseful of furniture with the same theme—French provincial light-colored wood with gold accents, overstuffed chairs, and couches of velvet or with floral patterns. But it was obvious that this was now a home dedicated to children; there were bright-colored toys, pedal cars and trikes, dolls, and stuffed animals everwhere. Halloween was a little more than a week past, and four little "Cat-in-the-Hat" costumes in plastic bags hung on a curtain rod above the sliding door to the Florida room and pool.

Technician Bob Creager processed the west side of the house, starting with the exterior door to the garage, using superglue to raise any latent prints that might be there. In the utility room there was so much blood on the floor he had trouble getting around. "But I went up to the dryer, and I got a print right at the edge of the rim," Creager said.

He also saw a bullet casing on top of the dryer. While the crime-scene technicians worked, the other investigators stayed out of their way. The fewer people at a crime scene, the better. Ron Albritton and Chris Iorio waited in the front yard and introduced themselves to Jamie Bellush. He was a big man and powerful-looking, but now he had tears running down his cheeks. When he saw the detectives, he asked them if he needed an attorney.

"Well," Iorio answered, a little taken aback, "it's up to you. We need to talk with you to get some information so we can start the investigation."

Jamie nodded readily and agreed to go with Iorio and Albritton to the sheriff's station on Ringling Boulevard. He asked only that his pastor be present during the interview, and Iorio said that would be fine. Reverend Landry could follow the sheriff's car in his own vehicle.

It was 6:58 P.M. when Albritton and Iorio interviewed Jamie. He probably knew the old axiom that detectives always look at those closest to the victim first, but he didn't seem unduly nervous. Rather, he appeared to be in shock, a man concentrating on putting one foot ahead of the other. Still, they had to talk to him at this moment; Albritton and Iorio had no idea what the family dynamics were or what could have led to such a violent murder.

Jamie explained that he and Sheila had been married about four years and had four children—the quadruplets—together. He also had two stepchildren living with him, although the younger girl, Daryl, twelve, was currently attending the Eckerd Camp, where she was getting counseling.

"I've attempted to adopt both the girls, but I got a lot of resistance from Sheila's ex-husband, Allen Blackthorne," Jamie said, adding that he *had* started to adopt them a few months earlier, and they both used his last name now.

Asked to describe what he remembered of his day—this long, long Friday—Jamie struggled to focus. He had gotten up about six thirty and fed the babies, he said. At seven he had awakened Stevie and then gone to take a shower and get dressed for work. A half hour later he had left in his company car, the blue Chevrolet coupe that was parked now in front of the Markridge house.

"I stopped at Mail Boxes, Etc., at Paradise Plaza," Jamie remembered, "and then I ate breakfast at Einstein's Bagels."

Concentrating hard, Jamie was even able to recall exactly what he had eaten for breakfast. After that, he said, he went to a storage warehouse on Clark Road, where he loaded up the trunk of his car with Pfizer samples for the interviews he had lined up that day. His first appointments were in Fort Myers, some eighty miles south of Sarasota. He wasn't sure just what time he arrived, but he gave the detectives the names of the doctors he had visited there. They could figure out his timetable that way.

"I ate lunch at Hooters in Fort Myers," Jamie said, "and I remember the waitress's name was Mary."

He opened his wallet and gave the detectives the yellow copy of his credit-card receipt from Hooters. After lunch, he said, he had one more appointment with a physician and then he had called a friend of his from a pay phone. "Around two thirty," he added, "I decided to head for home. It was Friday afternoon, and I didn't want to work much later than that."

Rather than retrace his drive down on I-75, Jamie said, he had chosen to go back on U.S. 41 because it was a lot more scenic. It passed through Punta Gorda, over the Charlotte Harbor bridge and then curved west along the Bay of Mexico. It paralleled I-75, and the water views were worth the little extra time it took.

"I got a page when I was on Bee Ridge Road," Jamie told the detectives. "It was a deputy—I can't remember his name—and he said there was a family emergency and I should come home. I thought one of the babies had fallen into the pool, but when I got to my house, one of the deputies told me my wife was dead. I knelt down and asked the deputies to pray with me."

Asked if he knew of anyone who might want to harm his wife, Jamie, too, brought up her former husband, Allen Blackthorne. He told Albritton and Iorio that they had nothing but problems with Allen and recounted the endless court battles over Stevie and Daryl. He characterized Allen as "very vindictive" and said he was positive that he would be the most likely person behind Sheila's murder.

"It was our gut call from our experience that this guy didn't do it," Iorio recalled, speaking of Jamie. "Between Ron and me, we've interviewed a lot of people, and we were basically betting our reputations. You always start with the inner circle and work outward, so we started with Jamie. We looked at each other after talking to him for the longest time and we *knew* he didn't do it. There were a lot of other things we could have done with him that would have delayed our getting to Texas. We agreed that we had to look further."

Jamie also mentioned another suspect. A man named Marty Cecchi,* who worked as a pool man and had once lived in the Markridge house. He couldn't give a definite reason why he thought of Cecchi, but he felt the guy was a little strange and warranted a visit from the Sarasota investigators.

It was 9:49 that night when Albritton and Iorio concluded their interview with Jamie. They had talked to him for almost three hours, and he appeared to be totally open with them. He was sure he could validate every place he had been since he left home that morning if that proved to be necessary. They would talk to him again, but they did not consider him a suspect—He wasn't even a "person of interest."

Meanwhile, the forensics team was swarming over the home where Jamie and Sheila had lived; Jamie didn't think he could go back there again—not ever. The Baptist church stepped in to help. Members arranged for him to stay at the Hampton Inn that was close to Gulf Gate and insisted on paying for his lodging. He was far too upset to see his children and his stepdaughter; he was still trying to accept his own loss.

Jamie called Kerry Bladorn to give her the terrible news that her sister was dead. "I said, 'You liar,' " Kerry remembered. "And then I realized that it was true—that what Sheila had always feared had happened. She was so afraid sometimes that she wouldn't live to raise the quadruplets, but then she seemed to be okay and she believed that she would live, after all."

Kerry hadn't been able to visit Sheila during this very week, even though her sister had tried to persuade her. She wondered if she might be dead too, had she gone to Sarasota—or if she could have saved Sheila. Now she and Rick made plans to fly to Sarasota at once. Kerry had four children of her own, and she rarely left them, especially her newest son, Patrick, who was just two months younger than Sheila's quadruplets. But there was no question that she had to go to comfort Sheila's children. She and Rick were on a plane headed to Sarasota before Kerry really let herself realize that her sister, her best friend, her buddy—no matter how far apart they sometimes were—was dead. She wondered how anyone could have tracked Sheila down when she and Jamie had been so careful to hide their location.

And it had all been for nothing.

Sheila's mother, Gene, had lost yet another child in November. She thought she would die from the pain of it. She took a little comfort as she read Sheila's favorite Bible passage, Psalm 37:

"Fret not thyself because of
evildoers, neither be thou
envious against the workers of iniquity.
For they shall soon be cut down
like the grass, and wither as the green herb. . . .
Rest in the Lord, and wait
patiently for him; fret not thyself because of
him who prospereth in his way, because of the man
who bringeth wicked devices to pass.
Cease from anger, and forsake
wrath: fret not thyself in any wise to do evil.
For evildoers shall be cut off:
but those who wait upon the Lord,
they shall inherit the earth."

Gene read the psalm over and over. It was as if Sheila were sending her a message, telling her that it would be all right, but she didn't see how anything would ever be all right again.

■

NEAR midnight on Friday, still on the day of Sheila's murder, Ron Albritton and Chris Iorio met with other detectives working the probe to exchange the information they had so far.

The two Sarasota detectives were about to plunge into a case that would occupy much of their time for the next thirty months. They had totally different backgrounds, but they would work smoothly together. Lieutenant Ron Albritton was a native Floridian, raised in Hardee County, cattle country whose county seat was Wauchula, a name that means "buzzard's nest" in Seminole. He had been with the sheriff's department for twenty-three years and had a B.A. degree in criminology from Florida State University. He had worked in almost every unit in Sarasota County from narcotics to polygraphy. He loved everything about Sarasota, including the climate, and he was an ardent golfer and fisherman.

Detective Chris Iorio, forty-one, had bright blue eyes and a crew cut prematurely flecked with gray. He still had the powerful shoulders of the football player and champion javelin thrower he once was. Raised in Penn Hills, Pennsylvania, a Pittsburgh suburb, he went to college in Charleston, South Carolina, on a track scholarship. "All I ever wanted to be was a Pennsylvania state trooper," he said. "I passed the tests, but I didn't get hired because of minority quotas, so I gave up on it."

Iorio ended up in Florida because he fell in love with Janice, a native Sarasotan, and moved there after they were married. They soon had two children. Iorio was twenty-eight years old when he decided to try again to become a state trooper—this time in Florida. He worked for the Florida highway patrol for two years, grew tired of traffic stops and tickets, and then hired on with the Sarasota sheriff's office in 1986. Like Albritton, he was in his element as a detective. The only thing he never got used to was the hot weather.

Within eight hours of the discovery of Sheila Bellush's body, Crime Stoppers tips were pouring in, along with bits of information from the investigators who had been heel-and-toeing it on a neighborhood canvass in Gulf Gate throughout the evening. There were numerous leads about "suspicious" vehicles seen near the house on Markridge, and members of the Crime Suppression Unit were following up on those through the night. But there was nothing solid enough for them to work on.

Chris Iorio was back at the murder scene at 12:34 A.M.—Saturday, November 8. He and criminalist Lisa Lanham of the Forensics Unit discussed where the attack on Sheila Bellush had begun. The most blood was in the utility room, and it looked as if Sheila had first encountered her killer there. Iorio saw a bullet hole in the utility-room wall about five feet above the floor. The path of the bullet was through the utility-room wall, across the dining room—which Stevie had been using as her bedroom—into a mirror on the opposite wall.

Lanham told him about the .45-caliber shell casing on top of the dryer. On its own, the casing didn't have a great deal of evidentiary value, but if they found the gun that had fired it, they would be able to compare extractor and ejector marks stamped on the casing with test-fired bullets.

The reason only one bullet had been fired seemed to be explained by a white hand towel, sooty from gunpowder. The shooter had evidently used it to muffle the sound of the gunshot, but the towel was black and burned where it had been sucked into the muzzle of the gun, making the weapon useless until someone managed to extricate it. With Sheila fighting back—as she apparently did, even with the bullet wound in her face—her killer would have had to look for another weapon. There was an empty spot in the magnetic knife rack on the kitchen wall. She had probably been stabbed with her own knife.

Long after midnight Iorio went home to check on his children and grab a few hours' sleep. At nine o'clock he was at the medical examiner's office to observe the postmortem exam of Sheila Bellush. David Winterhalter of the ME's office, Lieutenant Bruce Whitehead, and Lisa Lanham would also observe. They knew from viewing an X ray that the bullet fired into Sheila's right cheekbone had shattered her jaw before it exited at the base of her neck, leaving fragmented particles behind.

Sheila was photographed in her clothes before the autopsy began. She wore blue jeans with a black belt, a blue thermal short-sleeved shirt, black panties, and a lacy white bra. All of the garments above her waist were saturated with blood.

It was obvious that she had taken pride in her appearance. Her fingernails were freshly polished and her hair shiny clean where it was not stained with blood. She was so slender that it was almost impossible to believe that she had carried four babies at once. During the postmortem examination the scars from her plastic surgery were barely visible. Two tiny well-healed incisions indicated that she had breast implants, and the cesarean and tummy-tuck scars were only thin lines.

Sheila still wore an expensive diamond engagement ring and wedding band and a thick gold bracelet. If her attacker had been bent on robbery, why would he have left them behind?

Chris Iorio bagged the two car keys found in her right front jeans pocket into evidence; they were for the Ford van that was still parked in the driveway on Markridge. He also noted a grocery list and a dollar bill in that pocket.

Lisa Lanham took Sheila's finger- and palm prints for elimination purposes. Every flat surface back in her house had black dust on it from the search for prints.

Dr. Wilson Broussard, Jr., the forensic pathologist who performed the autopsy, pointed out the defense wounds on Sheila's arms and hands. The deepest thrust—probably from the filleting knife—had gone completely through her right hand. Her throat had been savagely cut, from left to right and right to left. The first four-inch slash had severed Sheila's internal right jugular vein. The second was five inches long. It had begun as a superficial cut, but then went deeper, severing the jugular vein on the left side too. The brutal slash ended at the right side of the cervical vertebrae at the C-4 level. It did not appear to have been a paralyzing wound, however.

The single gunshot wound that broke her jaw had bled profusely, but the blood had not spurted from Sheila's throat wounds; it had been from the veins, not from the arteries. Venous blood characteristically bleeds in a steady flow rather than an arterial jet. Although Sheila had ultimately lost most of the blood in her body, it had taken a while for exsanguination (bleeding out) to occur.

As she lay now on the autopsy table, Sheila was still beautiful, her eyes clear and her face serene. Unlike some murder victims, there was no terror etched on her face. She had put up a tremendous fight, but as she died, she had perhaps seen another world—the heaven she had always believed in despite the emotional pain in her life. But that was little comfort for those who were trying to find her killer and for those who loved her.

Chris Iorio asked if Sheila might have lived for a while after she was wounded. Yes, probably. The medical examiner speculated that she might have been saved if someone had gotten there in time.

Sheila had not given up easily. There were other wounds—numerous nonfatal stabs and scrapes, bruises on both knees, and two heavy blunt-force blows to her head that had left her scalp torn and caused her brain to hemorrhage. These were consistent with blows from the butt of a gun.

The Sarasota County detectives would be extremely careful *not* to reveal the extent of Sheila's injuries, nor the cause of death. If they should find someone with guilty knowledge, that information would separate the compulsive confessors from those who knew the truth.

But what was the motivation for such violence? Examination and laboratory tests would reveal no vaginal bruising or sperm to indicate that Sheila had been raped. Nothing had been stolen from her home. But someone had kept beating and stabbing her long after she was fatally injured. And that someone had a heart icy enough to walk away and leave four babies alone with their bleeding mother. Even with life jackets on, they could all have drowned in the pool.

They were too young to be witnesses, but they had seen what happened. One of her tiny boys was already worrying about "Mommy's bad boo-boo," and another said, "The bad man hurt Mommy."

Would they ever again sleep without nightmares?

_____Chapter Twenty-five_____

SAN ANTONIO, Texas, is in a different time zone from Sarasota, Florida—an hour earlier. On the endless afternoon and night of November 7, 1997, there was a great deal of activity in both regions, and understandably, communication was somewhat garbled. The rumors from Sarasota were horrifying, and those in San Antonio who heard the first reports wanted to believe that they weren't true.

At that point in time, Lisa Lanham and the team of Sarasota County forensic technicians were going over the white-and-yellow house on Markridge inch by inch. Other investigators were widening the circle around the murder scene, asking residents if they remembered anything—*anything*—unusual the day before. Ron Albritton and Chris Iorio were questioning Jamie Bellush, and the babies were being tenderly cared for by Stephanie Hayes and other women from the Baptist church. Reporters from Sarasota and St. Petersburg were trying to verify what had happened in time for their deadlines.

Twelve hundred miles away, Allen Blackthorne had spent that first Friday in November doing what he always did on a weekday. He was playing golf—this time at the Bandit golf course near Lake McQueeney with his favorite golf partner, Danny Rocha. Ray Cevallos, another member of their regular foursome, was set to play with them that day, but when he got there, they had teed off without him, and disgusted, he drove away.

Allen had to be home early because he and Maureen were going out that evening for the first time since Jacob's birth by cesarean section on September 23. It was their anniversary, the one they always celebrated; the anniversary of the night Allen asked Maureen to marry him.

November 7. A special day for both of them.

Allen's secretary, Virginia L'Heureux, had volunteered to sit with Brandon and Jacob as her anniversary gift to her employers, and their maid/nanny, Celia Blanco, was also in the house when Allen came home early. Since he had married Maureen, Virginia didn't have as many duties as she once had, although he assured her he still needed an assistant. Sometimes Maureen, Virginia, and Celia watched television together in the afternoons—enjoying especially the antics on the *Jerry Springer Show.*

Allen came home from his golf game and left again shortly thereafter, telling Virginia that he needed to buy Maureen flowers and a present. When he came back bearing gifts, he and Maureen took showers and dressed for their anniversary date. Allen had reservations at Ruth's Chris Steak House, but they didn't plan to go anywhere after dinner; Maureen didn't like to leave her children for long, especially her new baby.

The first hint that something terrible had happened in Florida came through a phone call to the Blackthorne home from Lori Bendseil, one of their attorneys. She phoned Maureen to say that a former associate of hers—who worked with Sheila's attorney, Ken Nunley—had heard a rumor that Sheila was dead.

Virginia recalled that Allen and Maureen gave little credence to that report and went ahead with their plans for the evening. Coincidentally, they encountered Lori and her husband, Ray Perez—the man who had begged Allen not to give up his parental rights two months earlier—at the steakhouse. Lori repeated the now strong rumors from Sarasota. Allen and Maureen reportedly began to wonder if it might be true. Neither expressed grief or horror—not then and not later. Allen and his fourth wife had no love for Sheila, but publicly they denied any real animosity toward her.

When they got home, Allen placed a call to Kim Hall, an RS Medical employee who was assigned to the territory that included Sarasota. He and Kim had spoken on the phone more often than usual during September and October, and now he left a message on her answering machine, asking that she watch the late news in Sarasota and get back to him if there was any coverage on his ex-wife.

Any chance that Sheila's murder was a only a rumor disappeared as Allen and Maureen watched their local TV news at 11 P.M. The screen flickered with views of a white-and-yellow house beneath a sky

roiling with dark clouds. Jamie and Stevie appeared, hugging and crying, as well as a street full of police cars and paramedics' vans. "I will
never forget it," Maureen would recall. "In our living room, sitting on
the couch, I looked at Allen and said, 'Time to get a lawyer.' Everything was just *boom!*"

Allen said later that he was chagrined and alarmed to hear himself named as a prime suspect in his ex-wife's brutal death, which he
said was, of course, ridiculous. He had been in San Antonio all week,
and scores of people had seen him. There was no way he could have
killed Sheila, nor would he want to: "She was the mother of my two
daughters."

Nevertheless, Allen hired one of San Antonio's top criminal defense attorneys the next morning. He would let Roy Barrera, Jr., field
the flurry of questions the news media were tossing at him. And
he supposed he might have to eventually talk to Florida investigators too.

Barrera was an unruffled spokesman, handsome and polished. In
an interview with the San Antonio *Express-News,* he said, "Rumors
were flying that authorities in Sarasota were coming here to arrest
[Allen]." But he had immediately contacted the investigators in Sarasota, and they told him Allen was not a suspect. "I have no clue as to
what happened," Allen's attorney said. "Sooner or later, they'll want
to talk to him. He is as shocked and surprised as anyone else by what
happened."

For all intents and purposes, Stevie and Daryl were orphans now,
but neither Allen nor Maureen made any attempt to contact the girls
in their bereavement. Roy Barrera had advised them not to. Actually,
Stevie was the only daughter who knew at this point that her mother
was dead. Radio and television reports were still being kept from
Daryl, until she could be with her remaining family when she heard
the terrible news.

SHEILA's body temperature, the amount of rigor mortis, and the livid-
ity in her tissues—the purplish red striations on the lower body after
the heart stops beating—all indicated that she had probably been
dead since well before noon on Friday.

Ron Albritton and Chris Iorio checked with the doctors' offices
that Jamie had called on the day Sheila died. They ascertained that
Jamie had been, just as he said, two hours from Sarasota at that time
and seen by a number of receptionists and physicians.

When Iorio returned to the sheriff's office, he learned that a possible eyewitness had been in the Gulf Gate neighborhood Friday

morning. The man reported seeing a strange car. Nervous as he was, Jake Mast had told sheriff's officers about seeing the white sports car with the license plate YBR-62G. He remembered a dark-haired man wearing camouflage clothes who had somehow frightened him. The investigators who conducted the door-to-door canvass had also found two women in the neighborhood who described a stranger walking near Markridge, a well-built, youngish man who had worn what appeared to be fatigues with a variegated camouflage pattern.

Iorio attempted to run the plate number through Florida computers to determine the registered owner. He was frustrated to find that the computers were down. Mast had been so busy memorizing the letters and numbers that he hadn't noticed the color of the plate. When the state computers were back on-line, there were no hits on YBR-62G. Either it was an out-of-state car, or Mast had been mistaken on one or more digits. That didn't mean they couldn't identify the owner eventually; they would just have to sort through many states and endless combinations.

At 2:56 on Saturday afternoon, Iorio returned a call he had received from a Bexar County, Texas, investigator named Fred McDermott. He got McDermott's answering machine and left a message, wondering what the Texas detective might have to tell him. He knew that both Jamie Bellush and Sheila's daughter Stevie had talked about bitter feelings between Allen Blackthorne and the victim, but acrimony and recrimination weren't that unusual in a divorce situation. Besides, Blackthorne apparently had a number of people who would swear he was in San Antonio all day on Friday.

Detective Cecilia Francis told Albritton and Iorio that she believed the pool man that Jamie had mentioned—Marty Cecchi—might be a viable suspect. She said he had, indeed, lived in the Markridge house just before the Bellushes moved in and knew the layout well; he also worked for them in pool maintenance and lawn care. Moreover, Francis had found Cecchi extremely nervous when she questioned him and felt a second interview was warranted.

Cecchi was a familiar sight in the Gulf Gate neighborhood and wouldn't have stood out. He might well have noted how attractive Sheila was when he worked on her pool and would probably even be aware that Jamie was out of town. Or he might even have had his eye on Sheila's teenage daughters, who looked a little older than their true age.

Cecchi was very jumpy when Iorio approached him for a second interview. He acknowledged that he *was* familiar with the family who lived in the house he once rented, although he didn't know their names. He did know Stevie and Daryl by name, however. But Cecchi, who was about thirty, was able to give Iorio an alibi for most of Friday, and he agreed willingly to have his fingerprints taken for elimination purposes. He also let Lisa Lanham pluck a few hairs from his head and didn't balk when Iorio accompanied him to a restroom to observe him while he gave up pubic hair exemplars. Cecchi posed for photographs, and there were no obvious bruises or scratches on his body. However, they would have to check out his alibis for Friday before he could be completely dismissed as a suspect.

Since Sheila and Jamie had moved so recently from Texas, the license-plate number on the white Mitsubishi was entered into Texas computers. This time there was a match. The printout that came back showed that the plate belonged to a white Mitsubishi Eclipse with a registered owner: Maria Del Toro of La Pryor, Texas. La Pryor was a small town west of San Antonio, near Eagle Pass on the Mexican border. Maria Del Toro was a woman in her sixties, and she had not reported her car as stolen.

What was her car doing in Sarasota, Florida, parked a block away from the scene of a brutal murder?

If this investigation was a paint-by-numbers picture, the swaths of color were scattered so far apart that there was no image emerging that made any kind of sense. Even so, Albritton and Iorio kept moving ahead, convinced that they would find closer links.

And they did. Sometimes the strongest witnesses appear out of nowhere—or at least from a direction investigators have yet to home in on. Sergeant Lowen from the Sarasota County District One Office called Iorio to say that an employee of a medical supply company wanted to talk to the detectives. Iorio and Cecilia Francis drove to Kim Hall's house at 11 A.M. on Sunday morning, November 9. Kim said she worked for the RS Medical company as an independent sales rep. The company sold electromuscular stimulators and part of her job included instructing patients who had prescriptions for the devices.

"I don't know Allen Blackthorne at all well," she began, "but he came to Sarasota once in May 1995 to ride with me for a day and 'beat the drum' for the company. Since then, I've seen him at sales meetings, although he didn't attend many."

"Was he your supervisor?" Iorio asked.

Kim Hall shook her head. "I saw him in Maui when I was one of the top ten salespeople in the company and won a trip to Hawaii. I met him, his wife Maureen, and their little boy Brandon in the hotel lobby."

1

Sheila Bellush believed in true love and family, but she lived with a terrible premonition.

Verma Gene Willams Anderson, Sheila's mother, in her younger days in Mississippi.

2

Major Frances Anthony Walsh, Jr., Gene's second husband and the father of her girls: Cathy, Sheila, and Kerry.

3

Sheila Leigh Walsh,
Gene's most petite—and
stubborn—daughter.

4

Don Smith,
Gene's third
husband. Her
girls considered
him their real
"Dad."

5

Kerry (left) and Sheila were very close, but Kerry distrusted Allen Van Houte, even though her sister was deeply in love with him.

"Guy" Van Houte (right) with his father, Robert. Early on, Guy quit living up to his father's expectations.

Allen Van Houte, about seven, was abandoned by his father before he was born.

8

Guy Van Houte with two of his sons from his third marriage, Randy (left), and Bruce (right).

9

Allen (right) at fifteen with a friend. An awkward, nerdy kid with big ears, he seemed to fit in nowhere.

Allen's mother, Karen, with two of his half-siblings, Marilyn and Randy. Left with one arm, Karen could still paint and train horses.

11

Allen (left) seventeen, with his uncle Tom Oliver. The Olivers gave him a home for a few years until he moved on.

Allen holds his baby daughter, Stevie, his first child with Sheila. They are in Gene's doll workshop. (1984)

Sheila on a plane to Hawaii. She was not as starry-eyed over Allen as she once was—but she agreed to leave the mainland with him, hoping things would get better. (1984)

1

Allen, on a cruise ship, hardly resembled the awkward teenager he once was. He was on his way to becoming a multimillionaire.

Kerry (left) and Sheila in Hawaii (1985). Kerry was shocked to find her sister pregnant for the second time, rail-thin, and bruised.

16

Sheila (right) and her sister Cathy, after Sheila escaped from Allen and drove home to Oregon. Emaciated and battered, she looked twenty years older than she was.

Sheila and Stevie pose by the pool at the Brandon Oaks apartment complex. Sheila, now divorced, fought Allen in court for support for her girls. It was an endless battle. (1990)

18

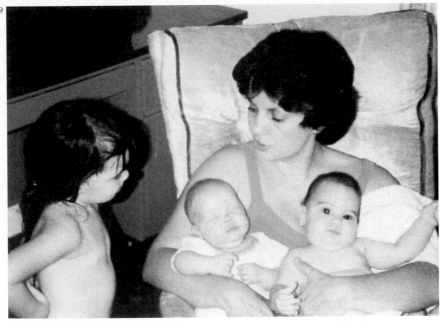

After Sue Tuffiash, Sheila's dear friend at Brandon Oaks, was murdered by her ex-husband, her own fears grew stronger. There seemed no place to hide.

Stevie (left), Sheila, and Daryl at Christmas, 1991. Sheila seemed happy, but she was terrified that Allen would take her girls away from her.

Sheila finally found happiness with Jamie Bellush in 1995. Through in vitro fertilization, she conceived not one—but four—babies.

The Bellush family in 1997: (left rear) Jamie, Sheila, Stevie (standing), and Daryl; and the quadruplets (left to right) Joey, Courtney, Timmy, and Frankie.

3

The Florida room in the Bellushs' rental house in Sarasota. Detectives found the quadruplets' dry diapers on this table. The babies wore only life jackets.

A Sarasota County Sheriff's photo showed the terrible struggle Sheila put up after being shot and stabbed until she fell, dying, at her kitchen door. Stevie found her mother's body.

The bloodied phone gave mute evidence that Sheila almost managed to call for help, but it was too late and she had lost too much blood.

Joey Del Toro's Mitsubishi Eclipse was a treasure trove of physical evidence when investigators searched it in Austin, Texas, the weekend after Sheila's murder 1,200 miles away.

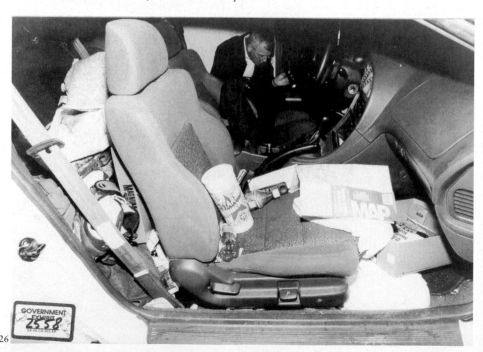

Allen Blackthorne, Sheila's combative ex-husband, soon became a prime suspect in her murder—even though he never left San Antonio on the day she died in Sarasota.

27

28

Allen, worth a reported $50 million, lived with his new wife, Maureen, and their two young sons in this lavish "Pink Palace" in San Antonio. At forty, he no longer worked, preferring to play golf every weekday.

Danny Rocha, a gambler and golf hustler, often heard Allen complain that Sheila was beating his two older daughters and had to be stopped.

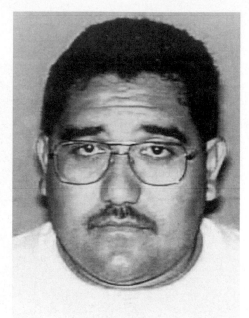

29

30

Before he started betting on golf games with Allen, Danny, his wife, and three small sons shared this modest home with his aunt Otilia.

Six months later Danny was able to buy this large house in a fine neighborhood. Winning thousands of dollars a day on the golf course, he obviously owed Allen big-time.

Sammy Gonzales was not the "sharpest knife in the drawer," but he had connections.

Joey Del Toro, a ladies' man and one-time football star, turned to cocaine. Was he Sheila's killer? Why would he drive 1,200 miles to murder a woman who was a complete stranger to him?

Sarasota Sheriff's Detectives Chris Iorio (left) and Lieutenant Ron Albritton on the grounds of the Sarasota Baptist Church. They were at the scene of Sheila's murder and worked for three years to solve the case.

Forensic Technician Lisa Lanham headed the crime-scene search to find clues to Sheila's killer. She took four-hundred photographs that were essential to the detectives.

Texas Ranger Gary De Los Santos entered the probe of Sheila's murder to offer a temporary assist to Sarasota detectives. He became the prime Texas investigator and worked on the case for three years.

Texas Ranger Analyst Melanie Schramm (left), Sergeant John Martin and Lieutenant Ray Cano of Company D in San Antonio helped to discover who was really responsible for Sheila's death.

Florida State Attorney Charlie Roberts, along with fellow State Attorney Henry Lee, prosecuted Danny Rocha for his part in a deadly plot.

Jesse Salazar (left) of the San Antonio Police Department, FBI Special Agent Mike Appleby, and San Antonio detective Richard Urbanek arrested Allen Blackthorne as he strolled off the golf course at the Oak Hills Country Club.

Allen and Maureen Blackthorne on their way to court in a civil case brought by Jamie Bellush. They told reporters they were confident that they would prove Allen had nothing whatsoever to do with his ex-wife's murder.

Assistant U.S. Attorneys Richard Durbin (left) and John Murphy joined with Bexar County Chief Criminal Deputy Prosecutor Michael Bernard (right) to face a million-dollar defense team hired by Allen Blackthorne.

Federal Judge Edward Prado presided over Allen Blackthorne's explosive trial, tempering his knowledge of the law with humor that lessened the tension.

43

The John H. Wood U.S. Courthouse in San Antonio, where Allen Blackthorne faced a jury of his peers. The trial was held in a courtroom with state-of-the-art electronics.

This photograph is one of several prints found by an FBI search team in Allen Blackthorne's office. The pictures of Daryl's birthday party were given to a hit man so he could identify Sheila Bellush.

The Bladorn family today. Rick and Kerry with their children. Back row (left to right): Daryl, Rick, Kerry, and Kelly. Front row (left to right): Christopher, Ryan, and Patrick.

Deputy U. S. Marshal Bobby Hogeland led Allen Blackthorne from the
Wackenhut jail van to the federal courthouse during his trial in June 2000.

Since Allen Blackthorne was only an acquaintance, Hall said she was surprised when he'd paged her in September 1997, only two months earlier. "It came in as an urgent page," she told the detectives. "I remember it was September 22 because it was my birthday."

"What did he want?"

"He said his ex-wife had stolen his kids and fled the state of Texas with them. He said he had to serve her with some legal papers in a child-custody battle. He was adamant that he had to find her immediately. Her name was Sheila Bellush. He wanted me to help find her. He was very upset. He told me that his daughter Daryl was only eleven, and she had called him from a phone booth near Lido Beach and sounded disoriented. He wanted me to go there and look for her."

"Did you agree?" Iorio asked.

"No. I said that wasn't a very good idea," Kim said. "I told him I didn't think it was part of my job to look for people in Sarasota. I suggested that he call the police or hire a private investigator."

For the moment Allen had agreed to do that, but then he tried one more time to convince Kim Hall to spy on Sheila for him. He asked her to drive to the Baptist church on Sunday and wait in the parking lot until she saw a family with quadruplets. Then he wanted her to follow them home and get their address.

Kim demurred again, and Allen finally agreed that spying wasn't her job. He asked one favor, however. "He wanted me to tear the PI section out of the yellow pages of the phone book and fax them to him," Kim said. She agreed to do that and said she sent Blackthorne page 578 from the 1997 GTE yellow pages.

A day or so later, she told the detectives, she had received an Airborne Express delivery at her residence. Curious, she opened the package and found two videotapes. "I looked at the tapes, and they were news reports from Texas that showed Sheila Bellush as a suspect in the battery of one of her children. Allen wanted me to know what Sheila looked like so I could identify her if I saw her."

"Was that the last time you heard from him about looking for Sheila?" Iorio asked.

"No. Allen left another message. I had an appointment at a doctor's office, and I've learned the best way to get their attention is to feed them," Kim said with a smile. "So I often take lunch in to the staff before I demonstrate our muscle device. Somehow Allen found me there on my cell phone. He was very excited and he said, 'I have an address! It's on South Tamiami Trail. *Please* go check it out and see if that's where Sheila is living.' "

Kim Hall was chagrined that Allen wasn't getting her message to leave her out of his personal dramas, but she agreed because the address happened to be right across the street from the doctor's office. She called Allen back and told him it wasn't a house at all; it was a Mail Boxes, Etc. outlet.

"I know," Allen said glumly. "The PI just told us that."

Allen left Kim alone after that, until November 7. "Two days ago, on Friday night, my caller ID showed that I had a call from a Texas area code," she told the detectives. "The display said it was Maureen Weingeist calling—that's Allen's wife. There was no message left, though. There *was* a message from the same number left at five minutes after ten. It was Allen's secretary, Virginia. She said that Allen needed me to call back as soon as I could. He wanted me to watch the eleven-o'clock news, and if I couldn't call him back that night, to be sure and call him in the morning. I didn't call him until about nine thirty the next day."

Kim reached Maureen first, who said bluntly, "Sheila's dead."

"*What?*" Kim gasped.

"His ex is dead," Maureen repeated. "Here's Allen."

"Oh, my God," Kim blurted. "Allen, are you okay?"

"Allen said that his ex-wife had been murdered," Kim told Iorio, "and he was 'just sick' about it. I asked him if he was going to come and get his kids."

Kim felt that Allen was faking an emotional reaction. "There was no real despair in his voice or any kind of sympathy for his ex-wife," she said. "His voice sounded very level. Then he said, 'Sheila loved her coke.' "

"That's a high-crime area there, isn't it?" Allen had asked her, and Kim told Iorio she felt he was trying to put words in her mouth, because Sarasota was not a high-crime area.

The morning after Sheila's murder, Allen was eager to know what the Sarasota *Herald-Tribune* had to say about it. He asked Kim to get her paper and read its coverage of the murder aloud to him. She did.

"He kept saying, 'This is making me sick' as I read it," Kim said, "but he didn't *sound* sick." When she was finished, she asked if Allen wanted her to send the newspaper to him, but he said he didn't need to see it.

Chris Iorio took photographs of Kim Hall's caller ID display, showing the calls made from Allen Blackthorne's house and the times they were placed.

It seemed bizarre. Blackthorne sounded more like a playwright waiting for the reviews after opening night than he did a grieving ex-husband. He had made Kim Hall read every word of the newspaper coverage and all the sidebars on Sheila's murder. And he never told her that he had given up custody and all rights to his daughters many weeks before he called to ask her to find their mother's address.

What good would Sheila's address have done him at that point? He had no legal right to contact Stevie and Daryl or to visit them. He had absolutely no right to know where they were living. Chris Iorio believed that Allen Blackthorne must have had some other reason to locate the Bellushes.

_____Chapter Twenty-six_____

KERRY AND RICK BLADORN arrived in Sarasota on Saturday afternoon, November 8. On Sunday morning they waited at the Baptist church with Jamie and the Reverends Mike Landry and Ames Pittman. Daryl was on her way from the Eckerd Camp, accompanied by three counselors who told her only that there were "family problems" they couldn't discuss. Daryl, like Jamie, was afraid that something was wrong with one of the quadruplets. The whole family had been so worried when they seemed too small to survive. Afterward, when they could crawl and walk, both Stevie and Daryl were taught to guard the babies' safety; all of the family had to keep an eye on them, continually counting, so that one of them wouldn't slip away and be injured, or even kidnapped.

When Daryl walked into the private meeting room in the church, she felt the tension in the air at once. Her eyes lit on her aunt Kerry and uncle Rick, and she was certain that something awful had happened to one of the babies. She didn't notice at first that her mother wasn't there.

Daryl looked around the room, bewildered, until Jamie grabbed her hand and put her on his lap. "Honey," he began slowly, "I hate to tell you this, but your mother . . . your mother has been brutally murdered."

Daryl reacted violently, leaping from Jamie's lap and running behind a couch, where she curled into a fetal position and sobbed as if her heart were breaking. She had never in her life thought that she would lose her mother, and her stepfather's words had shocked her beyond anything she had ever known.

The others in the room waited, sensing that Daryl had to cry for as long as she needed to and that no comforting would help. Finally she was able to focus on her relatives and the pastors, and with her voice breaking, she whispered, "I don't want to say this, but I think my dad did it. You need to tell the detectives that."

Daryl said almost exactly the same words that her sister Stevie had said earlier, voicing the same suspicions that Jamie had. A second husband might be expected to suspect the first husband who had caused so much dissension, but these girls were flesh of Allen Blackthorne's flesh. He was their natural father, but they both spoke of him as a man capable of the cruelest kind of murder.

Sarasota County detective Mark Brewer was chosen to speak with Sheila's two older daughters. Brewer's regular assignment was to investigate crimes against children, and he knew how to talk to frightened kids. He wasn't a large man, and he was not at all threatening. Daryl told him why she felt her father was behind her mother's murder. She admitted that, although she was forbidden to do so, she hadn't cut off communications with Allen. Lonely at the Y, and then feeling isolated at the Eckerd Camp—Camp E-Ninni-Hasse—Daryl had called her father at the 800 number he gave her, and both he and Maureen had urged her to stay in touch. Allen told her that he was worried about her, that he needed to know where she was so he could be sure she was okay. And he was just as insistent about knowing where her mother was living. How could he help Daryl, he argued, if he didn't know her mother and Jamie's address?

In truth, Daryl didn't know the Bellushes' address. She visited there on weekends, but she didn't know the house number, and she wasn't even sure about the name of the street. All she knew that fall of 1997 was that she couldn't live full-time with her mother and her siblings, and her father was a long way away. The 800 number Allen gave her was a lifeline. When things got really lonesome, she could call her daddy. She had just turned twelve, and though her father explained to her that he had been forced to give up his rights as her parent, she didn't really understand that. He was being so nice to her on the phone, assuring her that he missed her, that he was trying to find her.

Sheila and Jamie had told Daryl that she mustn't give out information about where they lived, and she tried to keep that secret. But gradually Allen winnowed information out of her. She found phone booths where she could call, and once, she told him that she was with a group of children at a place called Lido Beach in Florida. That didn't seem so bad; it wasn't where her mother lived. She also called from the Baptist church and from another phone booth near her mother's house.

Allen asked her to describe what she saw there, and Daryl told him about a Laundromat, a minimart, and an ice-cream store, just little bits of information that didn't seem like betraying her mother and stepfather. She was a child, and she didn't realize how many clues she was giving away. But now that her mother was dead, Daryl came to the horrible conclusion that she might have led her father right to her mother. The last time she talked to Allen was in mid-October, and he told her he wanted to come and see her for Christmas. "But how can I do that, sweetheart," he asked, "if I don't know where to find you?" And Daryl was so happy to know her daddy was coming that she forgot the huge secret she was not supposed to tell. She gave him a street name. She knew it was "Mark—something," and she described the house, white with yellow trim on the windows and the front door.

Allen had always been the consummate salesman—persuasive and charming. Even adults believed him; using his charisma and salesmanship, he had made a fortune. One twelve-year-old girl was no match for him when he was determined to learn Sheila's location.

Once Daryl told him the name of the street, she never heard from him again. Even so, she clung to her belief that he was going to come and see her at Christmas.

Not any longer.

Mark Brewer interviewed Kerry and Rick Bladorn. He learned more about the terrible marriage that Sheila had lived through with Allen and of Allen's threats that he would never let her take his children away from him.

With his world ripped to pieces, Jamie was a man on fire. His parents and siblings were extremely supportive as he sobbed and wondered aloud how he could ever take care of four babies by himself. They assured him he could come home to Newton, New Jersey, to the big, cozy house on the lakeshore where he had grown up. They would help him raise the children, and so would other members of their family and their friends.

Jamie planned to take Stevie with him to Newton, but he couldn't imagine taking Daryl. In his mind, it was always Daryl who had sparked so many of their troubles during the summer just past. She had been sneaky about telling the Adays that her mother beat her. She had been so determined to see her real father that Sheila was half crazy with her lies and exaggerations. If Daryl hadn't gone tattling to the neighbors, Sheila wouldn't have been arrested and brought into court, and they probably wouldn't have had to move to Florida.

Somehow Jamie could not see that Daryl was only a child, a child manipulated by a master. When he learned that she might have been responsible for telling Allen where they lived, he said flatly that she could never live with him, Stevie, Frankie, Joey, Timmy, and Courtney.

"Jamie expected that Daryl would go back to Camp E-Ninni-Hasse," Kerry recalled. "Rick talked to Jamie and found out that he never expected to see Daryl again. She wasn't going to New Jersey— ever. The Eckerd Camp could take care of her."

Tragedy piled onto tragedy, and Jamie was suffused with rage and self-pity. He had found the love of his life, his beautiful Sheila, mother of his four perfect babies, and now it was all gone.

Rick Bladorn was a softhearted, loving man. He didn't believe for a minute that Jamie was serious about abandoning Daryl; it was only his shock and sorrow talking.

As Sheila's family wrestled with the emotional aftermath of her murder, the Sarasota sheriff's investigators worked nearly around the clock looking for her killer. The homicide probe was accelerating, and a shadowy pattern *was* emerging. They learned that Maria Del Toro of La Pryor, Texas, had no reason to report her Mitsubishi Eclipse missing. It was not a car she herself drove. She had purchased it for her grandson, José Luis, who was called Joey.

Joey was only nine months old when his parents went off on their own pursuit of happiness and left the little brown-eyed boy behind. For twenty years Maria and her husband raised him as their own child. They were, perhaps, more indulgent than they had been with his father. Joey was so handsome, so full of fun and, in his high school years, such a wonderful athlete. He was a football star, and all the girls were crazy about him.

Yes, he got into trouble sometimes, but all he had to do was sweet-talk his grandmother the way he sweet-talked all the females in his life, and she couldn't resist giving him what he wanted. Even after she was widowed, Maria managed to pay for his college and buy the other things he wanted. The white Eclipse was one of the things he'd wanted.

"He was raised in a Christian home," she said, "with much love. José Luis is a very happy young man with many friends."

Among those friends were a plethora of girlfriends, and none of them seemed to be jealous. Joey Del Toro was a bumblebee buzzing from one flower to the next. They were all glad to see him when he came back to them. In the autumn of 1997 Joey had a job at a weight-loss spa down near the border at Corpus Christi, where he was popular with the older ladies who came to shed some of their fat and be pampered. In a white T-shirt that showed his muscles and tight pants that hugged his thighs, he gave them something pretty to look at.

Joey had had a little trouble over drugs—his grandmother wasn't sure just what it was about—so he was supposed to go to jail on the weekends until he worked off his fine. She thought that was where he was on the weekend of November 7. When she learned that he had called in with an excuse why he couldn't report in that weekend, his grandmother told Texas Ranger Sal Abreo that Joey was probably with one of his girlfriends. She gave the ranger some names and addresses in Austin. He might be with Anna Morales on East Oltorf Street, or with Carol Arreola at her apartment at 4501 East Riverside Drive.

Austin was only about an hour's drive from San Antonio, at least for someone who drove as fast as Joey Del Toro. Texas was big country, and no one considered traveling to Austin or "Corpus" or even Houston as much of a trip.

Working with Detective Manny Fuentes of the Austin Police Department, Texas Rangers from the Department of Public Safety staked out the addresses where Joey Del Toro might show up. And on Sunday, November 9, there it was. The white Mitsubishi Eclipse—covered with road dust, its interior jammed with junk, clothes, and garbage—was parked in front of Carol Arreola's apartment. None of the officers on the stakeouts had seen Joey himself, but they wasted no time in asking for a search warrant for the sleek white car with the license plate YBR-62G. They didn't expect to find much that would tie Del Toro to Sheila Bellush's murder—any self-respecting killer would certainly have dumped obvious evidence. But most killers had no concept of the danger of trace evidence—prints and hairs and fibers. And *that* was what they devoutly hoped to find.

In Sarasota, mourners were planning a service for Sheila. Her death was so unexpected that it would be Thursday, November 13, before all of her friends from far away could be there. The Sarasota Baptist Church was a massive building with a sanctuary that could accommodate hundreds. Even so, Pastor Mike Landry hoped that it would be large enough.

Stevie and the quadruplets continued to stay in Stephanie Hayes's house, Daryl went back to Eckerd Camp until the funeral, and Rick and Kerry and Gene and Don were lodged at the Hampton Inn, where Jamie was staying. They were all in limbo, as if somehow their worlds might start up again and none of what they were living through was really true.

INITIALLY it was difficult for detectives in two states to determine who would have jurisdiction over the Sheila Bellush case. Allen Blackthorne was the prime suspect, but there were witnesses who could verify that he had never left San Antonio on the day of the murder.

"I had concerns," Ron Albritton said, "that if there was a conspiracy that involved people in Texas, it might mean that the crime that occurred started out there and just ended in Sarasota. So I wasn't sure if it was Texas authorities assisting us or if we were assisting them. Or were we doing a joint investigation?"

It appeared to be the last option. With the Florida investigation well established, Albritton and Iorio packed their bags, and long before dawn on Monday morning, November 10, they caught a flight to Dallas. Everything they had found thus far pointed toward Texas as the state where they might find Sheila's killer.

Arriving in Dallas at 10:20, Albritton hurried to a pay phone and asked Texas Ranger crime analyst Bobbi Shaw, to check out any information on a José Del Toro, a.k.a. Juan Del Toro, and to have his photographs and fingerprints overnighted from Bexar County to the Sarasota County Sheriff's Office. Albritton also asked that Florida State Attorney Charlie Roberts be briefed on the information they had gathered so far, and checked to see if anyone had made contact with Detective Fred McDermott of Bexar County. And he wanted all the eyewitness reports of those who had seen the white car in Gulf Gate validated.

It wasn't easy coordinating a murder investigation in two different states, but it certainly appeared that the elusive Joey Del Toro had been in both Florida and Texas during the vital time periods from Thursday to Saturday. A maid at the Hampton Inn in Sarasota had found a .45-caliber bullet in a room she was cleaning, and she turned it in to the front desk. The new motel wasn't far from Gulf Gate, and on the night before Sheila was killed, one of its rooms had been occupied by a José Del Toro. He had shown his driver's license to prove that he was of age and could rent a hotel room.

By noon on that Monday, Del Toro's fingerprints and palm prints were faxed from Austin to Sarasota to use for comparison with some latent prints found in the utility room of the Markridge Road murder house. If the fax wasn't clear enough for absolute identification, copies would arrive by the next morning. A lay-down of photographs of young Hispanic men with short hair was prepared, with a photo of Del Toro included in the number three position.

The Sarasota investigators knew what Del Toro looked like, but they had no idea what his connection might be to Sheila Bellush, or to Allen Blackthorne for that matter. It would take some time to fill in the blanks on Joey.

Albritton and Iorio began by contacting two Texas Rangers who had been sitting on the address where the white Mitsubishi Eclipse was parked. Ranger Sergeant Joe Hutson and Ranger James Denman assured them that the car hadn't moved since at least the night before. Hutson had watched it continually, and no one had approached it.

"Before we got there," Iorio admitted, "I didn't even know that there still *were* Texas Rangers; I'd only seen them in western movies. But they were great, and we learned to respect them in a hurry."

The Texas Rangers are legendary in their state. They work under the auspices of the Texas Department of Public Safety, but there is a special luster to their badges, and their awesome reputation is un-equaled by any other state law-enforcement agency. At any given time there are only 107 Texas Rangers, including supervisors. Unless a ranger retires or dies in service, there are no openings. Since the days when they protected Texas from Indian warriors, Hispanic invaders, or renegade white men, the rangers have been considered the cream of the crop, lawmen who can work alone if they have to—and often do.

The favorite folktale about Texas Rangers stems from the last century, when there was a ferocious riot in the border city of El Paso. The townspeople called for help from the rangers and waited expec-tantly for the train bearing reinforcements to arrive. One lone ranger stepped from the train. Asked where the rest of his force was, he smiled thinly. "One riot? One ranger," he replied, and then set about cleaning up the streets of El Paso.

More than a century later Joe Hutson and James Denman wore the familiar ten-gallon Texas Ranger hat and the distinctive star badge. They were there to help in the murder probe any way they could, although they rode in squad cars now and not on horseback.

Albritton and Iorio arrived at the apartment on East Riverside in Austin at 3:30 Monday afternoon and were introduced to a pretty Hispanic woman in her early twenties. Her name was Carol Arreola, and she invited the investigators into the apartment she shared with two roommates, Olga Gonzalez and Keren Martin. She was very cooperative, explaining that she was a criminal justice major in col-lege. She signed waivers giving permission for her apartment to be searched. Nevertheless, the investigators set about obtaining a search warrant. None of them was willing to risk losing evidence that might be considered "fruit of the poisoned tree" if a clever defense lawyer nitpicked about the lack of a warrant.

Carol Arreola said that she knew Joey Del Toro, but that he didn't live in the apartment. He never had. But he had stopped by her place over the past several days. On Saturday morning she gave him a key to her apartment—she knew him well enough to trust him, even though she and her roomates would be away for most of the weekend. She said she recognized Joey's car, parked in front of her apartment, when she returned on Sunday night, but Joey had apparently left.

Olga Gonzalez recalled seeing Joey on Thursday morning. He had come to see Carol, but she wasn't there, so Olga left for class, leaving Joey in their apartment.

Neither girl knew where Joey had gone after Thursday morning, but Olga said she came home on Sunday night and was sure he had stayed there because their apartment was a mess. His sloppiness was a bone of contention between Carol and her roommates; they didn't care if he left his stuff in Carol's room, but they were annoyed when he left signs of partying in the rest of their neat apartment. Olga had picked up the clothing Joey left around and thrown it on the floor of Carol's room.

"Does this Joey Del Toro use drugs?" Albritton asked.

"I've seen him smoke marijuana and snort cocaine."

The investigators headed for Carol Arreola's bedroom, studiously ignoring a framed burlap bag stamped 50 KILOS, SUPERIOR QUALITY SEEDLESS MARIJUANA, ORGANICALLY GROWN IN CALIFORNIA, U.S.A. that hung on the wall outside her door. They weren't on a drug raid; they were looking for a killer.

Carol's room was small, economically furnished with a metal bed, a desk, and wicker-and-glass knickknack shelves with photos, candles, and stuffed animals. There was a Mexican sun-god plaque over her bed and a framed print of Edvard Munch's *The Scream* on one wall. The books stacked in a cubbyhole in her desk were textbooks: *Criminal Law,* and *Arrest, Search and Seizure,* as well as other volumes familiar to cops.

The one jarring note in Carol's room was a pile of clothing on the beige carpet. There was a khaki duffel bag with heavy military boots sticking out, T-shirts, boxer shorts, jeans, and something that sent a thrill along Albritton's and Iorio's nerves—clothing made of the familiar green-black-beige-brown amorphous shapes of camouflage wear.

Carol followed the detectives to the Austin Police Department to give a formal statement about Joey Del Toro. As they did with all their interviews on this murder case, Albritton and Iorio videotaped her statement. She said she had known Joey Del Toro since the previous December, and they dated, and were still dating, but only as "friends." Iorio doubted that was true, but he didn't press her. It didn't matter.

Asked about the last time she had seen Del Toro before he came to her apartment on Saturday, Carol said he'd come by on Thursday, or perhaps Wednesday. It was some time between noon and 3:00 P.M. He had been with his cousin Sammy Gonzales. She knew Sammy slightly and believed he worked at a golf range in San Antonio. He drove a black pickup truck.

Carol saw Joey again on Saturday at a girlfriend's house, and had given him her apartment key because he needed a place to stay. "I told him he knew the rules," she added. But from the looks of her apartment, Joey hadn't paid much attention; he had trashed it as he always did.

On Monday, the day this interview took place, Carol heard from Joey again at about 2:30 A.M. He was phoning to ask a favor. "He wanted me to get rid of the clothes and boots he left in my apartment," she said, "and a duffel bag that was in his car. He said I should make all those things 'disappear.' "

"Those were the clothes we saw in your bedroom?" Iorio asked.

She nodded. Because she was preparing for a career in criminal justice, Carol said she didn't want to get herself in trouble. She didn't know why Joey seemed so nervous during his last call, but he sounded as if he was crying as he begged her to dispose of his things. Obviously, she had not thrown his clothes away, and she said she hadn't touched his car either. As far as she knew, everything was just as he left it.

"Why do you think we're talking to you, Carol?" Chris Iorio asked.

"I feel that maybe Joey's involved in a very serious crime," she answered.

"Do you have any direct knowledge of a crime?"

"Joey called me on Friday evening," Carol said slowly. "He told me he had done something very wrong, but that's all he said. He told me he was in Atlanta, calling from his cell phone. He asked me to call his mother [really his grandmother] and charge a flight from Atlanta to Austin. I did talk to her, and she said someone had called her already about charging an airplane ticket on her credit card, but she wouldn't do it."

"When did the phone calls from Joey start?"

"They began about six p.m. on Friday the seventh, and he kept calling me from his cell phone. He was very insistent about getting that flight, and he said he was going to book it in Sammy's name, but that he'd be using the ticket. I finally asked him what he was going to do with his car, and he said he was going to leave it in the Atlanta airport."

Carol had suggested that if Joey was too tired to drive, he should go somewhere and sleep, but he said he was going to drive straight back to Texas. He had been driving a lot, apparently. "He said he had done something he shouldn't have done, but he wouldn't tell me what. I felt very nervous about it."

Chris Iorio saw that Carol Arreola was, indeed, nervous. Asked what Joey did for a living, she thought he collected money "from doctors and lawyers at a golf course Sammy was involved with. If Joey's in any kind of trouble, Sammy would know about it." From time to time, Joey had hinted to her about being involved in some organization so powerful that he couldn't get out of it. "He said they were important people at the country club," Carol told the detectives, "and they wouldn't let him get out."

Iorio asked Carol if she would take a polygraph examination, and she agreed at once. He asked her if she would lie for Joey, even if it meant she might go to jail.

"No, sir, I would not."

Obviously Joey Del Toro had no shortage of female friends. Anna Morales, rumored to be his current girlfriend, had called Carol's earlier on Monday and asked Olga Gonzalez if she could drop by and pick up some clothes that Joey had left. Olga had told her to come ahead, but Anna never showed up.

Anna Morales talked with Iorio and Joe Hutson. She said she and Joey were dating and volunteered that she had information about a homicide he was involved in.

"Do you know what kind of trouble José is in?"

"Yes."

"Can you tell us the whole story?" Iorio asked.

"The *whole* story?"

The two detectives nodded.

Anna was a talkative girl, and it took her a while to get to the point. "Joey told me that he had to go visit his cousin and he would be back in three or four days, and he and I were then supposed to go to a party in Park Station, but he told me that something had come up. He had to go out of town. I asked him why, and he said it was for business."

Anna suspected Joey might be cheating on her, and she peeked into his wallet. She didn't find any girls' phone numbers, but she did find $700 and two packets of cocaine. When she confronted him about the cocaine, Joey told her it was for a friend.

"Was it crack cocaine?" Iorio asked.

"No, it was powder cocaine that hadn't been cut yet."

Asked if Joey had called her from Florida, Anna nodded. "My caller ID showed it was a minimart called Sun Haven."

Anna hadn't saved the number, and she'd never heard of Sun Haven. But Iorio knew right where it was. It was close to Gulf Gate in Sarasota. He called the District One station back in Sarasota and asked detectives to follow up on the information with a photo of Del Toro.

Anna had also received several calls from Joey on the night of November 7, but she wasn't home. Her girlfriend Annette had answered the phone, and Joey asked Annette to call the jail and tell them that he wouldn't be able to report in for his weekend stay. He wanted her to tell them that one of his relatives in California had died. But the jail wouldn't take an excuse from Annette, so Joey said he'd make a call from his cell phone. Joey Del Toro was leaving a phone trail a mile wide or, more accurately, 1200 miles long.

Anna had finally located Joey at Sammy Gonzales's sister's house. "I told him that he was going to have to turn himself in for whatever he did. If he didn't, please don't come to my place, because I didn't want to be involved."

Sergeant Joe Hutson asked Anna if Joey had asked her to get rid of his clothes in Carol Arreola's apartment, and to clean out his car. She nodded. "He wanted me to burn his clothes and the other stuff. He also said to get the gun from a bag in his car, a green bag. It was a chrome automatic, with three clips. I went over there to do it, but I saw all the police cars and I just drove on by."

Anna recalled that before he went to Florida, Joey had visited Sammy Gonzales. "When he came back, he was real happy and excited because he had to go to Florida for a few days."

"Did Sammy go with him?" Iorio asked.

"I don't know."

Anna said she had some phone numbers where Joey might be

reached; she felt he would probably be with his cousin Sammy in San Antonio, or that he might even have gone to Mexico. She was sure, though, that he wouldn't stay there long. "Joey likes the good life, and he can't live that kind of life in Mexico."

Whoever Joey Del Toro was, and whatever his connection to Sheila Bellush, he was certainly rising rapidly to the top of the detectives' murder-suspect list.

Frightened, Carol Arreola kept adding to her statement. Back in front of Iorio's video camera, she admitted asking Joey what he had been up to when she gave him her apartment key on Saturday, November 8. "He told me he had done something like a hit man would do. He said he went to Florida, and he knew what it looked like to be looking into a woman's eyes that he was just about to harm . . ." She didn't know quite what to make of his confession, but Carol believed the incident Joey described to her had happened about two weeks earlier. Joey also told her the woman he hurt was having problems with her ex-husband, who was the person who ordered the hit.

Iorio and Albritton believed that Joey Del Toro was describing the murder of Sheila Bellush, a murder that had happened only the day before the bizarre conversation Carol had with Joey.

Carol Arreola told the Florida detectives that she had held back this information out of fear for her own safety. She was afraid that whoever hired Joey might order her killed too.

"I explained that was a valid consideration," Iorio said, "but we needed to get all the information we could from her."

Carol said that the victim's ex-husband had hired Joey because he was having some problems with his children and an ex-wife. She also knew that the woman Joey hurt was married to someone else.

It all tied in. Joey Del Toro had to have been talking about Sheila Bellush's murder, and if the hit was ordered by her ex-husband, she had only one: Allen Blackthorne. Ron Albritton and Chris Iorio were elated, but they knew they were a long way from arresting and charging Blackthorne. All they had at the moment were statements from witnesses twice removed from the murder itself. Hearsay statements. They had to back them up with solid evidence.

The white Mitsubishi was towed to the Texas State Department of Public Safety crime lab in Austin. DPS crime-lab technician Jody Williams conducted the search. It wasn't difficult. The car was a movable cache of evidence. Joey had undoubtedly been in Sarasota. He had been seen there within the time frame of Sheila Bellush's murder, and he would have had to pass by dumps, swamps, beaches, empty lots, and fields on his return trip to Texas—myriad spots where evidence could have been jettisoned.

But he had brought everything back with him. "Usually," Iorio recalled, "when you do a search warrant, you get one or two things that you're looking for. We got *everything.*"

"As detectives, you make a list of what you'd like to get from the crime scene, the things you could *hope* to encounter as items of evidence," Albritton added. "We got the whole shopping list."

The interior of the car was crammed with fast-food bags, empty soft-drink bottles, clothes still on hangers, a suitcase, and crumpled papers. But there was more. Albritton and Iorio could barely believe their luck as they noted the items Jody Williams took out of the Mitsubishi Eclipse and bagged into evidence:

- A Colt government model .45-caliber automatic handgun in a holster, along with three ammunition clips. One clip was full, and the other two were partially empty. (Found in a green backpack on the driver's seat.)
- A tan-colored Hampton Inn towel.
- A crumpled piece of white paper with scribbled directions to Markridge Road. (The paper had orange lettering on the top that read "Jim's Auto Salvage, Sebring, Florida.")
- A Rand McNally interstate regional map, folded open at Florida. There were two phone numbers jotted in the margin: 473-4180 and 448-7000.
- A shoe box from the Sports Authority that had once held a pair of black Magnum boots. The price sticker was on the side: $54.99.
- A receipt from the Sports Authority listing a purchase on November 6 of pants, camouflage mask, BDU top, camouflage T-shirt, and high-tech boots.
- A Tesa motel-room entry card (similar to those used at the Hampton Inn).
- A receipt from the Hampton Inn in Sarasota, Florida, for one night's lodging for José Del Toro on November 6.
- A camouflage ski mask made of knitted khaki-and-orange material, a grotesque mask that revealed only the wearer's eyes in a snakelike head.

In addition, Jody Williams's sharp eyes detected what appeared to be a dried blood smear on the front of the driver's seat. It looked to be transferred blood from the trousers of the driver. There might be enough to test for DNA.

Joey Del Toro had entertained himself with music for the 2400-mile round trip from Texas to Florida. One tape was country-western singer Tracy Lawrence's "Alibi." The other was Kenny Rogers's "Breathless." Given the scenario the investigators pictured in their minds, the choice of music was ironic. All the alibis in the world weren't likely to erase the impact of the evidence left in Joey Del Toro's car.

ALTHOUGH the Florida detectives were a little leery of Anna Morales's offer to help them locate Joey, she seemed to be sincere. "We had to weigh the order in which we talked to people," Iorio said. "If you talk to the wrong person first, they could all shut down. So we tried to be very careful."

Anna Morales was a vital witness. She called them at the DPS crime lab to say that she had located Sammy Gonzales. "He returned my page," she said.

Sergeant Joe Hutson urged her to find out where Joey Del Toro was. "The best way is to talk with Sammy," she said. "If I set up a meet with him in San Antonio, I think he'll bring Joey with him."

Anna headed toward San Antonio, and Texas Rangers from the DPS office there agreed to provide surveillance. If Sammy showed up alone, they would do nothing; as far as they knew, he had no connection to Sheila Bellush's murder. However, if Joey Del Toro should appear, the San Antonio rangers would arrest him.

Ron Albritton and Chris Iorio were convinced that Joey Del Toro was the man they wanted, but they didn't have a motive. Yes, he'd had $700 in his wallet, but who would kill a young mother for $700? As far as Joey's friends knew, he had never even mentioned the name Sheila Bellush. Nor had his cousin Sammy. Having so much evidence linking a suspect to murder but no motive was a backward way to work a homicide case. They had to believe that in the end it would all make sense.

The Austin police checked out the two local numbers written on the map of Florida found in Joey's car. One was for the probation office in Austin, and the other was the Travis County Juvenile Court Probation and Parole Office. Joey had a record involving drugs, but no one recalled that he had ever been mean or violent; he was a lover and a drugger.

He wasn't a killer.

Or was he?

_____Chapter Twenty-seven_____

TEXAS RANGER GERARDO DE LOS SANTOS never expected to be deeply involved in a homicide that had occurred so far from his home territory. All Texas Rangers are on hand to help with investigations whose tentacles reach into their state, but most such requests are for temporary and limited assistance. Gerardo "Gary" De Los Santos was about to step into a murder investigation that could well become the one case that stood out above all others in a long career.

De Los Santos was born in Laredo on July 4, 1957. His mother, Olga, called him Guero, which means "light complected" in Spanish. His father, Frank, was the district manager for Borden's milk and cheese products, but as Gerardo grew up, he realized that his father loved his small ranch more than anything else. Theirs was a very close family, and all the children were subtly and gently turned toward public service. Gerardo was born smack-dab in the middle of his siblings; he had an older brother and sister and a younger brother and sister. His brother Frank joined the Laredo Police Department, his older sister, Sara, became a registered nurse, and his younger sister, Norma, a fingerprint analyst for the U.S. Border Patrol. His younger brother, George, followed their father into management at Borden's.

Gary De Los Santos didn't grow up wanting to be a cop; from the time he could remember, his ambition was to be a game warden. To prepare for that, he got his associate of arts degree in law enforcement right after high school. The problem was that he was still only nineteen and too young to be a game warden.

"And then I was out driving with my father one day," he recalled, "and a black-and-white went by. That's what we call the trooper cars from the Department of Public Safety. That sounded like a good job too, and I joined the DPS on Pearl Harbor day, 1977. I was still only twenty."

De Los Santos worked TLE—Traffic and Stolen Vehicles—and CLE—Criminal Law Enforcement—and Special Crimes and Narcotics. He found himself drawn to criminal law far more than he was to traffic details. He forgot all about being a game warden; he had found his niche.

All Texas Rangers come from the Department of Public Safety, but not all DPS officers become rangers. The rangers probably have a more colorful history than any other law-enforcement agency in America. In 1823, when Texas was part of Mexico, Stephen Austin recruited ten volunteers to "Range" over wide areas to protect the Texas frontier. They were formally established on November 24, 1835, with three companies of fifty-six men, with a captain and two lieutenants, as the Texas Revolution flamed across the territory. They got $1.25 a day for "pay, rations, clothing, and horse service." Their ranks swelled to 850 men in 1838, far more than the 107 rangers in 2001. The early rangers fought to protect the Texas borders from being overrun by Mexico. "Even today, near the border," De Los Santos said, "there is still some hostility toward the rangers."

Over the next 165 years the Texas Rangers would hunt down some of the most infamous criminals and folk heroes known in the annals of crime—from Sam Bass to Bonnie Parker and Clyde Barrow, from John Wesley Hardin to David Koresh in the Waco cult tragedy.

Today the Texas Rangers are a very special part of the Texas DPS. They have to be commissioned law-enforcement officers for at least eight years, and four of those years must be with the DPS. Whenever a Texas Ranger position opens up, there are, of course, large numbers of applicants. Only those whose test scores rank in the top four or five spots move on to the interview board.

"It took me three tries on the test," De Los Santos recalled. "The second try I was ninth, and they took the top five. The third try, I was number two."

He was thirty-one years old when he was promoted on March 1, 1989. De Los Santos was assigned to Rio Grande City, 150 miles south of Laredo on the Mexican border across from Ciudad Camargo.

He met his wife, Leslie, through default. "I was really trying to date her sister, Bertha," he admitted, "but she was engaged, and so she introduced me to Leslie, the youngest of the four sisters in her family."

Today Leslie only laughs at her husband's less-than-romantic recall of their courtship. But it wasn't long before the two realized they were perfect for one another and it didn't matter how they met. Leslie, who worked for a time as a victims' advocate, is now a pharmaceutical sales rep for AstraZeneca, makers of Prilosec, Atacand and Inderal. They have one son, Gerardo Jr., now in his twenties, who attends college with a 4.0 grade average and wants to be a policeman when he graduates.

In his dozen years as a Texas Ranger, Gerardo Sr. would have widely diverse assignments. He served as one of then-Governor George W. Bush's bodyguards and appreciated the personal interest

Bush took in all the men and women who guarded him. "He knew your name and your kids' names," he said.

De Los Santos has also had experiences much less palatable; he was on the investigative team after the Waco cult suicidal disaster, digging in the scorched earth for the remains of Koresh's followers, who barricaded themselves—and their children—into the besieged cult headquarters and chose death by fire rather than surrender.

"I don't know—maybe I'm different—but I don't let the emotional part of it get to me," De Los Santos said. "I just put that part aside, and I don't think of it. I'm there to do a job, and that's what I do. No tears. No personal involvement."

Maybe he protested too much. The great big man in the great big hat seemed too intuitive and far too empathetic to be as removed from the pathos he encountered as he claimed to be.

De Los Santos passed the sergeant's exam and, later, the lieutenant's exam in the Texas Rangers. That is always a two-edged sword for any detective who thrives on working crime scenes and interrogating suspects. The higher the rank, the more isolated they can become from the very work they love the most.

But in November 1997 De Los Santos was a sergeant assigned to Company D, the San Antonio branch of the Texas Rangers, his office housed in a bright green building on South New Braunfels, a structure also used for driver's license orientation classes. The man dwarfed his office, where one wall held a pair of deer antlers that Leslie, wouldn't allow in their house, along with a painting of his late father's ranch.

"The last time my father visited his ranch," he remembered, "he turned back and looked at it for a long time as if he was memorizing it. Maybe he knew he wouldn't be back."

His father died soon after, and a friend painted the ranch, superimposing the image of Gary's father's face in the sky looking down.

Lieutenant Ray Cano was Gary De Los Santos's supervisor in the San Antonio Texas Rangers' office. Cano contacted De Los Santos on the Monday evening after Sheila Bellush's murder to tell him that Texas Ranger Joe Hutson in Austin needed assistance in locating a fugitive from justice wanted for murder by the Sarasota County sheriff's office. Cano filled De Los Santos in on the case background, and he—like everyone else living in San Antonio—remembered the "Quad Mom" who had often been on television.

The fugitive was José Luis Del Toro, Jr., born on April 26, 1976. According to his girlfriend Anna Morales, nineteen, Del Toro was probably in the San Antonio area. In fact, Anna was supposed to meet Del Toro and a friend of his at a Texaco station at the intersection of South Military Road and Interstate 35 between nine and ten that night.

And so it was Cano, De Los Santos, and several state troopers who staked out that location while Chris Iorio and Ron Albritton were still talking to potential witnesses up in Austin. For De Los Santos, it seemed to be a one-night assignment. Morales was supposedly cooperating with the police, and the rangers watched as she arrived at the Texaco station at 9:10 P.M. in a green Chevy pickup. She used the pay phone and then got into her truck. They followed her at a discreet distance and then waited while she went into a Taco Cabano restaurant. An hour later the surveillance was called off. Hutson phoned Cano to say that he'd heard from Morales. Del Toro's cousin Sammy Gonzales had spotted the officers and was afraid to show up. "Sammy called Anna on her cell phone and warned her that cops were following her and he couldn't meet her."

If Gonzales was innocent in the Florida murder, he would have had no reason to be so hinky about the cops. But maybe Joey Del Toro *was* with him as Anna had predicted.

De Los Santos arranged to meet secretly with Anna Morales, and he asked her to call Sammy again and urge him to meet her at a burger joint off San Pedro Street. She agreed, but her three calls to Gonzales's pager went unanswered.

The search for the elusive Joey Del Toro continued. Albritton and Iorio had no doubt that Del Toro had been the shooter. The evidence found in his abandoned Mitsubishi Eclipse placed him at the murder scene. They'd checked with the gas station a few blocks from Gulf Gate where he had asked for directions to the Markridge address; he had even kept the map the attendant had drawn for him. Not only had he left an unfired .45-caliber bullet in the room he stayed in, he also kept his key and his receipt from the Hampton Inn. He bought boots and camouflage clothes in Sarasota in a store right across from the Hampton Inn and kept the receipt. He'd left as many clues connecting him to Sheila Bellush's murder as Hansel and Gretel left breadcrumbs behind when they were captured by the witch. It was probably Del Toro's fingerprint on the dryer in Sheila's utility room, and in all likelihood the gun in the green bag in his car would be matched to the bullet Lisa Lanham found on the kitchen floor next to Sheila's body.

But the Florida detectives, the Austin police, and the Texas

Rangers needed to talk to Del Toro. Who had sent him from Texas to Florida on a murderous mission?

On Tuesday, November 11, Iorio and Albritton and Texas authorities met again with Anna Morales, Del Toro's favorite girlfriend. They told her that a warrant for his arrest for murder had been entered into the NCIC (National Crime Information Center) computers, and she shook her head in disbelief. She was still bemused that the man she knew as a charming and often unreliable rogue would actually hurt a woman physically. Everybody liked Joey. Still, Anna promised that she would help find him. He and his friends used pagers and cell phones, and she was sure that it was only a matter of time before she connected with someone who knew where he was. Carol Arreola gave them Sammy Gonzales's pager number and said that Sammy drove a shiny black pickup truck that was his proudest possession. Both Joey and Sammy often came up from San Antonio to Austin to "party."

Texas Ranger Brooks Long, stationed at Eagle Pass on the Mexican border, contacted Joey Del Toro's grandmother in La Pryor and asked her about Sammy Gonzales. She said that Sammy and Joey were blood cousins, once removed. Sammy's parents owned a business at Military Road and Flores Streets in San Antonio.

They were getting tantalizingly close to Del Toro. Anna Morales reported that he had left a message on her machine: "I need to talk to you. I'll call back at ten p.m.," he said.

Rangers set up surveillance at Morales's apartment by 6:30 P.M. on that Tuesday night, four days after Sheila's murder. For the second night in a row, they hoped Anna could lure Joey out of hiding. As Ron Albritton entered the apartment, Sergeant Sal Abreo signaled that Anna was on the phone with Joey. They were speaking in Spanish, which Abreo translated for Albritton.

It was Del Toro on the phone all right, but he wasn't calling from anywhere in Texas. This wasn't a surprise to Abreo or De Los Santos. A phone trap had been set on Anna's phone, which showed he was calling from the La Quinta Inn in Piedras Negras, Coahuila, Mexico, just across the U.S.-Mexico border from Eagle Pass, Texas. Del Toro was telling Anna Morales that he would be at the inn overnight before he headed into central Mexico.

That was not good news. The Mexican authorities might or might not be willing to arrest Del Toro and hand him over to American authorities. More often than not, politics, money, the mood of a judge, or even the weather on the Mexican side might dictate if, and how, extradition would take place. In the worst of all scenarios, Joey Del Toro might simply disappear into the bowels of Mexico, never to be seen again.

One bright note came when a man named Fernando Montez* walked voluntarily into the Austin Police Department to tell officers he had loaned Joey Del Toro a gun that might have been used in a homicide. Montez had been stunned when he heard the rumors about Joey. "Joey told me he needed a gun to 'take care of a problem,' " Montez said in a statement.

"Did he say *what* problem?" Detective E. Pedraza asked.

"No, and I didn't ask him."

The consensus among Joey Del Toro's friends was that he borrowed the gun to take care of something to do with drugs. The acquisition and consumption of cocaine and marijuana was Joey's paramount interest. That, and pretty women.

As he talked on the phone now with Anna, Joey asked her to cross the border and meet him at La Cabanita's and Jeans nightclub in Piedras Negras at 8:00 P.M. It suddenly looked as if it might be coming together; they would have the man who killed Sheila Bellush within four days of her murder. Ranger Brooks Long was in Eagle Pass, and apparently the Mexican police were willing to assist in capturing Del Toro.

Up in San Antonio, Gary De Los Santos set out to find Sammy Gonzales. Just before five on Tuesday afternoon, he went to the Fox Run Apartments, where Sammy was supposed to live, and observed a black 1997 Nissan pickup truck. The license plates came back registered to Sammy Gonzales.

De Los Santos made no attempt to contact Gonzales. He would wait until Joey Del Toro was arrested in Piedras Negras. He knew where to find Gonzales day or night, and he didn't appear to be going anywhere.

But luck was against them. The weather interfered with Anna's rendezvous with Joey. The Texas Rangers' plane carrying her to Eagle Pass ran into a violent storm and had to divert to Del Rio, Texas, to land. That meant more than an hour's drive to where Anna was to meet Joey. She was late, and Joey wasn't there. Although the La Quinta Inn was under surveillance by the Piedras Negras police and possibly the Coahuila judicial state police. Del Toro had managed to slip away unseen. He had shown up at the restaurant all right, but he was cagey and waited only fifteen minutes.

The next day was Wednesday, November 12, and the investigators' disappointment at coming so close to Del Toro, only to lose him because of a renegade storm, was palpable. With every day that passed, the chance that he would move farther into Mexico increased. There was some encouraging news, however. Sammy Gonzales phoned the San Antonio Texas Rangers' office and left a message for Gary De Los Santos. He said that if De Los Santos wanted to talk with him, all he had to do was call his parents and they would get hold of him at work.

De Los Santos already knew where Gonzales worked: the Precision Driving Range, where he helped golfers with their equipment and repaired bags. He was intrigued that Gonzales seemed so willing to talk to him.

Still assuming that his job in the investigation of Sheila Bellush's murder was only temporary, De Los Santos called Ron Albritton to offer assistance they might need. Albritton and Chris Iorio were happy to brief him on the case so far. There was no question now that Joey Del Toro had not only been in Sarasota, they had proof that placed him *inside the murder house*. The fingerprint found on the dryer had now been positively identified as his.

"Jamie Bellush says they never met," Iorio told De Los Santos. "He never even heard of Del Toro. And everyone who knows them says that what Joey's involved in, Sammy's in too."

"What about a motive?" De Los Santos asked Albritton.

"All we can get so far is that Joey told one of his girlfriends that he knows what it's like to look in the eyes of a woman he's about to harm, and this woman he *did* harm was having problems with her ex-husband; that's the person who ordered the hit. The ex-husband is supposed to have been concerned about their children—they had two girls together."

It wasn't difficult to identify the ex-husband. It kept coming back to Allen Blackthorne. Jamie, Stevie, and Daryl had all blamed him. He lived in San Antonio, and his name had been mentioned in the media within twenty-four hours of Sheila's murder.

But rumors were only rumors; the lay public had no idea what it would take to unearth the truth and then gather evidence to substantiate it. For that matter, neither did the investigative team, which seemed to grow every day. One thing the Sarasota detectives knew—they could use someone like Gary De Los Santos, an experienced homicide detective who knew San Antonio and south Texas like he knew his own backyard.

_____*Chapter Twenty-eight*_____

SHEILA HADN'T BEEN DEAD a week yet, although it seemed like months. Her memorial services would be held in Sarasota. Sarasota County Sheriff Geoffrey Monge gave a press conference to announce that an arrest warrant had been issued charging José Del Toro with the murder of Sheila Bellush. For some reason, media writers referred to Del Toro as a "drifter," an inapplicable description. Joey had a home, a job, a family, and dozens of friends. He didn't drift, but he often traveled the dusty roads of Texas in search of the next party. For the moment Del Toro wasn't drifting; he was rabbiting, apparently putting as much distance between himself and the Texas and Florida investigators as he could.

Even as this headline news flash went out in Florida and Texas, Texas Rangers still clustered at the border near Piedras Negras, prepared to take custody of Joey Del Toro as he was handed over by the Mexican police. Just because Del Toro hadn't waited around to see Anna Morales, it didn't mean that he wouldn't be caught. He hadn't done anything clever yet to cover up his connection to Sheila's murder. He was bound to make a mistake.

WHILE the Sarasota detectives, the Austin police, and the Texas Rangers looked for Joey Del Toro—a task that had seemed easy at first and was rapidly becoming disheartening—the services for Sheila were held in Sarasota.

Now that it no longer mattered, everyone knew where Sheila was. The rest of her family and her dozens of friends flew across America. They hadn't been able to save her from the dark shadows that she feared, but they would be with her one last time to honor her and say good-bye. As the dozens of mourners headed toward Sarasota, the sky opened up. Sarasota was drenched, drowned, buffeted by winds, and the lowlands flooded. The road into the parking lot of the Sarasota Baptist church was underwater. It had rained on Sheila's wedding day with Jamie, and it rained at her memorial services.

Minda Reece and Kelly McGonigal, two of Sheila's old friends who had tried to help her in her struggles with Allen, flew into Sarasota from Texas. "I remember the rain that never stopped," Minda said. "We rented a car and drove to the church in a blinding storm, and the church parking lot and even the road were underwater from all the rain. The weather matched the way we felt."

Sheila had always been so good to them; she was the most loyal friend they had ever known. Yes, there were many times that Sheila was frightened and desperately poor and needed them to help her keep her girls safe from their father, but when things were good for her, she shared that too. "Sheila would bring her friends to me for makeovers," Kelly, Sheila's hair dresser, recalled. "She got as much fun out of it as they did. And she took us all out to lunch in really nice restaurants afterward. Whether she was poor or rich, we knew that Sheila's friends meant a lot to her, and she meant so much to us."

Jamie had planned a memorial for Sheila that was both loving and heart-rending. His face reflected humor and loss as he told more than two hundred people in the packed church about meeting Sheila on the Southwest flight in Phoenix, and about their first secret marriage in their living room in San Antonio.

He recalled how they had decided to turn to in vitro fertilization so they could have children, and how thrilled they had been to learn they were going to have *four* babies. Jamie brought each of the four toddlers forward to introduce them to the crowd in the church. "They have a mommy who is an angel," he said as the sound of barely stifled sobs filled the sanctuary.

The Bellushes had been in Sarasota such a short time that there were many in the church who didn't know them. Jamie projected slides on a screen to show his family in happier days, and the sound of rain drumming against the roof gave a mournful counterpoint to the happy family pictures and the songs that were special to Sheila.

Stevie, very thin and pale, walked tentatively toward the lectern. She spoke of the last time she saw her mother alive. "[That morning] she told me how much she loved me, and that just stayed in my mind all day until I came home after school. Before I got out of the car, I gave her a kiss," Stevie said, "and I said I loved her. I'm glad I got to say good-bye."

Daryl had been driven to Sarasota again by her counselors from the Eckerd Camp, but she didn't speak to the people in the church; she was too upset.

It had never occurred to Daryl that she wouldn't be moving to New Jersey with her older sister and the babies; they were all she had left now. Indeed, the pastor of the Baptist church believed that Jamie had gone before a judge in Manatee County to be sure he had custody of both his stepdaughters. Reverend Landry told the press that the girls would have become wards of the state of Florida if Jamie hadn't stepped in.

But Daryl wasn't going with the rest of the family. Jamie had already made up his mind that Allen was guilty. Because of that, he could barely stand to look at Daryl. If only she hadn't told Allen the landmarks that let him locate the Bellushes' house, Jamie believed, Sheila would still be alive. Even Daryl admitted that she had talked to her father.

Shocked to learn that Jamie blamed Daryl, Rick Bladorn couldn't bear to tell her that she was going to be left behind. "I made a decision. I didn't even ask Kerry," he said. "I could see that there was a lot of blame being laid on Daryl by Jamie and his family, that they felt she was somehow responsible for Sheila's murder because Allen had pried information out of her. Well, I had been too close to Sheila in my life to ever let that happen to her daughter. There are some things you just cannot do. I couldn't let that little girl go back to Eckerd with strangers and become a ward of the state. She was only twelve years old. I told Daryl she was coming to Oregon with us."

Kerry agreed immediately with Rick that they would take Daryl home with them. Sheila would have wept in heaven if she knew that Daryl had been banned from the Bellush family. Jamie, Rick, and Kerry went to the judge. In the hearing, Jamie was granted guardianship of Stevie, and Kerry was granted custody of Daryl. Somehow Rick and Kerry would manage, even though they weren't in the least well off and already had four children waiting for them in Oregon.

Kerry had promised to go with Jamie, Stevie, and the babies to Newton, where she would help out until Jamie found someone to care for Frankie, Timmy, Joey, and Courtney and they got into a routine.

"I brought Daryl home with me on Kerry's ticket," Rick said. "We flew into Portland, and I took Daryl by the school where her cousins Kelly and Ryan were going—and where she would go. I wanted her to know right away that we all loved her, and that she had a place to live and a place to go to school. Then we went shopping to get her some clothes. She had nothing—nothing at all to wear."

Daryl had once had nice clothes, but so much had happened to her since the night in early September when Pat Aday called the Bexar County sheriff on Sheila. Daryl had been in The Bridge, on the plane to Sarasota, in the Y shelter, in the Eckerd Camp, and, after spending most weekends with her family in Sarasota, she was almost ready to come home for good when her mother was killed. By the middle of November her clothes and the life she had known got lost along the way.

Rick and Kerry Bladorn were very young. Kerry wasn't thirty yet, and Rick wasn't much older. But from that moment on, Daryl was part of their family. Her cousin Kelly was a year younger than Daryl and the only girl among three brothers—Ryan and the "little boys," Christopher and Patrick. Now there was another girl in the family, and it wouldn't have been surprising if Kelly's nose was out of joint from having an instant big sister. But Sheila and Kerry had always seen to it that their children knew each other and loved each other. It seemed the most natural thing in the world that Kerry would step in to take Sheila's place the best way she could. The cousins got along.

For the moment, though—with Kerry in New Jersey—it was Rick who had to balance five children ranging in age from twenty months to twelve years and his job repairing and selling cars. Somehow he did it.

They didn't have the perfect space for an expanding family. Kerry and Rick were living in a double-wide mobile home, saving money for the big house they hoped to build. Rick's parents, who spent several months of each year in poor areas in the Southwest doing charitable work for the Mobile Missionaries Assistance Program (MMAP), lived nearby.

_____Chapter Twenty-nine_____

SHEILA'S MEMORIAL SERVICES went on endlessly, as if Jamie could not bear to let her go. There could be no closure when those who loved her could dry their tears and look ahead. In truth, there never would be until her killer or killers were arrested and convicted.

On Tuesday, November 17, Don and Gene Smith, their oldest daughter, Cathy, Don's daughter, Amy, Rick, and his youngest son, Patrick, flew to New Jersey for Sheila's funeral service in the Newton Presbyterian church. Jamie chose a simple pine casket for Sheila, and he and Stevie bought her burial clothes at the Gap. They wanted something that Sheila would have been comfortable wearing: jeans, a black turtleneck pullover, and a sweater.

Kerry tried to help Jamie put some kind of life together without his wife. She remembered what a short time it had been since she and Sheila had visited their father's grave after their grandmother's funeral. They paid their respects to Francis Anthony Walsh, who was a few years younger than Sheila was when he died. He was thirty-two.

It was the first time Sheila had seen her father's grave. "She cried for almost an hour," Kerry said. "And then she told me she knew she would die when she was thirty-five. And she was right. I don't know *how* she knew." But they weren't sad for long; they gloried in being young, two sisters together, laughing and taking pictures next to their rented convertible on that sunny day. Never in a million years did Kerry really believe that she would watch her sister lowered into the ground only seven years later. But on November 20 she said good-bye to Sheila.

Kerry was angry. They were supposed to be sharing their children as they grew up and spending holidays with each other. As frightened and desperate as Sheila had been over the previous decade, she had always had an indomitable will to survive. Kerry had counted on that, but even Sheila hadn't been equal to whatever malevolent force had crept into her home. All their dreams for the future had disappeared like smoke in an autumn wind.

Kerry stayed in Newton, until she was reasonably sure that with Jamie's parents, his sister-in-law, a hired nanny, and Stevie's help after school, the quadruplets would be well cared for. She held Joey when he woke at night, terrified by dreams no tiny boy should ever have, and rocked him, knowing that she was the closest thing to his mommy there was.

She had always loved Sheila's babies, and now it was extremely hard to leave them. They all had their own personalities. Timmy spoke first and was the first to do anything. Frankie would need casts to straighten his legs from his "scrunched position" in Sheila's womb, and he tended to walk on his "tippy-toes." Little Courtney was the most reserved, and Joey seemed the most devastated by the loss—and perhaps the terrible memories—created by Sheila's murder.

Jamie's parents were generous to him; they all shared living space for a while so they could help him with the quads. Then they moved out and gave him the full use of the big house on the lake where he had grown up. Jamie and the quadruplets were related to them by blood. Stevie was the odd girl out, although she tried to belong. She carried a picture of her mother with her always. Thirteen is a difficult age as girls enter puberty, even when life is normal. Stevie, too, lived with horrific images in her mind; she was living in her third house in less than three months, in a strange town, and going to a school where she didn't know anyone. She was alternately depressed and raucous.

Eventually Sheila's family accepted what they had to accept. Sheila was gone. The detectives investigating her murder had named a chief suspect, and the case seemed to be moving forward. They had never heard of José Del Toro. It seemed impossible that a complete stranger had killed Sheila.

No one could have known then how complicated it would be or

how long it would take to prove the real motivation behind her murder. There would be too many times when those who loved her believed that some of the players in what came to be called the "Black Cow" plot and the puppeteer behind the horror were going to walk away untouched.

_____Chapter Thirty_____

SAMMY GONZALES seemed an unlikely source of information, but all of Joey Del Toro's girlfriends insisted the two cousins were very close and where Joey was, Sammy could often be found too. Gary De Los Santos learned that Sammy, at twenty-seven, was working at a job where most high school or college kids began their working careers. He was a gofer, someone who was almost invisible to the wealthy golfers who practiced their swings at the Precision Driving Range.

Some said that Sammy wasn't the sharpest knife in the drawer and that he was easily influenced by men he admired. His social life depended upon his being a tagalong. He was close to his parents, a good son, but certainly not a high achiever in life. And Sammy was scared to death. Although De Los Santos didn't know it until much later, Sammy had run home to his mother and father after he got a shocking phone call about his cousin Joey.

"Sammy slept that night between his parents in their bed," De Los Santos said. "Like a little kid with a nightmare."

On the evening of November 12, Rangers Gary De Los Santos, Sal Abreo, and Ray Cano met Sammy for the first time. He was a stocky man with a wide, almost childlike face. Gary asked him if he was willing to talk about Joey. Would he tell them what Joey had to do with the murder of a woman named Sheila in Florida? After De Los Santos assured him he could drive his own truck out to the Texas Rangers' office on South New Braunfels Road, Sammy agreed.

Sammy followed the rangers in his cherished black pickup truck. He seemed perfectly willing to have Ron Albritton and Chris Iorio join the group. The Sarasota investigators were, of course, consumed with curiosity about what this witness might say.

De Los Santos advised Sammy that he was not under arrest and that he was perfectly free to stop the interview and leave any time he wanted. And then he eased into the conversation by asking Sammy about his work. Sammy seemed very proud of his job at Precision; he had only begun it on a full-time basis two days earlier. He was responsible for locking up at night, but otherwise he would do pretty much what he had always done. "Before this job," Sammy said, "I worked at the San Antonio Country Club repairing clubs."

"When did you see Joey last?" De Los Santos asked.

"Monday morning."

"November tenth?"

Sammy nodded. "I picked him up about two thirty a.m. at one of his girlfriends' houses on McCullough Street, and I dropped him off at a Diamond Shamrock gas station down the street."

Sammy said the girlfriend's name was Magaly Cantu and added that he had partied with Joey in Austin on Saturday, November 8, after he picked him up at the Country Club Creek Apartments (where Carol Arreola lived and where Joey had abandoned his white Eclipse). Sammy said the pair had come back to San Antonio that night and partied until Sunday morning.

Sammy remembered that Anna Morales wanted to meet with him at the gas station Monday night, but he'd been sure he saw a police car, and he was too frightened. He said he had just learned, through another girl, that Joey had killed somebody. This had been shocking news. Sammy shook his head. No, he didn't know anything about any murder in Florida.

The investigators doubted that, but Sammy opened his eyes wide with innocence. He just wasn't smart enough to joust with these lawmen, all of whom were highly skilled interrogators.

Chris Iorio and Sal Abreo advised Sammy of his rights under Miranda, and he waived them.

"It would be better for you, Sammy," De Los Santos said, "if you told the truth." It was apparent that Sammy felt a connection to De Los Santos and was less talkative when Abreo questioned him. This was no time for egos; in interrogations, good detectives know when to pull back and let natural selection work.

Sammy appeared to be thinking hard. He took a deep breath, and slowly began to open the curtains, just a little, on a horrific scenario. The Florida detectives and the Texas Rangers knew widely diverse facts connected to Sheila Bellush's murder, but they didn't know how they intertwined or where the matrix was. Certainly, they had heard strong statements about the capacity for evil of a San Antonio multimillionaire, but they had never seen the man, and they were a long way from proving those theories. As Allen Blackthorne's attorney pointed out, his client had spent the day and night of

November 7 in San Antonio, behaving normally and seen by myriad witnesses.

Now, for the first time, the investigators were poised at the edge of a black stage where Sheila Bellush's last moments were played out. Most of all, they hoped they might find out *why* it was necessary for Sheila to die.

Sammy began his narrative by recalling a time several months earlier. He said a friend of his, Danny Rocha, had asked him if he would be willing to beat a woman. Sammy said he couldn't hurt a woman, but he thought his cousin Joey might do it.

Rocha gave Sammy an address in Boerne, Texas, where the woman supposedly lived. Sammy admitted that he had gone to Boerne by himself, looking for the house. "See, we had this picture of the woman and a little girl so we would know what she looked like— Danny got that. I went back twice with Joey, but things never worked out," Sammy said.

"Where did Danny get the picture?" Iorio asked.

"He got it from the person who wanted the woman beaten."

When Sammy and Joey went back to Boerne a third time, Sammy said, they peeked in the window and saw that there was hardly any furniture inside. It looked as though nobody was living in the house. They learned the woman had moved. "Danny found that out," Sammy said.

Sammy was tiptoeing around the edges of his story, trying, as any suspect does, to minimize his own involvement.

"They always do that," De Los Santos commented later. "None of them tell everything at once. They think that they can tell you the story in a way where they don't look so bad. They leave things out. They make what they did sound better than it was. You get to where you *know* you're hearing a cleaned-up version of the truth."

De Los Santos kept his face empty of judgment. Sammy said he thought that the plan would be canceled because the woman was gone, but on November 4 Danny Rocha told him that the deal was still on. Sammy, Joey, and Danny met that night at a bar called the Pan American Golf Association Club, a Hispanic club. "Danny gave Joey $500 up-front money so he could get to Florida and beat the woman."

Sammy added that he himself had never gotten any money, but he thought Danny Rocha had. "I don't know how much."

Asked if Allen Blackthorne had ordered the woman's beating, Sammy claimed ignorance.

"You know Allen Blackthorne?" De Los Santos asked.

Sammy shook his head. "Never met him. I wouldn't know him if I was looking at him."

Little beads of moisture were forming on Sammy's forehead. Asked to describe the house he'd visited in Boerne, he said it was "two-story, with a front porch with rails facing the street. It had a garage on the right side, and a driveway leading all the way from the street to the garage."

"What color?"

"Brick . . . kind of blue trim . . . no fence."

The investigators asked Sammy how Joey got the address in Florida. He thought the person who ordered the beating had given that to Joey. "I didn't know that there was going to be a murder," Sammy added, the sweat dripping down his face now.

The details were becoming harder to pull out. Sammy said that Joey had gone to Florida by himself. On Friday, the day of the murder, Joey had paged him about 4:30, but Sammy didn't return it because he was at work. Later he had talked to Joey. "He wanted me to get him some plane tickets, but his grandmother wouldn't put them on her credit card, so he drove to Austin instead."

Haltingly Sammy said that after Joey came back on Saturday, he had admitted shooting and cutting a woman. "He said he stabbed her instead of shooting her again because the gun made too much noise."

Bingo! Sammy Gonzales knew how Sheila died. It had never been in the papers or on television. It had been so closely guarded that many of the Sarasota officers didn't even know. Chris Iorio looked at Gary De Los Santos and nodded slightly.

But Sammy said Joey insisted that the woman was still alive when he left her, and her kids were on the couch. He said he was surprised that Joey wasn't upset about what he had done. He'd just gone ahead and spent the weekend partying, ending up at Magaly Cantu's house in San Antonio.

"So he called me at two thirty in the morning—Monday—from Magaly's and told me to come pick him up," Sammy continued, "and I took him to the Greyhound bus station, and he got on a bus for Laredo."

And, from there, it would have been a simple matter for Joey Del Toro to cross into Mexico. It was a grotesque story—as sketchy as Sammy Gonzales was on details—and it sickened the investigators. Sammy agreed to tape his version of Sheila Bellush's death. Chris Iorio kept the original audiocassette, and Gary De Los Santos kept a copy of it. It was a ghastly kernel of what had happened. And it was only the beginning.

They had one new name: Danny Rocha. Danny appeared to be the link closest to the person who had ordered the hit. That person was likely to be Allen Blackthorne, but they still couldn't prove it. They had yet to talk to the man or even to catch a glimpse of him.

Early Thursday morning De Los Santos asked Ranger Analyst Melanie Schramm, to put together a comprehensive report on Daniel Rocha, along with his driver's-license photograph. He had done a cursory check, and he already knew that there was at least one Daniel Rocha in San Antonio: Daniel Alex Rocha, white male, born July 15, 1969, who lived at 222 Wickes Street.

De Los Santos sent Ranger Marrie Garcia to that address to sit surveillance at the house. If this was the right Danny Rocha, he would probably be getting mighty nervous about now. Garcia reported back that a blue minivan and a cream-colored Honda were parked in front of the house.

Within half an hour, Ray Cano got a phone call from Steve Hilbig, the Bexar County district attorney. Hilbig had received a call from a local attorney, Gerald Goldstein, who said he had a client with information on the Bellush murder. Goldstein declined to give the name of his client, however.

One of the best ways to assure that murderous plots succeed is to keep the cast of characters to a minimum; it was beginning to look as though whoever was behind Sheila's execution had involved way too many people—and that most of them were not good at keeping secrets.

Melanie Schramm came up with more information on Daniel Rocha. Four years earlier he had worked at the Precision Golf Driving Range. His present employment was vague, but she had found a second address for him; 1330 Summit Creek. Ranger and San Antonio Police Department surveillance was established at both addresses, but they would wait until they learned more about Daniel Rocha before they approached him.

JOEY Del Toro had apparently needed the comfort of friendly female voices as he traveled across the Southeast. On Thursday, November 13, Texas Ranger Ted Poling of Garland received a phone call from yet another young woman. Ileana Cerda lived in Fort Worth, hundreds of miles from San Antonio or even Austin. But with Del Toro's name all over the news, Ileana realized that his seemingly innocuous phone calls to her, beginning on the night of the murder, might have some importance to the police.

Gary De Los Santos called Ileana, and she told him about her friendship with Del Toro. She met him on her twenty-first birthday in 1995 in College Station, where they were both attending Texas A.&M. They'd dated only for a little while, but they had continued to talk on the phone over the last two years. "Joey dropped out of college last spring semester," Ileana said. "Until November seventh I hadn't heard from him for two months."

Joey had called her at 9:58 P.M. on Friday, and they chatted for about ten minutes. "I had to hang up because someone was at my door, and he said he would call me back later," Ileana said.

At 11:30 Joey did call back. He told her he was driving through Alabama on his way back to Texas. He explained he had been "taking care of business," but he didn't elaborate.

"Joey called me the next day, Saturday, and just asked what I was doing," Ileana said. "He was about a hundred miles past Fort Worth then, and I asked him why he hadn't stopped to see me, but he said he needed to get to Austin. He said he would call me later."

Ileana Cerda said she called Joey's cell phone a couple more times that morning, and they had "normal conversations." But when she called Joey on Monday, November 10, his phone was turned off. And on Tuesday she found it was disconnected.

"Do you know where he is now?" De Los Santos asked.

"I have no idea."

De Los Santos knew; Joey Del Toro was somewhere in Mexico. That was a very big country for a man to be lost in. And obviously Joey had no desire to be found.

ANY number of anonymous tipsters were calling in information on the Bellush murder, and each one had to be checked out. Some were ridiculously off the mark. But one said that Allen Blackthorne had conspired with Danny Rocha and someone named "Oink" to have Allen's ex-wife killed, and that Blackthorne had paid $400,000 to have it done.

Another call came in from Vicksburg, Mississippi, with a slightly different version. That caller said Sheila Bellush was killed because she treated kids so badly. The figure for the hit was much less: "Fifty thousand dollars, and Danny kept four thousand" The common denominator, however, was the name Danny, reportedly a sometime thug and bookie—*Danny Rocha.*

More definite information came from an unlikely source when De Los Santos and Iorio went to the small house at 222 Wickes. In this modest but very neat home, they found Otilia Rocha, who identified herself as Danny Rocha's aunt. It was immediately obvious that Rocha's aunt Tillie was hesitant to talk to the investigators and that she didn't want to tell them where Danny was. She said he had a sweet wife, Eva, and three little boys. They had all lived with her until recently, when they moved into their own home.

But as De Los Santos impressed upon Otilia Rocha that it was essential that they talk to her nephew, she began to speak, stress etched on her face, just as it had been on Joey Del Toro's grandmother's.

Otilia said that Danny had called a family meeting two days before. He told his family that he was in serious trouble and that he was involved in something that meant he would be going to jail. He needed to borrow money so that he could hire an attorney.

"What was his attorney's name?" De Los Santos asked.

"Goldstein. Danny said he wanted to come in and confess to the police," Otilia said.

Goldstein was the attorney who had called the Bexar County prosecutor. That fit. But just what Danny needed to confess Otilia wasn't sure.

Asked if she had ever met a man named Allen Blackthorne, Otilia nodded. She had gone to his house on Halloween with Danny and his little boys. He was one of Danny's friends.

And then Danny Rocha's aunt said that she knew "for a fact" that Blackthorne had given Joey Del Toro $4000 to kill his ex-wife. But she shrank back when Chris Iorio asked her if she would give a formal statement. No, she would not. She couldn't do that to Danny.

There were steps backward, but they were getting closer to the truth with every interview.

Sammy Gonzales was asked to come back in and fill in some of the chinks in his story. Once more, he listened to his Miranda rights and once more he waived them. He agreed to take De Los Santos and Iorio to the house where he'd been told Sheila Bellush lived. At Sammy's direction, they headed northwest of San Antonio to Boerne. As they drove, they got a call from Ron Albritton. He and Ray Cano were following up on the lead out of Mississippi. It was the anonymous caller who gave the price for a hit on Sheila Bellush as $50,000. That was for Danny—the first link in the plot—who was then supposed to subcontract the job to the real hit man.

Albritton had asked where they could find Danny, and the caller directed them to an address on Summit Creek and told them to stand right in front of that house. The house next door would be Danny's. "He's packing right now to leave the country."

Albritton and Cano raced to the address specified, but they found only an empty house.

Miles away, Iorio and De Los Santos let Sammy lead them to a neighborhood of new houses on big lots, and finally to a house at 27243 Boerne Glen. It matched the description he had given them earlier: brick, blue trim. Neither De Los Santos nor Iorio had ever been to the Bellushes' Boerne house before; they couldn't have found it without Sammy's directions, which proved he wasn't lying to them.

On the drive back from Boerne Glen, Sammy Gonzales admitted that he'd left out some details in his first statement. "I gave Joey $500 before he went to Florida—Danny gave it to me. After it was over, Danny gave me another $3500 to give to Joey."

It was like pulling teeth, but the truth had begun to seep out. De Los Santos and Iorio knew full well that it might be a long time before it gushed out in its entirety.

They had no idea how long that would be.

Sammy Gonzales said he had no doubt that it was Allen Blackthorne who had ordered that his ex-wife be beaten. "But I didn't think he wanted her killed."

Now Sammy admitted that Blackthorne wasn't a complete stranger to him. He didn't know him as well as he knew Danny, but he said he had seen Blackthorne play golf with Danny many times. "[That Friday night] when Danny went over to Allen's to get the $3500 for Joey, Allen told him that the lady got killed. Danny was shocked, I think, and he told me not to say anything to anybody."

"How did Allen know that she was dead?" De Los Santos asked.

"Somebody called him up and told him."

Sammy admitted in this round of questioning that Joey told him he had parked his car a few blocks from the victim's house in Florida. He'd had trouble finding it, and had to stop to ask directions. The detectives were already aware of that. He'd left the directions in his car.

"Did he know that the victim had children?" Iorio asked.

"Yeah. We both knew that."

_____Chapter Thirty-one_____

SAMMY GONZALES had an interesting way of telling a story. He took his time, adding minute details as if he were actually seeing pictures and hearing a voice in his head. He could not be hurried, nor could he jump into the middle of a recollection; he apparently needed to start at the beginning.

It made De Los Santos and Iorio impatient, but they held their tongues. Sammy was the weakest link in a chain, but they needed to hear what he had to say before they moved on. They knew they might have to re-interview him a number of times before they learned all he could tell them about this truly heinous plot. Sammy's hesitation was obviously because he was loyal to Danny Rocha; he didn't want to say anything that would put the blame on Danny.

"Danny will roll over on you," Iorio told Sammy. "Don't think he won't if he thinks it will make him look better. He's going to talk, and it would be better for you if you tell us now."

Sammy looked doubtful. He was Tio Sammy to Danny's three little boys. He was like family; naïvely he didn't think Danny would ever betray him.

A week after Sheila Bellush's murder, Gary De Los Santos took Chris Iorio and Ron Albritton to the last address listed for the still mysterious Allen Blackthorne. They went to 13271 Hunter's Lark. It was a lovely house, but an empty one. There was a FOR SALE sign on the lawn. De Los Santos asked Ranger Analyst Melanie Schramm to begin looking for more information on Blackthorne. It was possible that he had left San Antonio, although his attorney had indicated that he had no reason to leave; he had no connection whatsoever to the tragedy in Florida.

The trio of investigators went back to 1330 Summit Creek, Danny Rocha's new house. It, too, was empty of life. Neighbors said they hadn't seen anyone there for at least two days.

An hour later they found Danny; he was at his aunt Tillie's house, standing on her front porch with members of his family. He was wearing a T-shirt, sweatpants, and socks without shoes. He didn't seem surprised to see them and agreed to go to the San Antonio Police Department to talk with them. But he said he was too nervous to drive and asked if they would drive him. He also asked if he could change his clothes, brush his teeth, and put on shoes. The detectives waited while he did that.

Once at police headquarters, however, Danny Rocha said he would cooperate and tell everything he knew about the Sheila Bellush case, but he wanted his attorney present. Indeed, he was so amiable that he willingly agreed to pose for a Polaroid photo arm in arm with Gary De Los Santos as if the two were buddies. Chris Iorio snapped it. He had a reason for wanting that photograph.

It wasn't going to be as easy to hear Rocha's story as they had hoped. Gerald Goldstein, Rocha's attorney, spoke to him and then asked to talk with Ron Albritton. Goldstein said he needed to talk to Charlie Roberts, the Florida state attorney who would likely be the prosecutor in any Sarasota County trial. By the time Albritton called Roberts again, the momentum had stalled.

"I already have a fax from Goldstein's office," Roberts said. "His client is invoking his right not to be questioned."

The calls between Danny Rocha's attorney, Charlie Roberts, and Bexar County D.A. Steve Hilbig continued through the afternoon. Goldstein sought a plea bargain for Danny, who, he said, could provide corroborating evidence against the person who had actually ordered the attack on Sheila Bellush. Naturally, Rocha wanted something in return. This wasn't unusual; prosecutors realize that they occasionally have to seek lesser punishment for suspects if it means the difference between a conviction or dangerous defendants walking free. There were many, many phone calls between the negotiators in two states. In the end, Goldstein and Rocha decided he wasn't ready to talk yet. Rocha wanted to be taken home.

He wasn't under arrest, and the frustrated detectives had no choice but to drive him there. But he wasn't going to leave Bexar County; his whereabouts were being monitored.

THE Comprehensive Report on Allen Blackthorne, a.k.a. Allen Van Houte, came in from Ranger Analyst Schramm. Blackthorne sounded far more interesting to the investigators than Rocha, Gonzales, and Del Toro combined. Heretofore, they had been penny-ante lawbreakers at best—or rather, worst. But Blackthorne had an extensive history of police contacts and a checkered marital history. He was an extremely wealthy man, despite going through a couple of bankruptcies, and he had used several Social Security numbers. The detectives noted that he was currently married for the fourth time, after acrimonious divorces from his first three wives. He was nothing if not litigious. Sheila Bellush had been his third wife, and they had apparently battled in one courtroom or another for a decade after their divorce.

Just as his lawyer had predicted, Blackthorne hadn't left San Antonio; he had only moved to a bigger house. Melanie Schramm found records that showed he was living in Shavano Creek, one of the most upscale neighborhoods in Bexar County, at 223 Box Oak.

As anxious as they were to look Blackthorne in the eye, Iorio and De Los Santos forced themselves to wait until they had as much information as possible. They needed to choreograph their interviews so that they didn't spook the next witnesses in line. They kept their third scheduled interview with Sammy Gonzales and weren't surprised that he now admitted even more details. That was Sammy's pattern. De Los Santos jotted notes of the newest revelations.

"According to Gonzales," Gary wrote, "another $10,000 was offered to Del Toro if he went ahead and just *killed* Sheila so Allen could get his daughters back. Gonzales hasn't said this before in an effort to protect himself, but mostly to protect Rocha.

"In reference to Gonzales and Rocha's compensation [for their alleged participation in the crime], Blackthorne was supposed to build a golf course that Rocha was going to manage, and Gonzales would be hired to work there. The golf course was to cost millions, and Rocha would be very well taken care of if 'the job' was done.

"Rocha was able to afford his big new house in Summit Creek because he is a bookie and also makes a lot of money collecting bets at local golf courses. The person who finances Rocha is named George—last name unknown—goes by the nickname Oink."

But Sammy Gonzales was still holding back, trying not to say anything that would make Danny Rocha look bad. He evidently thought he could switch the detectives' focus to Oink.

"You know that Danny's been talking to us, don't you?" Iorio asked.

Sammy shook his head. He didn't believe that.

Iorio pulled out the Polaroid that showed Rocha and De Los Santos posing with grins on their faces and their arms on each other's shoulders. On this day of questioning, De Los Santos had deliberately worn the same clothes that he wore in the photo.

"See," Iorio said. "Look at Danny smiling. He's not holding back to protect *you*."

Sammy looked confused at first, and then he looked angry. The picture convinced him that he'd been betrayed and that Danny Rocha was telling the police everything.

THE plot was growing as thick as tar. Blackthorne had apparently dangled a number of carrots in front of the men he had chosen to rid himself of his ex-wife and get his children back.

Joey Del Toro was still missing. Even with everyone pointing their fingers at him as the actual executioner of Sheila Bellush, and with the evidence found in his abandoned car, it seemed bizarre that he could have carried out such savage butchery on a woman. Joey wasn't a woman-beater; he was a lover. Every day brought more pretty women who adored Joey. None of them could believe that he would hurt a female, much less kill her. He certainly wasn't a constant lover, but he was so sweet that all of his women forgave his lapses in fidelity.

The count of young women who had been in touch with Joey the weekend after Sheila's death was at a half dozen so far: Carol Arreola, her roommates Olga Gonzalez and Keren Martin, Anna Morales and Magaly Cantu, *her* roommate—Gail Harriman—and Ileana Cerda. There would be many more. Joey was the personification of a ladies' man.

Sammy Gonzales kept adding to his story, and so did the women who had talked to Joey on the phone over the five days before, during and after November 7. Magaly Cantu said she'd only known Joey for a a week before his return from Florida, but she was happy when he called her on Saturday night, November 8, to party with him. Now she admitted that he and Sammy had spent the weekend at her house in San Antonio with her and her roommate, Gail.

"We just hung around and drank beer," Magaly said. "Neither Joey or Sammy seemed bothered or upset, and they didn't say anything about being in trouble."

On Sunday, Sammy had left at noon to go to work, and Joey and the two girls went to the North Star Mall. Joey had a lot of cash on him, in hundreds and fifty-dollar bills. He was generous; he bought clothes for both girls, but he spent $700 on clothes for himself.

"Didn't you wonder where he got all that cash?" De Los Santos asked.

Magaly shook her head. "I assumed he was into drugs some way and that's why he had so much money."

On Sunday night, November 9, Joey took the girls to a nightclub. He still seemed in a good mood and under no stress. "At two thirty a.m., though," Magaly said, "Joey got a page from Sammy. And then Sammy picked him up. I think that's when he took Joey to the bus station to go to Laredo."

Asked if there was anything—anything at all—unusual about Joey Del Toro during that weekend after Sheila Bellush's murder, Magaly Cantu nodded. "He had a scratch on his forehead, on the left side, that went all the way to his eyelid. It looked like a fresh fingernail scratch. But he said he got hit by a beer bottle when he was trying to collect some money from some people and a fight broke out. Then he said he got the money from collecting gambling debts, that he gets thirty to forty percent of everything he collects."

In actual fact, Joey Del Toro wasn't a gambling collector. Sammy Gonzales, however, fancied himself a collector/bodyguard, but he was neither. The detectives found out that Danny Rocha sometimes let

Sammy go with him on the Wednesdays he visited the losers and the winners who placed bets with him. Danny evidently did carry a lot of cash on him then, and Sammy liked to think that he "covered Danny's back."

Magaly Cantu promised to call the investigators if she heard from Joey.

A ticket seller at the Greyhound bus station said there *was* a bus that left daily from Laredo for Mexico at 6:20 A.M., but they just sold tickets; they didn't ask for ID, and they couldn't differentiate Joey Del Toro from hundreds of others who rode the early morning bus out of the country.

Magaly Cantu was as good as her word. A few days later she *did* find a message on her answering machine from Del Toro. He left her a phone number in Mexico. She called him back but failed to jot down the number. "He wouldn't tell me where he was," she said.

Magaly knew now that Joey was suspected of a gruesome murder, a murder that happened a day before the weekend he spent in her apartment. "Why did you *do* it?" she breathed into the phone.

Joey told her he had no choice. "Someone" had come to Austin and abducted him at gunpoint, taking him to some lake he wasn't sure he could ever find again. There, Joey explained, they had given him the address of a woman who was to be killed. "They said they would hurt my family," he told Magaly, "unless I did what they told me to do."

IT was galling for Ron Albritton, Chris Iorio, and Gary De Los Santos to get the information they needed in such piecemeal fashion. Not one of their witnesses had come forth with the whole story on the first telling. They sensed that they were dealing with the Three Stooges of murder, a trio of klutzy plotters who had made mistake after mistake—and *still* Joey Del Toro was loose and Allen Blackthorne's participation in the murder scenario was obscured.

They didn't believe for a minute that anyone forced Joey to commit a murder by threatening his family. Joey moved in drug circles, but his actual job was at a spa in Corpus Christi. He made a living helping overweight rich women work out.

To date, there was absolutely no indication that any of the three suspects—Gonzales, Rocha, and Del Toro—had a personal connection to Sheila Bellush prior to her murder. They moved in completely different circles. She was a decade or more older than they were, not a drug user, not a gambler, not even a golfer. Why would any one of them want her injured or dead?

Usually a crime is solved because detectives are able to deduce a motive for murder. In a sense, the murder of Sheila Bellush might just be solved because the first three suspects had no motive at all to kill her.

THANKSGIVING was fast approaching, and Ron Albritton and Chris Iorio hadn't been home for a long time. Although Sheila's murder occurred in their territory, the main thrust of their investigation was in Texas. Along with Gary De Los Santos, they were working around the clock. De Los Santos had come on board to aid the Florida investigation, but he'd soon found himself a permanent member of the team. It was obvious that Sammy Gonzales preferred to talk with him, but it was far more than that; De Los Santos was a superb investigator and a workhorse. None of the three detectives could even imagine managing this burgeoning case without the others. They were all obsessed with it and with the memory of Sheila Bellush.

It seemed that they were closing in on their targets. On Sunday, November 16, 1997, Iorio and Albritton prepared probable-cause affidavits preparatory to obtaining arrest warrants for conspiracy to commit murder, based on Florida state law, for Sammy Gonzales and Danny Rocha.

Danny smelled trouble in the air. He was in the process of turning his grand new house back to the man he bought it from. He asked friends to look after Eva and his three boys if he wasn't around to care for them.

Maybe the trio of detectives was finally going to get lucky. Later that day Magaly Cantu reported that Joey was trying to reach her again. He'd left the same number as before and the name Adrian. De Los Santos immediately called Ranger Brooks Long at Eagle Pass and asked him to contact Mexican authorities with the information.

Long found that the number was in Monterrey, Nuevo León, 141 miles south of Laredo. Ron Albritton telephoned the American consulate in Mexico City and requested assistance in locating José Luis Del Toro. He described the tall, muscular suspect, saying that he would probably stand out in a crowd. If the Mexican police agreed to cooperate, it was possible that Del Toro could be arrested and extradited to the United States soon.

_____Chapter Thirty-two_____

THE TIME HAD COME to call on Allen Blackthorne. It was 6:30 on that Sunday evening in November when Gary De Los Santos, Ron

Albritton, and Chris Iorio arrived at the magnificent pink mansion in Shavano Creek. They pulled into the curving driveway that ran between the house and the velvet green lawn. When they rang the bell, a maid answered and summoned her mistress, Maureen Blackthorne. They identified themselves and asked to see her husband. Maureen was pleasant, if not particularly glad to see them. She explained that Allen was out picking something up at the store, but she expected him back any moment. "Won't you come in and wait for him?" she said.

As if on cue, the phone rang, and Maureen answered it, identifying the caller as Roy Barrera, Jr., Allen's attorney. She held the phone out. "He would like to speak to one of you, please," she said.

Albritton took the phone, nodding, and began speaking in one-syllable words. As he talked with Barrera, Allen Blackthorne walked in, and Iorio and De Los Santos introduced themselves. They noted that he seemed extremely nervous and almost "dazed" to see detectives in his house.

Albritton wasn't surprised when Roy Barrera, Jr., declared that he could not allow his client to be interviewed unless he was present. He requested that the three investigators leave the Blackthorne residence.

They did.

"Allen must have seen us from his car as we pulled into their driveway," Albritton said. "He just kept on driving by and called his attorney, and Barrera was on the line almost as soon as we got in the house."

But they had seen Allen Blackthorne face-to-face now. That seemed important. They saw a tall, tanned, and handsome man who lived in luxury beyond anything the average man could imagine. There was no comparison between the virtual palace he lived in and the tiny houses where Sammy Gonzales and Otilia Rocha lived. Even Danny Rocha's new brick house couldn't begin to compare with the pink mansion.

Allen Blackthorne had all of this, and an attractive young wife and two small sons. It seemed impossible that he would risk losing it to settle some old score. He had tried to appear calm, but the very sight of three lawmen had apparently shaken him up badly. They wondered what he was hiding and why he wanted them blocked from talking to him.

They could wait.

On Monday, November 17, arrest warrants for Danny Rocha and Sammy Gonzales were issued out of Florida. Based on the Florida charges, De Los Santos prepared fugitive warrants to be served in Texas, and then he and Iorio set out to look for the two men. Sammy wasn't at his apartment, but they found him at the Precision Driving Range and placed him under arrest.

Shortly after that, Ron Albritton and Ranger John Martin located Danny Rocha at his aunt Otilia's house. Neither prisoner was surprised; they had been waiting for the axe to fall. Crestfallen, the men were taken to the Texas Rangers' office on South New Braunfels Road for questioning.

Sammy gave them a few more details, although he refused to sign a statement. He admitted to De Los Santos that Joey Del Toro had known full well that he was going to Florida to kill Sheila Bellush. "He asked me for a gun," he said.

Sammy had no gun, but he added that he thought Oink had been with them when Joey asked for the weapon.

Danny Rocha invoked his right to remain silent until he spoke to his attorney. The two men—these links between Joey Del Toro and the person who wanted Sheila Bellush dead—were booked into the Bexar County jail. It had been only ten days since her murder, but the investigators had no particular sense of triumph in accomplishing the arrests so quickly. They didn't have the killer, and they didn't have the instigator of the plot that Sammy had described. Allen Blackthorne still played golf and enjoyed his sumptuous lifestyle, and Joey Del Toro was like a fox, never staying in one place long enough for them to drive him to earth.

MAGALY Cantu told the detectives that she was still getting a number of phone calls that registered only as "out of the area" on her answering machine. In one twenty-five-minute period on Sunday, she'd had four, with three more calls on Monday. The message always asked her to call a number. The first time she tried, someone picked up but did not speak. Four minutes later a man answered, but it wasn't Joey. The man told her she'd called a cell phone registered to a business called the Auto Plaza. When she asked for Adrian Joey's code name, the man said he wasn't in. She left a message that she had called.

With one more call, Magaly learned that the phone was currently in a neighborhood known as Campos Verdes in Piedras Negras. Joey had left Monterrey and was right across the border from Eagle Pass, Texas. How long he might stay there was anybody's guess.

Three days later Joey was still on the run. But the Ranger investigators were given a letter a student had accidentally left in a school computer lab in Eagle Pass. The girl was writing to Joey. They scratched their heads; the fugitive seemed to have an endless supply of young women.

"Dear Joey," the E-mail read, "I understand why you are running, but if you didn't do it, why *are* you running? I'm afraid the police will come looking for me and think I am part of it. I have enclosed the money you asked for. I want to see you but I know it's not safe right now."

The girl, Tami Kent*, wrote to Joey that the police in Piedras Negras knew about his phone calls. She enclosed directions to a ranch where friends of her family lived. He could hide there. If he was still there by Thursday, she would come to the ranch to see him.

When Brooks Long located Tami, she gave him a three-page statement. She said she was in her computer class waiting to get on the Internet shortly before 5:00 P.M. on November 17 when a man came up to her. She described him as "Five six, two hundred and fifty pounds, dark complexion, mustache, bulldog face with big eyes, black hair with a little bit of gray."

Ranger Long knew that Danny Rocha and Sammy Gonzales were in jail at that time and had no idea who the "bulldog face" man was. At first Tami had denied that she knew anyone named Del Toro, but then she admitted she knew Joey. The stranger said he had been sent by Joey to ask a favor. "Joey wants to borrow $600. He'll pay you back," he said.

Tami had agreed to get the money. The man told her he would be back to pick it up and he could take her to Joey.

"He wanted it by Wednesday the nineteenth, and he told me not to say anything to anyone," Tami said. "I typed out the letter to Joey, but I was afraid of the man, and I didn't even go to class. I ended up tearing up the letter." But the E-mail file had remained in the school computer.

Joey's time as a free man was running out. The next day, Ranger Ray Cano received a call from Special Agent Isaias Lopez of the Immigration and Naturalization Service (INS), stationed in Monterrey. A million people live in Monterrey, in the foothills of the Sierra Madre. A man less desperate to talk with his women friends could have gotten lost in that region, but Joey Toro needed constant contact with them. And now Lopez and Commandante José De La Rosa of the Nuevo León State Judicial Police and twenty of his agents were holding surveillance on the house where Joey was believed to be hiding among the group of Salvadoran students who lived there.

A pen register had been placed on the phone Joey used to call Magaly Cantu. The phone trap had intercepted Magaly's number often. It had also trapped some sixty calls to Vera Cruz. It might be that Joey was preparing to travel deeper into Mexico to that city on the Gulf of Mexico, and from there take a boat to anywhere. If they didn't get him now, they might never find him.

Magaly Cantu continued to cooperate with the police. She agreed to call the number Del Toro gave her again. At 3:55 P.M. on Thursday, November 20, she finally reached him. Ranger Ray Cano learned that they were talking in Spanish. Special Agent Lopez was recording the call. They began to speak in English when Joey told Magaly that he was wanted on both sides of the border.

The Rangers, INS agents, and Mexican police urged Magaly to keep Joey on the phone as long as possible. Joey was getting edgy, though. As the call stretched to forty-five minutes, he asked Magaly to go to a public phone and call him back in an hour. She stalled.

It was 4:42 P.M. "Ask her to ask him if he is on the first or second floor of the building," Lopez urged. "We are outside watching."

Magaly couldn't get an answer out of Joey. She could only tell Ranger Martin that she heard a television in the background.

At 4:47 P.M. Cano phoned Lopez and said it was imperative that they apprehend Del Toro before nightfall.

"The judicial police are in place. They are on standby," Lopez assured him.

At 4:57 P.M. Lopez called Cano and told him the best news the ranger lieutenant had heard for weeks. "Joey Del Toro has been apprehended without incident. He will be taken to the INS for processing."

Ironically, Del Toro was not charged with murder in Mexico; he was arrested for being in the country illegally. He had been there for more than seventy-two hours without a visa.

At Ranger headquarters in San Antonio, Gary De Los Santos heard the good news. But there was no word about what, if anything, Joey was telling the INS agents and the Neuvo León judicial police. And there was no indication of when he would be extradited to the United States. It would be dicey until they actually had Joey Del Toro in an American jail.

At 2:00 P.M. the next day, Ray Cano learned there was a chance that Del Toro would be taken to Nuevo Laredo, Tamaulipas, Mexico, and deported to U.S. soil in Laredo, Webb County, Texas. There was great excitement on the Texas side of the line, but nobody was high-fiving yet.

And with good reason. By eight that night, INS special agent Lopez in Monterrey called Cano and said that the word was not good.

It appeared that Joey Del Toro had changed his mind, or perhaps the Mexican authorities had changed their minds. His deportation as an illegal alien was out of the question now, and Del Toro was going for extradition proceedings instead. For the moment the plan was for the prisoner to be taken to Mexico City to be detained at a prison there to await the proceedings.

That meant it would be at least sixty days before Joey Del Toro might cross the border into the United States. The investigation, which had rolled along with the fluidity of a ball bearing on a seamless track, had just hit the wall and bounced. But while Joey waited in a less than luxurious Mexican jail, the men who had hoped to talk to him accepted the detour and turned their attention to other methods of learning about Allen Blackthorne.

PART FIVE

The Long Haul

Chapter Thirty-three

THE WORLD WENT ON without Sheila, who lay now beneath the snow in the Yellow Frame Cemetery fifteen miles from Newton, New Jersey, but the tragedy of losing her etched acidlike pain on the souls of those she left behind. All she had ever wanted was a happy family, and now her family was scattered across the country. Jamie Bellush never went back to the house on Markridge Road. Stevie, Frankie, Joey, Timmy, and Courtney lived with him in Newton. Stevie was going to the high school her stepfather once attended. Daryl was three thousand miles away, living with Rick and Kerry Bladorn and their four children near Salem, Oregon. The girls were no longer close—their father had seen to that as he worked his divisive tactics even on his own daughters—and they rarely corresponded. Where Kerry and Sheila had always comforted and supported each other, Stevie and Daryl went on as if each had no sister.

Daryl plunged into school and sports, and she consistently got A's. The behavior problems she had once exhibited disappeared now that she was no longer under her father's influence. The Bladorns opened their hearts and arms and drew Daryl into their family.

It wasn't as easy for Stevie. As the weeks passed, she always loved her toddler half siblings, but she also yearned for time just to be young. Most of her youth and belief in happy endings had disappeared in that god-awful moment when she found her mother's body in a wash of blood.

Now Stevie and Jamie were sometimes at loggerheads. "It's really hard here," she told a reporter. "I don't get along extremely well with Jamie or his parents. I get so frustrated because I feel like he doesn't help out with the kids. I want to sit down and just cry. *I* want to be a kid. I want to go to the movies. I want to go to friends' houses."

Stevie carried her mother's picture, with Jamie's image folded under at the crease so it didn't show. Like Daryl, she had been in three schools in a year, and both sisters had known complete rejection by their biological father. Bad enough—but Stevie had to fight nightmares, too, of horror that might never fade.

Sheila's clothes, her shoes, the makeup she had loved to experiment with, were all packed in boxes stored in the attic of the Newton house. Jamie could not bear to open them. He dealt with his grief by granting media interviews in which he blasted Sheila's killers. He buried himself in working long hours for Pfizer, and he even created a Web site, where he wrote the story of his love affair with Sheila, her murder, and his life as he currently lived it. He posted dozens of photographs of his early life and his family with Sheila, and new pictures of the quadruplets; it was almost as if he wanted to prove to himself and others that the halcyon days had once existed. Jamie heard from people all over America, and he spent many evenings on the Internet trying to forget the emptiness of a leftover life without the wife he had planned to grow old with.

With their second birthday approaching, no one could know what Sheila's quadruplets remembered of her murder. They were very intelligent, and surely they remembered something. But at their age they couldn't verbalize what they might have seen as they sat on the couch, watching their mother as she struggled desperately with a stranger in a scary mask. Sammy Gonzales had said that Joey told him the babies were awake and watching as he attacked their mother.

If she looked down on them from heaven, as many in her family believed she did, Sheila knew that her babies were safe with their daddy, and that Stevie and Daryl were with family. She had always been a spiritual woman with devout faith in God, and her mother and sisters comforted each other with their sure knowledge that Sheila *was* in heaven.

In the end, only two elements could even begin to heal the emotional wounds left when Sheila died—time and the arrest and punishment of those who killed her. Three men she never knew were in jail, charged with her murder. One man she knew only too well was caught in the laser light of an investigation the like of which Florida and Texas had never seen before: *Allen.*

ALLEN Blackthorne had skated free of real trouble his whole life. Heretofore his vanquished opponents had been people who loved him, people who were attracted to the wealth he wore like a golden magnet, vulnerable people who trusted him, and even the children he'd fathered. The only person who had ever defeated him in court was Sheila—and she was dead now. Ultimately, Allen always won and moved confidently on to the next battle.

Perhaps not this time. Now Allen's opponents were men and women who had nothing to gain beyond the satisfaction that they had done their jobs well and had avenged the death of a young mother. Moreover, Allen faced adversaries who could be just as cunning as he was, and manipulative too, if it served the law. They worked for the modest wages that public servants earn, and they didn't want his money; they could not be bought off. They weren't afraid of him, and they certainly had no affection for him.

But Allen Blackthorne had enough money to buy the best team of criminal defense lawyers in the country if he should need them. He had been nervous and surprised when Chris Iorio, Ron Albritton, and Gary De Los Santos showed up in his front foyer, but he was back in fighting form again. He had regained his balance.

And yet, even as he did, the line of prosecutors and investigators who vowed to bring him down grew longer. Some—like Bill Blagg, U.S. Attorney for the San Antonio region, and his top assistants, John Murphy and Richard Durbin—had offered their help early on, and were waiting in the wings. San Antonio Police Department detectives and FBI agents watched the case with interest. For the moment, Bexar County D.A. Steve Hilbig was handling the San Antonio part of the case, along with the Texas Rangers, but reinforcements were in place.

THE first three suspects in Sheila Bellush's murder were rounded up in thirteen days. The fourth would take longer than anyone might ever have thought.

Allen Blackthorne had never told the absolute truth about his life. Even people who thought they knew him well were oddly misinformed. He was expert at smoke and mirrors, changing aspects of his background by tweaking his history here and there. In the darkest sense, he was a self-made man. But even he left a trail, no matter how he tried to obscure it.

Allen's criminal record existed as the prime source of fact, and the investigators began with that and with his four marriages—all fact, although Allen would deny that one marriage had ever existed. Exposing the rest of his life would take precise and minute examination; it would be akin to unbraiding a complex wire made up of dozens of leads.

A golf assistant at the Oak Hills Country Club phoned the Ranger office in San Antonio and said he had information about Danny Rocha and Allen Blackthorne. Gary De Los Santos interviewed him and learned that Allen had been a member of Oak Hills for two or three years, sponsored by a local dentist. Allen had later submitted the names of two golfers he wanted to sponsor: Danny Rocha and Ray Cevallos. The Oak Hills board turned Danny down, but accepted Cevallos, an affluent businessman in his fifties.

Allen was a frequent player on the Oak Hills course, and his group often included Cevallos and Rocha, along with a physician and several businessmen. De Los Santos learned that almost all golfers put down wagers as they played, but the pro at Oak Hills said he rarely saw the kind of bets that Allen's foursome wagered. "Rocha always carried a wad of hundred-dollar bills," he said, "and he liked to show it off. I've heard that Blackthorne has written checks to Rocha up to $30,000."

Thirty thousand dollars. That seemed incredible to the ranger, but the golf pro said that that was the word around the country club. Allen Blackthorne was a golfing maniac, addicted to the game and to high-stakes betting. He was also a man with a violent temper when things didn't go his way. He had destroyed golf clubs and even smashed a golf cart on one occasion.

De Los Santos and Iorio established that Allen and Danny Rocha played golf together several times a week. That was their obvious connection. As the two detectives made their way from one golf course to another in the San Antonio area, they found that both men were well known. Rocha, once a champion, was the better golfer by far, but he didn't mind playing with Blackthorne—the money was good.

They visited the Pan American—the Hispanic golf club. They learned that Danny Rocha had given a talk to the members on Tuesday, November 4—three days before Sheila's murder. The public relations representative for the club told them he had seen Sammy Gonzales with Rocha that night. They were with another man, a man he thought was Sammy's cousin Joey Del Toro.

"Was Oink there too?" Gary asked.

"He might have been. He's here a lot."

Asked to describe the mysterious Oink, the PR man said he was in his seventies and his real name was George Hendrix.

De Los Santos checked for driver's-license information on Hendrix and found an address for him at an apartment on Broadway. Hendrix's sparse criminal record was for small-time gambling and bookmaking. That didn't mean he wasn't a force in the Mexican mafia, one who had never been identified. He could even be the key man in planning the hit on Sheila Bellush. But a visit to the man called Oink dissuaded Iorio and De Los Santos of that notion. The manager told them that Hendrix had lived in the apartment house since 1980 and pointed out an older car in the parking lot that belonged to him. The two detectives staked out the building, and it wasn't long before they noticed an elderly man emerge from Hendrix's apartment.

George Hendrix didn't look like a viable member of a death plot. He was an old man, living in a modest apartment. He admitted that he took bets, but said his income wasn't much. He was Danny Rocha's financial backer, but he figured they had *lost* money in 1997. "Danny earns ten percent of my take," he said. "He might have made two or three thousand dollars this year."

Hendrix looked genuinely baffled when they asked him about Danny Rocha's involvement in a murder. He didn't know what they were talking about. Iorio asked him if he was familiar with a man named Allen Blackthorne. He nodded, but said, "I've never met him personally."

When they left the small apartment, Iorio and De Los Santos were convinced that Danny hadn't made enough money from this small-time bookie operation to buy groceries, much less to account for the down payments on his new house on Summit Creek. Sammy Gonzales had been garrulous about Danny's business, but he clearly knew nothing about it.

Their investigation suggested that Danny had depended on his golf winnings from Allen Blackthorne to support his newly affluent lifestyle. Winning thousands of dollars several times a week could explain Rocha's wealth. He must have thought he hit the mother lode when he met Allen Blackthorne. But Danny and Eva and their three boys hadn't even lived in their fine brick house for six months before it was all over.

Now he was in jail, and his wife and boys were back with his aunt Otilia. "It looks like Allen called in his markers," De Los Santos said of Blackthorne's hold over Rocha. "He needed Danny for more than a golf partner."

Rick Speights, the next-door neighbor that Rocha had considered a brother, was eager to talk about what he knew, quite possibly because he was afraid he might become a suspect in Sheila Bellush's murder if he didn't. He told Gary De Los Santos that he had met both Danny Rocha and Allen Blackthorne through Ray Cevallos, whom Speights also played golf with. They were introduced at the Oak Hills Country Club in the early fall of 1996.

Rick said he suggested to Danny that he buy the house next door to him in the spring of 1997. Rick had often placed bets with Danny, and he estimated from what Danny said that his income from his bookmaking operation was between $150,000 to $250,000 a year.

De Los Santos said nothing. He and Iorio knew that Danny Rocha had exaggerated his income ten- to twenty-fold, and Speights had bought it. According to Rick, Danny took him into his confidence as they drank beer one night in July at the gap in their fence. Danny told him about the bizarre trip he took to Oregon with Allen Blackthorne. "Allen came right out and asked him to find someone to kill his ex-wife," Speights said. "I told Danny to leave it alone. I told him Allen was crazy. He said Allen wanted his kids back."

"Did Danny say anything about the trip with Allen after that night?" De Los Santos asked.

"Nope. He never mentioned it again."

Rick said he came to know Danny far better than he did Allen Blackthorne. But he admitted he'd gone to Allen's house a few days after the massive media coverage of Sheila Bellush's arrest for allegedly beating her daughter.

"Danny and I went over to Allen's to see his new car," Rick said. "He had a white Mitsubishi 3000 GT two-door convertible. He told us he paid $71,000 in cash for it. And he bought a Montero SUV in cash for his wife too."

Rick said that while he and Danny were at Allen's pink mansion, Allen put a videotape into his VCR. It showed all the television news coverage of Sheila Bellush's arrest. Maureen was present when Allen told his two visitors, "You see what kind of a bitch I used to be married to."

Neither Danny nor Rick knew what to say, and Rick had no idea why Allen had shown them the tape.

A few days later, on Saturday morning, Rick said his wife woke him up and asked him what Allen's ex-wife's name was.

"I told her I didn't know, and she asked me, 'Was it Sheila Bellush?' "

Rick said he recognized the name then. "My wife had just read the newspaper and told me that Sheila Bellush had been murdered in Sarasota. I immediately thought of what Danny told me when he came back from the trip to Portland with Allen."

Rick told De Los Santos that he called Danny and asked him to come outside, where he showed him the paper. He asked him if he had anything to do with the woman's murder. "He said he didn't."

But three days later Danny met Rick again at their mutual fence line. "He told me he was in trouble," Rick said, "and he needed my advice. I told him not to tell me anything that I couldn't repeat."

Danny asked Rick to do something for him. He might need Rick to sell his truck, and to talk to Randy Robertson, who held Danny's mortgage, about getting his equity out of the house to give to his wife, Eva.

"I might get arrested," Danny told Rick, the sweat glistening on his forehead. Rick didn't ask him why. He assumed, though, that it had something to do with the murder of Sheila Bellush.

According to Rick, Danny was in a panic, and his anxiety had increased with every day that passed during the week after Sheila's murder. Even though Rick didn't want to know details, Danny persisted. "He told me he met with Sammy and asked him if he knew anyone who would go to Florida and beat up Allen's ex-wife. Whoever did it was supposed to leave a message with her: 'Allen wants his kids back, and this is only the beginning.' "

Sammy wouldn't hurt a woman, but he said his cousin might do it. Danny told Rick that Sammy got $50,000 but that his cousin only got $4000. "Danny told me that he didn't get any of the money," Rick said.

On the Friday after the murder, November 14, Rick said he made a collection of a bet for Danny and delivered the money to him at his aunt's house. Danny was running even more scared and asked to borrow a gun for protection. "He was afraid Del Toro would come looking for him if he ran out of money. That's the first time I ever heard the name Del Toro," Rick said. "I lied to Danny and said I didn't have any weapons. I told him I didn't want to talk about the murder anymore because it was making my family nuts."

At 6:00 P.M. on that same Friday, Rick Speights got a call from Allen Blackthorne, a most unusual circumstance. Allen asked Rick what was going on with him. "I told him, 'Nothing. What's going on with you?' "

Allen sounded calm and remarked that he thought all the interest in Sheila's murder was dying down. Now that the police knew where Del Toro was, he figured they would leave him alone.

If Allen was at ease, Danny Rocha was a wreck, and he wasn't answering his phone. Rick said Danny could see Allen's number on his caller ID and he was sure he had spotted Allen driving Maureen's car in his neighborhood. That was what made up his mind to move his family back to his aunt Tillie's.

Rick was nervous too. He told De Los Santos about Allen's hook in Danny—the promise of a 25 percent interest in a $20 million golf course Allen was going to build. "I heard Allen tell Danny that he could manage it."

Speights was being cooperative now, but De Los Santos could not help thinking how different the ending might have been if he had only come forward *before* Sheila Bellush was murdered. How could anyone aware of the vicious plot in progress remain silent?

CHRIS Iorio took a statement from Randy Robertson about his real estate dealings with Danny Rocha. Robertson said he had been led to believe that Danny was a solid citizen who owned a home-remodeling business. He had agreed to hold the mortgage, but asked that Danny pay half his equity up-front, which he did. Danny told him he had re-modeled a house in Alamo Heights and sold it to get the money for the down payment on the Summit Creek house. "The mortgage payments were $1100 a month, and they came out of his checking account," Robertson said.

The house deal with Danny Rocha closed on June 13, 1997. Danny simply took over the seller's payments. That way there was nothing written down to make the IRS wonder where his money came from.

Robertson said Danny contacted him the week after Sheila Bellush's murder. He said he would probably be going to jail and wouldn't be able to finish paying for the house. "I trusted some guys I know in business. Something went terribly wrong," Danny told Robertson. "And it turned out I couldn't trust them after all."

Now that Danny *was* in jail, along with Sammy and Joey, Chris Iorio and Gary De Los Santos were finding that all roads led back to Allen Blackthorne, if in a somewhat circuitous fashion. And they needed more than that; they needed solid ties that could not be ripped apart. Yes, they could prove that Allen spent much of his time with Danny Rocha over the last year, but that wasn't enough. It wasn't even enough that Allen hated his ex-wife. A lot of men hated their ex-wives. Allen had never left San Antonio during the vital time period when Sheila was murdered, and they still had only hearsay information about a plot to kill her.

JAMIE Bellush insisted that he and Sheila had taken their family and literally *escaped* to Sarasota to hide from Allen. Sheila had been terribly afraid of him, and yet Allen had only rarely been in her physical presence in the ten years since their divorce.

There was Daryl. She had been tricked into giving her father hints about where they lived, but she never knew the address. But Allen hadn't just relied upon Daryl. The investigators began to find more and more connections between Allen and people he apparently thought could help him locate Sheila. As they began to connect the dots, they had a dawning inkling of how relentless Allen's search for Sheila had been.

Kim Hall, the RS Medical saleswoman in Sarasota, had told Iorio that Allen wanted *her* to find Sheila, and when she refused, he'd asked for the phone numbers and addresses of private investigators. Had he found one? Daryl had given her father half a street name and some information about an ice-cream parlor and a Laundromat. But Del Toro had left a map behind in his car with directions and a complete address of the yellow-and-white house. He evidently had found it once and driven by when he first arrived in Sarasota. But then he got lost and had to go to a service-station operator for help.

"She gave him directions that a local would use—a shortcut," Iorio told De Los Santos. "And she said he kept insisting that he had to go down I-41 to get there—so somebody outside Sarasota gave him his original instructions."

GARY De Los Santos executed administrative subpoenas for the telephone records for twenty-three phone numbers for the time period between June 1, 1997, through November 21, 1997. Most laymen don't realize that phone calls can be trapped *before the fact* as well as after. It was going to be an awesome task to match calls to particular phones, but it was essential to the probe. By 1997 most people didn't have just have one phone; they had home phones, cell phones, pagers, fax phones, and two or three phone lines in a house if they were rich enough to pay the bill. Even Sammy Gonzales, a lowly bag boy at a golf range, had two phones, a pager, and a cell phone. Joey Del Toro had a cell phone, which he obviously used continually, and he had access to his grandmother's phone. Allen Blackthorne had no fewer than six phones, all of them cordless. Add to that the phones of girlfriends that Joey called both before and after Sheila's murder and there was the possibility that with tedious checking and cross-checking De Los Santos could get an hour-by-hour picture of exactly where Joey had been and whom he had talked to.

By adding golf courses and tee times and players' rosters in the San Antonio area, the peregrinations of Allen Blackthorne and Danny Rocha were also easy to chart. The two men had played golf together several times a week. Everyone leaves paper trails that they are completely unaware of; Allen, Danny, Joey, and even Sammy left a more cluttered path than most. Wagers on the golf course are usually settled by the end of the day's play, often by personal checks. According to those who knew both men, Allen Blackthorne had lost a lot of money to Danny Rocha.

"He was a horrible golfer," Danny would sometimes say. "He thinks he's good, but he's *horrible*."

De Los Santos, Albritton, and Iorio spent the two days before Thanksgiving, 1997, visiting still more golf courses. Allen and Danny had played at the San Antonio Country Club in May 1997 because Oak Hills was closed for renovation. Interestingly, Joey Del Toro had worked at the same club six months before.

When they arrived at The Bandit golf course in New Braunfels, they found that it had opened for business on November 1, 1997. On November 7, even as Sheila Bellush lay murdered in her kitchen in Sarasota 1200 miles away, tee-time records—salvaged just in time from a trash can—showed that Allen and Danny teed off at 10:30 A.M. in a foursome with two other men.

Sammy Gonzales spent November 7, his first day on the job, at the Precision Driving Range.

Only Joey Del Toro was absent from his job in Corpus Christi and, subsequently, from the jail where he was supposed to be spending the weekend.

As Gary De Los Santos pored over the voluminous telephone records for the people whose whereabouts and phone calls were vital to the investigation, he began to track Joey along his route from San Antonio to Sarasota and, after Sheila Bellush's murder, up to Atlanta, Georgia, before he headed west again along a slightly more northerly route back to Austin.

Joey might as well have traced his deadly journey in blood across a map of the southern United States. It was that clear.

_____*Chapter Thirty-four*_____

WHILE THE DETECTIVES continued their reconstruction of
Allen Blackthorne's life, the three men arrested for conspiracy to murder his ex-wife moved ponderously through the justice system.

On December 3, 1997, a Bexar County grand jury indicted
Sammy Gonzales for criminal solicitation to commit capital murder,
a capital felony, for Sheila Bellush's murder. Sammy finally realized
that his great and good friend Danny Rocha would do nothing to
protect him. He entered a guilty plea on the Texas indictment and
agreed to testify for the state in any and all proceedings in the future.
He also agreed to plead guilty in Florida. In return for this, the state of
Texas would recommend that Sammy serve no more than thirty years
in prison. With time off for good behavior, it would be considerably
less.

On December 15 Sammy gave an eight-page confession to Gary
De Los Santos, with the blessing of his attorney. Once more Gary read
Sammy his rights under Miranda. And now Sammy, alone with Gary
De Los Santos, detailed the plan that had escalated to the point of
bloody murder.

De Los Santos summed it up later in his follow-up report:

Gonzales was first approached by Daniel Rocha in the latter part of
July of this year [1997] in reference to Rocha wanting Gonzales to
do him a favor by beating up a woman. In exchange, the person who
wanted this woman beaten up would be willing to pay $20,000. At
this first contact with Gonzales, Rocha would not identify the person wanting to contract the beating, but mentioned the person was
the ex-husband of the target. The reason given to Gonzales was
[that] the woman was physically abusing his daughter.

Sammy Gonzales was not a man to embroider a story; he laid out
the facts in stark simplicity. He admitted that he told Danny he would
think about his proposal and let him know later. A week or so later
Danny and Sammy did meet again, and Sammy told Danny that he
couldn't do it. Rocha then asked him to find someone who could do
it. Sammy said he didn't know if he could, but Rocha pressed on and
told him he needed to know soon. Sammy said he might have a cousin
who would do it. Danny told him that if he liked, he could keep
$15,000 and give his cousin only $5000. He promised Sammy that he

would get the victim's address, and Sammy asked that he also get photographs of her.

Sammy said Danny gave him an address and two pictures of the victim-to-be a few days later. This time, he named the man who wanted his ex-wife beaten. It was Allen Blackthorne. Danny put the heat on a little, telling Sammy that Allen had found someone who would do it for $5000, but if it didn't work and his ex-wife continued to beat his daughter, he would be ordering another attack and that would mean another $5000. He suggested that Sammy could keep $1000 for himself and only give his cousin $4000. To prove he was serious, Danny gave Sammy $4000 in hundred-dollar bills, "He gave it to me to hold," Sammy told De Los Santos, "because he said he might end up spending it if he had it."

Up to that point, Sammy said he hadn't made any effort to find someone to do the job. Now he called his cousin Joey Del Toro in Corpus Christi and asked him if he could find someone willing to beat someone up for $3000. Joey said he would do it himself and came to San Antonio to meet with Sammy. The two men had actually driven up to Boerne, and they thought they saw the blond woman in the photographs leaving the house in Boerne Glen.

"Joey wanted to do it right then," Sammy told De Los Santos, "but I deliberately took too long going back to the house and she was gone." Danny was under pressure, and he called Sammy a few days later and told him to read a newspaper article about Sheila Bellush, who was being accused of beating one of her daughters. "That's the first time I even knew her name," Sammy said.

A few days later Danny called him and told him that they had to carry out the beating very soon, because the target was getting ready to move to Florida. Like two bumbling movie villains, Sammy and Joey made several attempts to find Sheila Bellush. They drove past her house and peeked in the windows.

Sammy said he believed the whole thing would be called off, but Danny called him and said the deal was back on. Blackthorne was going to hire a private investigator to find Sheila's address in Florida. Over the next few weeks Danny provided Sammy with videos of the news broadcasts about Sheila's arrest.

For a little while, Sammy forgot about it. In mid-October he drove his mother to New Jersey to see relatives. But then Danny called him to tell him the PI had found Sheila's address and he needed Sammy's cousin to go to Florida to carry out the beating.

"I told him I didn't think he'd go all the way to Florida," Sammy said, "unless he got $5000 *plus* expenses. Danny told me then that

Allen was willing to pay an extra $10,000 *if* he got his daughter back—no questions asked."

Sammy told Danny that the woman would have to be beaten up "pretty bad" and she might even die. "Danny told me that Allen knew she could die," Sammy said. "He never told me that she shouldn't be killed."

It was an ugly story. Sammy Gonzales was recalling conversations about punishing a woman with four little toddlers, a woman who was barely five feet tall and weighed less than a hundred pounds. And they had discussed it calmly, haggling only over money and "expenses."

Joey Del Toro was a mass of muscle, six feet tall, an athlete who kept himself in great shape. How could they have believed that if he beat such a tiny woman, he wouldn't do her grievous, and probably fatal, harm? De Los Santos kept his face empty of expression, but he wondered why one of these men hadn't said, "No!"

After six and a half weeks of intense investigation, with Christmas fast approaching, the tall ranger was hearing the real story behind Sheila Bellush's murder. Sammy Gonzales had a bland, almost innocent face, but he seemed completely unaware of the hideous thing they had done.

And they had done it deliberately, with much advance planning. On November 4, three days before Sheila died, Sammy said he met with Danny and Joey at the Pan American Golf Association Club to discuss the plan. De Los Santos had seen the building; it was nothing like the Oak Hills Country Club, with its sweeping lawns and high walls. The Pan American Club was a ramshackle building with a corrugated tin roof, attached to a burger joint. On that Tuesday night Danny gave Joey $500 in hundred-dollar bills for expenses on his Florida trip, along with an address for Sheila Bellush. He mentioned the "incentive" pay of $10,000 if Allen got his daughter back, and Joey said that it might be easier if he just went ahead and shot the victim, although that might kill her. *If she dies, she dies.* That was the consensus among the plotters. The beating had escalated into something far worse.

According to Sammy, Danny said, "It's up to you how you do it. If she dies, it probably *would* be the easiest way for you to get your money."

AND so Joey set off on his mission of murder the next morning. Sammy said he received a phone call from Joey on Wednesday, November 5, as he headed for Florida. On Thursday, Sammy got another call. Joey was already in Sarasota, and he was checking things out to figure the best time to confront Sheila Bellush. He told Sammy to call him on his cell phone the next day.

When Sammy reached Joey's cell phone a day later, Joey said nervously that the job was done; the woman was dead. Joey said he'd had to buy some things to expedite the job, and he told Sammy he would need another $3000 to cover that. The instructions from the top man had stipulated Joey should "dress casual." And he'd translated that to mean camouflage, so he bought the whole outfit.

On that black Friday, Sammy said he met with Danny Rocha and told him it was done. And Danny had gone to Allen Blackthorne and told him, and asked for more money. According to Danny, Allen said they'd "messed up," but Danny hadn't explained what that meant to Sammy. However, Danny had gotten an additional $3500 to give to Joey.

The rest of Sammy's statement to Gary De Los Santos covered information that the investigators already knew from talking to the women who had partied with Joey and whom he had solicited to cover his tracks. The Texas Rangers, the Austin police, and the Sarasota County Sheriff's Office had followed Joey Del Toro's sloppy trail through Austin, San Antonio, and finally into Mexico on a bus.

SAMMY Gonzales was scheduled to go before the grand jury the following day. He would have an opportunity to read his statement again, make any corrections he might have, and sign it before a notary. He did that and then appeared before the grand jury.

Shortly thereafter, Sammy was taken back to the Bexar County jail. As the result of Sammy's testimony, Danny Rocha was indicted for criminal solicitation to commit capital murder.

The next day, a week before Christmas Eve, Sammy Gonzales entered his plea of guilty to the Texas charges.

Danny Rocha, charged in both Texas and Florida, acted at first as if he, too, would seek a plea bargain. Since the investigators felt that Danny was the man directly connected to Allen Blackthorne, his testimony and admissions could be essential to the case. He seemed a shoo-in for a plea bargain too. Con-wise inmates noted that Danny was scared, afraid of the Mexican mafia inside jail, and heartbroken that he would not see his three boys grow up.

But Danny was cagey and considered himself far more cunning than the authorities. He played "Will he?/Won't he?" with both the Florida state attorneys, Charlie Roberts and Henry Lee, and the Bexar

County D.A., Steve Hilbig. Several conferences were set up with Danny's attorney, and the prosecutors were stunned to find Danny was convinced that he could win in court. In a plea bargain he would probably be paroled in nineteen years, the same sentence that Sammy Gonzales faced. If he went on to trial without giving any information to the investigators, he stood a good chance of being sentenced to life in prison.

Danny had talked a great deal *before* his arrest, calling family meetings at his aunt Otilia's house, telling Rick Speights far too many details, and according to Ray Cevallos, telling him the same story about the trip to Oregon where Allen Blackthorne had solicited Danny to find someone to beat up his ex-wife.

Cevallos told De Los Santos that he felt sorry for Danny after Sheila's murder. He loaned him $5000 and helped him obtain an attorney.

But now no one felt so sorry for Danny Rocha that they were willing to risk their own skins to protect him. One by one, they came to testify before the grand jury: Sammy, Rick Speights, Ray Cevallos, and even, reluctantly, his own aunt Otilia.

Both Danny and Sammy were now charged with conspiracy in two states. Sammy had rolled over quickly, but Danny still played his cards close to his vest. He was betting that Florida and Texas needed his testimony against Allen Blackthorne so badly that a plea bargain would *always* be an alternative for him. He was sure he could chip away at any sentence until he got it down to time he could serve comfortably.

He vastly overestimated his importance. Detectives were already out looking for other ways to trap the big game they hunted: Allen Blackthorne. If Danny waited too long to agree to testify against Blackthorne, he might just find himself out of options.

De Los Santos, Iorio, and Albritton didn't let up on their investigation as they worked continually to verify Sammy Gonzales's statements to De Los Santos and the grand jury. Sammy wasn't a clever man, but his memory was excellent. Once he entered into the plea bargain and testified before the grand jury, he had little to lose. Did he feel guilty about the dead woman in Florida? He seemed to have no emotional connection to Sheila Bellush. He had never seen her beyond her image in two blurry snapshots. He had heard from Joey that his cousin had shot her somewhere in the face and then cut her throat. He had seen a .45-caliber automatic that Joey said he used to shoot her, but that still didn't make Sheila real to Sammy.

She was a stranger. She was also apparently a stranger to Danny and to Joey. If Sammy was to be believed—and he seemed a guileless witness—all three of them had done it solely for the money.

That made it even more horrible somehow—a murder committed without conscience or any personal motive beyond greed. But there was more that the detectives had to prove. If the Three Stooges had done it for monetary gain and for the things they could buy—drugs, bigger houses, better golf clubs, faster cars, prettier women—how much worse was it to think that the man Sheila Bellush had once loved, the man whose two daughters she had borne, the man she had once cleaved to more than the parents who loved her, had coldly ordered her execution.

It certainly appeared that Allen Blackthorne was the Mr. Big with the cash who had orchestrated the murder plot. But when he was summoned to testify before the grand jury, he refused to answer questions. Roy Barrera, Jr., argued that his client was being hounded simply because he once had a stormy relationship with his ex-wife and was a golfing buddy of one of the men charged in her murder. Allen was only caught in a tornado of speculation—and that wasn't fair to him.

OUT in the rarefied air of Shavano Creek, Allen and Maureen seemed remarkably unconcerned about the ongoing investigation into Sheila's death. When reporters called, Allen was always good for a quote or two. He explained that it was utterly ridiculous to think he had anything to do with his ex-wife's murder. He hinted that the police should be looking at his ex-wife's widower, Jamie, instead of him. Allen spoke of himself as a simple man, devoted to his wife and his small sons. He had retired so he could spend more time with them. He liked to play golf, to take care of his lawn, to help his neighbors. He alluded to his hardscrabble childhood and his struggle to make it in the business world.

Allen did not talk to detectives, and they didn't pursue him for interviews. That would come, all in good time. But if Allen had hoped to maintain a low profile, it didn't happen. He had had enough media coverage to make him a public figure. After a time he seemed almost to enjoy his notoriety.

"Allen was the white O.J.," a neighbor said. "He was always talking about the case and protesting his innocence. *The case* became his and Maureen's main topic of conversation."

Whenever the TV vans or reporters showed up, Allen managed to be out in his yard, puttering around, or going to the neighbors to offer to help them with something. He certainly didn't hole up in his house.

"Allen golfed, worked in the yard, and sat in a rocker-recliner in the driveway and smoked," a resident of Shavano Creek recalled. "He practiced golf putts on his lawn, and most of them ended up in our yards, and he always wore a baseball cap and carried a big insulated cup that he got from 7-Eleven. We used to wonder if he was a secret drinker, but we found out it was full of Diet Coke. None of us ever saw him drink alcohol. Maureen was still running around seeing to the computers and other machines she had for sale in the garage."

The Blackthornes enjoyed the 1997 holiday season with their son Brandon and the new baby, Jake. They did not send so much as a Christmas card to Allen's daughters.

_____Chapter Thirty-five_____

GARY DE LOS SANTOS pored over the thick files in Bexar County court records that detailed the seemingly endless divorce and child-custody wars between Allen and Sheila. Even looking at the stilted legalese, he caught the rage that was continually re-ignited between the two, right down to the July 1997 date when Allen finally gave up all claim his daughters. If they were looking for motive—and they were—it was hate. Allen had hated Sheila so much that he didn't want her to have any happiness or any of *his* money.

Chris Iorio followed up on a tip about a man named Tom Oliver who lived in Vancouver, Washington. Clark County sheriff's detectives Scott Schnamer and J. Lebow interviewed Oliver, who said he was Allen Blackthorne's uncle by marriage. Since there was so little information about Blackthorne's early years or his life before San Antonio, Iorio was enthralled to hear what Oliver had to say.

Tom explained that Allen's real last name was Van Houte, and that he was a man who gravitated to power and money. Allen had grown into a powerful person, although the numerous businesses he had been involved in had not thrived—not until RS Medical. "He ran out on a lot of them [business ventures]," Oliver told the Washington detectives, "and he owed a lot of money to various people and banks."

Oliver recalled Sheila's fear when she left Allen and her calls to him and his wife, Debbie, from a church basement in San Antonio telling them how frightened she was.

"When was the last time you saw Allen?" Oliver was asked.

"About three weeks before Sheila's murder," he said. "Allen came to visit us, and he brought a video of his new house. He told us he was just paying the mortgage off, and the place was worth two or three million dollars."

Allen had spoken about Sheila, and told the Olivers that she was "into drugs" and having all sorts of problems. He explained that Stevie and Daryl did fine as long as they were with him, but they got into trouble when Sheila had them. He did not tell his aunt and uncle that he had given up custody of the girls a month or so earlier.

As he had so many times in the past, Allen had said of Sheila, "I think I'll just get rid of her."

Oliver said he mentioned some problems to Allen; a former business associate of his and Debbie's had stolen money and equipment from them. "Allen said, 'Just tell me what you want, and I'll get somebody to take care of him so he won't be around. I know of a Mexican bar where I can walk in and I can lay a note and the money on the table, and whatever the problem is, it will be taken care of on whatever date you say.' "

After that statement Allen had begun to talk about Sheila again. When his uncle asked him if he was going to run into complications with Sheila about the sale of his company—which was supposed to bring in a great deal of money, $99 million according to Allen—Allen said, "I've taken care of that. There will be no problem."

Tom Oliver had never met Danny Rocha, but Allen told him that he was going to loan him money, or perhaps he was going to hire him to manage a golf course Allen planned to build. "Allen was in a great mood," his uncle said, "because he'd been to the Indian gambling spots on the Oregon coast and he made $6000. He gave my daughter a $100 bill."

Tom Oliver also told the Clark County detectives about the fatal accident in which Allen had intentionally killed a motorcycle rider. "He had Sheila lie about it to the police. He made her say they were surrounded by a motorcycle gang."

There was much to learn about Allen's first forty-three years, and the investigators gathered bits of information here, memories there, and records of arrests, bankruptcies, divorces, constant moves from state to state. The handsome millionaire appeared to have come from such bleak poverty and emotional deprivation that the detectives were incredulous that he had somehow managed to amass such a huge fortune, most of it through his activities as a flim-flam man.

His college education was an elaborate lie, and most of the women who had been with him were scared to death of him. Here and there, they picked up references to Allen's sexual kinkiness and his obsession with dressing as a woman.

Everything they learned was fascinating, but nothing—so far—was enough to indict him for capital murder. They kept digging.

Joey Del Toro was interviewed by the Nuevo León State Judicial Police on November 20 shortly after his capture. Texas Ranger Israel Pacheco sent a copy of Joey's videotaped interview to Gary De Los Santos. It was two days before Christmas when he saw it. The interview was entirely in Spanish, but that was no problem for the bilingual De Los Santos. He nodded to himself as he watched the flickering image of the husky suspect. Like all of them, Joey was downplaying his part in Sheila Bellush's murder.

"He minimized at first too," De Los Santos said. "He gave four versions of her death and changed his story a little with each one."

In his first account Joey said that he was hired by Danny Rocha on November 4, 1997, but only to give Sheila a beating, for a fee of $3000. After he was given an address and a photograph, he drove to Sarasota, arriving on Friday, November 7. He said he went to the victim's house between 8:30 and 8:45 A.M. He watched the woman leave in a blue car, and he entered her house through a window near the kitchen and hid in the garage. When she came back ten minutes later, he admitted surprising her in the kitchen and striking her twice in the face with his fist. He claimed he had no weapons with him, and that she was alive when he left her house through the front door. He had immediately driven back to Texas and informed Danny Rocha that the "job was done."

Joey said he had spent the weekend in a motel so small it didn't have a name; then he went to the bus station Sunday morning to catch a bus headed for Mexico. He denied that he was under the influence of any drugs during his trip to Florida.

Joey omitted any reference to his cousin Sammy Gonzales in this, his first version. His second recall of the attack on Sheila was the same as the first, except he said that Danny Rocha had paid him upon his return to Texas. In his third version he mentioned that he had been wearing "military clothing and boots" when he entered the Bellush house. This time he admitted that Sheila was unconscious when he left her house.

In his fourth and final version Joey came up with a whole new suspect, a man named Jorge Lopez. Joey said that Danny Rocha introduced Lopez to him at some golf course in San Antonio and then paid him $3000 to beat Sheila Bellush so that Lopez could then do *his* job. In this fourth confession Joey said that he and Lopez went drinking at a bar called Paradise in San Antonio before they left to drive to Austin, where they slept that night in Joey's white Eclipse.

"At five a.m.," Joey said, "I drove Jorge to the intersection of Congress and Riverside and left him there so he could get a gun. I picked him up a half hour later, and we left for Florida."

The pair had bought a map and arrived in Sarasota on Friday. Joey said he left Jorge off near the victim's house, where he was supposed to wait in the backyard while Joey parked his car a block away. Both men had entered the house to wait for the victim. There, Joey said, he had hit the woman twice with his fist and knocked her unconscious.

"I knew what was going to happen next," Joey said on the video, trying to give the impression that he would have no part of killing the victim. "So I left the house and went back to my car. Then I picked Jorge up in back of the woman's house. I called Danny Rocha on his cell phone and told him the job was done."

After he described dropping Jorge Lopez off for a debriefing with Danny Rocha, Joey picked up on his earlier story of renting a motel room. He insisted that he only found out that the woman had died when he watched a television news show. Danny Rocha had later confirmed it. It was Rocha who told him that the victim's throat had been cut and she was shot. Joey said he panicked when Anna Morales told him that the police were looking for him. He quickly took the bus to Mexico.

Like the other suspects, Joey's confession named the victim's ex-husband as the author of the plot to have her hurt. But he insisted that he only knew this secondhand because Danny Rocha had told him that. "Her husband's name was Allen," he said.

Joey had named a fourth conspirator, but not one of the American investigators ever located the phantomlike Jorge Lopez. He was clearly a red herring, thrown in to minimize Joey's part in Sheila's brutal murder.

CHRISTMAS 1997 came and went in a blur for Gary De Los Santos. In December and January he continued to spend the major portion of his day on the telephone records, establishing a timeline. He concentrated on the cell phones listed to Sammy Gonzales, Joey Del Toro,

Danny Rocha, Anna Morales, Maria Del Toro, and Allen Black-thorne. He charted 170 calls that seemed to relate to the investigation. Some of the calls only substantiated what they already knew, but that was important—the more ways to back up the State's case, the better.

Joey Del Toro had been constitutionally unable to go for long without calling someone, and when he was under pressure, he was a compulsive caller. Allen Blackthorne had at least six phones, including four 800 lines.

On the day Sheila died, De Los Santos saw tragedy in a line of phone numbers, a time of death etched there. Joey called his girlfriend Anna Morales, at 9:29 A.M. There was a gap after that of four hours before Joey began calling a number of people: 1:37 P.M., 1:45 P.M., 1:47 P.M., 2:00 P.M., 2:43 P.M., 2:56 P.M.

At 3:01 Texas time—an hour later in Sarasota—Sammy Gonzales called Ron's Sun Haven Minute Mart in Sarasota. He was answering a page from Joey, but Joey was long gone by then. Ron's Minute Mart was less than a mile from Markridge Road. The phone in the booth outside rang on and on.

CHRIS Iorio, back in Sarasota now, retraced Joey's path through his jurisdiction: the Hampton Inn, the Sports Authority where he bought the camouflage outfit, the service station where he got directions to the Bellush house, all of the pay phones where Joey had made calls. He talked to the neighbors who had seen the stranger in camouflage uniform and also to neighbors who saw and heard nothing at all unusual on the morning of November 7.

As that dread Friday moved toward evening, Joey's calls had originated farther and farther north of Sarasota; he seemed to be heading up into Georgia, rather than turning west along the route he had taken when he drove toward Florida the day before. 3:59 P.M., 4:05 P.M., 4:06, 4:16, 4:21, 4:24, 4:38. Joey was calling Anna and Sammy, possibly to forget the ugly pictures in his brain as he raced north.

Then there were the calls from suburbs of Atlanta, verifying that Joey had wanted to fly home, as Sammy had said, and was looking for a credit card with which he could buy a plane ticket.

Joey Del Toro made thirty-eight phone calls on the day Sheila died and the day after. He received as many. He and his two partners in death for hire—Rocha and Gonzales—spoke often during that forty-eight-hour period. All of that confirmation helped weave the case tighter. But what fascinated De Los Santos and Iorio even more were the calls made from Allen Blackthorne's phones that showed a sudden peak in frequency to Florida numbers. Not on November 7, however. He was too clever for that.

It was tedious work tracing numbers, but De Los Santos kept at it. Local calls didn't appear on phone bills *unless* the caller was too lazy to look numbers up and simply dialed "Information," incurring a thirty-cent charge. Allen seemed to reach for Information automatically. At this point, De Los Santos could only guess the reason for the calls the suspect had made, but he would follow up and find out.

On September 6, the weekend that Sheila and Jamie Bellush moved to Florida, Allen had made three calls to A-1 Bail Bonds. Odd. There were also a number of calls to hotels and motels along Route 10 going east, as if someone was tracking the family as they tried to leave Texas undetected. What Allen was looking for might be almost impossible to ascertain. Two or three months after the fact, there wasn't much chance that motel desk clerks would remember a conversation with someone who called in, asking about guests.

On September 22, Allen made two calls to Sarasota and accepted an incoming 800 number call. De Los Santos zeroed in on the calls that intrigued him, marking them for further investigation. The investigative team already knew that Allen had been in touch with Daryl through his 800 number and that he had solicited Kim Hall to help him look for the Bellush family.

On October 5, there were another two 800 incoming. Both of these proved to be from Sarasota, Florida; they were probably the calls that Daryl made to her father from a phone booth at Lido Beach and from the YMCA shelter. She said Allen had urged her to keep in touch because he was worried about her, but when Daryl called, he had only quizzed her for clues to her mother's address.

Beginning on October 6, there was a flurry of calls from numbers billed to Allen Blackthorne, most of them to Sarasota. Within a month of Sheila's desperate escape from San Antonio, he obviously knew where she was—the city, if not the exact location.

De Los Santos and his counterparts in Florida, Chris Iorio and Ron Albritton, were fascinated by Allen's sudden interest in communication with citizens of Sarasota. Kim Hall refused to help him find the Bellush family, but she had faxed him a local yellow page that listed private investigators. And, indeed, phone records showed that someone at the Blackthorne numbers *had* called a handful of private eyes in Sarasota as well as public utility companies serving that area.

A couple of the PIs recalled talking with a man who wanted to find his ex-wife. However, most private investigators will not search for missing spouses unless they see court orders that indicate child-custody violations or other legal reasons for the search. When they told the caller this, he hung up without leaving his name.

One of the numbers called was Chuck Chambers's Investigations of Bradenton, Florida, a city a few miles north of Sarasota. But when Chris Iorio contacted Chambers, he refused to disclose the name of his client, unless he was ordered to do so by a court of law, because of agency/client confidentiality.

As Iorio and De Los Santos probed deeper, they could see the pattern, and it was chilling. During the first part of October, Allen was getting closer and closer to Sheila. On October 11 he had called Emily's Homemade Ice Cream Parlor in Sarasota, 0.8 miles from the Bellush house on Markridge. It wasn't far from Ron's Sun Haven Minute Mart. Allen was closing in.

On October 11 someone called A-1 Bail Bonds in San Antonio again. A day later Allen's cell number called Danny Rocha from Waco, Texas. On October 25 he used his charge card to call Danny from a pay phone just north of the Houston airport. The next day he called him from the Shilo Inn in Portland, Oregon. Four hours later he called Danny from Lincoln City, Oregon, a Pacific Coast town not far from Siletz, where Allen had lived as a teenager. There were more calls from Lincoln City to Danny. That must have been the same trip where Allen had visited his aunt and uncle, the Olivers—the trip where he won $6000 at the Indian casino.

De Los Santos verified that Allen was in the Northwest for an RS Medical meeting, but he still wondered why the Shavano Creek millionaire was so attached to a golf hustler that he would call him that often. More likely, these were calls from a man who had located a target and was now anxious to have his mission carried out.

Sammy Gonzales had given dates and times; these were mirrored now in the phone records in front of De Los Santos. The numbers he starred were the most intriguing. In San Antonio and in Sarasota, detectives set out to find out why these subscribers had received phone calls from a man named Allen Blackthorne.

Early on Friday, January 2, 1998, De Los Santos arrived at A-1 Bail Bonds on West Martin Street in San Antonio. There were calls to A-1 from two of the many phones listed in Allen's name. De Los Santos quickly established that this was the company that had posted Sheila's bail when she was arrested on September 1. When she left the state of Texas, she gave the bail-bond company her new address: 15 Paradise Plaza, #203, in Sarasota, Florida. The company was unaware that it was not a real address but a cubbyhole maintained by Mail Boxes, Etc. Still, Sheila had called in regularly on the days she was required to do so. And, of course, she had shown up as promised to be arraigned.

The most De Los Santos could hope for was that A-1 Bail Bonds might keep a log of incoming calls. Manager James Byars nodded: Yes, they did. "We keep audio records too," he offered.

"You *record* calls?" De Los Santos asked excitedly.

"We do," Byars said, adding that they didn't save the audio records forever. Eventually they recorded over old tapes. He promised to look through the tapes to see if he could find the calls that had come in from the Blackthorne residence.

Three days later Byars called De Los Santos. The tapes still existed, and he had found the calls in question. They sounded like the same caller—a male. "The guy never identified himself," Byars said. That didn't matter. It seemed a miracle that the tapes were available. They could figure out later who the caller was.

Ron Albritton faxed the yellow pages section on Sarasota PIs to De Los Santos. Several of the numbers listed there correlated with calls made from Allen's numbers. He was stalking her by phone, De Los Santos thought. He probably never even had to leave the comfort of the recliner chair in his garage, but he was busy on the phone—beginning some mornings at 5:00 A.M. He seemed obsessed with locating the Bellushes, mostly concentrating on Sheila. Allen had seen to it that she was arrested on a trumped-up charge, and that was the final straw that effectively drove her and Jamie out of San Antonio. However, once she was gone, Allen—or someone with access to his phone lines—had tracked her to within a half mile of the rental house on Markridge.

Why? Allen Blackthorne had everything a man could want. A new family. A mansion. Endless days to play golf in the sunshine. He was rich, and he had successfully divested himself of any obligation to his two oldest daughters. He was free and clear. Why then had he continued to harass, torment, and shadow Sheila?

MIDWAY through January 1998, Gary De Los Santos phoned Virginia L'Heureux, Allen's secretary. He knew through the ranger analyst Melanie Schramm that the Texas Attorney General's Financial Crime Division was watching Blackthorne's bank accounts for signs of staging—the regular withdrawal of large amounts of money in cash. Virginia had attempted to withdraw $11,000 from the San Antonio Federal Credit Union on October 24, asking for $9000 in cash and a $2000 check. When she was told that a currency-transaction report would have to be filled out, Allen's secretary changed her mind and took only the $9000.

The timing of the attempted withdrawal was interesting. De Los Santos noted that it was *after* Allen had found out Sheila's address in Florida and, of course, two weeks before her murder.

Now Virginia told him that she was just walking out to go to work, and would talk with him later in the day. By three that afternoon, however, De Los Santos had a message from a San Antonio attorney, Patrick Stollmeier, who said he represented Virginia and would need to be present when she spoke with De Los Santos. An appointment was set for a week hence.

Meanwhile, A-1 Bail Bonds had turned over their audiotapes of the anonymous caller. *If* the investigators and a team of prosecutors ever managed to charge Allen Blackthorne and he came to trial, De Los Santos suspected that these tapes might be vitally important, and he carefully put them into evidence.

Florida State Attorney Charlie Roberts, Ron Albritton, and Chris Iorio were anxious to find out if it was Allen who had hired Chuck Chambers, the private investigator from Bradenton, Florida. Chambers voluntarily released two packages, said to contain evidence linked to Allen, to the Sarasota County investigators, and they were placed, unopened, in the Sarasota sheriff's office's property room.

On January 28, Sarasota Circuit Judge Bob McDonald released the packages to the detectives. The chain of evidence of the mysterious packages was maintained meticulously. Forensic technician Lisa Lanham photographed the packages and their contents as Iorio and Albritton opened them. Inside were two commercially dubbed videotapes that showed Sheila as she appeared in court to face charges of child abuse.

The Chambers agency would know exactly what Sheila looked like from those tapes. Albritton and Iorio questioned Matthew Hunt, one of Chuck Chambers's investigators. He told them the first call came from a woman who said she was Allen Blackthorne's assistant, and she asked that any arrangements be confidential. After she was reassured, Blackthorne himself got on the phone. He explained that he wanted his ex-wife, Sheila Bellush, located. One of his daughters had called him from the Sarasota Baptist church in distress, but she wasn't able to tell him where her mother was living. Sheila, Allen told Hunt, was wanted in Texas for skipping out on her bond, and there was a warrant for her arrest.

"I asked him why he didn't call the sheriff's department," Hunt said. "He told me, 'Because I don't know her address.' "

Hunt said he himself had called the Sarasota County Sheriff's Department and discovered there was no warrant out for a Sheila Bellush. He'd called Blackthorne to tell him this. But Allen explained that it was only because an investigator on Sheila's case was preparing a warrant that had yet to be processed. "He told me the paperwork was already done, but he still needed to know her address."

Hunt said it was actually October 11 when the Chambers agency confirmed the address where Sheila was living. It wasn't hard; they knew the location of the minimart, the ice-cream parlor and the Laundromat that Daryl had mentioned. There was only one street with "Mark" in the name. Hunt bought a bouquet of flowers from a Publix Market near Gulf Gate, and he and an associate pretended that they were delivering flowers and had the wrong address. They rang the doorbell at the white house with yellow shutters and actually talked to Jamie Bellush. They gave Allen the address on Markridge and told him that Sheila was definitely living there.

Allen seemed satisfied and paid the agency with a credit card.

If the case began as a net with loosely woven strands, those strands were growing tighter and closer all the time, so tight that soon no one could escape. Even though she was not killed until three weeks and six days later, Gary De Los Santos realized that Sheila was as good as dead on that October day when her ex-husband found her.

But was motive, a series of confessions by two other suspects, witness statements, a dark psychological profile, prior bad acts, and an interlocking map of phone calls enough to prove conspiracy to commit murder? Allen and Maureen clearly didn't think so, although they had no idea how much the investigators already knew about Allen. They continued to give confident interviews and go about their lives as they always had.

_____Chapter Thirty-six_____

JOEY DEL TORO remained in Mexico. There were rumors that a big chunk of money had been paid to dissuade someone from extraditing him to the United States. No one could prove that someone on behalf of Allen Blackthorne had sealed a successful pact with Mexican authorities, but Joey sat tight in prison, safe for the moment from prosecution and unapproachable by American investigators. He was housed in the Reclusorio Oriente in Mexico City, a prison that had taco vendors and shoeshines available, far more casual than any stateside confinement would be, but much removed from his former lifestyle.

Joey's grandmother complained that she no longer wanted to make payments on a Mitsubishi Eclipse she couldn't even drive. She asked that the car she bought for Joey be returned to her. Chris Iorio explained that was not likely to happen. The car was a treasure trove of evidence.

Jamie Bellush requested the return of other physical evidence: Sheila's wedding and engagement rings and her earrings, the jewelry she had been wearing when she died. That request was granted. Someday Sheila's three daughters—Stevie, Daryl, and tiny Courtney—could share these sentimental bequests from their mother.

Gary De Los Santos noted that one of the videotapes about Sheila contained an interview with Bexar County detective Fred McDermott. While tapping a thick stack of what looked like police files, McDermott spoke with a news anchor. Anyone watching would think that Sheila had a lengthy record of child abuse. And, of course, that wasn't true.

De Los Santos talked with McDermott. He acknowledged he worked for Allen Blackthorne in a private capacity after he had investigated the child-endangerment charges against Sheila. McDermott said that most of his information about Sheila and her treatment of her two older daughters came directly from Allen. He had explained to McDermott that he had no choice but to give up his parental rights so that Sheila wouldn't interrogate the girls and beat them after they returned from visits to his home. McDermott said he had also located the Bellushes' address in Sarasota, but despite Allen's demands to know what it was, he insisted he never gave it to him.

Even when Child Protective Services cleared Sheila of any wrongdoing, McDermott said he believed he had enough evidence to pursue the case, and he had made calls looking for Daryl in the Y camp and searching for Sheila. "When we learned Sheila had been murdered," he said, "our investigation ceased."

Ironically, now that it was too late, the Bexar County detective said that he suspected Allen immediately when he heard that Sheila had been killed.

Allen had had any number of people assisting him, some unknowingly, in his determined pursuit of Sheila. It was February 1998 before De Los Santos was finally able to talk with Virginia L'Heureux.

She came to their meeting without legal representation; her attorney was now representing Maureen Blackthorne, and that would be a conflict of interest, so she was speaking for herself. Virginia said she had nothing to hide, although Allen wasn't pleased that she was talking to De Los Santos. That didn't matter, as she no longer worked for Allen. Virginia had been cast adrift. Allen had officially "retired" and told her he didn't need a secretary.

The Blackthornes had promised to find Virginia another attorney after Maureen took hers, but they hadn't come up with one. Nor had Allen handed over the title to the car she had purchased with him as the co-signer.

Virginia said that Pat Stollmeier, now Maureen's lawyer, had questioned her about what she knew that might possibly hurt Allen. "The only thing I could think of," she recalled to De Los Santos, "was a time in 1992 when Allen came back from one of his and Sheila's custody battles. He said, 'I could have her [Sheila] go to Mexico and have somebody do away with her.' I thought he was joking."

Virginia was a soft-faced woman, a religious woman who tended to see the best in people. Her friends had begged her to resign from her job a long time ago, but she had been loyal to Allen. She seemed fearful now, although she was apparently more afraid of a backlash from the Blackthornes than she was of talking to a Texas Ranger. Virginia's job with Allen had begun long before he met and married Maureen. In the beginning, she was a girl Friday to a wealthy bachelor. She had become a secretary and friend to both him and Maureen.

Virginia recalled making the reservations for Allen and Danny Rocha to fly to Portland on July 27, 1997. The men played golf together frequently, and she knew Danny was a bookie. "He came over to Allen's house often to make copies of sports sheets on Allen's copier," she said.

Virginia also said she had personally seen a check as high as $6000 made out to Danny, and she had once cashed a $5000 check to get money to give to him for a gambling debt of Allen's.

In October, Allen had asked her to tape all the newscasts about Sheila's arrest, including McDermott's remarks about her fugitive status, and then have Videos of San Antonio make five copies.

"Why did he do that?" De Los Santos asked.

"He was thinking of sending them to Sheila's husband's boss, and their neighbors in Sarasota, to show what kind of person she was."

"What did he do with them?"

"I don't know."

Virginia said she was also asked to find a private investigator in Sarasota to locate Daryl. "But Allen already knew where she was," she said, "because she called him once or twice from the Sarasota Baptist church. Then he had me call that church and pretend I was a member who wanted to send a welcome card to the lady with the quadruplets, and I needed her address. They told me that the family hadn't filled out a 'member of the parish' card yet."

"Why did he want the address?"

"I have no idea, unless he wanted to see Daryl or know where to contact her."

"Did he mention his other daughter, Stevie?"

"No, he never mentioned her."

Allen had used Virginia to make the initial contact with the Chuck Chambers agency. When they asked for information on Sheila's and Jamie's backgrounds, Allen whispered to her the information he read off his divorce decree: Sheila's birth date and her Social Security number.

Virginia remembered the night of Sheila's murder when she was baby-sitting in the Blackthornes' house in Shavano Creek. She learned that Sheila had been murdered in a phone call from one of Allen's lawyers. She said that neither Allen nor Maureen seemed upset when she told them about it. They'd heard the rumor earlier from Lori Bendseil. Shortly thereafter, Danny Rocha had shown up.

"Why was he there that night?" De Los Santos asked with interest.

"I asked Maureen that later," Virginia said, "after I talked to an attorney when you first called me. And she said Danny came by that night to borrow money. I asked her why he didn't borrow money earlier when he and Allen were playing golf."

Maureen had shrugged off that question. Later there were other things that had made Virginia curious and concerned. After Rocha, Gonzales, and Del Toro were named as the prime suspects by the media, Maureen remarked that the police were probably going to make a big deal about November 4. Virginia said she didn't understand, and Maureen told her that was the day the news broadcasts said that Rocha hired Joey Del Toro.

"She reminded me that on that day a girl, who said her name was Virginia too, came over here and made some copies of betting sheets for Danny. She said she was his secretary. I know it wasn't his wife, because I know Eva Rocha—she's been at Allen and Maureen's," Virginia said. "Then Maureen said that November fourth was also the date Allen went to Danny's house to help him build a fence or something."

That was very odd, because Allen didn't do anything around his own house except work on his precious grass. Virginia said she began to feel that Maureen was trying to program her memory. Then about two weeks before her job ended, she was in the garage talking to the Blackthornes as they smoked. Allen said he was worried because he had left a piece of paper with Sheila's Sarasota address written on it on his desk. He was concerned because he'd suddenly remembered that Danny Rocha might have been sitting at his desk.

"I told him I was sorry for letting Danny sit at his desk, but he had sat there numerous times before and Allen never said anything."

"Did you ever see a piece of paper like that?" De Los Santos asked.

Virginia shook her head. "All of these things happened after they learned that you wanted to talk with me. Allen talked about Sheila's address being in plain sight, and about wanting to build a golf course. And Maureen mentioned that possibly Ray Cevallos and Danny Rocha had planned to blackmail Allen."

On Virginia's last day in Allen's employ, Maureen had asked her to clean off Allen's desk. On top of a pile of papers in the middle of the desk, there was a letter of some sort, typed in capital letters. She had read a little of it, enough to see that it was purportedly from Danny Rocha to Allen about their friendship. It spoke of the golf course Allen would build when he retired, and how Danny had come from a poor Mexican family to a grand house in Stone Oak. He lamented that he had been rejected for membership in Oak Hills Country Club and that he wouldn't be able to play golf with Allen anymore.

"I was being too nosy," Virginia confessed to De Los Santos, "and I didn't finish reading it. But I somehow felt that they meant for me to read it, telling me to clean the desk, and having it right there."

De Los Santos had obtained search warrants for the Blackthornes' bank records. From their Security Service Federal Credit Union account alone, there were twenty-eight cash withdrawals from January 30, 1997, to December 12, amounting to approximately $316,000, in addition to hundreds of checks written. Virginia explained that the cash was mostly for Allen and Maureen's "pocket change" because they liked to have a good deal of money on them at all times. Theirs was a world of extreme wealth and privilege. Allen's biggest extravagance was, of course, golf.

De Los Santos talked to caddies and golf pros and fellow golfers who accompanied Allen on his weekday golf sessions. Even though he lost eighty-five percent of the time, it didn't seem to bother him; he would still press for double or nothing. They said that sometimes Danny Rocha deliberately let him win, knowing he would catch up later in the week.

It was beginning to came together. De Los Santos, along with Iorio and Albritton, worked the case as all superior detectives must. First they winnowed out good information from bad and discovered the secrets that the suspects didn't want them to know. Then they documented everything they could, building a three- or four-layer impervious shell around each bit of evidence, even circumstantial evidence and witness statements.

____Chapter Thirty-seven____

SAMMY GONZALES would never go to trial as a defendant; he had accepted a plea bargain hammered out by Florida State Attorneys Charlie Roberts and Henry Lee. On February 12, 1998, in exchange for agreeing to testify against his co-conspirators, Sammy got the sentence he'd been promised. The Florida prosecutors had worked out the intricate details with Bexar County, Texas, prosecutors. On June 12 he pleaded guilty in Florida to solicitation to commit capital murder, and he was sentenced to nineteen years in prison, a sentence that would run concurrently with any sentence that might result from an additional conviction for him on Texas charges.

Like Chris Iorio and Ron Albritton, Gary De Los Santos felt a sense of satisfaction, but he kept right on investigating Allen Blackthorne. The biggest fish wasn't caught yet. The Bexar County grand jury continued to meet, question witnesses, and consider evidence, but none of that activity appeared to bother Allen.

Danny Rocha had been in a Florida jail awaiting trial since March. He continued to play games with prosecutors in both states, sure that his testimony against Allen was so vital to them that he could write his own ticket. He *was* shocked and hurt, however, when he learned that Rick Speights had given incriminating statements about him in grand-jury testimony.

Speights told De Los Santos about the mail he received from Rocha. Danny accused him of cooperating with the police so he could collect the Crime Stoppers' reward, and in his next letter Speights detected a subtle threat, one that made him fear for his family. "Danny wants me to lie for him on the witness stand," Speights said.

"Why didn't you report that sooner?" De Los Santos asked.

"I felt like I'd already caused enough trouble for Danny and his family."

Danny knew his chance of getting home soon would fade if Rick kept incriminating him. He warned his former neighbor and best friend that his testimony could mean life in prison for him. Danny had asked Rick to be a male figure in his three little boys' lives, and Rick was trying to keep an eye on them. Now Danny was "hurt" and wanted a promise of Rick's loyalty before he "allowed" him to influence his children. Speights told De Los Santos he was trying to help Eva Rocha by collecting gambling money owed to Danny and taking it to her.

Danny wrote to Rick that he refused to do nineteen years the way Sammy was. His wife would divorce him, and members of his family might die if he went to prison for almost twenty years; he intended to fight for a complete acquittal. In his letters Danny blamed prosecutors for seeking "the spotlight" and ignoring the real culprit behind the plan, even though they had plenty of evidence against him, but he stopped short of naming Blackthorne.

Danny rightly suspected the state's case consisted of testimony by Ray Cevallos, Sammy Gonzales, and Rick Speights, and suggested that Rick could have a "memory lapse" that would render his grand-jury testimony useless. "Loss of memory isn't a lie," Danny wrote, suggesting a scenario more favorable to his case. Perhaps Rick might access some "new memories"—memories that said it was Sammy who talked to him about Sheila's death, and not Danny after all. Danny told Rick to say that the Texas Rangers had lied to him and threatened to put him in jail if he didn't tell them what they wanted to hear.

Danny had not given nearly as much thought to the prospect of beating and killing Sheila as he now gave to blaming her murder on someone other than himself. Stuck in a Florida jail, he thought of nothing else.

THERE were few headlines about Sheila Bellush's murder through the summer of 1998; Sammy Gonzales had pleaded guilty, Danny Rocha was still playing cat-and-mouse with prosecutors and they seemed a long way from a trial. Joey Del Toro remained in Mexico.

In mid-June, Jamie Bellush erupted, frustrated that those he felt were primarily responsible for Sheila's death were going unpunished.

He gave press conferences and announced that he was going to demand that Joey Del Toro be extradited. "It tears my guts up," he told Leanora Minai, an investigative reporter from the St. Petersburg *Times*. "This guy shot my wife through the face and cut her throat in front of my quadruplets. *Why* is he still in Mexico?"

Jamie was scheduled to appear on the *Today* show within the hour to debate a representative of the Mexican government, and then head to the Mexican embassy in Washington, D.C., where he planned to picket and pass out fliers while he held a banner reading BOYCOTT MEXICO! THEY ARE HARBORING JOSÉ LUIS DEL TORO, WHO MURDERED SHEILA BELLUSH, MY WIFE, IN COLD BLOOD!

The full impact of losing Sheila had sunk in. Beyond his grief, Jamie was beside himself trying to care for his four toddlers and Stevie. On the morning Minai interviewed Jamie, he was exhausted from lack of sleep. Timmy had croup, and he had been up with him most of the night. He was grateful for his mother, who came to look after Timmy, but Jamie worried when he had to leave him. He was on the road for Pfizer most days, and when he got home, exhausted, his children ran to him, demanding attention and wanting to be held. Stevie wasn't happy either.

Sometimes Jamie just walked to his study and locked the door, losing himself on the Internet. He was lonesome and realized that he couldn't raise his family alone. He wrote back to some of the women who responded to his Web site.

Stevie was outraged at the idea that Jamie was probably going to see other women; she wanted him to remain faithful to her mother's memory forever. The two of them butted heads often. Jamie was angry with Stevie if she came home a few minutes late from a sports event or a dance. Stevie was furious with her stepfather when he made himself a sandwich and left crumbs and dirty dishes after she'd cleaned the kitchen for the night.

And Stevie carried with her, always, the insistent belief that she was reliving her mother's life and that she, too, was doomed. She didn't tell anyone about her dark thoughts, but she wrote them in her purple-covered journal.

Neither Stevie nor Jamie had ever expected that their lives would turn out the way they had. It was worse, somehow, because they both believed that Allen was the one behind Sheila's murder, and it seemed that no one cared and nothing was being done. The world was going on as if that terrible day in November had never happened. Rather than being a comfort to one another, Sheila's oldest daughter and her widower grew further apart. Their home was nothing like a television series with a widowed father, a perky teenage stepdaughter, and four adorable toddlers.

There weren't many laughs, it was real life, and Sheila's presence was sorely missed.

In Oregon, Kerry and Rick Bladorn were still living in their double-wide mobile home with their four children and Daryl. Rick moved his inventory of used cars onto their land so he could be home more. Kerry continued to sell Mary Kay, and in between, they found themselves constantly shuttling one child or another to games and school activities. Their home wasn't television material either, but their marriage was strong as iron, and they loved all the kids.

Daryl missed her mother, and Kerry understood that: She missed Sheila too.

Daryl wrote her autobiography for an English class:

Before my Mom died, I was a sweet innocent child. Up until then, I always thought that everyone was good, and my personality reflected that. I looked at the world through rose-colored glasses. Also, I was gullible to a fault. Now, however, I am not so naïve. While there are still good people in this world, there are also a lot of bad ones. I'm not a pessimist, and I am quite optimistic about the future; however, I will make whatever future *I* choose, and I won't rely on people to get me there.

And a poem:

That Room

Sitting on my bed,
I watch the minutes tick by
I get a thought in my head
And I start to cry.
Twelve years with you,
And now you're dead.
All I knew and all I wanted
Died too.

Your laughing eyes,
Your honey voice,
It chokes me up when I remember.
If you were here,
You would hold me tight.
Then you would say "It'll be all right."

Your smiling face,
Your warm embrace
Gone in an instant.

They say they know I'll be okay.
What the heck do they know.
They don't live each day
With pain, and think
Of the day you went away.

Sitting on my bed,
I bow my head.
Twelve years and now you're dead.
My thoughts provoke
Unfunny jokes.
And now I am in that room with you.

Both of Sheila's girls received Social Security benefits from her account, but it wasn't nearly enough to pay for their myriad needs. There *was* money in a trust for their college tuition, money that Allen had been forced to pay after one of Sheila's more successful court battles. Other than that, Allen did nothing at all to help them. Neither Stevie nor Daryl got so much as a postcard from him after their mother's death.

EVEN though it often seemed that nothing was happening in the investigation of Sheila's murder, that wasn't true. In Sarasota, Danny Rocha was moving toward trial. In San Antonio, Gary De Los Santos was still verifying or eliminating rumors and suspicions. He had all of the Blackthornes' bank records now, along with copies of credit-card and phone bills.

There would be several watershed moments in the investigation into Sheila Bellush's murder. Allen and Maureen grew restive in June 1998. Maybe it was more nerve-racking for them *not* to be questioned by the police after Sammy agreed to testify against others in the murder plot. Danny Rocha's lawyer had released Sammy Gonzales's sworn statements that implicated Allen too.

Charlie Roberts felt that information would jeopardize the ongoing investigation and "impair the ability of the state attorney's office to prosecute potential codefendants." But Sarasota Circuit Judge Bob McDonald felt that any damage to a fair trial was "too speculative."

Worse for Allen was Judge McDonald's unsealing of 200 pages of investigative reports, including transcripts from an interview with Stevie Bellush in which she said she suspected her father of killing her mother. One of Allen's current San Antonio attorneys, Anthony Nicholas, Barrera's partner, derided that notion and any suggestion that Allen would ever have aligned himself with the likes of Rocha, Gonzales, and Del Toro. "To me, it's obvious Rocha wanted to ingratiate himself to Allen, so he took it upon himself to do all these things," Nicholas offered. "Putting two and two together, Rocha knew something about the prior relationship with Sheila and the two girls, so I think he just decided to *help* Allen. Allen didn't ask him to do any of that stuff. If you were going to have somebody killed or murdered and you have all this money, would you ask the Three Stooges? I mean—hell—you'd hire a professional first."

But there it was in black and white in the recently unsealed copies of Texas Ranger follow-up reports. On November 29, 1997, the report read "Blackthorne's arrest is anticipated in the near future."

The average man *would* be sweating.

In June of 1998, Allen and Maureen began to look for a highly visible criminal defense attorney. They tried to retain Gerry Spence, the flamboyant Wyoming lawyer known for his big hats, his fringed suede jackets, and his courtroom victories. But Spence wasn't available.

The Blackthornes settled on Richard Lubin of West Palm Beach, Florida. Lubin, fifty-three, was a dynamic and savvy criminal defense attorney with a long list of clients who had made headlines. Among them were members of the extended Kennedy-Skakel families, including Rushton Skakel, father of Michael Skakel, who was accused of the Martha Moxley murder, another wealthy man and his wife involved in a murder for hire, and several of the richest residents of West Palm Beach who had fallen on hard legal times after combining alcohol and driving. Lubin was a lawyers' lawyer, representing even F. Lee Bailey in his tussle with the government over $2 million in legal fees Bailey had collected from a client convicted of fraud. Lubin—and Bailey—won.

Richard Lubin was very, very good at what he did, and he didn't come cheap. No one would ever know for sure, but the word on the street was that he agreed to represent Allen for $800,000, plus expenses. With Richard Lubin representing them, Allen and Maureen now had a connection to class and fame they had not known before.

"Allen Blackthorne vehemently denies any involvement whatsoever in the death of Sheila Bellush," Lubin said, coming out fighting.

He was unflappable and brushed off reporters' questions about Allen's involvement. "Gonzales's statement is like a game of telephone," he said deprecatingly. "Gonzales *says* that Rocha *says* that Blackthorne *said* that somebody should beat [Sheila Bellush] up. If there's one thing we should know, it's that statements made by people who are looking at the death penalty should not be accepted at face value. There's very often a motive involved."

Lubin stressed that Blackthorne was still in San Antonio and had no plans to go anywhere. "I really don't think this investigation is going to lead to an arrest and indictment of Allen Blackthorne," he said with a smile.

Charlie Roberts, just as unflappable, said, "Our goal has been to identify *everyone* involved in this case, and the investigation will continue until everyone *is* ID'd."

THE long summer of 1998 passed. The Blackthornes seemed to have taken heart with Richard Lubin and his staff supporting them. They still worked hard to make friends, something that was more difficult now than ever. Although Maureen remained close to Pat Aday, she and Allen craved more of a social life.

"Anyone new moving in, you would see Allen and Maureen walking over with a welcome basket," an old-timer on Box Oak said. "The thing that no one can understand is that Allen seemed like such a great guy. It was Maureen who was outrageous. She called one of our neighbors who had a house for sale because she was interested in buying it. The woman explained that she had already sold it, and Maureen asked several times, 'How much did you get for it?' and the woman finally said, 'That's none of your business.' Well, Maureen just went off on her and said, 'Do you *know* who I am? I live in the big, *big,* pink house across the street from you, and I can find out for myself what you got for your house.'

"Things like that seemed to embarrass Allen. But it didn't stop Maureen. She fought over dogs and over her maids dating or staying out late. Her emotions were right on the surface, while Allen was a deep pool. She just wanted to be in control of everything and everybody."

Even though they sometimes found her behavior cloying and unpredictable, when Maureen's joint birthday with a neighbor came around on November 17, 1998, another neighbor took them both out to lunch at La Scala, the restaurant where Maureen first met Allen. "Maureen spent the whole time talking about their case," the hostess said. "She even got a call from Richard Lubin on her cell phone and spent a long time talking to him in the middle of lunch."

_____Chapter Thirty-eight _____

WHILE ALLEN'S ATTORNEYS were denying any illicit connections between their client and Danny Rocha, Danny sent letters to newspapers in San Antonio and Sarasota, claiming that he had tried to cooperate with prosecutors, that he had made five proffers. He couldn't understand why the state of Florida was still going to take him to trial. "It was not supposed to happen this way," Danny wrote. "I am guilty [only] of the conspiracy to commit assault. Unlike Gonzales and Del Toro, I have a wife and children. I could never participate in the murder of a mother."

Danny had been offered the same plea bargain that Sammy took—nineteen years. That wasn't good enough for him. Moreover, he felt he had been hoodwinked by Allen Blackthorne. "I think Blackthorne's back there at home in San Antonio and he is loving it," Danny said. "[Sheila] is murdered. He's not in jail. He's not looking at any prosecution, and I think he's laughing at me."

And that might very well have been true. Danny had always considered himself a clever man, able to spot someone who meant to deceive him, but he had been playing way out of his league in an arena whose danger he never saw.

Charlie Roberts said mildly that "Mr. Rocha can take a polygraph and give a full, complete, and truthful statement at any time." That, Danny Rocha did not care to do. Instead, he dug himself a deeper hole. He kept sending letters from jail—continuing his attempts to change witness testimony—to his good friend Rick Speights.

ON November 7, 1998, a year after Sheila's murder, Jamie Bellush talked to reporters, telling them how painful it was for him to stand by the bad of a sick child. "I thought," he said with tears in his eyes, "that this wasn't meant to be done alone. Sheila should be here with me. If Sheila was killed in a car accident or died of a heart attack, at least there would be some bit of closure to it."

He told them how Timmy and Joey, three years old now, had let go of a balloon and watched it float high overhead. "They said they were sending it to Mommy."

Jamie struck back in the only way he could at the moment. He filed a wrongful-death lawsuit against *all four of* the conspiracy suspects in Sheila's death: Danny Rocha, Sammy Gonzales, Joey Del Toro, and Allen Blackthorne, claiming that "money and hate" were the basis for the murder plot against Sheila.

Danny was broke, and so were Sammy and Joey; they weren't likely targets for a civil suit. And Danny had far more to worry about than monetary damages. He was due to go on trial in Sarasota that month. But it was postponed, and he continued to give press conferences and joust with prosecutors over a plea bargain. In the end—and much to his surprise—Danny found himself just about out of any leverage he might have had with prosecutors. The sweet plea bargain he had counted on well nigh evaporated.

His trial in Judge Nancy Donellan's 13th Judicial Circuit courtroom in the Sarasota County Judicial Center finally began on January 11, 1999. So long delayed, it moved along with surprising velocity. A jury was seated by the end of the first day, Monday. The state and the defense made their opening remarks on Tuesday morning.

Charlie Roberts was not given to histrionics. He came across as a good man and a very intelligent man, soft-spoken but with an encyclopedic grasp of the facts in the Sheila Bellush murder. Now, along with Henry Lee, Roberts would have to explain to the Florida jurors how a nefarious plot hatched in Texas had ended with a brutal murder in Sarasota County. It would be a challenge to describe the meetings, calls, rehearsals, payoffs, and human connections that were as tangled as an old-fashioned PBX switchboard.

Moreover, this would be of necessity the trial of *two* men; in order to prove Danny Rocha guilty, Roberts and Lee would have to convince the jury that Joey Del Toro—who still sat in a Mexican prison—had killed Sheila Bellush. No one on the Florida prosecuting team believed that Danny was a hands-on killer, but they needed to show that if he hadn't pulled some deadly strings, Sheila would probably still be alive.

Roberts hit the jurors hard and early with the ugliness and cruelty of Sheila's death. "This is the case of the murder of a woman named Sheila Bellush who had her throat slashed on both sides of her neck with a kitchen knife and was shot in the face because the defendant—the defendant here—told the killer, José Luis Del Toro, Jr., quote, 'Yeah, it would be easier to go ahead and shoot her; there's $10,000 more for you if she can't take care of her kids anymore.' "

When Roberts continued, Allen Blackthorne's name came up for the first time in a court of law as the mastermind of murder. "Daniel

Rocha met a wealthy man named Allen Blackthorne, who, in very plain and simple words, *despised* his ex-wife," Roberts said. "Plain and simple terms—he *hated* her. He despised her so much that he concocted stories about her abusing their two children, and, in fact, encouraged the children to exaggerate and lie about alleged abuse committed on them by his ex-wife Sheila Bellush, none of which was true."

Charlie Roberts didn't go in for verbose oratory. The loss of the victim was so shocking, the greed of the defendant spoke for itself, and the evidence gathered by the Sarasota sheriff's detectives and criminalists was so compelling that Roberts's opening statement distilled the whole terrible case against Danny Rocha into a court reporter's transcript of only thirty-seven pages.

Even so, the jurors paled and winced as his words created ghastly pictures in their minds.

This was not the usual murder trial; it was more sophisticated legally, and Roberts wanted to be sure the jurors understood the three ways principal first-degree murder could be proved. The testimony to come would show that all of them applied to Rocha. "One: The evidence will show he assisted, encouraged, or paid—or promised to pay—Del Toro to shoot Sheila Bellush by saying, 'It's the easiest way to get your $10,000.' Two: He assisted, encouraged, paid—or promised to pay—Del Toro to do harm to Sheila Bellush, the foreseeable consequence of which was her death.

"And finally, by giving him the address where she could be found—her home—he assisted Del Toro in committing a burglary, entering the residence without the permission of the owner, to commit a crime. Therein, by giving the address, during the course of that burglary, Sheila Bellush was killed.

"The evidence will show that Rocha's sole motivation was greed and the good life. The death of a woman he never met was a small price to pay."

The jurors could consider separate charges: murder in the first degree, principal to murder in the first degree, and conspiracy to commit murder in the first degree.

Defense Attorney Jack McGill's opening remarks indicated that he wouldn't attempt to prove that Rocha was completely innocent. But he maintained that Rocha was profoundly "shocked" when he heard Sheila was dead. And he stressed that, of course, Danny Rocha had never imagined that that might happen.

GARY De Los Santos had flown to Sarasota to testify in Rocha's trial. He, Ron Albritton, and Chris Iorio would spend most of the trial waiting outside the courtroom, barred from hearing what was said beyond the closed doors because they were to be witnesses. It was often this way; those who were the most professionally, and emotionally, involved in a case could not watch the fruition of their efforts.

Testimony started on Tuesday afternoon, January 12, 1999, with Karen Nardi, the 911 operator who took Stevie Bellush's call fourteen months earlier. Charlie Roberts played the tape of Stevie's call, and her agonized sobs echoed throughout the courtroom. The tape spoke for itself.

Stevie was the next witness. She wore a black sweater, and her hair—the same dark shade as her father's—was long and straight, her face chalky pale. She testified about her family's history in a clear voice. For one so young, she had a veneer of steel about her, as if she would not let herself cry.

"Did you ever witness your biological father, Allen Blackthorne, physically abusing your mother?" Roberts asked.

McGill objected and was overruled.

"I did."

"Stevie, would you describe to the members of the jury how your mom treated you and Daryl?

McGill objected on grounds of irrelevancy, and he was overruled again.

"She was very loving and she tried to do the best thing possible. She was always trying to understand if we had a problem—where we were coming from. As far as our schooling and therapy goes, she tried to keep it very organized."

"Did your mom ever abuse you or Daryl?"

"In no way—*no*," Stevie answered, refusing to waver.

When Stevie seemed ready, Roberts asked her about the afternoon she found her mother dead. She recalled her chilling search through the house, finally ending at the kitchen. "I turned to the left and faced the utility room and she was laying (sic) right there in the entrance of the kitchen."

"Could you point with the pin to the approximate area where you saw her?

"She was lying between the dishwasher and this . . ."

"Okay. And what did you see?" It was difficult for the prosecutor to have to ask this, but he had to.

"Leading from the utility room," Stevie said softly, her mind totally back to that moment of horror, "there was a trail of blood, and I saw her laying (sic) between the two counters. She was slumped over, and there was blood everywhere. And I looked at the counter, and the phone was off the hook. There was a drawer open. There were two drawers open, silverware drawers."

Gene Smith, her handkerchief held to her face, watched her granddaughter. Her husband, Don, was there, and so were Jamie Bellush and Kerry Bladorn. Hearing about Sheila's terrible death was an indescribable ordeal for them.

"I hung up the phone really quickly, and I stood there. And then I walked out of the kitchen area and back to the bedroom, picked up the phone, and dialed 911. I didn't believe it as I was calling, so I hung up, like, on the first ring, walked back to the kitchen, you know, looked at the scene again and picked up the phone and dialed 911 . . . 911 was [already] there."

Responding to Roberts's questions, Stevie said she had mentioned her father to the first officers to arrive. "I told them I thought Allen Blackthorne had something to do with this, and they then asked me if he actually came down and did it himself. And I said no—he probably hired somebody or had somebody else do it."

Jack McGill cross-examined Stevie, a dicey foray at best. The jury was clearly concerned about her. Stevie agreed with the defense attorney's characterization of her father as "manipulative." She said she had never seen or met Danny Rocha.

HENRY Lee questioned the officers who had responded to the 911 dispatch: Sarasota police officer Todd Thurow, first, who identified the gruesome color photographs of Sheila's body and the blood trail from the utility room, across the kitchen, ending where she lay. Most laymen have never seen the body of a victim, and these photographs were horrific. The jurors passed them down the rows of the jury box, gulping as they looked down.

Chris Laster, a paramedic, took the stand next.

"What did you observe inside?" Henry Lee asked.

"I walked through the kitchen area. I saw four small children, some with blood on them, walking around the house naked."

"Did [Sheila] appear to be deceased?"

Laster explained the signs that indicated she had been dead for hours.

It was a long afternoon, but the witnesses followed one another briskly. The case was building. Neighbors and workmen in the area recalled seeing the tall man in the camouflage outfit. So far, Danny Rocha seemed at ease. The state was only proving the case against Joey Del Toro; nothing pointed to *him*.

Bob Creager, the Sarasota County fingerprint and trace-evidence expert, explained how he had dusted every surface inside the murder house for latent prints. He had joined Corporal William Kuchar and technician Lisa Lanham to process the crime scene; he was the last member of the evidence team to arrive.

"I stayed behind and loaded up what we call major crime-scene equipment—we don't ordinarily carry it in our vans—alternate light sources, everything from extra evidence bags to barriers, different things. It was around five . . . five thirty p.m. when I got there, starting to get dark. It was cloudy, and we were afraid it was going to rain, so we did our outdoor stuff first."

Creager identified the latent print he had lifted from Sheila's dryer. Lieutenant Bruce Whitehead, an expert in fingerprint identification, testified that he had compared the dryer print to Joey Del Toro's print. "I positively identified the number five right little finger of José Luis Del Toro as the donor of the latent print lifted from the dryer."

"Absolute identification?"

"Yes," Whitehead said. "Absolutely."

McGill hadn't cross-examined any of the state's expert witnesses. The second day of Danny Rocha's trial was over.

The first witness the next morning was Sammy Gonzales, who wore bright red jail scrubs. Once Tio Sammy to Danny's three little boys, Sammy was very dangerous to him now. Danny stared intently at his old friend as if he could somehow ferret out what he was going to say. Roberts questioned the amiable-looking convict on the stand. Sammy described meeting Danny. "First, when I met him," he said, "it was just coincidence. It just grew further as we became good friends, and toward the end we were having Christmases and Thanksgivings together like a family."

But as Roberts asked him about the events that began in August of 1997, it was quickly apparent that Sammy was not going to let friendship keep him from telling the truth. Ponderously he recounted a heinous plot for the jurors. "[Danny] kept persisting, persisting," he testified. "At that time, I told him I can try to find somebody."

It was not a good morning for Danny Rocha, and he appeared to sink in his seat, his thick short neck and jutting jaw almost disappearing into his dark blue suit, as his name seemed to be in every sentence. With only slight changes, Sammy told the jurors what he had told Gary De Los Santos in November 1997. However, this was the first time the public heard of the intricacies of Allen Blackthorne's alleged proposals to Danny. Sammy said it was their fourth or fifth conversation before Danny mentioned the head man of the plot as "Allen."

Sammy admitted bringing his cousin José Luis Del Toro into the scheming. To be sure they kept focused, Sammy testified that Danny added fuel to the fire by giving him newspaper articles and a video about Sheila's arrest for child abuse. But he and Joey had little luck finding Sheila, even with all their abortive trips to Boerne.

Although Danny had given Sammy and Joey $4000 to hurt Sheila, he grew so impatient with them he took it back.

"Did he give you *anything* out of the $4000?" Roberts asked.

"Correct. He gave me twenty dollars."

"Just a twenty-dollar bill?"

"Correct. He gave me twenty dollars, and he gave Del Toro twenty dollars for gas."

Sammy was serving nineteen years in prison; his fate was set. He was keeping his promise, however, to testify against the other men involved in the plot to kill Sheila. There was still a naïveté about him. He apparently didn't grasp how he had been twisted, manipulated, and hounded. It didn't erase his guilt; it only made Danny seem guiltier.

"I'd like to move ahead now," Roberts said, "to early October. Did the defendant make contact with you then?"

"Correct."

"And how was that done—with a page again?"

"Yes. He called me and said he had some stuff to give me, and he said, 'Why don't you come over? I'll give you some stuff, have some dinner with Eva and the kids.' We ate, and then he gave me a whole bunch of golf shirts—and gave me another videotape of Sheila."

Now Danny told Sammy that Allen had Sheila's address in Florida. He asked Sammy if he wanted to go there, and when he declined, Danny asked if his cousin would go. The price was back up. There would be a $10,000 incentive if Allen got his daughter back.

"When the defendant told you about this $10,000 incentive," Roberts asked, "Did he give you any kind of suggestion as to how it should be done?"

"He mentioned words—'beat her up.' He used a lot of bad words. He said 'chingasos,' and he said, 'Do whatever you want to do—the way you want to do it.'"

"I told Danny," Sammy continued, "that in order for Allen to get his daughter back, Sheila would have to get beaten up pretty bad. And that's when I told Danny about she could die of her injuries, and Danny said, 'Yeah, it's a possibility.'"

"At that point," Roberts asked, "did you ask him if Allen knew that she could die?"

"Yes, I did. That's when Danny said, 'Yeah, he does.' "

Sammy said he began to look for Joey without success. In early November, Joey finally paged him. He was in Austin, and he asked Sammy to come up there. "I told him that Danny was looking for him, and he said, 'Is it still on?' I said, 'Yes, it's still on. He said, 'I'll be right there.' "

It was Tuesday, November 4.

Unaware that the ante had been upped by $10,000, Joey was willing to do it for $3000. And so they met that evening—Sammy and Joey and Danny—at the Pan American Golf clubhouse. "We sat down at the table," Sammy said. "We were drinking at that time."

"Did he talk money at this point?" Roberts asked.

"Danny told him, 'I'll pay you $4000 and expenses.' "

"Was it a surprise for you—the amount? Did you think it was going to be something else?"

Sammy answered that he expected $5000, and then the $10,000 bonus.

Joey asked how he was supposed to carry out his assignment and also help Allen get his daughter's custody back. Danny was vague, and Joey asked if he was supposed to bring proof.

Sammy testified, "Yeah, Danny said, 'Just take some pictures of her face.' And that's when Joey told him, 'Is it easier for me to just go ahead and shoot her?' And Danny told him, 'Yes, whatever is easier for you. That's what you can do. It's the easiest way to get the $10,000.' "

Sammy Gonzales testified that he remembered Friday, November 7, 1997, all too well. He knew Joey was in Sarasota, and he got a page from him sometime in the middle of the day. He thought it was about 12:30 Texas time. "When I called him back, he told me, 'Sam, don't ask no questions. Just listen to me. It's done.' And that's when I told him, 'What do you mean it's done?' [He said] She's dead.' And I told him, 'She's dead?' He goes, 'Yes, she's dead.' "

Oddly, when Sammy told Danny that Sheila was dead, he seemed surprised. "I don't remember exactly what words he said," Sammy testified. "He mumbled a lot. He was kind of in shock, a crazed kind of shock. Like he kind of said, 'He really *did* it?' "

Danny Rocha panicked. Had he been sleepwalking through all the plans and scenarios designed to get rid of Sheila? How could he not realize that the plan, once set in motion, was inexorable? Perhaps he had never allowed himself to think about the bloody result? Sammy testified that Danny said he had to go to Allen Blackthorne's house, but he was back in an hour because Allen couldn't see him then.

Sammy testified that he took $3500 that Danny gave him to Joey Del Toro at Carol Arreola's apartment in Austin.

"Did Del Toro give you any money?" Roberts asked Sammy.

"He gave me a hundred dollars."

"Out of this whole event, all the money that was discussed, all the money that was handed to you by the defendant, can you tell the members of the jury how much you got?"

"A hundred and twenty dollars."

"And was the hundred given back [to Joey]?"

"Yes, sir."

"How much were you left with?"

"Twenty dollars."

On cross-examination, Jack McGill concentrated on what the term *chingasos* actually meant. He got Sammy to say that it could be something as innocuous as an argument on the phone.

"Okay," McGill said, "and Danny told you this the first time when he talked about the lady in Texas, this is simple and *chingasos*. Correct?"

"Correct."

"That's the term he used? Simple and *chingasos*?"

"Correct."

On redirect, Charlie Roberts asked Sammy Gonzales just what charge he had pled guilty to. "In that deposition you gave to Chris Iorio [on November 14], you talked about the $10,000 incentive. You also talked about the Del Toro statement 'Wouldn't it be easier if I just shot her?' You pled guilty to conspiracy to commit first degree murder. Is that right?"

"Correct."

"Not conspiracy to commit battery?"

"Correct."

"Not conspiracy to commit assault?"

"Correct."

IT was Wednesday afternoon. The state witnesses continued: Ray Cevallos, who had seen Rocha, Gonzales, and Del Toro in the Pan American clubhouse on November 4. Dapper and expensively dressed, Cevallos was old enough to be Danny Rocha's father, and he owned a golf-supply business and a flowershop in San Antonio. It was Cevallos who helped raise money for Danny's legal defense. He had played golf often with Danny and Allen.

Henry Lee asked Cevallos about the range of gambling bets

among the men he played with. He answered, "Anywhere from a hundred to a thousand per hole."

"Would it be fair to say that Mr. Blackthorne was not as good a golfer as Mr. Rocha?" Lee asked.

"Well, the handicap would state that in itself," Cevallos answered. "Mr. Blackthorne is about a ten to twelve handicapper, while Mr. Rocha is about a one."

One by one, Danny Rocha's former friends took the witness stand against him. Rick Speights, whom he had begged to lie, told all of the secret things they had discussed in the evenings in their backyards. It was shocking for spectators to hear just how many people had had some inkling or even full knowledge of the plan to beat and/or kill Sheila. And yet no one had come forward to save her.

Chris Iorio waited in the corridor for three days, his bulging case file beside him. He and Gary De Los Santos had unearthed the greater part of the evidence for this trial, but for now they were only two cogs in a giant synchronized wheel that was the state's case. Ironically, Iorio would testify only about the search of Joey Del Toro's white Mitsubishi and about finding the camouflage clothing and combat boots that Joey purchased in Sarasota. "We found many items," Iorio said. "We found a map from the Sarasota area. We found directions on a piece of paper that was tied to our area here in Sarasota, found a weapon and three clips that we were later able to identify as the weapon used."

None of the jurors could possibly realize how much work the detective had done to elicit the physical evidence that now came into the trial: the clothing, boots, contents of the car, Sports Authority receipts, the Hampton Inn receipt for the night of November 6, 1997, the green backpack that held the death gun. And yet Iorio was on the witness stand for mere minutes. He was back in the corridor, almost shocked to realize how quickly his testimony was over. That was the way a trial could go—hours of sometimes wearying testimony to lay the groundwork and then startling testimony like Iorio's that allowed vital evidence to be entered into the record.

De Los Santos teased Iorio gently for overpreparing for his few minutes in the witness chair.

His time was coming.

The forensic technicians and criminalists were back on the stand. William Kuchar recalled sealing the evidence Iorio and the Austin police had gathered, keeping the chain of evidence sacrosanct. Lisa Lanham was the forensic technician designated to be the lead at the

murder scene. She had taken the terrible photos in the Bellush home—
every corner of every room—and the pictures of Sheila, dried blood
curtaining her face, as she lay on her back where she had fallen, her
right leg extended and the left jackknifed beneath her.

Lisa was a slender young woman with dark hair cut in a soft cap
around her head. She didn't look like someone who could stomach
the abattoir the Sarasota sheriff's staff faced on that dread day in November. But she could cope with the horror of homicide, and she
had—many times before and after that stormy Friday night in November 1997.

"I'd like you to now tell the members of the jury what observa-
tions you made of the scene immediately around the body, as well as
any items of evidence that you felt were relevant that you observed in
the kitchen or in the utility room."

"The area around the body—there was a large amount of blood.
There was also an apparent projectile on the floor." Lisa said that a
bullet had gone through the utility-room wall, across the dining room
used as Stevie's bedroom, and then bounced off a mirror, tumbling
through a half door, and ironically falling where Sheila had fallen.

"You mean the actual bullet, *an* actual bullet?"

"Yes."

Lisa had attended Sheila's autopsy and received a sample of her
blood to be kept under refrigeration until it could be compared to a
suspect's blood.

Charlie Roberts and Henry Lee were presenting a careful case
with a flowing timeline so that the jury would know every sequence of
the probe into Sheila Bellush's death. They could follow the evidence
and the testimony for themselves. Experts followed experts to explain
what trace evidence had been identified—or not identified.

Lieutenant Bruce Whitehead was recalled. He had fingerprint
cards with latents raised on the gun found in Joey Del Toro's car in
Austin, Texas. One latent print had been lifted off the safety lever of
the pistol and the other from the frame below the slide on the serial
number side. Joey's fingers had left both prints.

The foundation of this trial was to prove Joey a killer. The state
had connected him to Danny, and peripherally to Allen. The jurors
had to believe beyond a reasonable doubt that Joey Del Toro had
killed Sheila before they could convict Danny Rocha.

Amanda Numbers, the clerk on duty at the Hampton Inn in Sarasota, recalled meeting Joey Del Toro. "He came to the desk. He didn't
look old enough to rent a room, because you have to be twenty-one,

so I asked him for his driver's license. I made a photocopy of it, and I stapled it to the reg card." Joey had checked in at 7:28 on the evening of November 6 and checked out on the morning of November 7. He might as well have taken out an ad in the Sarasota newspaper announcing that he was in town; he had left a blazing trail of receipts and phone calls that led the investigators right back to him.

It was Wednesday afternoon when Gary De Los Santos was called as a witness. His months of investigation were, at least for this trial's purposes, reduced to ten pages of transcript. He had taken the statements from Rick Speights and Ray Cevallos and delivered Danny's letter requesting that Rick lie for him. Roberts asked De Los Santos about that, and if he had attempted to talk with Allen Blackthorne. He had indeed.

"Would he speak to you?"

"No, sir."

De Los Santos was no glory hound. He didn't care what part he played in this trial. He believed that Sammy, Danny, and Joey were all guilty of carrying the baton in the vengeful relay to have Sheila killed. He also believed that the instigator still played golf in San Antonio. If *that* man was ever brought to trial, only then would he be satisfied that he had done his job.

And then the trial had an abrupt recess. After listening to Sammy's testimony and hearing his name being drawn ever more deeply into the plot, Danny was worried. Halfway through Wednesday afternoon he told Jack McGill that he wanted to plea-bargain. At this eleventh hour, he said he was finally ready to tell the complete truth. Judge Donellan dismissed the jurors early. Puzzled, they filed out, unaware of what was happening.

It could have been all over at that point. A special meeting was held, and De Los Santos, Iorio, and Albritton met with Charlie Roberts and Henry Lee and Sarasota County D.A. Earl Mooreland. Rocha's attorney had given his consent for them to interview his client.

The three detectives talked with Danny in the Sarasota County jail at six that evening. The interview began with Danny telling them what *he* wanted. Rather bizarrely, he still believed that he could dictate the length of his sentence and where he would serve his time. He particularly wanted a sentence shorter than Sammy Gonzales's.

"First, he wanted four to seven years," Henry Lee recalled. "We said no. Then he was up to twelve. We said no. We told him all along, the minimum was nineteen—just like Sammy's."

But he wouldn't even consider nineteen years. Since Allen was still free, Danny stubbornly believed that he could fling down the final card in a game of legal poker—and win. De Los Santos tried to explain to him that it was not going to be like that. "Look at the jury, man," he urged. "Look at their faces."

Danny didn't seem to hear him. He kept laying out his terms. "I'm a gambler," Danny said easily. "I like the odds."

"Those aren't Mexicans on the jury," De Los Santos said. "You're not on your turf. You're not in control of this courtroom. You are *fucked,* man."

And slowly it dawned on Danny that he had been a rank amateur playing in a game with a true professional sociopath. He had been manipulated by the man he thought *he* controlled. *He* was the one on trial for murder. His face wasn't as confident, and his shoulders sagged a little. Now, at last, was Danny Rocha going to tell them the truth to save himself from life in prison?

As he spoke, Danny followed the scenario that Sammy had been telling the investigators for more than a year. He agreed that Sheila's murder had been for hire and that Allen Blackthorne was behind it all. This was the very first time that Danny had talked in any depth about the murder plot and the first time he went into detail about Allen. It looked hopeful. He said Allen had concocted the story about Sheila being a child abuser to use as a backup plan if they all got arrested.

It was true, Danny acknowledged, that he and Allen had first discussed the plan on the trip to Oregon in late July. He added that Maureen Blackthorne had been in on the murder for hire scheme and said that she was the one who came up with the code word Black Cow. Danny admitted that he had gone along with the scheme because he wanted that 25 percent of Allen's dream golf course.

At first, he said, Allen wanted Sheila shot twice in the head, but then he "got cold feet" just before Sheila moved to Florida. Then Allen said he only wanted her "tortured and crippled," but he wanted her to have numerous beatings at $5000 per beating. At the Pan American Club meeting, Danny said, he was the one who told Joey Del Toro to shoot Sheila twice in the head—on Blackthorne's orders.

The payoff varied from $10,000 to $50,000 to $250,000 for the sports bar. Danny Rocha was scornful of Rick Speights's testimony. He implicated Rick in the plot too, saying he knew about it all along and had even suggested an alternative hit man who worked at a golf course in Mississippi.

"I never did get any money for my part," Danny finished. He said he would be willing to take a lie-detector test to validate his statement.

It was nine o'clock in the evening, but the detectives contacted Ranger Lieutenant Ray Cano and Ranger John Martin and asked them to meet the plane carrying Ray Cevallos and Rick Speights back to San Antonio. All through the night various investigators attempted to verify Danny's newest stories, and they could not. Sammy Gonzales looked puzzled when Chris Iorio asked him what Black Cow meant; he'd never heard the term before.

When Danny was hooked up to the polygraph at noon on Thursday, January 14, he looked nervous. He said that parts of his story were "bullshit." He admitted that Rick Speights had wanted nothing to do with the murder plot. He said he had received $10,000 in hundred-dollar bills from Allen the Monday after Sheila was murdered. He was supposed to give it to Joey Del Toro, but he kept it instead, using it to pay part of his attorney's fee. He had asked for the money on the night of Sheila's murder, but Allen didn't have that much on him then. Danny agreed that Allen had never said in so many words that they should kill Sheila, but his meaning was always clear.

James O'Conner, who was hired by the defense, monitored the tracings of the polygraph. Two hours later O'Conner reported that Danny Rocha showed deception on several questions: (1) "Did Allen Blackthorne tell you the best way to do it was to kill Sheila and put two bullets in her head?" (2) "Did Allen tell you the best way of doing it was to kill Sheila Bellush?" and (3) "Did Allen specifically tell you there would be a $50,000 incentive if Sheila Bellush was killed?" Danny had answered yes to all three.

He was still lying. He flunked the polygraph six times. There was no question that Danny was telling the truth when he said he knew what Allen wanted, but he apparently wasn't completely truthful in the terms he quoted. He had promised to tell the complete truth to save his own skin. And he lied. He embellished. The monetary discussions had changed so often that maybe even he didn't remember them all at this point.

Danny Rocha was angling for a shorter sentence, but he had just destroyed his chance for that. His trial continued.

Was it possible that Allen Blackthorne was *not* involved in Sheila's death? Or had Danny added so many false details to implicate him that he had succeeded only in strengthening the case against himself and weakening it against Allen?

Later Henry Lee spoke to Sarasota *Herald-Tribune* reporter John Tedesco about his department's frustrations in dealing with Rocha.

"We wanted to work with him from day one," Lee said. "We always knew he was the key. He refused. All we've insisted on all along was that he give us a complete and truthful statement."

Now it was revealed that Charlie Roberts had even flown to San Antonio when Rocha was arrested, ten days after Sheila's murder. He had offered the nineteen-year deal then, but Rocha balked. "We met three different times," Lee said, "and he gave us three different stories. We checked out each of his stories. None of them were true."

Lee looked tired, as he said, "The story kept changing. The detectives stayed with him for four or five hours and finally gave up."

DANNY Rocha, who had just blown his last chance, was back at the defense table on Thursday afternoon. And the evidence against him and his alleged co-conspirators piled up relentlessly.

Peter Tsingalles, the Florida Department of Law Enforcement's crime-laboratory serologist, took the witness stand. He was an expert in the analysis of body fluids and the DNA markers that can be isolated from them. He opened an evidence packet containing two tubes of blood and identified them as Sheila Bellush's. Next he identified the contents of a container marked "Exhibit 38" as a pair of camouflage pants.

"Did you find human blood on those camouflage pants?" Roberts asked.

"Yes, I did," Tsingalles said. "The DNA profile from the Exhibit 3T stain [from the pants] was consistent with the DNA profile from 36-M, which was the stain card from Sheila Bellush." Tsingalles had also found Sheila's blood on the left military-style boot Del Toro wore on November 7.

Terrance LaVoy, a senior crime-lab analyst for the FDLE and an expert in firearm and tool identification, told the jurors about comparing the gun in the white Mitsubishi with the shell casing and slug found at the murder scene. He showed them the gun. "This particular firearm is a .45-caliber semiautomatic pistol that was manufactured by the Colt firearms company."

"Did you test-fire that weapon?"

"I did. I test-fired it six different times."

Under a scanning comparison microscope, LaVoy had compared the bullets from his test firing with the bullet that broke Sheila's jaw. They had both been fired by the same gun. He did the same with the casings and found the extractor and ejector marks on the bottom of the casings identical. The gun Joey Del Toro borrowed in Texas was the gun used in Sheila's murder.

"Call Sergeant Gary De Los Santos," the court clerk said, recalling him to the stand. De Los Santos, fluent in Spanish, was asked about the term so foreign to this Florida jury: *chingasos*. Roberts sought to correct any suggestion that it meant something as mild as a verbal argument.

"Would you please define the term to the members of the jury?"

"*Chingasos* is Spanish slang which would literally mean 'butt blows,' blows striking somebody," De Los Santos explained.

"Does that term employ the use only of physical force as opposed to verbal force?"

"Just physical force."

Dr. Wilson Broussard, Jr., the forensic pathologist who performed the autopsy on Sheila Bellush's body the morning after her death was to be the final witness for the state. Whatever the term *chingasos* meant, there was nothing "simple" or mild about what her killer had done to her. The jurors had seen Sheila Bellush as she was in life as well as the photographs of how she looked when thirteen-year-old Stevie found her. Dr. Broussard gave them an excruciatingly detailed view of the injuries he had found at the postmortem.

In response to Henry Lee's questions, Broussard said he had gone to the murder scene on November 7 at 8:00 P.M. and witnessed the victim. His first impressions were verified as he proceeded with the formal autopsy. "The most fatal injuries, in my opinion, were a combination of three major injuries—a gunshot wound to the face and two major incise wounds, [by that] I mean cuts with sharp force injuries to the neck. The combination of these three disrupted major vasculature in the body. The exsanguination—the loss of blood—due to these three major injuries was the cause of death."

Dr. Broussard also described numerous defense wounds, characteristically found on the hands and arms. One stab wound had gone completely through Sheila's hand at the base of her little finger. There were both incised wounds (longer than they are deep) and penetrating wounds to her hands. They would not have been fatal, but they had bled copiously.

"Did you notice any injuries to the head?"

"Yes. On the back of the head there were two large lacerations and associated contusion or bruising underneath the scalp in that region. There were also recent contusions or bruises on the knees, both sides."

All of them, Dr. Broussard felt, had been sustained near the time of Sheila's death. As he testified, the autopsy pictures were introduced, numbered forty-eight through sixty.

Such pictures are stunning to lay persons; they are part of almost every homicide trial. If, as the state implied, the man on trial had been carrying out the orders of an ex-husband full of hatred and the need for brutal revenge, Allen Blackthorne had gotten what he wanted. Could the jury, unfamiliar with the tangled story before the trial, and still with only a glimpse of the mysterious Blackthorne's involvement, grasp what had gone on?

Pointing to one of the clinically specific photos, Dr. Broussard described the bullet wound. "This is the entrance wound. It enters the right-cheek region, travels through the soft tissue, fractures the angle of the jaw, lacerates minor vasculature [veins], facial arteries, soft tissue, passes around the level of the fourth cervical vertebra, which stays lateral, doesn't go through the vertebral bodies or damage the spinal cord—and exits the back of the neck here."

"Would this woman have been immediately incapacitated?" Lee asked.

"Yes. The .45-caliber being a powerful handgun, the energy wave can cause a shock [to the heart] or concussion. It would not necessarily make her totally unconscious, but I would think it would be consistent with probably incapacitating her and shocking to the point of dropping to the floor."

"Would it have been fatal had she not obtained medical treatment?" Lee asked.

"Yes, because of the bleeding. It would have been a slower process if she hadn't sustained other wounds. If someone could have gotten to the phone and called for help, [she could] have survived this wound."

The two long, relatively shallow cuts on either side of Sheila's neck had not reached the deep carotid arteries, but sliced through the jugular veins, right and left, creating more bleeding. The cut on the right side went deeper and slammed into vertebrae in her neck. That would explain the bent knife. The severed jugular veins bled too. "That would cause significant bleeding," Dr. Broussard testified. "Without medical attention, [this] would eventually prove fatal."

"Do you have an opinion," Lee asked, "as to how long someone would remain conscious or survive after sustaining all three of these wounds you just described?"

"I would think it would be at least several minutes."

"And after several minutes, there would be—"

"Probably [she] would slip into unconsciousness, and as the heart would continue to beat, the bleeding would continue."

"And then [she would] eventually die?"

"Correct."

The blows to Sheila's head had probably been dealt by her killer with some blunt force, or she could have fallen twice and hit her head on something in the kitchen or utility room.

Fourteen months after Sheila's death, the courtroom was hushed with the horror of it. But Henry Lee couldn't stop. The jurors needed to know what all of the conniving and payoffs had led to; they had to understand what Sheila had suffered as she tried in vain to save her babies and herself. Lee led Dr. Broussard through the myriad details of the defense wounds.

Sheila's feet had been bare and stained red when she came to the medical examiner's office. "When you see the blood on the bottom of someone's feet," Broussard explained, "you obviously know they've walked through it."

"Upright and struggling?"

"Consistent with that."

It wasn't that far from the utility room to the far edge of the kitchen—perhaps twelve feet—but it would have seemed endless to a woman fighting to stay conscious, her feet entangled in clothing from the laundry, probably with a little boy clinging to one leg and a powerful man lunging at her with a knife. That Sheila had even managed to reach the wall phone was somehow miraculous. But she lost consciousness as she tried to dial for help.

"Did you also do a drug screen as part of the process?"

"Yes, we did," Dr. Broussard said.

"What were the results?"

"They were negative. The blood alcohol, urine drug screen, disclosed no drugs."

The state rested its case.

ON Friday morning, January 15, 1999, the jury waited to hear the defense witnesses, but there were none. Danny Rocha chose not to take the stand and acknowledged before Judge Donellan that he knew he had the right to do so. There was no one else who would say that he was an innocent in this case. The defense rested without calling a single witness.

The time had come to move on to final arguments.

Few would disagree that Joey Del Toro was guilty of killing Sheila Bellush. Jack McGill did not dispute the facts in the case against his client. In his argument, however, he pointed to Danny as a man in the dark—a man who was "in shock" when he heard that Sheila had been killed. McGill repeated, "*He was in shock!*"

McGill looked at the jurors. "If you find basically that Danny Rocha had no conscious intent that the homicide be committed, then you have to find him not guilty. Look to see if he did some act, word, or intended to incite, cause, or encourage the other person to do it."

McGill characterized Sheila's murder as "the act of a madman, the act of someone who's gone berserk, looking at the scene, looking at the manner in which it happened, looking at the cuts, the gun, obviously not something that was planned, reasonably foreseeable, nor was it the act of someone who is rationally carrying out some plan."

Perhaps not, but then again it might well be that the "madman" had only been a klutz, an amateur hit man hired by far more cunning minds than his own.

CHARLIE Roberts began the final arguments for the state of Florida: "Members of the jury, in early August of 1997, that man—the defendant—told Rick Speights, 'Allen Blackthorne asked me if I knew anyone who would kill his ex-wife, Sheila Bellush.' That was the testimony you heard in court. You did not hear only that he said he wanted her dead, as Mr. McGill said in his closing argument. The words were specific: 'Do you know anyone who would *kill* my ex-wife?' Not scare. Not beat. *Kill.*

"From that time on, until November 4, 1997, that man persisted and pestered Sam Gonzales to find someone to beat Sheila Bellush. The defendant is not on trial for the attempted beating that was to occur in Boerne, Texas. He is on trial for the *murder* of Sheila Bellush that occurred in Sarasota, Florida, on November 7, 1997."

Roberts went back over the plotting and the denouement of the crime. There was no question, he stressed, that Joey Del Toro had killed Sheila Bellush as an "independent act" of his own volition. "This is a clear-cut case of murder in the first degree," he told the jury. It didn't matter that Danny Rocha was playing golf in Texas as Sheila Bellush fought for her life in Florida. He was as guilty as the man with the gun and the knife.

Charlie Roberts asked finally, "I'd like to leave you with one question and answer, and I'll give you the answer first. The answer is 'Yes.' The question is 'Would Frankie, Timmy, Courtney, Joey, Stevie, and Daryl's mother be alive today if it weren't for that man over there?'"

Although Jack McGill spoke forcefully and cogently in rebuttal to Charlie Roberts's arguments, that *Jeopardy*-like answer and question still rang in the courtroom.

The jurors were excused to begin deliberations at 11:40 A.M. on Friday, January 15, 1999. One juror had an immediate question, sent out on a piece of paper: "Why wasn't Blackthorne arrested?"

Judge Donellan explained to them that the answer to that was not their responsibility. Allen Blackthorne's status had no relevancy in this case. "I implore you," she said, "do not consider that as part of your deliberations."

The rule of thumb is that the longer a jury stays out, the more optimistic the defense becomes. Danny Rocha and Jack McGill didn't have time to get their hopes up. The jury was back in less than five hours. It was still Friday afternoon. They had found Rocha guilty of first-degree murder and guilty of conspiracy to commit murder in the third degree.

The "gambler" had guessed wrong. Rocha heard the verdicts and bowed his head.

On February 19 he appeared before Judge Donellan for sentencing. When she asked if Rocha had anything to say before sentencing, his attorney said no. And then the judge said that *she* had some questions for Rocha. "Who made you God?" she asked. "Who gave you the right to plan to inflict pain on another human life, let alone to take another's life? You did both because you wanted to play God, because you wanted a piece of a golf course. Now your life, too, is over the way you dreamed it or lived it or knew it. It cannot be redeemed. But is there redemption for you? Perhaps, if you consciously remember the beautiful life you've taken and the other lives you've ruined."

Judge Donellan was as shocked as anyone in her courtroom at the cold-blooded plan to take away Sheila's life. Now she meted out Danny Rocha's punishment: life in prison, without parole, and 13.3 years for conspiracy to commit aggravated battery. He was still charged with solicitation to commit capital murder in Bexar County, Texas. Like Sheila's children, Danny Rocha's three little boys would grow up without a parent; he would have his life, but it would be a life in prison, more than a thousand miles away from them and his wife, Eva.

But the question jotted down by an anonymous juror in Sarasota was the one that consumed those who loved Sheila, and haunted the detectives who had rounded up three of the four suspects. *Why wasn't Blackthorne arrested?*

_____*Chapter Thirty-nine*_____

AT LONG LAST, the focus of the investigation was squarely on Allen Blackthorne. If he thought the unpleasantness and suspicions would go away after Danny Rocha was convicted, he was wrong. Although Joey Del Toro was still in a Mexican prison and had not yet faced a jury, proof of his guilt had been dutifully reported by newspapers and wire services all over America. And so had the implication that Allen Blackthorne was the master plotter of the whole ugly scheme.

It was 1999 and Bexar County got a new district attorney: Judge Susan Reed. Her chief criminal deputy, Michael Bernard, was assigned to the investigation of Allen Blackthorne, along with the D.A.'s investigator, Buster Burch. They joined Gary De Los Santos. Reed was interested in putting the investigation of Blackthorne into high gear. So was Bill Blagg, the U.S. Attorney for the San Antonio region. He and his top assistants, John Murphy and Richard Durbin, had been watching the case for twenty months. Because the murder plot had been hatched in San Antonio, Texas, and carried out in Sarasota, Florida, it involved interstate commerce, and the crime was, in essence, on wheels. Both Reed's and Blagg's offices had the legal right and—as each of them felt—the moral obligation to work to find every member of the conspiracy.

Moreover, there was a relatively new and little-known statute that made it a federal crime to commit domestic abuse *across* state lines. If the detectives and prosecutors could prove that Sheila was killed because her former husband tracked her to Florida from Texas and was the driving force in this despicable crime, Allen Blackthorne might well be convicted of not only state but federal charges. It would be an important legal victory for abused women all over America; too many battered wives flee to other states to escape husbands and lovers who terrorize them—only to realize they have no place to hide. Federal convictions are hard-nosed; prisoners must serve at least 85 percent of their sentences, as opposed to 66⅔ percent in most state prisons. And if Allen should be found guilty in a federal court, he might very well get the death penalty.

Quietly FBI special agent Michael Appleby and San Antonio Police Department detectives Richard Urbanek and Jesse Salazar began to attend meetings on the continuing probe.

Outwardly Allen did not seem at all fazed that the case was still open. District Attorney Reed's office put her investigators on his trail, and Buster Burch began to explore Allen's background too. He and De Los Santos widened the perimeters designed to trap the millionaire golfer. They discovered that Allen was working hard to shift suspicion to Jamie Bellush and to distance himself from Danny Rocha, whom he termed a congenital liar. He maintained that he had talked to a number of his golf partners about what a terrible mother Sheila was and how worried he was about his daughters. One doctor Allen golfed with recalled that Allen hired his own PI to investigate Jamie Bellush.

Allen was looking for ways to connect Joey Del Toro to Bellush, and he spoke of what seemed very tenuous links. Allen said that Jamie had once supplied Pfizer drugs to a pharmacy where Joey worked. He told the physician he golfed with that Jamie had known Sammy Gonzales because Jamie had played golf at the San Antonio Country Club. He said that Jamie also golfed with Danny Rocha.

"Why didn't Allen tell someone that before now?" De Los Santos asked the doctor.

"I have no idea," the doctor said. When De Los Santos asked him not to mention that they had talked, the physician refused, saying he considered Allen his friend and he wouldn't lie to him.

It was the spring of 1999, and at the moment, the Blackthornes were in Florida. In Shavano Creek, Jeanette, the neighbor who shared a birthday with Maureen, had an odd experience with the Blackthornes when they were staying in a Florida condo while Allen golfed. At nine one evening, Maureen called Jeanette and asked her to go into the office in their house and change the settings on her four phone lines. She said the Hispanic couple who were looking after the house couldn't figure the phones out. So Jeanette went over, and the couple let her in. "When I got to the phones, I couldn't miss seeing this piece of paper right next to them," Jeanette said. "Someone had written on it with dark broad strokes, and it read, 'Rocha is a fucking liar!' "

As she stood there, the phone rang immediately, and it was Maureen, checking to see that the phones worked. "It was so easy to fix the phones," Jeanette said. "Only a matter of pushing two buttons. Maureen spoke fluent Spanish, and she could have told her house-sitters what to do. Later I suspected that she just wanted to get me over there to read that note about Rocha to get me on her side."

Jeanette didn't know that Virginia L'Heureux had an almost identical experience when she was asked to clean Allen's desk on the last day she worked for him—and found the letter signed "Danny" there.

The Blackthornes were on the offensive.

But so were De Los Santos, Burch, and myriad prosecutors. The Texas Ranger and the Bexar County D.A.'s investigator flew to Newton, New Jersey, to talk to Jamie Bellush and his stepdaughter, Stevie. Stevie had excellent and pathetic recall of her parents' marriage. She remembered her father beating her mother with a belt on one occasion when the police came. She knew that her father had tried to drown her mother by sticking her head in the toilet bowl, and that he had once tried to run over her.

He hadn't treated his two older daughters much better than he did their mother. Stevie recalled Allen's sexual abuse of her when she was very small, not more than three. "He beat Daryl and me once when the toilet accidentally overflowed at his house. He held us down and hit us with a metal bow and arrow. We had bruises on our stomachs, back and sides. We didn't report it."

Asked if her mother had ever disciplined them physically, Stevie said she had spanked them, "but it was nothing like my father. I got along fine with my mother." She denied that Sheila had ever been out of control when she spanked Daryl.

The two investigators talked with Jamie Bellush. He said he knew nothing firsthand about Sheila's marriage to Allen—only what she had told him. According to Sheila, Allen had very kinky sexual behavior and wanted to hire male prostitutes to have sex with her. He had also hit her, once breaking his own hand when he struck her in the face. "He threatened to throw acid in her face if she ever left him," Jamie said quietly.

"You ever know any of the three other guys involved in Sheila's death?" Buster Burch asked.

Jamie shook his head. "None of them."

"You never played golf with Danny Rocha?"

"I never even saw the man before."

Allen's campaign to paint Jamie as the real mastermind behind Sheila's murder continued. Pat Stollmeier, one of Maureen's attorneys, submitted in District Judge Pat Boone's court that Bellush's attorney, Ken Nunley, was withholding evidence of his involvement. Allen's legal team said they had a timeline that suggested that it was *Jamie* who planned his wife's murder. They had an affidavit from a man who said he had seen someone who looked like Jamie meeting a man fitting Del Toro's description in an Arby's restaurant in Sarasota, Florida. Stollmeier took the sworn statement from the Sarasota man, who said he witnessed the Arby's meeting between two men at 8:30 A.M. on November 7, 1997. He identified the single photo of Del Toro the attorney showed him as the younger man and the three photos of Bellush as the other man he saw. He said the taller, heavier man had worn a short-sleeved sports shirt and the younger man camouflage clothing. The witness said they were looking at a piece of paper and pointing at it.

The witness, a seventy-year-old retired army sergeant, also reported he'd seen the younger man arrive in a white or gray car with Texas license plates. No one said how he managed to contact Maureen's attorneys. Chris Iorio and Ron Albritton had already verified Jamie's account of his time on November 7, and he had been removed from the suspect list almost immediately.

"After two years," Iorio said, "I had to go back and do it again. I talked to the doctors' staffs and I talked to the guy in Arby's. He described the camouflage uniform, but that information had been in all the papers. When I asked him to tell me the colors of the 'camo' he saw, he had it all wrong; he gave me the camouflage colors they wore in Korea when he was in the army. And I saw the photos he identified as Jamie; they were so dark that all you could really say was that he had two eyes, a mouth, and a nose."

The witness later retracted his statement.

Defense investigators, identifying themselves as police officers had questioned doctors' receptionists in Fort Myers, trying to pinpoint just what times Jamie had been in their clinics on November 7. Most remembered the jovial drug rep who had shown them pictures of his quadruplets, but two years later it was difficult for them to isolate exact times. The defense maintained that Jamie had no alibi for the time that Sheila was murdered. "James Bellush had a three-hour time period where he is unaccounted for," one of Allen's attorneys said. "[His] alibis are not checking out."

One piece of the Blackthorne attorneys' circumstantial evidence was the fact that Sammy Gonzales had driven his mother to New Jersey to visit relatives in October 1997, and that was the same state where Jamie's parents lived.

Lots of people live in New Jersey.

Allen had mounted an offensive of his own, determined to boomerang Jamie's charge that he was "Mr. Big" in the murder plot. Fancy footwork and glib accusations had always worked for Allen before, and he had a phalanx of attorneys running interference for him.

ON March 4, 1999, Jamie and Allen met for the first time in a courtroom. It was not, however, at a murder trial. Jamie asserted in this civil hearing before a bankruptcy-court judge that Allen had deliberately hidden assets from Sheila while he conspired to first harass and then murder her. "[In 1991] Blackthorne claimed he was bankrupt," Jamie's lawsuit read. "And yet eight years later he is a multimillionaire. Many of the assets reported on his schedules were not reported in the divorce."

Jamie's hatred for Allen was palpable, and the courtroom virtually vibrated with hostility. Jamie often prefaced his responses to Judge Boone's questions with, "The day Mr. Blackthorne had my wife killed . . ."

Maureen appeared distressed by this and whispered worriedly to Allen, who only smiled and said softly, "It's okay." Allen, wearing a tailored charcoal-gray suit, sat confidently in the courtroom while Jamie stared at him coldly.

Sheila's widower said that Allen was not responding to discovery motions.

"Have *we* been the ones delaying everything in court?" Allen asked with exaggerated innocence. "We've been the ones pushing it."

The judge's ruling was that Jamie could try to locate property belonging to Sheila, but he could not collect on debts stemming from Allen's bankruptcy. Allen's lawyers claimed a larger victory when they said that since Jamie could not collect any bankruptcy debts, that eliminated any motive for Allen to have had Sheila killed. In a bitter decision for Jamie, the judge ordered him to pay some of Allen's legal fees, which totaled $4800.

ALLEN remained obsessed with golf. The one tournament he wanted to win had so far eluded him—it was the four-day spring golf tournament at the Oak Hills Country Club, culminating in the Black and White Ball. If he won this tournament, he believed that he would at last be accepted and respected at Oak Hills. In other years Allen had tried to bring Danny Rocha into the club as a member and been turned down. Danny's handicap would have offset Allen's mediocre skills on the links. In the spring of 1999 he imported a professional golf pro in his twenties as his partner and deliberately lied about the ringer's handicap. Allen and his partner won. But Allen was deemed a golf cheater. The tournament was supposed to be for club members only, and Allen was the only member who had *bought* himself a professional golfer. When the winners were announced at the Black and White Ball after the tournament, the trophy award ceremony became an organized ostracism of Allen's unsportsmanlike contact.

"They were booing him," a member recalled. "They clapped, but it was that dull thud of clap, pause, clap, pause, clap. Maureen was furious that anyone should treat Allen that way and began to tell club members off."

Oak Hills members were so outraged that Allen's trophy would be displayed in the room reserved for past winners that they simply closed the room down while they decided what to do. "They had trophies there from 1946, but they stopped the whole tradition rather than put Allen's trophy up," a member said. "Now they've simply skipped 1999. Even the plaque with the winners' names goes from 1998 to 2000. It would kill Allen to know that."

Maureen seemed angrier than Allen was; he continued to play golf five days a week. Except for his hatred of Sheila, he never appeared to carry a grudge.

THE Bexar County grand jury reopened its investigation into Sheila's murder during the week of May 10, 1999, issuing subpoenas for new witnesses, some of them Allen's acquaintances. When Allen was summoned to the grand jury and refused to answer questions, the television cameras caught him smiling broadly, confidence oozing from every pore. His clothing was perfect, his teeth gleamed white against his tan, and he looked as if he really wanted to talk to the reporters. He was the epitome of the nice guy who had somehow found himself in an awkward situation, but one that would certainly be straightened out soon. Indeed, he looked for all the world like a movie star or a politician ducking the press, but waving his hand apologetically.

Other footage followed Allen and Maureen down the hall; they held hands and leaned toward one another, two lovers against a storm. And still they smiled.

The murder of Sheila Bellush had been carried all across America on the wire services. Coincidentally, the intense journalistic investigation of the Blackthorne-Bellush case by *48 Hours* for CBS showed on Thursday, May 13, during the week of the revived grand-jury hearings. Heretofore, Allen had refused all interviews "on the record," but this venue seemed to appeal to him; he had finally found a platform he deemed worthy of his participation. He granted Peter Van Sant an interview. *48 hours* cameras went with Allen to the golf course, and he obviously reveled in that, striding across the greens, the wind riffling his thick hair as he reached into the holes to retrieve a ball and selected the best club for his next swing.

For his one-on-one interview, Allen wore a dark suit, a crisp white shirt, and a yellow power tie with a discreet navy-blue pattern. He also wore an expression befitting a totally innocent man and revealed just the proper degree of shock, his eyes opening wider, when Van Sant asked him, "Did you kill your wife?"

"*Never,*" Allen said flatly. "No way. I didn't want her murdered or hurt—ever. There was no threat of any kind. Period."

Asked to describe himself, Allen half-smiled. "I'm a husband. I'm a father. I'm a golfer. We're a strong family. My wife is *awesome*. My kids are great."

"Why would Danny Rocha want to kill her?" Van Sant asked.

"I don't have any idea," Allen said, mystified. "I don't have any idea what's going on with Danny."

"How did Danny Rocha get Sheila's address?"

"Oh, I haven't got a clue," Allen said dismissively. "I have no idea. Damn it, I'm going to prove myself innocent."

Van Sant kept pushing, but Allen was impervious. "You can look me in the eye," the *48 Hours* correspondent asked, "and say you had *nothing* to do with it?"

Allen stared back at him without blinking. "I had nothing to do with it."

The rest of the hour-long documentary showed Sheila's fore-shortened life. Her wedding reception with Jamie flashed across the screen; no one had to exaggerate how lovely she was. *48 Hours'* host Dan Rather didn't mention how Allen had attempted to ruin her second wedding by serving her with court papers.

The camera cut from Sheila and Jamie to Sheila and Kerry, the four babies, Stevie and Daryl, all the good times. In the San Antonio television news, Sheila held all four newborns and sighed happily, "The first week out of the hospital was *scary!*" One shot of Sheila kept coming back, showing her cornflower-blue eyes fringed with dark lashes. She looked very pretty and very tiny.

The bad times were there too, although the Sarasota County sheriff's photographs that were shown were taken several feet away from Sheila's body and blinked on the screen so rapidly that viewers couldn't really focus on them or linger long on the blood splashed all over the kitchen floor.

There was Joey Del Toro, still fighting extradition in Mexico, when he was the handsome young football star in a high school photo with "Coyotes" emblazoned on his jersey. There was Sammy Gonzales as he testified in Sarasota, Florida. And then there was Danny Rocha. Again, how long would he keep talking without really admitting his part in Sheila's death? Now Danny wore the same red jail scrubs that Sammy had worn when he testified against him, and his voice was somehow a whine as he said, "I didn't participate in that. I didn't know a trigger was gonna be pulled. Allen Blackthorne is more responsible. I was just helping a friend."

And back to Allen's insistence, "I didn't want her murdered or hurt—ever."

IN San Antonio the federal prosecutors, John Murphy and Richard Durbin, watched *48 Hours* and were infuriated by Allen's "arrogance." Along with their boss, Bill Blagg, they had been eager to get into the probe of Blackthorne from the beginning. They didn't know what kind of reception they would receive from the Florida authorities but suspected that their interest might not be welcome.

"We were wrong," John Murphy said. "Charlie Roberts and Henry Lee welcomed our participation."

With the San Antonio Assistant U.S. Attorneys' entrance into the continuing investigation of Blackthorne, the FBI came aboard too. Although he had been with the bureau for twenty-four years, Mike Appleby didn't fit the perception of a typical FBI agent; he was a laid-back man with little pretension. Appleby considered Richard Urbanek, a San Antonio police detective, his partner and had for years. He was currently assigned to the San Antonio division's violent-crime squad, whose investigations involved gang-related murders, organized-crime murders, and murders involving interstate travel. In San Antonio, at least, there were none of the turf tussles that so often mark interaction between federal and local investigators; they needed each other too much.

The various agencies joined in a Safe Streets Task Force, and they worked any number of high-profile cases. When a challenging case came along, it was only a matter of "getting the team back together" for Urbanek, Appleby, and Jesse Salazar, also a San Antonio detective. They wore a number of hats; Salazar and Urbanek were cross-designated deputy U.S. marshals on occasion, assigned to the FBI.

While Allen was being confident and charming with the media, a blue-ribbon team was mobilizing against him. Now Blackthorne was up against the Bexar County D.A.'s office, the Texas Rangers, the San Antonio Police Department, the FBI, the assistant U.S. Attorney's office (reporting to *their* boss, Janet Reno), the Florida state attorneys, and the Sarasota County Sheriff's Office.

So far Allen had benefited from Texas statutes that didn't allow conviction based solely on the testimony of an accomplice. That was one of the reasons that the Florida trial went first. Now, not only was Texas determined to find additional evidence against him, but the federal government was tracking him too.

It was only a matter of time, as law-enforcement officers from all these jurisdictions fanned out across America to talk to potential witnesses in a Texas trial where the defendant would be Allen Blackthorne himself and not one of his rumored underlings.

Since grand-jury hearings are secret, that spring of 1999 the media could only report on who slipped into the room. Gary De Los Santos testified, along with some of Allen's golfing partners, members of exclusive country clubs, and a former caddie.

Emboldened by his appearance on *48 Hours,* Allen began to speak often with newspaper and television reporters. "Eighteen months have passed," he said fervently, "and this investigation has left people hanging. All we want is someone to look at the truth."

He was about to get what he asked for. District Attorney Susan Reed responded, "We have already issued an invitation through his attorney [for Blackthorne] to talk, and there's a grand jury three days out of the week down here. And if he'd like to come down in front of that grand jury, we'd be very willing to accommodate that."

The invitation went unanswered. Allen said that he had offered to take a polygraph to prove his innocence, showing reporters a copy of a letter his attorney had sent to a Sarasota County detective in which he offered to take a lie-detector test. It read, "Who do you suggest for the polygraph examination?"

He claimed his offer was not accepted. Richard Lubin added, "Allen has been investigated every which way you can possibly be investigated. I'd like somebody to say finally, 'We had good reason to suspect you, but now we realize you had nothing to do with it.' "

Gary De Los Santos snorted. "I've always had an open door," he said. "If he wants to take a polygraph, I'll sure as hell give him a polygraph."

Chapter Forty

ONCE ALLEN BEGAN to talk to the media, he grew steadily more effusive. His neighbors had long noted that he was drawn to the arrival of media vans and cars like a moth to a flame. Even before he began to speak to reporters, he almost always came outside, fully aware that he was being photographed. Now, in mid-1999, as the two-year anniversary of Sheila's murder lay ahead, Allen was bursting with comments on his case. Some of his revelations would have been better kept to himself. As he left one of the civil hearings in Jamie's suit against him, he commented to reporters that if Joey Del Toro had committed the murder by himself, he would certainly have had more blood on his camouflage fatigues than court records indicated.

Allen was far from an expert on bloodstains. He was talking through his hat, but one wondered why he had spent so much time pondering the evidence. "There was only a speck of blood on Del Toro's clothing," he said. "You tell me where the blood is."

"On your hands," a courthouse habitué whispered under her breath. Neither Allen nor the reporters heard.

Allen spoke amiably to reporters, aware of the need to give them quotable comments. "I'm trying to dispel one lie at a time," he said. "Every time I dispel one, it's like weeds in your yard—three more pop up. But that's okay. I'm good at pulling weeds."

The picture Allen painted of himself was that of the complete family man. He welcomed posing for photographs with Maureen and was given to sentimental one-liners like, "I'm the luckiest guy in the world."

IT was ironic that a man who'd done such a thorough job of hiding his past now had so many people delving into it. No one could have hidden dark secrets for long with the number of agencies involved, and neither could Allen Blackthorne.

On June 28, 1999, twenty months after Sheila's murder, D.A. investigator Buster Burch finally located Ellen, the first of Allen's wives. He found her living in a tiny northwestern town, her last name changed, her determination to stay anonymous paramount in her mind. She agreed, however, to talk with Susan Reed, Michael Bernard, and Burch.

Ellen, who was now forty-five, shuddered as she recalled the violence of her marriage to Allen. The boy she fell in love with at Bible-study meetings had become a monster. She said she suffered several beatings and once almost died of strangulation when Allen put his hands on her throat and squeezed until the capillaries in her eyes burst, peppering the whites with the tiny dots of blood called petechiae. "I went to a doctor," she recalled, "but when he asked who had choked me, I left."

Ellen said she had been much too afraid of Allen to tell the police what he had done to her. Things were bad enough as it was. He had kicked her in the stomach when she was pregnant, and that baby was aborted. It was humiliating for Ellen to tell strangers about Allen; few people could understand the consummate evil that roiled just beneath the surface of his mind. His sexual appetites had been bizarre and perverted.

Finding Mary Kelley was even more difficult. She lived on the West Coast too, but she didn't want to talk about Allen—not to anyone. She was still frightened that he might find her and carry out the threats she had heard so often. The only way to get the essential feedback from Mary that might help bring about Allen's arrest was to subpoena her to testify before the Bexar County grand jury. *That* was more terrifying for her than giving a voluntary statement.

She agreed to talk with them. In late August 1999, Mary met with Bernard, Burch, and Gary De Los Santos in the Texas Ranger headquarters in San Antonio. It was clear she didn't want to be in the same state as her ex-husband, even one as big as Texas—as if he would somehow be able to find her and hurt her again.

Mary recalled the man she married in November, twenty years earlier. He had been very controlling, she said. On two occasions he had physically assaulted her, grabbing her by the hair and slamming her against the wall. He slapped her in the face, threw furniture around their home, and punched holes in the wall.

The physical attacks were not the worst. Mary said that twice, when she threatened to leave Allen, he told her he would hire someone to hurt her children while she watched—but she would be tied up so she couldn't move to help them. That shocked her because, although Allen had been very cruel to her he had always been nice to her children. She told the investigators that she finally managed to sneak away from him. She hadn't seen Allen for eighteen years and hoped never to see him again. Now that he was a suspect in the murder of the wife he married after her, she was even more afraid of him.

One woman in Allen's past who seemed the least damaged was Rafaela Tyler*, who had given birth to his daughter out of wedlock in the early '90s. She had also been with him the shortest length of time; Rafaela was Allen's administrative assistant in San Antonio when he still worked for RS Medical. She worked in his home office from August 1990 to March 1991. She told Gary De Los Santos that her relationship with Allen soon became intimate. This was a few years after his divorce but during his ongoing custody battle with Sheila.

When Rafaela became pregnant by Allen, he ordered her to have an abortion—something she refused to do. "He fired me soon after that," she said. She had asked for child support, and surprisingly, he had agreed to that without a court order. "He sends me $400 a month regularly. All I asked was that he never try to see our daughter."

Rafaela said she had never heard Allen threaten to harm Sheila, although he had often called her ugly names.

Sheila, Allen's third wife, could no longer tell them about their marriage, but there were dozens of people who could. Indeed, detectives couldn't find anyone who described Sheila and Allen's marriage as anything but a catastrophe. But that still wasn't enough to charge him with her murder. John Murphy and Richard Durbin, along with Mike Bernard and D.A. Susan Reed, knew that hearsay testimony would be shot down by any defense attorney worth his salt. They were careful to find enough witnesses who had actually seen Allen mistreat Sheila and his first two daughters with their own eyes.

Daryl told them about the same incident that Stevie had. When the toilet overflowed in his house, her father was furious. "He threw me against the wall a few times," Daryl said, "and I got a bump on my head and a black eye. Then he sat on Stevie and shook her and just pounded her into the ground. When he couldn't find his car keys, he hit us with this metal arrow thing."

"Did your mother know this happened?" De Los Santos asked her.

Daryl nodded. But Sheila had been too afraid to call the police on Allen. Daryl tried to explain to the ranger that it was almost impossible to overcome her father's control. "Once I was there at his house for my weekly visit, and I got homesick and told my father I wanted to go home. I called my mom, and he just took the phone away from me and hung it up. He told me I wasn't going anywhere, and he said my mom didn't really care about me. Then he grabbed me by the arms and put me in my room. When my mom got there, I ran to the door and tried to leave with her.

"But my mom had me by the arms, and my dad grabbed my feet, and they were having a tug-of-war with me. My dad said if my mom let go, he would too—but when my mom let go, he pulled me into his house and locked the door on my mom."

As the minute examination of Allen's life continued, De Los Santos got a tip that an employee of a Christian day-care school had information. The woman said that both Stevie and Daryl had attended the school from August 1990 to September 1991. The little girls would have been about five and six then.

"They were dropped off after school by their school bus," the woman told De Los Santos, "and either their mother or their father would pick them up. The parents fought all the time, and he used foul language with complete disregard for the children around him."

The most troubling thing for the witness was the way Stevie was after she spent a weekend with her father. The woman was embarrassed as she said, "Stevie would be dirty and smelly. There was a smell of, well . . . *sex* on her clothing and on her when I held her on my lap. When I tried to ask her if she needed help or was afraid of something, she just said that her father didn't want her talking about it."

THE civil suit Jamie Bellush had filled against Allen went ahead, despite Allen's sardonic sneer when he spoke of it as frivolous and his continued position that it was Sheila's widower who wanted her dead—and-certainly not himself.

Jamie Bellush was in court again, via a videotaped deposition in early July 1999. "It was easy to point the finger in Allen's direction anyway, wasn't it?" John Curney, yet another of Allen and Maureen's attorneys, asked him.

"I didn't think anybody else would want to harm my wife, sir," Jamie replied.

"Certainly not you," Curney said sarcastically.

"Absolutely not, sir."

It was a long and angry deposition; for ten hours Jamie jousted with Curney. Even Bill Clinton's deposition in the Paula Jones case was only six hours long. Now Allen's attorneys lashed into Jamie for putting suspicion on their client from the very first day.

When the hearing was finally over, Allen and Maureen were exuberant. "I said once before that this case has been about lies—a lot of lies," Allen told reporters, and he used his weed analogy again. "We've got to go out and pull each one of those lies out of the ground—just like you would a weed, one at a time—and expose them."

Allen said he realized his and Sheila's strife-ridden divorce and their lengthy custody battles had made it easy for Jamie to try to put the blame on him. "The story sounded good," he said, "[but] it was a hell of a good lie."

And then like a dam slowly giving way, the trickles that connected Allen and Maureen to bloody murder became torrents, and the stone wall that kept Allen inviolate from all harm began to weaken. Finally, word came that Mexico had agreed to extradite Joey Del Toro. He didn't have to fear the death penalty; Sarasota authorities had been forced to waive any threat of capital punishment before Mexico would agree to turn him over.

Iorio and Albritton were given short notice that Joey was already in the air on a Mexican military plane; he was due to arrive in Miami on the evening of July 13, 1999. They left Sarasota immediately for the 200-mile drive to Miami, worried that they wouldn't get there in time. They needn't have been concerned. It was two in the morning before the Mexican plane taxied to a stop. Chris Iorio and Ron Albritton stood by to take Joey into custody. They waited all night as Joey went from one government agency to another—the FBI, U.S. Customs—and finally they saw the man they'd hunted for so long.

"We expected him to look skinny and haggard," Iorio recalled, "because he'd been in a prison where the food wasn't supposed to be very good. But he surprised us. He looked healthy and muscular; he was in great shape."

It was 6:00 A.M. before the Sarasota detectives got to talk to Del Toro. They interviewed him for an hour, or rather, they tried to interview him. The man whom they believed to be Sheila's killer responded to all their questions in a friendly enough fashion, but he said he couldn't answer on the advice of his attorney.

"We left him our cards," Iorio said, "and told him we'd be taking him to jail in Sarasota later in the day. He rode in the police van, and Ron and I followed behind it in our car. We didn't want him to have any chance to escape. We were even concerned that someone who didn't want Joey to talk might intercept the van."

Locked in the Sarasota County jail, where the ambience was far different from that of the Mexican prison where he'd spent twenty months, Joey was a no-bail prisoner. His family couldn't have raised bail money anyway; they couldn't even afford to pay an attorney. Sarasota County judge Judy Goldman accepted a not-guilty plea from his public defender. Del Toro himself did not appear in court. If a jury found him guilty of first-degree murder, he stood a good chance of spending the rest of his life in prison.

WHAT happened to Joey Del Toro meant little to the Blackthornes of San Antonio; they had distanced themselves from him. Allen and Maureen were so confident that their troubles were behind them that they granted a St. Petersburg *Times* reporter's request to come to their home for an interview. Leanora Minai had followed the case from the beginning, and she was intensely curious about the Blackthornes' world.

Minai found Allen at his usual post in a recliner in front of his garage, puffing on a cigarette and sipping on Diet Coke. He accepted compliments on his exquisite lawn and explained that he had planted Tiff 419 Bermuda grass and mowed it almost every day.

Other than that, the Blackthornes did virtually no real work around their estate. They had a pool man every Wednesday to tend to their 60,000-gallon swimming pool, which was triple the size of most family pools. They had maids and nannies to take care of the house and Brandon and Jacob. Allen explained that they were spending all their time concentrating on the case.

As if on cue, Maureen appeared after a swim and sat near Allen, fingers entwined with his, as he talked about love in response to Minai's question. "What is being in love?" he said. "It's a good question. I went a lot of my life not believing in the concept."

He glanced adoringly at Maureen and gave still another version of his life as an abused child, including variations on his favorite themes—his beating with a two-by-four by his mother and the story of how she once poured flammable liquid on him and set him on fire. This time he said "a man" had saved him, failing to mention it was one of his stepfathers. "He got the hell burned out of him," Allen added.

It was, or course, another lie. Leanora Minai didn't know that. This was the childhood that Allen espoused at the time, and he sounded as sincere as a priest.

In his biography of the day, he recalled only one wife before Sheila and said she had left him for her ex-husband after three weeks. Another untruth. He didn't give her name, so he might have been talking about either Ellen or Mary. Probably Mary.

Smoking one heavily filtered Vantage cigarette after another, Allen recalled meeting Sheila Leigh Walsh and finding her "almost too good to be true." He described her as gracious, accommodating, charming, and pretty—and compatible in every way. He had cooked; Sheila did the dishes. Two lovebirds. But it was all an image, a façade. This was not the marriage the real Sheila had endured for so long.

"The nicest thing she ever did for me was file for divorce," Allen finished bitterly. "I never loved her—*never.*"

Now he said he first learned about Sheila's murder as he watched television late on that night of November 7, 1997. He didn't mention all the earlier notifications he'd had. He was stoic as he remarked that he had "never shed a tear" over Sheila's death.

Leaving their boys with their nanny, the Blackthornes accompanied Minai to dinner at Koi Kawa, a San Antonio sushi bar, where they ate California rolls and shrimp tempura. They rode in Maureen's black Mitsubishi Montero with the license plate 43BOYS. Ricky

Martin's best-selling CD was on the stereo, and Allen sang along to Maureen about counting the minutes, seconds, hours until she was by his side again.

They certainly seemed madly in love, calling each other Mama and Papa and lighting each other's cigarettes. "There isn't anything that I don't love about Maureen," Allen told Minai. "I could sit for days and talk to Maureen and never grow tired. Physically, she's perfect. Emotionally, she's just ideal."

Like Allen, Maureen recalled events differently from other people. Now she said that it was she who had hired a private detective to check Allen out, and not her brother-in-law. "I want to know everything he's doing," she had specified. "I want to know if he's with hookers, ordering room service for one person or two. I want to know what movies he's watching."

The PI allegedly told her that Allen was doing none of those things. His only vice was gambling—playing blackjack at $600 a hand. "But now," she said beaming, "I know he's faithful."

Maureen admitted being a little concerned when Sheila and Jamie warned her about Allen's penchant for beating his wives and telling her that he had sexually molested Stevie.

"I got her on the phone," Allen cut in. "I said, 'If you want to break up with me, why don't you do it for the right reasons?' " And he told of bringing Maureen overflowing boxes of documents from his court battles with Sheila and asking her to read them all. "Then she called up and apologized to me."

They rewrote their timetable again about another spat, saying it had occurred after their marriage, although it was, in truth, before. Maureen, newly pregnant with Brandon, had refused to put her $100,000 savings in with Allen's money, and she ran off angry and tried to drive away. But Allen blocked her car's path and she called the police. They soon made up and pooled their money, Maureen said.

Detectives already knew about this, "spat." Maureen's former banker had told them how distraught she was on one occasion, confiding the most intimate details of her argument with Allen to a virtual stranger. The man was surprised when she broke down, but he said she never mentioned trouble with Allen again.

Always, always the Blackthornes presented their ideal partnership to the media, cutting and splicing and rearranging the facts to make them fit, gazing into each other's eyes.

When Minai asked Allen about golf, he waxed more enthusiastic than he had about his wife, going into anecdote after anecdote. It was obvious that this was a man who *lived* to play golf. He claimed that his handicap was sometimes as low as two. He bragged about winning the Black and White Championship at Oak Hills, but he acknowledged that he wasn't as welcome there as he had been. Good friends had told him club members were in corners talking about him.

That was true.

Allen said he didn't really mind being "gossip topic number one. It's no big deal. Truth is a process."

Headed for yet another set-to with Jamie Bellush in Bexar County's historic red stone courthouse, Allen was sanguine. Dressed in expensively casual clothes, with $200 designer sunglasses propped above his forehead, the omnipresent cigarette in his mouth, he obviously looked forward to the next legal tussle. Even though Jamie was once again testifying through a remote television feed, it was clear the men detested each other. Their lawyers shouted without pause, drowning each other out. The court reporter had trouble deciphering which was which.

In the end the judge ordered Allen and Maureen to turn over their 1997 IRS returns and bank statements. In the hallway afterward, Allen smiled to see the waiting television cameras. He looked directly toward the lens and declared his innocence once more.

"They love the limelight," a bailiff muttered. "Right up until the time they go to the penitentiary, they're going to enjoy it."

Perhaps that was true. Back at their mansion, Leanora Minai was a captive audience for hours of videotaped coverage of the Blackthornes' case. She noticed that they studied the tapes and their comments "like a football coach studies game film."

They had little else to do. Although the executives at the top of RS Medical, Inc., insisted that they had no ill will toward Allen, they admitted to Gary De Los Santos that his active participation in the company had steadily diminished. Between 1994 and 1997, when he was made vice president of special products, he didn't do much more than attend board meetings and help close deals on certain accounts. Shortly after Sheila's murder in November 1997, Allen resigned from the company, turning his stock over to Maureen, making her a very, very wealthy woman. It was rumored to be worth more than $50 million.

"Maureen," Leanora Minai asked, "have you ever asked Allen if he ordered Sheila's murder?"

"I don't have to," she replied.

Was it true, Minai pushed, what they were saying about Maureen's coming up with the phrase "Black Cow?"

"Let me share something with you," Maureen Blackthorne said, her voice hard. "Venezuela is in South America, but I did not grow up on a farm."

The Blackthornes' office had become a war room. Allen said he and Maureen put in forty-hour weeks there, organizing his defense—if it should come to that. They had neat binders cataloguing and cross-referencing every legal skirmish and witness's statement and/or testimony, noting who said what at what time. The walls were covered with charts, with yellow highlighter pointing out the elements that appeared to suggest that neither Allen nor Maureen could have had anything at all to do with Sheila's murder.

It was the two of them against the storm, but rather than being anxious or depressed, both clearly relished it. Perhaps Maureen was, indeed, absolutely perfect for Allen, just as he claimed.

For Minai's benefit, Allen tapped the charts with reminders of his innocence. "Why didn't they investigate Jamie's debts before the murder, and [find] that Jamie had several life insurance policies on Sheila? He was able to divert all attention from himself onto myself."

And then, stunningly, Allen began to act out Sheila's murder. "This was rage," he told Minai. "He stabs her like this, all the way to the spine. He cuts the bottom of her feet, her forearms. He takes a knife and drives it through the palm of her hand—some thirty-three cuts."

He was clearly loving the drama of it all. Was it possible that he also loved the thought of how Sheila had suffered?

_____*Chapter Forty-one* _____

ON NOVEMBER 5, 1999, the San Antonio *Express-News* headline read FEDS PROBING BELLUSH MURDER. Two years after Sheila died, the date was significant; it was again the first Friday in November. The headline was news to the lay population of San Antonio and Sarasota, but the feds had been involved in the investigation for some time. They had watched Allen Blackthorne's smug pronouncements and been frustrated that convolutions of Texas law had so far allowed him to remain free. In Allen, they had all the elements: motive, method, means, and opportunity to kill his ex-wife. Indeed, he was the *only* member of the four-suspect team with any reason at all to want Sheila dead. None of the investigators and prosecutors had turned up one witness who said that Danny Rocha, Sammy Gonzales, and Joey Del Toro even *knew* Sheila Bellush.

Despite Allen's insistence that Jamie Bellush was the most likely suspect, he had long since been eliminated. Nor was there any evidence to validate Allen's two-killer theory and the existence of Del Toro's mythical "Jorge."

But it had been two years, and murder leaves behind such profound pain that it often continues in one form or another for decades. Sheila's four babies were growing up without their mother, far from any of her relatives—save for Stevie, who was caught somewhere between childhood and womanhood, haunted by the images she still dreamed about, and virtually estranged from Jamie. She edged past his rules, and his rules—too strict already—became even more militaristic. He was so consumed by his need for revenge against Allen that he may not have seen Stevie's pain.

Gene Smith aged in double time, her grief over Sheila keeping her from enjoying the children she had left. Her diabetes was worse and her health began to fail.

If only Allen could be made to answer for Sheila's death, their families might heal. Perhaps not—but it was agonizing for those who loved Sheila to see Allen smiling back from newspapers and television sets, striding across a golf course or ducking into one of his new cars. His insouciance grated on everyone who had worked the case. The grand jury had failed so far to hand down an indictment, hampered by the fact that the two men who claimed to know the most were both incarcerated.

But federal courts have different rules. Jurors are allowed to consider accomplices' statements. With John Murphy and Richard Durbin on the case, the prosecution had room to move about. To keep within the parameters of his plea bargain, Sammy Gonzales had promised to testify whenever asked. It didn't matter if it was in a state court or a federal court.

Even Danny Rocha was hinting again that he *might* talk. But would he testify? He had nothing left to lose—or to gain, really. Slowly he finally began to reveal information that led investigators to the search for new, solid evidence.

City, county, state, and federal law-enforcement authorities often cooperate with one another in pushing a case to the surface, where it will float. The practice is sometimes called the silver-platter doctrine—one jurisdiction hands over evidence to another in a better position to pursue the case. It is like one football player tossing the ball to another player who has a better chance of crossing the goal line. It isn't always easy on the human beings involved. Prosecutors are not that different from CEOs in big business; they work their way up from misdemeanor cases to high-profile cases. When they get a big one, it is akin to bringing a major business deal to fruition.

Egos are involved, and turf wars sometimes erupt in law enforcement. Going after a suspect/defendant like Allen Blackthorne was a very big deal, indeed—no matter what more lofty human sympathy for the victim also came into play. It's hard to hand over a case "on a silver platter." In this instance, however, there was belief across the board that Allen Blackthorne had to be charged and face a jury of his peers. Egos didn't matter. Justice—or a good shot at justice—did.

John Murphy, first assistant to U.S. Attorney Bill Blagg and the number two federal prosecutor in the Western District, was overseeing the inquiry into Allen's alleged participation in the murder plot. Startlingly, Murphy's ex-wife had lived for a time with Allen a decade earlier. In a city as large as San Antonio, it was a stunning coincidence. But should that be a reason for Murphy to recuse himself from the federal prosecution team?

Margaret "Kitty" Murphy Hawkins and John Murphy were married from 1978 to 1981. Kitty had met Allen almost ten years later, and Murphy had been happily remarried for years. After two years of dating Allen, Kitty still spoke well of him, one of the few San Antonians who did. John Murphy examined his own motivation carefully and realized that he had no more animosity toward Allen than he had for any defendant. He stayed on the case.

The media tossed this news happily in the air, worrying it for a while to get as much mileage as possible. And it was yet another opportunity for Allen to give reporters a quote. "Is this like *Days of Our Lives?*" he asked. "Let me tell you something. This is *my* life, and these are the kinds of games that are being played."

Since Maureen, the nanny, and the maids—and Allen, when he was home—watched television soap operas, Allen was quite familiar with the popular *Days*. His own life had always been one of upheaval, and he was capable of using it to his advantage. He said he sincerely hoped that there was no bad blood between himself and Murphy. "He might feel a little love-scorned," Allen said sanctimoniously. "I hope his personal losses don't affect his professionalism."

If anyone was professional, it was John Murphy. Those who had worked beside him and even those who had been on the other side of a trial verified that. "He's just a prince of a guy," Wayne Speck, a recently retired Assistant U.S. Attorney, said. "I can't consider this being any kind of conflict. He and Kitty have been divorced for a long, long time."

Anthony Nicholas, a lawyer who once represented Allen and who knew Murphy well, agreed. "He's always been fair and upright. He's always been square with me."

John Murphy had a full head of prematurely white hair and a neat beard. His features were sharply handsome in profile, his eyes a piercing light blue, and his Irish complexion was given to flushing when he was angry. He was a frustration to reporters because he rarely, if ever, had a comment for them.

"I *couldn't* talk to them," he said later. "The defense can choose to speak before a case is finished. We can't."

Richard Durbin, also an assistant U.S. attorney, was a good foil for Murphy, and their styles meshed like expensive machinery. Tall and Lincolnesque, with brown eyes so warm that it was difficult to picture him angry, Durbin's mind was eidetic—capable of committing whole files to memory—although he would always deny that characterization or brush it off by saying he remembered only as long as he needed to. Both men were fathers of teenage daughters.

The third member of the federal prosecuting team was Michael Bernard, Susan Reed's chief criminal deputy, who would be cross-designated as a federal prosecutor for any criminal trial involving Allen Blackthorne. Bernard looked a lot like actor Jim Belushi, and he wore expensive suits that broke halfway below the knee, revealing the cowboy boots beneath. He had a twinkle in his eye, but he was tough when it came to cross-examination.

The forensic evidence found at the scene of Sheila's murder and the witnesses before, during, and after her death had been thoroughly investigated and continued to be probed. The D.A.'s office had visited Oregon, and so had Gary De Los Santos. John Murphy and Richard Durbin would also travel the well-worn paths between Texas, Oregon, New Jersey, and Florida.

Sometimes they arrived at a distant city late at night, only to find that their car and hotel reservations had been canceled. They slept sitting up or not at all. There were many early morning flights before the sun was up, and many nights that lasted until 4:00 A.M. One aspect of investigating any high-profile, seemingly endless case is the loss of sleep the detectives and prosecutors experience, the holidays never celebrated.

On one trip to New Jersey, Murphy and Durbin arrived in Newark without having eaten all day and found only one restaurant open. They recalled that trip. "The menu was not exactly what we were hoping for," Murphy said.

"Every course was meat," Durbin added. "No salad. No vegetables. Just meat." Fortunately, they weren't vegetarians.

Although they would become friends later, Kerry Bladorn smiled to remember how very formal Gary De Los Santos was when he visited the mobile home where she and Rick lived with their four children and Daryl. The ranger's size dwarfed the small rooms. "He wouldn't even let me give him a cup of coffee," Kerry said. "He was all business."

And when John Murphy and Richard Durbin arrived a few months later to question Kerry and Daryl as potential witnesses in a possible trial, they seemed so imposing to Kerry's three-year-old son that he tugged at her skirt and asked, "Mommy, which one's the *President*?"

EVEN as the case against Allen Blackthorne was heating up, the coverage in the San Antonio and Sarasota papers diminished. But after two years, just when it seemed that Allen was about to be arrested, nothing happened. The public certainly knew his name by now, and his face was familiar. San Antonians chose sides about his guilt or innocence. If the Blackthornes had ever had any pretensions about climbing the ladder of society, those hopes were dashed. They stayed close to the Adays, and Allen could still get a golf foursome together, but their neighbors watched them warily, and the gossip at the Oak Hills Country Club fairly sizzled.

The Blackthornes seemed to be supporting any number of attorneys. Jamie Bellush was pressing his civil suit, they were in constant touch with Richard Lubin—Allen's criminal defense attorney in West Palm Beach—and there were always little fires to put out.

The Bellush suit was due to come to trial on November 30, the Tuesday after the Thanksgiving Day holiday, but it was delayed for ninety days when Danny Rocha's attorney said that his testimony in such a case might tend to incriminate him and rob him of a fair trial in the charges he still faced in Bexar County.

The case was feeding on itself, with tentacles reaching everywhere. Allen voiced disappointment to the press. He said he'd been trying to get his case heard so he could live his life without rumor and innuendo following him everywhere he went. In the same breath he predicted that it would probably be years before Jamie's civil suit resumed.

"We may never get our day in court to clear our names and expose the truth in this case," Allen said plaintively. He and his attorneys blamed the federal prosecutors for the delay. "They're trying to buy time in hopes somebody cuts Danny Rocha some kind of a deal," John Curney, now representing Maureen Blackthorne, said. He felt that halting the civil suit would help them and hurt Allen. "You wouldn't want Rocha testifying anytime prior to any criminal case against Allen, because it gives Allen a free crack at cross-examining him before he goes to trial, and they all know that."

Allen railed at Judge Pat Boone and Jamie's attorneys. "They're the ones fighting this thing from going to court," he said. "This isn't just a continuance that they asked for. They wanted an abatement, so we couldn't do one more piece of discovery, so we couldn't gather one more piece of evidence. We're closing in on them, and they wanted to make sure they stopped us."

Allen could have been a brilliant attorney. Indeed, working attorneys who had faced him in custody and child-support hearings were amazed that he had no formal training in the law. And he had every reason in the world to become familiar with each facet of his own case.

In December 1999 Maureen and Allen shared their third lavish holiday season since Sheila's murder. If anything, Allen seemed more jaunty than ever. Although he still wouldn't talk to the grand jurors, he welcomed the media. They roared up en masse to his house on Box Oak shortly after Christmas. Susan Glenny was taking down her Christmas lights, and Allen opened his garage door, saw her, and hurried over to help. It was a great photo opportunity. "That was Allen," she sighed. "One time, the reporters showed up when he was inside, and he actually came out and mowed his grass."

Clint Glenny hadn't represented Allen for almost a year; he had left his employ when Allen simply failed to pay his legal bills. Susan had been right in insisting they let Allen pay for her fancy room in the maternity wing; that was all they ever got. Allen asked Glenny not to tell anyone why they'd parted ways, and Clint was as good as his word. Predictably, Allen seemed to bear his neighbor/former attorney no ill will.

MIKE Appleby and Gary De Los Santos were now working in tandem—the FBI agent with the federal government's case and the Texas Ranger with Bexar County. They got along well, and De Los Santos called Mike "Apple," as did most of the cops he worked with.

Appleby looked like a casting director's FBI agent, a cross between John Wayne and Clint Eastwood, with a deep and rumbling

Texas drawl. He didn't appear to take himself or the FBI's occasionally puffed-up image very seriously, preferring to hang out with Richard Urbanek, the San Antonio police detective who was his best friend as well as his partner.

Appleby did take the violent death of Sheila Bellush very seriously. As a talisman, he carried a picture of her in the pocket of his jacket. It was a photograph of the petite mother as she was hugely pregnant with her four babies, almost as wide as she was tall. She was smiling triumphantly. It reminded him of the reason they were all working so hard to avenge her death. Appleby didn't usually feel animosity toward the felons he tracked down, but, he admitted, that didn't apply with Allen Blackthorne.

In December 1999 Appleby flew to New Jersey to interview Jamie Bellush. He asked if Jamie had copies of some photographs that Danny Rocha had described. He was looking for a photo of Sheila with several children in some kind of a restaurant, perhaps a pizza parlor. One of the children in the photo with her could have been Daryl or Stevie. That was the picture that Danny said had ended up in Joey Del Toro's hands. But Joey had thrown it away a long time ago, one of the few items of physical evidence he had the sense to get rid of.

Jamie brought out a bunch of photographs, and he and Appleby sorted through them, until they found some that matched almost exactly the photos Rocha described. They were of a birthday party in Jungle Jim's Playland in San Antonio—Daryl's birthday, from the date on the photo. A man in a monkey suit stood behind Sheila and Daryl.

Later, when Appleby showed these pictures to Danny Rocha and Sammy Gonzales, they both identified them as very like the photos that Allen gave Danny to give to the killer.

Jamie didn't have the negatives. He hadn't taken the pictures. They were some Sheila had before their marriage.

As the millennium rolled in, the time had come at last. It was Tuesday, January 4, 2000. Despite dire predictions, nothing had exploded, and computers kept right on going. The world hadn't ended with the millennium after all, but it was soon to end for Allen Blackthorne—at least the world as he knew it. Mike Appleby and Gary De Los Santos planned to join in Allen's arrest, and Chris Iorio and Ron Albritton were on a plane headed for San Antonio so they too, could be present to see it happen. They all deserved to be there.

The grand jury had handed down sealed indictments charging Allen Blackthorne with two counts. "Count one: Conspiracy to use

Interstate Commerce Facilities in the Commission of Murder for Hire. Count two: Interstate Domestic Violence—Crossing State Line and Causing Another to Commit an Offense.

Conviction on count one meant death or life imprisonment and a $250,000 fine and on count two, life imprisonment."

The U.S. District Court for the Western District of Texas had Allen's personal data sheet filled in, noting the charges, the federal prosecutors (John Murphy and Richard Durbin, Jr.), the defense attorneys (David Botsford and Richard G. Lubin), Allen's address, and the recommendation that Allen be detained without bond.

The only tentative line came after "Date of Arrest." It read "To be arrested . . ."

_____Chapter Forty-two _____

ALTHOUGH MIKE APPLEBY was slated to be one of the arresting officers, it troubled him a little. "I never really felt it was our case," he said, referring to the FBI. "We adopted it, and it's not that I wasn't enthusiastic about it, but if anyone could read Gary De Los Santos's case file, they'd know who did the work in Texas to bring Blackthorne down."

The lead detectives were initially Chris Iorio and Ron Albritton, but Gary De Los Santos was their constant contact in Texas. And Appleby, Urbanek, and Salazar were fully aware that other agencies like the Texas Rangers and Bexar County, not to mention Sarasota County, had worked Sheila Bellush's murder for almost a year and a half before the FBI came in. They had no intention of swiping the cream off the top of the investigation by arresting Allen without those agencies being present. In particular, Mike Appleby wanted to have Gary De Los Santos make the arrest. He had every expectation that De Los Santos and Chris Iorio would be the ones who put handcuffs on Allen Blackthorne.

District Attorney Susan Reed had made one promise to the tall ranger who had dogged Allen Blackthorne's trail: "You'll be the one who arrests Allen." And De Los Santos had answered, "The bottom line is that we *get* Allen," but he had to admit to himself that he really wanted to be there when it all came to a crashing halt.

Allen's secret indictment by the federal government came down on Tuesday, January 4, 2000. The Bexar County indictment was supposed to come on Wednesday, with the attendant press conference. Chris Iorio and Ron Albritton bought their own plane tickets and headed west. They wanted to be there too.

By then, FBI agent Mike Appleby couldn't have cared less about the actual arrest; he was home in bed "sick as a dog" with the flu. But suddenly he got a call to meet De Los Santos at the Oak Hills Country Club; someone had leaked the information to the media about the secret federal indictment. They hoped that Iorio and Albritton would land in time, but they had to be prepared to arrest Allen if he heard the news. At the moment, he was happily playing golf, unaware that the net was about to drop over him.

With a high temperature and fighting nausea, Appleby dragged himself out of bed and joined De Los Santos, Urbanek, and Salazar in the parking lot of the Oak Hills Country Club. The Florida detectives' plane was still in the air; their flight had been delayed.

It was a sunny Texas winter day, and the quartet of investigators knew that Allen had teed off to play eighteen holes of golf; they could wait for him. So far, the arrest plans were low-key and on schedule. But then De Los Santos was summoned back to the county courthouse. Because word on the federal indictment had hit the street, reporters were calling the U.S. Attorney's Office to verify it, and the county arrest warrant wasn't complete.

The "silver-platter doctrine" went only so far; the Bexar County D.A.'s office wanted to share credit for the arrest. Blackthorne was such an incredibly huge trophy to catch, and De Los Santos was summoned to the historic red courthouse in downtown San Antonio to write a second affidavit for a *county* arrest warrant. It was a crushing disappointment for him to be pulled off the climax of the investigation when he had worked the case since the beginning. But politics got in the way.

Mike Appleby told De Los Santos not to sweat it; Allen wasn't going anywhere soon, and the FBI agent said he and his two-man crew would sit on Allen's car in the parking lot to be sure he didn't leave the country club. They would wait for De Los Santos to get back and join in the arrest. With any luck and a good tailwind, Iorio and Albritton would make it too.

While De Los Santos was typing his affidavit, Appleby, Urbanek, and Salazar watched all the likely exits from the golf course. The moment was approaching when Allen would realize that he wasn't above the system after all; it was a moment that the detectives who had been on the case the longest deserved to witness.

The *Express-News* described the scene later as a "caravan of federal agents wearing bulletproof vests . . . about a dozen plainclothes agents milled about, sending hand signals to each other and talking on cell phones." But Appleby remarked later that the media coverage was a little sensational. The only reporters who'd found the trio of arresting officers were "two little gals, two cub reporters who were running around the parking lot."

"Jesse went and got a soda water," Urbanek said, " 'cause we knew we had plenty of time. We only had three cars. We were in touch by radio—killing time. Every time Apple drove up, we stayed away from him. We didn't want to catch what he had. There weren't any 'secret hand signals'; we were just waiting for Blackthorne to come out, and waiting for Gary to get there."

Appleby, Urbanek, and Salazar sat in the parking lot or drove slowly around the grounds for an hour and a half, but De Los Santos was still trapped writing his arrest affidavit. It must have been akin to a frustration nightmare where everything floats in slow motion.

"We knew Allen was going to play eighteen holes," Urbanek said, "and we knew the approximate time he'd be walking out. And then someone at the club called Gary and said Allen was going to play another nine, because he was down some money. That was good news, but it was about four in the afternoon, and in January in San Antonio it's dark by five."

They were talking back and forth with De Los Santos, asking him how long he was going to be. But they began to get a little concerned. If the press knew about the arrest warrant, there was a chance that Maureen might hear it on the radio and call Allen on his cell phone. "It was possible that he'd just leave, and never come back to his car."

But Allen kept playing golf. De Los Santos wasn't back as the sky shaded from pink to gray and Allen came strolling out to the parking lot. They couldn't wait any longer.

"We didn't want to let him go home," Appleby said. "You never know. He might go home and we'd have a hostage situation. He might kill himself—kill Maureen. We didn't know."

Allen walked out with the two men he'd played with that day— Dr. Rod Lee and another man. He'd lost big, in what might well turn out to be the last golf game of his life. He was headed to his car for his checkbook to pay off his debt when Mike Appleby drove in front of the car, blocking it. At the same time, Salazar and Urbanek drove up behind him.

Urbanek walked up to Allen. "He was very, very timid," the San

Antonio detective recalled. "He said, 'I know what this is about. I've been told. Please, just don't do this here. Please don't handcuff me. I won't cause you any problems.' "

Allen didn't want to be humiliated in front of other Oak Hills members. The detectives gave him a small break. Urbanek put their prisoner in the back seat with him in Appleby's car, and they drove a hundred feet away so no one watched as they handcuffed him. They sat for a short time in the parking lot—the investigators and the stunned man in custody. They talked about golf. Even now, it was Allen's passion. Or maybe he just preferred to talk about golf rather than the subject at hand.

They drove Allen first to the FBI offices in the San Antonio Post Office building, where he was photographed and fingerprinted. He had $3800 in cash on him—some of the "pocket change" that Virginia L'Heureux had mentioned. They counted it on the hood of Appleby's unmarked FBI car and put it in the safe in an evidence envelope.

Finally finished with typing the detailed affidavit for Bexar County, De Los Santos joined them as they transported Allen to the Wackenhut custodial facility, a jail operated by the independent security company. De Los Santos had missed the moment that would have been the pinnacle of his career, but he let it go. The cameras caught Allen, and the captors whose size diminished him, as he was led, handcuffed, into Wackenhut, where he would be put on an FBI hold. Reporters called out and asked him how he would plead.

"What do you think?" Allen answered bleakly.

Reached at her home by phone, Maureen sounded confident. "At least it'll be over," she said. "We'll go to court. End of story. They're going to be hammered. At least it'll give us a forum to be able to do something and expose everything. Let me tell you something," she emphasized, "we're finally getting to a place where he can prove his innocence. It's going to be one way of putting an end to it."

Was it Pollyanna bravado, or did she believe what she was saying?

Mike Appleby went home and crawled back into bed. He called in sick the next morning, but his plans to surrender to the flu changed again. Allen was going to be arraigned that morning, but he wasn't on the van from Wackenhut that routinely transported prisoners to court hearings. John Murphy called Appleby and asked, "Where's Blackthorne?"

"He's on his way over in the van," Appleby groaned.

"No, he isn't," the federal prosecutor said. "You've got to go get him."

Still pale green and feverish, Appleby reluctantly got out of bed once more to fetch Blackthorne. He called De Los Santos to join him on the way to the jail, but he was back at the D.A.'s office in grand jury. So Appleby picked Allen up at Wackenhut. He wasn't the man who had walked off the Oak Hills golf course twelve hours before. He no longer wore the expensive golf clothes he had on at arrest; he had on jail-issue dull gray scrubs and a white T-shirt. No jewelry, no $200 sunglasses. Indeed, photographs still exist of seven-year-old Allen in raggedy clothes standing next to an old shed someplace in Oregon. The ghost of that stoic child appeared in the face of the man in handcuffs. Allen Blackthorne appeared stunned to find himself reduced to the status of a prisoner.

"I was nice," Appleby recalled. "We don't hard-ass anybody. We don't grab them and throw them around. We generally aren't mad at anybody, although this was the first guy in all my years I've ever *been* mad at because of what he did. We've handled the Mexican mafia—Urbanek's handled serial killers—but we've never been *mad* before."

Still, Appleby didn't betray his emotions; he was civil with Allen. "We're in the car, I'm sick—and he's a chain-smoker," he recalled. He asked Allen if he wanted a cigarette, and when he nodded, Appleby pulled off Durango Street near the federal courthouse. This might be Allen's last cigarette for a while. He puffed nervously, inhaling deeply as he held the cigarette in cuffed hands.

Appleby recalled, "We'd been talking golf the night before, but now Blackthorne asked me 'What's going to happen to me?' "

"Let me explain," Appleby said matter-of-factly. "I'll take you to the marshal's office. A pretrial services person is going to interview you, get your background, see how much money you've got and all, and then you're going to be brought before a magistrate."

Allen let out a whooshing sigh, but as Appleby studied his face, he somehow pulled himself together. Out of the blue, Allen asked, "Have you ever played golf in Idaho?"

"His world was coming to an end," the FBI agent recalled with amazement, "and he's talking about playing golf in Idaho."

Allen was calm as he appeared before U.S. Magistrate Pam Mathy to hear himself charged with using interstate commerce facilities in the commission of murder for hire, and interstate domestic violence.

Maureen was there for him—as always—attractive and poised. Allen turned to her and said softly, "Hi, baby." He stopped short of blowing her a kiss.

Allen did not enter a plea. When Judge Mathy read over Allen's record of *not* obeying court orders and probation stipulations, she ruled that there would be no bail on the federal charges and $3 million on the state charges (Bexar County) of murder. He could have come up with $3 million easily enough, but he couldn't fight the "no bail."

And then Allen was back in the Wackenhut facility in a stark cell, where he could have a smoke only when his guards said he could.

"This case is about domestic violence," U.S. Attorney Bill Blagg said to reporters later. "We don't live in caves anymore. Women aren't possessions. They have rights. They are human beings. In this case, we are talking about brutality, violence, and death."

Although Richard Lubin still represented Allen, Austin attorney David Botsford was his attorney du jour at his arraignment. Botsford was an expert in Texas law, and he once represented the late Karla Fay Tucker in her failed appeals to avoid the death sentence. She died by lethal injection on February 3, 1998, the first woman to be executed in Texas in 135 years.

The media scrambled now for ever more intimate views of Allen Blackthorne's life. The elements of the complicated murder case were reprised for anyone who might not have lived in San Antonio or Sarasota in 1997. Allen had been his own spin doctor as he presented his life to television and newspaper reporters. His description of his childhood was anything but storybook, and now and it became even more convoluted as reporters found his far-flung relatives. His half brothers Nick, Randy, and Bruce, spoke for their father, Sheldon "Guy" Van Houte, but Guy himself remained elusive.

Allen had always been able to move on to a new phase of his life when the old one grew uncomfortable. Locked up in Wackenhut, he could no longer do that. But he quickly learned to get around many of the rules. Prisoners who wanted to smoke in their cells could get up on their cots and blow the smoke into the air vents to hide the smell from the guards. And Allen had food brought in so he didn't have to exist on the bland and starchy diet that Wackenhut offered.

He could make collect calls and conferred frequently with his attorneys. Outwardly he kept to the same party line that Maureen voiced at his arrest. He was looking forward to a trial that would completely exonerate him.

_____Chapter Forty-three_____

ALTHOUGH THE PUBLIC didn't realize it, the case against Allen Blackthorne had mushroomed. His defense team kept up an assured façade, stressing always that they, too, were anxious to go to trial so his name could finally be cleared.

On January 27, 2000, Mike Appleby wrote a meticulous search warrant; the time had come to search the Blackthorne house. Given his choice, Appleby would rather have gone in with only Richard Urbanek, Jesse Salazar, and Gary De Los Santos. "We could have done it without all the hoopla," he said, "but the FBI has Evidence Response Teams and they're good." It was just that the four detectives knew each other and the case so well that they worked together without speaking, each one knowing what should come next. Still, the pink palace was huge, and there were many places to search.

Appleby's search warrant described the exterior of the house at 223 Box Oak in detail so that there would be no mistake about the address and the items to be seized:

1. Books, records, receipts, notes, ledgers, bank statements/ records, letters, and other papers relating to Allen Blackthorne's daily contacts, both business and social, to include records identifying bank accounts, wire transfers, and/or locations of safe-deposit boxes, from the beginning of 1997 through mid-1999.
2. Telephone and address books or papers which reflect names, addresses, or telephone numbers of associates of Allen Blackthorne, as well as correspondence between Allen Blackthorne and associates, including Daniel Rocha.
3. Photographs, including negatives, depicting Sheila Bellush and others attending a child's birthday party.
4. Tape recordings of telephone calls made to and from A-1/ Veloz Bail Bonds during September and October 1997.
5. A CD ROM containing street maps of cities in the United States.

The search team didn't expect that Maureen Blackthorne was going to be happy to see them. They figured she would be even less enthusiastic to have her massive home crawling with the FBI and San Antonio police detectives, and one big Texas Ranger.

And they were right.

With her husband in jail awaiting trial, Maureen was jittery—
and angry to have her home invaded. She had appeared very self-
assured at Allen's arraignment, but that confidence was gone—at
least for the moment—when she found the searchers at her door. She
phoned her attorney, John Curney, who drove immediately to her
Shavano Creek house and asked to speak to her. He demanded to see
a copy of the search warrant and affidavit. When Appleby politely declined and asked Curney to leave the house during the search, the
lawyer waited outside for half an hour until Maureen came out to
show him the warrant. He warned her not to talk to any of the in-
truders inside.

In all, there were eleven law-enforcement personnel swarming
over the Blackthorne house, including Appleby, De Los Santos, Urbanek, Salazar, Buster Burch, and six members of the FBI evidence
search team. Appleby relied heavily on De Los Santos's report of the
events that had occurred before the FBI came into the picture, and Appleby had also interviewed Danny Rocha.

The Blackthornes' telephone records and known bank records
had already been seized, but there were other items that might still be
in the house. Rocha said he'd sent a letter to "B. K. Cow, c/o Law officers of Black and Ely" at the Box Oak address. It was a way for him
to send something from jail marked "legal mail" so that it wouldn't
be read by a censor. And it was undoubtedly intended as a subtle
threat to the Blackthornes that Rocha intended to talk to detectives.

When he was on *48 Hours,* Allen had made a point of displaying
his voluminous collection of papers and materials on his case. Appleby believed that the Blackthornes had probably saved a lot of
things that they wouldn't want the police to find, some of it long forgotten and dusty—and devastating to the defense.

"Oftentimes," he wrote in his affidavit for a search warrant,
"these individuals do not even realize the incriminating nature of the
documents they keep." In the past Appleby had found treasure troves
of physical evidence making perfect paper trails that connected the
suspect and his crime.

De Los Santos's investigation turned up evidence that the Blackthornes had purchased a Rand McNally atlas with a bonus CD ROM
attached, a disk that might well help someone find streets in Sarasota,
Florida, or anywhere else in America, for that matter. Virginia
L' Heureux had mentioned a stack of videotapes of Sheila's legal troubles after her arrest—tapes Allen wanted her to send to Sheila's new
neighbors and Jamie's boss at Pfizer.

Appleby knew from an IRS agent that Maureen had written checks to Rocha totaling $9000 on about October 10, 1997. Were the canceled checks still in the Blackthornes' office? And the investigators still wondered who had paid the attorneys who represented Joey Del Toro in Mexico? Those lawyers had succeeded in blocking Del Toro's extradition to the United States for twenty months. Joey's grandmother didn't have enough money to pay attorneys, but someone else, who didn't want American detectives questioning Joey, apparently did.

Perhaps most of all, the searchers wanted to find the photographs that Allen had reportedly given to Danny Rocha so that a hit man could recognize Sheila. Appleby was determined to find another set of those pictures, and the negatives if possible, during the January 27, 2000, search.

Every one of the Blackthornes' attorneys—an ever growing list—had received a copy of the search warrant. Appleby assured Richard Lubin and the others that anything that seemed to be a "work product" of the Blackthornes' own investigation for their defense would be sealed.

And it was. Maureen pointed out certain files, notepads, and computer disks that she and Allen had been preparing for Richard Lubin, and they were set aside.

As the searchers worked their way through the huge house, they noted that the maids had cleaned it thoroughly. Everything was neat and in line. In the spacious master bedroom, Jesse Salazar saw that Maureen and Allen each had a walk-in closet as big as most bedrooms—hers to the right, his to the left. They also had their own sections of a large and luxurious bathroom with a tub in the center. All of Maureen's shoes and purses were lined up and arranged by color and size; all of her clothing was on hangers pointing the same way.

Allen's closet was similarly neat, but Salazar found some rather bizarre items. There was an electric cattle prod and two suitcases filled with what the searchers termed "adult novelties": dildos in several skin tones, vibrators, women's wigs, and large-sized lingerie.

Apparently the statements from Allen's earlier wives about his sexual peculiarities were not exaggerated. It wasn't illegal to have private sex toys, but it seemed strange that a couple who must have known they were under suspicion and might be liable to a search wouldn't have stored the sex suitcases somewhere else. The searchers took photographs of them.

Without Allen, Maureen had lost much of her spark; she wore no makeup, and even her body language was different—subdued and somehow defeated. Perhaps she had believed his bravado and his scoffing quotes. Conversely, the searchers wondered if she might have been afraid of him.

Richard Urbanek was an experienced homicide detective, and he and Appleby had talked about how Maureen might respond if she didn't have Allen nearby to censor her. They suspected that she might have been just as physically abused as Ellen, Mary, and Sheila, forced to do what her husband wanted.

"We thought we might pitch Maureen to see if she would talk," Appleby said. "But, man, was that a closed door!"

Urbanek nodded. "A closed door from the very first."

The Blackthornes had a great deal of cash in their home: $11,300. Maureen explained that easily. They had the cash in case banks were closed because of a Y2K millennium crisis. Lots of people had prepared the same way for the widespread computer outages that doomsayers predicted; it was just that the Blackthornes had so much *more* money than most people.

The main section of the house was almost unlived-in, as pristine as a model home for sale, with its theme rooms and matching murals and numerous paintings on the walls. It was a showplace of excess.

"Their garage was who they really were," Jesse Salazar commented. "The maids didn't clean the garage. It looked like any garage before a sale, with junk thrown all over. One drawer had old greens receipts from golf courses going back to 1996, piles of them."

"They had a computer set up in the garage," Urbanek said, "and a telephone. And a really big ashtray."

The office yielded almost more than they could have hoped for. There was a blue plastic file box there with a jumble of photographs in it. Appleby looked through the color shots and held his breath. And there they were—what appeared to be another set of prints of the birthday party at Jungle Jim's Playland—the same pictures Appleby had seen at Jamie's house in New Jersey, the pictures that Danny Rocha had described. The negatives were there too. A younger Allen was in some of the photographs, along with Effie Woods—Sheila's longtime friend who was always there to help her. Daryl's birthday party appeared to have taken place during a period of détente, probably around 1990–91.

Appleby compared the prints with the negatives to see if they matched and were all there. He found that there *were* prints missing for two of the negatives. Where were they? From the negatives, it looked as if the photographs were of Sheila, a child, and someone in a monkey suit. Were they the pictures that Danny gave to Joey Del Toro so that he could be sure he was murdering the right woman?

It would seem so. Sheila had her picture taken scores of times, but if Allen had saved any of them, they weren't in his house now—only the silly birthday-party pictures taken eight or nine years ago.

In the end the search team bagged and labeled thirty-one items of possible evidentiary value, ranging from handwritten notes to videotapes, business cards to phone-call books, and bank records, including two canceled checks totaling $87,000 written to unknown parties. There was a sheet of paper from a computer printer titled "Current Trip," a location generated by the Rand McNally CD. It depicted a map of streets that led to 3120 Markridge Road, Sarasota, Florida.

As the sudden spring heat spread over San Antonio, Allen's attorneys flooded the U.S. district court judge assigned to the case with motions. Judge Edward Prado would preside over Allen's trial. He was a remarkable man of keen intelligence, hilarious wit, and a presence that discouraged both defendants and attorneys from *ever* forgetting who was in charge of his courtroom.

Like many young lawyers, Edward Prado started out in 1972 prosecuting misdemeanors for Bexar County, but he rose rapidly through the justice system. In 1984, Ronald Reagan appointed him to his federal judgeship. On February 10, 2000, Judge Prado set a March 6 trial date for Allen, giving each side just under four weeks to prepare. Later he relented and pushed the trial date ahead to June 5, coincidentally Allen's forty-fifth birthday.

Those who knew Prado realized that, short of a natural disaster, this date was firm. "When the judge says he's going to trial on June fifth," Deputy U.S. Marshal Joseph Johnson, assigned to the Western District Court, said, "he's going to trial on June fifth, so don't make any other plans."

State, county, and federal authorities had been building the case for two years and four months. The Blackthornes had retained seven or eight attorneys over that period, and now Richard Lubin's defense team geared up.

By the first week of March, Allen had long since tired of the constraints of incarceration. Despite the prosecutors' testimony that he was a dangerous man with a maniacal temper, as well as the on-the-record statements of his first two wives and the growing mountain of evidence against him, he wanted to go home until his trial. And he had the solution to how that could be managed.

He proposed conditions of release that he felt would assuage anyone's doubts. Unlike most prisoners, Allen could pay for his own guards. First of all, he and Maureen would execute an "appearance and compliance bond" containing the following conditions:

1. 24-hour electronic monitoring of Blackthorne (voice track or otherwise).
2. 24-hour house arrest/home confinement of Blackthorne.
3. Installation of a separate phone line at defendant's residence that does not have call waiting, call forwarding, etc., so that a representative of U.S. Pretrial Services, the U.S. Marshal and/or this court could contact Blackthorne directly with each such call to be tape recorded by U.S. Pretrial Services and/or the U.S. Marshal to verify that Blackthorne either answered the phone or spoke to the representative who called him.
4. An off-duty law-enforcement officer, paid for by the defendant, stationed immediately outside the Blackthorne residence to prevent defendant from leaving the residence and to record the names of all persons entering the residence.

Further, Allen would put up a personal-recognizance bond of $500,000, and Maureen would match that. Allen said his passport had already expired, and Maureen was ready to surrender hers. The Blackthornes were even willing to place all their assets under the court's control, and Allen promised not to phone or mail any of the people who were "allegedly afraid" of him.

The long document described all the doors and high walls around his property, earnestly arguing that he could not walk away without being seen. It was an outrageous request, but Allen had always believed that money could buy him anything he wanted. Not this time. Judge Prado ruled that he would remain in Wackenhut until his trial.

There the specter of the death penalty hung over Allen Blackthorne. If he should be convicted of the charges against him, it would be up to U.S. Attorney General Janet Reno herself to decide if the death penalty was a possible punishment.

THERE were two trials scheduled for the summer of 2000. First, Allen Blackthorne's in San Antonio, and within a week of its ending—however it ended—Joey Del Toro's trial in Sarasota. Initially Gary De Los Santos and Chris Iorio planned to fly the physical evidence from Sarasota County to San Antonio in a Texas Rangers plane.

"But we thought about it," Iorio said, "and we realized what a catastrophe it would be if the plane crashed. All that evidence could be lost, and both Blackthorne and Del Toro might go free."

"So we drove it," De Los Santos said. "Chris and Ron and I drove from Sarasota to San Antonio with all the evidence under our constant control."

They drove straight through, spelling each other at the wheel. As soon as the Blackthorne trial ended, they would drive the evidence back to Sarasota for Del Toro's trial.

By this time, the three men were fast friends, although Iorio and Albritton had terrorized De Los Santos on a Sarasota golf course when a huge alligator appeared. "We had him pose for a picture with it, and then we told him that it could run faster than a man could," Iorio said laughing. "That's true, but not for very far or very long. They don't have alligators in Bexar County, Texas, and Gary wasn't real happy to be posing with this one."

PART SIX

June 2000, San Antonio

Chapter Forty-four

THE JOHN H. WOOD, JR., U.S. Courthouse of the Western District of Texas, named for "Maximum John" Wood—a federal judge murdered in San Antonio in 1979 by a group of men that included Charles Harrelson, father of actor Woody Harrelson—is a most remarkable building, a structural legacy handed down from HemisFair, the 1968 World's Fair: It is a round building in every sense; even its courtrooms are circular, and the gallery seating is pie-shaped rather than rectangular. The west side is all windows that reflect blue sky and clouds, and the lobby soars many stories high. The building, which sits in the shadow of another HemisFair wonder, the 750-foot Tower of the Americas, appears ready to lift off like an airy, three-story spaceship.

The light becomes shadowy as one moves inside, and the uninitiated get lost in a morass of corridors, round and round. There are no windows in the courtrooms or in the offices of the judges and the court workers who are their support system, but compared to the relentless Texas sun and the humid, pounding rain—which alternate in June—the air inside is deliciously icy. Those who would avoid media cameras can bypass the glass doors in front; there are secret pathways leading off hidden corridors. Jail vans deliver and pick up defendants at closed-off sally ports where telephoto lenses have to be focused rapidly to catch their manacled images.

Walls outside the three floors of courtrooms ring a deep center well, and they are lined with portraits of judges who have served the Western District of Texas since 1880.

During the first week of June 2000, security was even tighter than usual in the U.S. Courthouse, but the men who moved visitors and trial participants through the metal detectors just inside the main doors were unfailingly polite and friendly as they searched purses and briefcases and set cameras aside. Deputy U.S. marshals guarded the courtrooms themselves. They were under the command of Jack Dean, a former Texas Ranger, who had hired Gary De Los Santos. Dean was a formidable presence, a handsome man in his sixties, towering at six feet four, with ramrod-straight posture and thick white hair.

There was a wonderful juxtaposition of Texas history and the computer age in HemisFair Park. Perhaps a hundred feet behind the courthouse, a little farmhouse typical of the nineteenth century was surrounded by a cottage garden of old-fashioned flowers. Court watchers headed for the cafeteria in the Federal Office Building, east of the courthouse, didn't have to stretch much to imagine a pioneer farm wife rejoicing in the blooms from precious seeds and starts carried across the country: mimosa trees, petunias, phlox, portulaca, and roses.

But *inside* Judge Edward Prado's courtroom, on the third floor of the U.S. Courthouse, there were state-of-the-art electronic systems astounding to those who spend half their lives in one trial or another. Both the prosecution and the defense tables had computer monitors, as did the jury box; even the gallery had monitors so spectators could see evidence as it was introduced, something entirely new for most observers, who were accustomed to stretching their necks to catch a glimpse of physical evidence. Judge Prado could touch a button and lower a large screen opposite the jury box to enhance images, as a witness or attorney used a laser beam to point out significant aspects of photographs, maps, or documents—or even videotapes.

Between the attorneys' tables there was a solid pedestal containing a sound system without equal in any courtroom. Judge Prado, a computer aficionado, taught members of the judiciary this audio-visual science of the twenty-first-century courtroom. Other courtrooms seemed as outdated as a court reporter who used Gregg shorthand. Evidence or testimony in the trial of Allen Blackthorne would be instantly available and understood, seen and heard not only by the jurors but also by the spectators in the gallery.

For almost three years, dozens of people had been consumed with the mystery of Sheila Bellush's murder. They would all come together in Judge Prado's courtroom, traveling from Florida and Oregon and New Jersey and Washington State, from homes and law-enforcement agencies and prisons, television and radio stations, newspapers. In a courtroom with only four rows that grew shorter as the room rounded, space on the unyielding benches—the only old-fashioned touch—was precious. So many people in a relatively small room created their own heat, but as Judge Prado explained, "I don't want anyone falling asleep." Air conditioning in the courtroom made it chilly enough for most women to wear sweaters.

As in all trials, the participants chose their spots: the media from San Antonio and Sarasota, *People* magazine, the Associated Press, and this writer were directed to the first two rows on the right side, behind the defense table. For all the space-age technology, there were no cameras allowed. Journalists scrunched over so that Brigitte Woosley, the courtroom artist who had just finished drawing the Waco trial, got the aisle seat in the second row on the right side of the courtroom. Maureen Blackthorne preferred to sit with the media; that put her closest to her husband.

On the left side Gary De Los Santos, Michael Appleby, Bill Blagg, Mike Carlisle (an FBI agent), D.A. Susan Reed, and others directly involved in bringing Allen to trial took up the front row. Behind them were Sheila's family: Gene and Don Smith, Gene's sisters Betty and Julie and their husbands, nieces and nephews, Effie Wood and her daughter. Ironically, Chris Iorio had to sit outside this courtroom, too, until he was called to testify. He was good-natured as he waited at a table just to the right of the elevators, watching the participants come and go. No one knew more about Sheila Bellush's murder.

The back rows of the courtroom held spectators, and when the lines became too long, there was an overflow courtroom across the center well with its own screen.

And so it began.

ON June 5, his forty-fifth birthday, Allen Blackthorne arrived at the courthouse in handcuffs and wearing jail scrubs. But when he entered the courtroom, he wore a navy-blue suit, a white shirt and diagonally striped tie, and wire-rimmed glasses. He smiled frequently and sardonically, showing his now perfect teeth, all of them implants or capped to repair the damage of a childhood with no dental care. He had so many attorneys that an extra table was added to make their battle station L-shaped. Richard Lubin sat at the far left, then Allen, Kurt Volker (Lubin's associate), David Botsford, Jack Pytel, and finally Lubin's paralegal assistant, a statuesque blonde some of the male law-enforcement officers had dubbed Brunhilde. Even though the transcripts of Tracy Ray and Glyn Poage, Judge Prado's court reporters, appeared instantly on the monitors on the attorneys' desks, Lubin's paralegal typed it herself on a laptop computer.

Maureen's attitude in the courtroom was supremely confident. She mouthed messages to her husband and conferred with his attorneys whenever there was a break. Sitting in the midst of reporters, she whispered to them often, "See—see how much bad publicity Allen's had? All of those prospective jurors have read about him again and again. How do they expect him to have a fair trial?"

Maureen was much thinner than she had been in photographs taken months before. Her dark jacket and white skirt hung on her. And yet it was obvious that she enjoyed her role as the wife of the defendant. She beamed at Richard Lubin when he beckoned to her or gave her sheaves of records. She was in the inner circle of power. Either the Blackthornes were well rehearsed to appear serene about the outcome of this high-profile case, or they truly believed that it was only a matter of weeks before Allen was acquitted. At the beginning of the trial, Maureen spoke to reporters as if they were old friends who were on her side.

Judge Prado would do the voir dire—the questioning of potential jurors—himself. There were only two prosecutors the first day; John Murphy's father had died and he was away for the funeral. Richard Durbin and Michael Bernard would handle things as the jury was picked. Once that was done, the trial that had taken so long to begin would be delayed for yet another week.

All judges have their own style, and Edward Prado was a dynamo, often a comedian, who burst from his chambers with athletic energy. With his powerful personality and long black robe, he seemed six feet tall, although in actuality he was several inches shorter. He moved around the courtroom as he questioned the jury pool of 146 residents from several counties surrounding San Antonio. The pool was three times as large as it would have been for a low-profile trial. Prado sat on his bench, strode around the room, leaned on the lectern, and sometimes even dropped to a chair, one leg slung over the chair's arm. He knew that most of the prospective jurors were nervous, tentative, and bewildered as they walked into a courtroom where the tension was palpable. He defused the situation with his running patter, rapid-fire questions, and jokes.

But there was no question at all about who was in charge of the courtroom. Although Judge Prado told one woman from the jury pool that she was really trying out for *Who Wants to Be a Millionaire* and pushed buttons on his audio system to play fight songs from Texas A&M or his own alma mater, the University of Texas, to make other possible jurors feel at home, he knew exactly what he was doing and which questions he needed to ask to weed out those too influenced by the media coverage of the Bellush/Blackthorne case. A solid sitting jury has few secrets. One by one, they answered questions like, Ever been a juror before? A witness in a case? A party to a case? Do you have a prior criminal record?

Surprisingly—or perhaps not—a number of the potential jurors had been victimized by criminal cases ranging from stalking to murder. A sister had been harassed. One man's father had killed an abusive son-in-law. Those people were eliminated, of course. A tall gray-haired man admitted spending a night in jail for stealing a bag of Cheetos decades earlier.

"That's what you get for going to Texas Tech," Prado jibed.

One man spoke longingly of the theft of his 1961 Volkswagen bug. "It was just a shell when I got it back," he told Prado. "They even took my eight-track tape player."

"And those are hard to find these days," Prado shot back as the courtroom filled with laughter.

A parish priest was willing to serve, even though it meant he might miss a scheduled trip to Europe. He was confused about the crime at hand—mixing it up with Susan Smith's drowning murder of her two sons.

Only three of the first ninety possible jurors were in the dark about Sheila Bellush and Allen Blackthorne. That was almost a given in San Antonio. But the man in his seventies, who watched television news four times a day, was probably more of a danger to the defense than the air-conditioner repairman in his early twenties.

A woman who said she could "throw up at pictures in *National Geographic*" appealed to the state; she was educated and listened to National Public Radio on her way to work. She didn't want to serve, but she allowed that she would if chosen.

For two days Judge Prado questioned prospective jurors, winnowing his list down to a doable number for the lawyers on both sides to challenge. The federal prosecutors were allotted seven challenges, while the defense had thirteen. The irrepressible judge played the theme from *Jeopardy* as the final cut was about to be made.

In the end, it seemed to come down to the sex of the jurors left. The defense wanted more males; the prosecution team naturally felt that Sheila's story would hit home with females. But who could really say? Fathers of daughters might feel for Sheila in her plight. The final jury that would decide Allen Blackthorne's fate had eight men and four women, with two male alternates. Ten were married. None had been divorced. Their average age was thirty-eight, with the youngest twenty-one and the oldest sixty-one. Some had college educations and some were blue-collar workers.

Prado warned them that they might need "bladders made of steel" and said he planned to get Porta-Potties for the lawyers, and then relented, pointing out the red buttons at their jury seats so they could signal when they needed a break.

By the end of the day on Tuesday, June 6, the jury was in place, but the trial itself would have to wait until the following Monday when John Murphy returned to make his opening remarks.

THE reporters filed out, the Florida group—Tom Spaulding and Carey Codd of the Sarasota *Herald-Tribune;* Jackie Barron of WFLA-TV and Kim Dean of WWSB, Sarasota; Isabel Mascarenas of WTSP-St. Petersburg and Leanora Minai of the St. Petersburg *Times*—debating whether to go home in the Interim.

Tom Spaulding had adopted a starving, fleabitten stray dog who hung around the courthouse; he took "Fred" with him on the plane to his new home in Sarasota and started looking for a dog-sitter. Loydean Thomas, Associated Press; Robert Stewart, *People;* Shari St. Clair and Paul Venema, KSAT; José Luis Alverdi, KVTV; and Mike Zientek of KENS-TV were all San Antonians. For an author from Seattle, the delay was a chance to become familiar with San Antonio.

But the trial delay was disappointing to everyone. It was akin to starting a race well only to be called back just as the adrenaline began pumping.

And in the Wackenhut jail facility, Allen waited, annoyed that it meant another week away from home. He didn't have to worry about the death penalty. Janet Reno had ruled that the federal government would not seek it. The word among the media was that she had waffled because of all the recent unsavory publicity over Elian Gonzales.

How long would the trial last? Some said two weeks—and some

said two months. That was the way with all trials. There was no use planning beyond the next day.

_____*Chapter Forty-five*_____

IT RAINED ON Monday, June 12, as Allen Blackthorne's trial began. At 9:38 A.M. Judge Prado asked the jury, "Is everybody dry?" Few in the courtroom *were* dry; the skies over East Durango Street had opened up just as they parked their cars and headed toward the courthouse. The air-conditioning turned damp clothes clammy, but the spectators barely noticed. Almost every eye was fixed on the defendant. If they expected him to look worried, they were disappointed; Allen was once again perfectly groomed, and he chatted with his attorneys, smiling, as if they were old friends at a pleasant social gathering.

First Assistant U.S. Attorney John Murphy rose to make his opening remarks, introducing his fellow prosecutors and the law-enforcement officers and district attorney's staff who sat behind the rail. "This case is being tried in the courtroom of the future," Murphy began. "One look at me and you can tell I'm a prosecutor of the past—my VCR still blinks the time."

That was the last of Murphy's humor as he spoke to the jurors about how a man known to be in San Antonio at the moment his ex-wife was murdered in Florida could be guilty of interstate murder for hire, and interstate domestic violence. Put in simple language, Murphy explained, it was "illegal to cause someone to travel [across state lines] to commit violence for reward—and succeed. To travel—and the murder was done for payment. Conspiracy is an agreement to commit a crime. And to prove [premeditated] murder itself, [the state has the burden] to show that the victim is dead and that it was planned beforehand." The federal statute that dealt with domestic violence was 2261, Title 18. It was illegal to cross a state line to "injure, harass or intimidate a spouse or partner. Whoever causes someone to commit an offense against the U.S. is as guilty as if he had done it all himself. He can cause another person to commit the crime, and he's just as responsible."

Murphy had committed the history of Sheila Bellush and Allen Blackthorne to memory, but he occasionally glanced down at the calendar he had filled in with significant dates. It was a horrendous story of a woman hounded and stalked and battered emotionally and physically until she died. Murphy described to the jurors what Sheila had been through. He began with her wedding to Allen in Salem, Oregon, in 1983 and moved through the years when Stevie and Daryl were born, their constant relocations to stay ahead of creditors, their divorce and the endless petty court battles. Theirs was such a grotesquely tangled story, bindweed growing through a rosebush, choking and finally obliterating it with hatred and controversy.

Murphy knew well the motivation behind Sheila's murder. "Allen Blackthorne lost every single time," the prosecutor said. "In the end, he gave up all his rights to his children *forever.*"

Allen Blackthorne was not, Murphy pointed out, a man who could stand losing. Despite Sheila's lack of money and her fear of him, she had kept pushing so that her girls could have enough to eat, medical care, a decent place to live, clothes, and an education. The jurors might have had surface awareness of the Bellush murder case, but no one outside Sheila's intimates and the detectives who put the case together had ever known how deliberate the plan had been, beginning with Allen's pitch to Danny Rocha and ending with Sheila's bloody murder four months later.

Murphy and Richard Durbin had studied a diagram that demonstrated the circle of domestic abuse. The outside ring read "Physical-VIOLENCE-Sexual" over and over. The matrix read "POWER AND CONTROL," and inside were the weapons used against thousands of women trapped in sick marriages: "Coercion and threats, intimidation, emotional abuse, isolation, minimizing, denying and blaming, using children, male privilege, economic abuse." Allen had employed all these cudgels against Sheila, and still she didn't break emotionally.

Sheila's body, crumpled in the doorway of her kitchen, her blue shirt stained mahogany with her own dried blood, her face hidden under a veil of red, flashed on the screen. The courtroom was silent . . . shocked.

"Was it a beating—or a murder?" Murphy asked. "Danny Rocha did a ton of stuff wrong. He always minimized his culpability, but he never changed who was behind it. This is a particularly ugly crime. And this is *not* a 'one witness' case."

Murphy knew that one of his prime witnesses was a known liar: Danny Rocha. If Danny *had* been the state's only witness, a conviction might be dicey. Danny had changed his story many times, but the essence of it was true. He had never once changed the name of the puppeteer, Allen Blackthorne, the man who *hired* Sheila's killer.

■

RICHARD Lubin rose and introduced the men at *his* table: Allen, of course, and Kurt Volker, David Botsford, Tom Gainer, Jack Pytel. He also introduced Maureen, having her stand for the jurors. His thin hair in short, tight curls, Lubin moved like a boxer, bobbing and weaving at the lectern as he emphasized his points. He was almost unctuous in his civility. And deprecating as he pooh-poohed Murphy's accusation of his client. He would show the jurors that Allen Blackthorne had nothing whatsoever to do with the death of his late ex-wife. "This is about a murder committed by Danny Rocha. Danny Rocha has done all of this," Lubin said. "He's an expert at the art of manipulation."

The defense's stance was that Danny Rocha, Sammy Gonzales, and Joey Del Toro were, indeed, guilty of murder. "But not Allen. Our case rests on Danny Rocha's credibility. He's already a convicted murderer and an admitted liar . . . a bookmaker, gambler, hustler. His whole life is a hustle." And that was true. None of the prosecutors could dispute that. Lubin continued to list Danny's lies, his efforts to avoid punishment, his letters from jail to "suborn perjury."

"Danny's a carnivore; Allen's a businessman, self-taught," Lubin said. "Golf and gambling were his weakness. Allen Blackthorne was [Danny's] pigeon—his ticket to ride. The stakes were large, and it was a problem. Allen usually lost, but sometimes Danny let him win. He had bigger plans: the sports bar and a new golf course. Allen Blackthorne is trusting in golf and in his life."

As he sat at the defense table listening to his attorney, Allen looked suitably humble and nodded slightly. He listened avidly as Lubin described him as a good man caught up in a "lousy marriage" who tried valiantly to take care of his children. "Allen Blackthorne went to Sheila's house hundreds and hundreds and hundreds of times to pick-up his kids," Lubin said. "No problem with that. Sheila bought a house in the same block with Allen. Allen had no money in the late '80s, but he always fought battles in court."

Lubin put a picture of Allen with his children on the screen. "He built himself up financially. He sued former associates [and] he got $258,000. He gave Sheila $188,000, keeping only $70,000 for himself. Then he met Maureen. Things were going great. He had a *great* life going. The girls were a heartache. It was good with Daryl, bad with Stevie and Jamie. Allen believed [Jamie] was overdisciplining the girls. He and Maureen had a heart-to-heart talk. 'Let's not tear apart our new family. Let's try another way.' "

And so Allen had given up his rights to his daughters, Lubin pointed out, but only very, very reluctantly. He and Maureen had vowed to protect their nuclear family, but mostly Allen had given up to save his girls from any more harm. He had done it because he didn't want them beaten any longer when they came home from his house. He wanted Sheila arrested *only* so she would get counseling.

Richard Lubin admitted to the jury that Allen had searched for Sheila and Jamie after they moved to Sarasota, but only because he was trying to save Daryl, who was crying out for help on the 800 number Allen had given her.

"He did hire an agency to find them, and he said, 'When you find her, go to the police and have her arrested.' He just wanted to protect his kids. He was not looking to hurt Sheila or scare her or kill her. Danny Rocha did it because he wanted Allen to be grateful to him. He didn't know Allen had given up custody—he wanted to impress him."

Lubin said that Sheila's death was, indeed, "a horrible murder— it was on the anniversary of their engagement. They learned of it on TV. Sheila's murder brought Allen only heartache. There's no reason at all for Allen to be involved. But he was a part of Rocha's scheme. Allen Blackthorne was not involved then and he's not now. He's not guilty."

THE trial had begun much as Danny Rocha's Sarasota trial had; it was, after all, the same crime with a different defendant. The jurors heard the state's first witness, the Sarasota dispatcher, followed by the terrible tape of Stevie's phone call for help as she stood over her mother's body.

The second witness was Stevie herself. She was a year and a half older than she was when she testified in Florida. Wearing a gray jumper and a sweater with white cuffs and collar, her long silky hair streaked blond in sections. Stevie seemed more contained as she answered questions in the lockjaw voice often affected by wealthy prep school girls. It was the first time she had been in the same room with her biological father in three years, and she was obviously determined to show him she could not care less about him.

As John Murphy questioned her, she gave her current living arrangement. "I live with my stepfather, James Bellush, and the quads: Frankie, Tim, Joe, and Courtney."

She answered questions about her biological parents, Sheila Leigh Bellush and Allen Van Houte/Allen Blackthorne.

"How do you refer to him?" Murphy asked.

"Allen."

"About how old were you [when your parents divorced]? Do you remember?"

"I was about three years old."

"Was there a time that you didn't live with either of your parents?"

"Right after the divorce. I was put in a shelter and lived there with foster parents."

Stevie explained that Daryl lived there too for a few months. After that, they lived with their mother in "a missionary apartment, basically a church-based apartment."

Stevie thought they had lived there about a year before they moved into Brandon Oaks.

"Did you want to live with your mom?"

"About that age, I had no preference."

"Did you eventually become unhappy [with your mom]?"

"Yes, when I was five or six—until about the third grade. I wanted to live with Allen."

"And why was that?"

"Basically, I just felt I would have more fun and more freedom living with Allen. He didn't have rules. Basically, Allen showered myself and my sister with gifts and money. You know, fifty dollars from the tooth fairy, stuff like that."

"Was there any bedtime?"

"No."

"Stay up as late as you want?"

"Yes."

"Did your mother have rules?"

"Yes, she did." Stevie said there were no video games or other equipment at her mother's house. Her mother and Allen were usually in some kind of conflict.

"Did your mother appear to be stressed?"

"Absolutely. She had to work constantly. You know, Allen, at a point in time would not pay child support, and she had to work two jobs, had to raise two kids by herself and fight legal battles."

Stevie's affect seemed contrived to sound as world-weary as someone three decades older than she was. She answered John Murphy's questions about the schools she had attended. First Nazarene when they lived at Brandon Oaks, and then Larkspur Elementary when they lived down the street from Allen.

"Would you go visit him?"

"Occasionally, yeah."

"Would that sometimes anger your mother?"

"Absolutely, yeah."

"In fact, one time your mother got particularly angry?"

"Yes, she did. Some type of conflict had occurred, and I went down the street to Allen's house, knocked on the door. No one was home. And my mother and Daryl were out looking for me, and it was raining. And so I finally went back home and hid in my closet, and eventually my mom and Daryl found me. She was scared because she didn't know where I was. They drove around for an hour trying to find me."

"What did she do?"

"She spanked me, and she left a nice-sized bruise on me. Well, Allen had always told me, you know, to go tell someone if anything ever happens, so I did. I went to the school nurse and told her, and she called Allen from there."

Stevie explained that her mother wasn't happy living down the block from Allen. They had moved to the little Brookhollow house when the witness was seven and her father had filed another custody hearing.

"Did you, in fact, testify?"

"Yes, I did."

"What did you testify to?"

Kurt Volker objected, but Judge Prado told Stevie she could answer.

"I testified in regards to who I wanted to live with and the sexual abuse charges."

Although Volker kept objecting, he was overruled. The answer Stevie gave was surprising. "I wanted to live with Allen at that point in time."

But Sheila had won. And Allen had disappeared for about three months.

"You didn't see or hear from him?"

"No phone calls, no child support, nothing."

Stevie answered questions about her mother's engagement to Jamie Bellush.

"How did you feel about that?" Murphy asked.

"I was excited for my mom, but not too enthusiastic about Jamie. He was rough, strict, and he had tough rules we had to follow."

Stevie and Daryl weren't used to following rules, and when they disobeyed, Stevie said, they were spanked with a belt or a spoon. Soon after, Allen married Maureen, and they both told her that Jamie's punishment was "child abuse" and urged her to report anything that might happen.

Stevie answered questions about the counselors she had seen over the years. There had been many. As she grew older, she had become disenchanted with her father.

"While you were living in Boerne, did you have a preference as to which parent you wanted to live with?" Murphy asked.

"Yes. It was my mother."

"What changed you?"

"Basically, I realized how manipulative and controlling—"

Kurt Volker was on his feet, objecting. This time, Judge Prado sustained the objection. As Stevie tried to answer the prosecutor's questions about why she felt closer to her mother, Volker objected again and again.

Finally allowed to answer, Stevie said, "Through the years, I realized or I saw all the things he had done to hurt her and all the ways he had tried to control her and control me and hurt me, and I finally decided I wasn't going to live with that anymore."

She had been in the eighth grade when her eyes were opened to her father's manipulation. She described for the jurors the sequence of events when she and Daryl started to disagree, Pat Aday's intrusion into their lives, and how frightening her father's stalking became. They had packed and left for Sarasota.

Daryl had spent weekends with them there, on leave from the Y camp. Daryl often begged to go "up the street" to the small shopping mall, and Stevie testified, "I was hanging out outside in front of the house with a girlfriend of mine, and Daryl—being the little sister—just wanted to tag along and hang out, and at one point said, 'Stevie, hey, can I go up the street, take your bike and go up the street to a gas station for candy or something?' "

"And you let her?"

"Not at first, but after an hour of her persistently bugging me about it, I finally said, 'All right! Go! But if you call Allen—' "

They both knew they weren't supposed to talk with their biological father, but Stevie wondered if Daryl was sneaking to call him. Daryl hadn't caught on to him yet.

"While you were in Florida," Murphy asked, "how was your mom's health?"

"My mom was extremely stressed-out. She lost about thirty pounds in about four weeks, and started on anxiety medication."

"What was she worried about?"

Again Volker objected.

Now John Murphy led Stevie back to the terrible day of November 7, 1997. She had told it so many times. The babies had been sitting in the little hallway next to their bedroom and the spare bathroom, and one was asleep on the floor. Disturbed, she had gone looking for her mother.

"It was very strange," Stevie said. "I found my mom laying (sic) on the floor in the doorway of the kitchen." Stevie nodded as Murphy pointed to the crime scene on the screen.

"What did she look like?"

"She was covered in blood. I could see that her throat was slit. She laid there, and there was blood everywhere . . . *everywhere.*"

"What did you do?"

"I was in shock when I first saw her. And I bent down and said to her, 'Mom, Mom.' And at first I thought she was playing a trick on me, you know. And so from there, I looked and saw that the phone, which was covered with blood, was off the hook. So I hung it up and went back into her room and picked up the phone."

Stevie identified photographs of the babies as they stood in the paramedics' van, little striations and flecks of dried blood still marking their skin. Although it had all been "a blur," she said, she had helped with them, taking off the life jackets, putting on diapers.

She had been thirteen. John Murphy asked her what she remembered most about her father and mother during the first thirteen years of her life.

"Just constant fighting and stress for my mom and manipulative and deceitful and hurtful."

"Did he ever tell you how he felt about her?"

"Yes. He said he hated her."

"Anything else?"

"When I was really young and I wanted to live with him, we would have conversations about her, and he would tell me that he hated her and my mother lied about him and made up lies about him and got people to lie about him in court, and he wouldn't care if she was killed. He wanted her dead."

"I'm sorry?" Murphy asked as her voice lowered.

"He said he wanted her dead."

"Do you see Allen in the courtroom today?"

"Yes, I do."

"Would you tell us where he is sitting and what he is wearing?"

"He is sitting second from the left, on your left, in a gray suit."

Allen didn't look up. It might have been a complete stranger sitting on the witness stand and not his daughter at all.

"When was the last time you saw Allen?"

"Ninety-seven."

"When?"

"I would say about June."

"Have you seen him since you moved?"

"To Sarasota?"

"Yes."

"No."

"Have you seen him since your mother died?"

"No."

"When was the last time you talked to or heard from Allen?"

"June of '97."

"Has he written to you?"

"No."

"Called you?"

"No."

"Sent you anything?"

"No."

Kurt Volker cross-examined Stevie. He attempted to get her to say that her mother had told her bad things about her father too.

"No. I *saw* things."

"During the divorce?"

"Before the divorce, but I didn't testify to that."

"And how old were you then?"

"Three."

"Can you remember that?"

"Yes." There was little doubt in an observer's mind that she did, indeed. The witness was only sixteen, but she was very bright and old beyond her years.

"From 1992 on, your father really had no personal contact at all with your mother?"

"I would not say that was correct."

"They used to communicate by mail, letters?"

"Phone."

"Fax?"

"Phone."

To questions about Jamie's corporal punishment, Stevie admitted he had slapped her. Yes, she had told Maureen that Jamie had slapped her and left "a little bruise on the corner of my eye."

A picture of a teenager's reddened leg showed on the screen. Volker wanted her to admit that Jamie had beaten her. "It is the defense position that Mr. Blackthorne felt that Jamie Bellush was the person that was responsible for beating his children. The prosecution is arguing that Allen killed his wife, and it is our position that's ludicrous, because if he had killed his wife, he would be turning his daughter over to this man who is leaving [bruises] like that. We just want to show she said he spanked her, but, I mean, my God, she's got some serious welts there."

Judge Prado allowed him to ask questions about spanking but warned him to be careful, "because you could be opening some doors to some other things."

Stevie was not an easy witness for the defense. When Volker brought up Pat Aday's complaint to the sheriff's deputy, she said she had seen her mom spank Daryl with a belt. Before that, Stevie said her mother had never spanked her or Daryl since she married Jamie.

Looking at photos of Daryl's alleged bruises, Stevie said, "This is from being spanked, and Daryl rolled over on her side purposely so my mom would spank her on the side of the leg. Daryl had naturally really red cheeks, and if you look at any picture previous to these, they are all the same color. I was watching my mom the entire time that Daryl and I and my mom were in the room. My mom *never* struck her in the face."

When Volker started to ask her about Daryl's being in a "behavioral camp until about a week after the terrible thing that happened to your mother," Stevie corrected him.

"My mom was *murdered*."

On redirect, John Murphy asked Stevie why Jamie had slapped her.

"It was for getting into trouble at school, not doing homework, or fighting with my little sister."

"The time you went to the Adays and had those pictures taken of your legs, was there some incident that provoked that?"

"I had candles in my room, and I left one on the edge of the nightstand lit, and I fell asleep with it burning. My mom and Jamie came up to my room and found it and freaked out."

As for Allen's contact with Sheila after 1992, Murphy asked Stevie if she remembered an incident when Allen picked her up for a trip to Oregon.

"I do. At the time we were living in Brookhollow and Allen pulled up in the driveway to pick me up. He wasn't taking Daryl. Daryl didn't want to go. My mom reached in the car to give me a hug, and he pulled out with the door open, and she ended up going to the hospital. He didn't stop to see if she was all right. He hit her in the side with the car door."

Asked if Allen had ever beaten her, Stevie nodded. "There was an incident with Allen where he beat me up pretty badly—and Maureen was there, and I had bruises on the back of my legs, on my back, on my arms, on my face."

"Did you try to hide them?"

"Yes, I did. We went to the country club—Allen took me—and I kept a shirt on over my bathing suit because the bruises were really bad on my back, and a lifeguard asked me what happened—when I took my shirt off. And I told him I was playing football and got bruised on my back."

Kurt Volker objected when Murphy asked what Allen had beaten her with, and Judge Prado sustained the objection.

Stevie was excused, and she left the courtroom without glancing at her father. Although the defense stipulated that they might recall her to the stand, she was allowed to leave San Antonio if she should choose to do so.

Brian Balance, one of the EMTs who responded to the scene on Markridge, followed Stevie to the stand. "A deputy sheriff was holding a child," he testified, "and he handed me a child and told me to take care of it."

Soon there were four toddlers and their half sister Stevie in the rescue rig. All the deputies could tell them was that they had a "possible murder" inside, and they needed the fire-rescue team to help with the babies. But when they went into the house to check the victim for signs of life, the witness said it was far too late.

Another graphic color photo of Sheila Bellush's body appeared on the monitors. It was a terrible sight, even for those experienced with violent death. Juror number one, who had said during voir dire that she could "throw up at pictures in *National Geographic,*" glanced down at the screen in front of her and quickly looked away, her hand covering her lips and chin.

JAMIE Bellush testified. As he recalled how he met Sheila, became engaged at Christmas 1992, and married her twice—once secretly and once in a formal ceremony—he was as tearful and emotional as his stepdaughter had been coldly controlled.

Their wedding rehearsal dinner was held on the Riverwalk. "The girls were due back from visitation to Allen's," Jamie said. "Allen wouldn't let them out of the car until Sheila was served with papers.

He and the process server were in the car and they high-fived and laughed after she was served."

Jamie felt that he was a "really good stepfather" and said he'd gotten Stevie and Daryl into soccer and band. They had their difficulties over rules and discipline, yes, but both girls were in therapy, and he and Sheila had begun family therapy in the late spring of 1997.

"Nothing was ever easy with Allen," Jamie said. "He wouldn't bring the girls to therapy. He would drop one girl off and keep the other. He wouldn't let them participate in activities when they were with him."

John Murphy asked Jamie about the in vitro process. "Did it work?"

Jamie smiled. "Big-time," he said, explaining that the quadruplets were nine weeks early and that Sheila had spent the last months of her pregnancy in the hospital on bed rest. Once home, Jamie said, they realized the Alamo Heights house wasn't large enough for six children, and they had bought the house in Boerne with a bridge loan from his father.

But, of course, theirs hadn't been a perfect life "Stevie and I always butted heads," Jamie said. After his marriage to Maureen, the troubles with Allen got worse. "Daryl used to be overjoyed that I was in her life, but after the quads were born, Stevie and I got along better and it was worse with Daryl."

Even so, there had been the candle incident, and once Jamie found Stevie in her closet with a boy. "She had no shirt on. I called the police on the boy, and I slapped Stevie."

Jamie said he always got along with the Praters, who lived to the right of their new house, and, initially, with the Adays. But later the Adays "harassed us all the time. They said we didn't feed our dogs, and that our fence line was on their property."

As Jamie testified, it was clear that Boerne was not the paradise they hoped it would be. When he got an offer of a better position with Pfizer in Florida, they were relieved. "We didn't have to live around [Allen] anymore."

Over Labor Day, Jamie said, he had stayed in Florida because a good friend had tickets on the fifty-yard line to see the Buccaneers play. Sheila had gone back to Texas after they looked for houses to rent. "I called home, and Sheila said, 'Jamie, I need you to come home. I'm being arrested.'

"I decided to take control of my family and move us to Sarasota," Jamie continued. "I rented a U-Haul and hid it from the Adays. We took only the essentials."

But nothing had gone right, even after they were away from San Antonio. Jamie said they couldn't have Daryl in the home with them. She stayed at the Y first, then was hospitalized, and finally went to the Eckerd wilderness camp, Camp E-Ninni-Hasse, for what was to be a longtime stay. The cost was $110 a day. Sheila herself consulted a physician in Nokomis, some miles south of Sarasota, and was diagnosed with anxiety.

To throw Allen off the trail, Jamie said, he flew back to Boerne to pack for the movers and had his personal phone line disconnected, but he left the business line in place. That way, no one could be sure that the house was vacant.

As Murphy asked him to recall November 7, Jamie began to choke up. He remembered every moment of that day. He'd gone to the storage company to load up his car with samples and saw Sheila's van go by, never knowing it was the last time he would see his wife alive. "I went down I-75 toward Fort Myers. I tried to get oriented, as I'd never worked Naples to St. Petersburg. I called only on psychiatrists and neurologists." He'd gotten back to Sarasota by five that afternoon. "I checked on the new house. There was no paint or carpet yet—the pool wasn't dug." He had already decided to keep their address at Mailboxes, Etc., and they were going to put the house they were building into a blind trust so that no one could trace them through public records.

"My pager went off as I was going home," Jamie testified. "I pulled into a gas station and returned the call. The message was from a Sarasota officer, and it said, 'Please call me right away.' When I did, he said, 'You need to come home right away.' I thought that one of the babies had fallen into the pool, but he said, 'No, sir, it's your wife.' I asked, 'Is she dead?' and he said, 'Yes, sir.' "

Tears streaked Jamie's face as he said he'd asked the officers at the scene if they were Christians and said, "Please pray with me."

He sobbed openly as he identified the photographs of his toddlers standing in the fire-department rig. Timmy, he said, who was the most verbal, talked about what had happened. "Mommy's got a bad boo-boo and the man did it." Asked if he had any financial help in raising Stevie, Jamie shook his head. Other than her mother's Social Security, he took care of her. There had, of course, been no help from Allen, nor any inquiry about how she was doing.

Richard Lubin cross-examined Jamie. He was a mercurial personality in court, his demeanor changing from polite inquiry to scathing disdain. He continually accused the witness of beating Allen's daughters.

"Didn't you discipline them with a belt—wooden spoons?"

"Yes, sir."

"And CPS advised that was not the way to do it?"

"Yes, sir. I think it was not in my best interest to do that anymore. I changed my mind and realized that stepparents shouldn't discipline that way."

"Weren't the police called over your beating of Stevie?"

"Yes."

"And didn't you say 'The hand is for love, and objects are for discipline?' "

"Yes, sir."

But Jamie said he had changed. He and Sheila had entered therapy, not because of internal pressures on their family but because of external pressures. They could have found a way were it not for Allen's continual undermining of their efforts to blend together the four babies and the two preteens and to modify the military-like discipline that Jamie thought was best. They were making progress despite everything. And then suddenly there *was* no family any longer.

As to their flight to Florida, Jamie disagreed with Lubin that they were running from the law and hiding from Deputy McDermott. "We were happy to be away from Allen," he said.

"Her bond papers said she could not leave Bexar County?" Lubin pressed.

That was true, but Sheila kept in touch with the bail company. Jamie said they felt that McDermott was in Allen's pocket. If not, it "sure was a strange coincidence" that he began to look for Daryl in Florida.

"You were a little bit traumatized when you talked to detectives?" Lubin asked.

Jamie stared back at him. "I'm *still* traumatized." He admitted that he had refused to let Daryl come back to the family. Yes, he felt that she had some responsibility in her mother's death—"minuscule responsibility" for telling her father where they were living.

"Even with Allen giving up all rights, Stevie and Daryl could speak to him?"

"We asked them not to."

"Was it warm or cold on November seventh?" Lubin asked suddenly.

"I was working in my shirtsleeves," Jamie replied.

"There was insurance on Sheila?"

"Three policies totaling $316,000."

"You were the breadwinner? You considered the two girls your children in that context?"

"Yes, sir."

"How much was Allen paying prior to the termination of his parental rights?"

"Around $1100 a month."

ON redirect, the state pointed out that Allen hadn't paid the child support himself: Under court order, it was mailed by RS Medical.

"What did you do with the life insurance?" Murphy asked.

"Every penny has been invested in an A. G. Edwards account for the children's education. The latest account value is $510,000."

"Did you leave Texas because of the criminal charges pending against Sheila?"

"No, sir," Jamie said firmly. "We left to get away from Mr. Blackthorne. That bond was pulled; our attorney paid it. Sheila called in whenever she had to."

"Did you have a basis for telling the detectives you thought it was Allen Blackthorne behind your wife's murder, for expressing your opinion to the officers?"

"Sheila told me—"

"Objection!" It was expected. Richard Lubin was not going to allow hearsay on such a vital point.

Jamie began again, "Sheila told me—"

Lubin still objected, and Jamie was angry. "No one can speak for Sheila here?" he asked.

Judge Prado ruled, perhaps reluctantly, that what Jamie was trying to say was indeed hearsay. "He cannot say what she said."

And that was true. Even so, there were many people in that courtroom who would, in their own way, speak for Sheila and reveal the kind of dread that walked with her for the last dozen years of her short life.

_____Chapter Forty-six_____

DANNY ROCHA was the next witness, for the state. Squat and dour, he looked older than his thirty years. He had been in custody since November 1999, and there was a flat bitterness about him as he told the jurors of his convictions for first-degree murder as a principal in the death of Sheila Bellush, and in the conspiracy to commit murder.

"I'm serving life without parole," he said in a monotone. "I've appealed it and it was denied. I'm gonna die in prison."

Danny acknowledged that he had nothing to lose and very little to gain by telling the truth now. He knew he wouldn't get out of prison in his lifetime. He was not a particularly appealing witness; he started out by admitting that he was a liar. That was a preemptive strike by the prosecution team because they knew that Richard Lubin would surely try to impeach this witness. Murphy, Durbin, and Bernard were aware they were going to hand a witness—who could be proven to be a man with the truth not in him—over to the defense for cross-examination. They could almost see Lubin salivating at the opportunity. Better to get it over with.

Danny Rocha gave the jury a quick review of his life. He moved to San Antonio in 1983, when he was fourteen. He changed high schools for his junior and senior years because of the golf program at MacArthur, playing on their golf team and winning a scholarship to San Jacinto Junior College in Houston. He later came back to San Antonio Community College and started working at the pro shop at the Chaparral Country Club in suburban Seguin. At that time, he was a bright young light in golfing in Texas.

It was clear that Rocha's whole world was golf—that, and gambling. On the golf teams at college and working in the bag room, cart barn, and driving range of various clubs and courses, he got better and better. "I was good enough to tour," Danny explained. "Not the PGA Tour, but lots of others. I played in tournaments as a professional. But you rarely get any money."

It was obvious that money was always important to Danny. He had married his wife, Eva, on January 30, 1991, when he was twenty-two, and they scraped by. He worked at the Precision Driving Range for the next three or four years, picking up balls at first, and then as manager. He and Eva went to California to see his extended family and to see if they liked it. "But it was too expensive," Danny testified.

In 1995 he found a way to make money as a gambler and a bookie. "I was making a lot of money compared to what I made at Precision. I was on the phone between five thirty and six thirty every night and for about five hours a day on weekends. I played golf the rest of the time."

"For fun?" John Murphy asked.

"I didn't play for fun, but I enjoyed gambling on the golf course.

We gambled for a minimum of a couple hundred to thousands of dollars. There was a circle of golfers who played Monday to Friday. I did extremely well—I'm a good handicapper."

Danny admitted that most people would consider him a golf hustler. "I wouldn't accept a bet I might lose," he said. "It was all for money."

And so he had met Allen Blackthorne through a caddie nicknamed Smell Good Jerry. "Allen had run out of people to gamble with at Oak Hills," Danny said. "I was suspicious at first. We tried to check him out to be sure he wasn't a great golfer. Some people said he'd been on the African tour. But he just seemed to be a wealthy member of Oak Hills who wanted to gamble."

Danny found that Allen was not only not a professional golfer, he was a remarkably inept amateur. "I evaluated him and saw that he was *horrible*. I couldn't believe what I was seeing. We had lots of bets. We bet per hole and doubled whenever we wanted to."

Danny recalled one early game with Allen where he had started well but was soon down $10,000. "He wanted to *press* the entire amount. If he lost the last hole, he could lose $24,000. At best, he'd break even."

Allen ended up owing Danny $8000 for one afternoon of golf, and the witness realized he had found someone who could pay him a small fortune in gambling debts if he worked Blackthorne just right. Danny said he was winning so regularly that he began to give Allen strokes. "It was never fair, but I made it fairer. I was giving him fourteen strokes and I was *still* beating him."

At the defense table, Allen shifted uneasily, and his prominent ears reddened. He appeared to be far more disturbed to be called a bad golfer than he was when Stevie called him a bad father.

The first day of testimony was very long, a precursor of what was to come. Judge Prado moved his trials along, making the most of the hours allotted to him. Some jurors commuted sixty miles because the Western District drew from so many counties. If he had to hold court from 8:00 A.M. to 8:00 P.M., this was one judge who would do it. The wooden benches grew harder as the day ebbed, but nobody left early and nobody got bored—there was nothing boring about the unfolding of a diabolical plot.

Outside, the air was still hot at 6:30 P.M., the lantana plants in giant concrete planters dusty and drooping. Reporters lined up two-dozen wide with their camera crews, back-pedaling to keep up with the lawyers and witnesses, all vying to get at least one good quote for the 11:00 P.M. news or the morning edition.

Maureen Blackthorne, surrounded by attorneys, lit a cigarette the moment she cleared the courthouse doors. She joked confidently, apparently convinced that her husband would be home by the Fourth of July, if not sooner. She was a seductive woman who leaned into men's personal space as she spoke to them, almost unconsciously flirtatious.

ON Tuesday morning, June 13, outside the presence of the jury, Judge Prado played "Appointed Forever," a parody recorded by the Travis County Texas Bar Association's musically and comedically talented Bar and Grill Singers. The tune was familiar: "Happy Together" by the Turtles, originally beginning "Imagine me and you, I do/I think about you day and night, it's only right," but the new words were hilarious:

> Imagine me as God, *I* do—
> I think about it day and night, it feels so right
> To be a federal district judge and know that I'm
> Appointed *forever!*

Prado flashed his wide smile as the song about the omnipotence of federal judges boomed in the courtroom.

> And even at the very worst.
> If you decide to take
>   me up to be reversed,
> You'll have to go to circuit court first,
> And that takes *forever!*

The Bar and Grill Singers donated profits from their CDs to a fund for those who couldn't afford to pay an attorney.

Beyond his natural talent at a clever quip, Judge Prado worked hard to keep balance in his courtroom. He could be abrupt with an attorney who pushed too far or tried to sneak something in, and he had no patience at all with tardiness. His energy was pervasive in a trial whose content virtually drained the spirit of anyone caught there, with its ghastly photographs and testimony that brought even worse mind pictures. Although the defense was not quick to smile at Prado's diversionary tactics, the gallery and the jurors appreciated them.

Danny Rocha was still on the stand that Tuesday morning. He was an instinctively cagey witness, "unsure" of just how much he had made from golf bets with Allen. John Murphy pushed him to be more specific. "How much would you make in an average week of golf gambling?"

"Within—Around a couple thousand a hole up to $10,000," Danny replied.

"What's the most you ever won?"

"The most," Danny hedged, "in a single day with Allen would be over $10,000 and under $30,000."

Murphy meticulously traced the day-by-day relationship between Danny Rocha and Allen Blackthorne. It was patently obvious that Allen had groomed Danny to do whatever he wanted by introducing him to a world he had only dreamed of.

With enough money to purchase his grand new house in Stone Oak and a glimpse of a different kind of life, Danny was ripe for payback time. He trusted his neighbor Rick Speights "like a brother" and told him everything. "We sat out late at night," Danny testified, "and talked of going into business together. I enjoyed my lifestyle, but it couldn't last. I was riding a wave but I wanted to be legit. I wanted to be like Allen with a legit business. Our lifestyle was alike, but Allen was far wealthier."

For hours Danny told the jurors of the plot outlined on a plane from San Antonio to Oregon. The "simple *chingasos*" had grown beyond all reason and all compassion. The investigators had heard this story of greed-driven violence many times; the jurors had not, and their deliberately blank expressions, like those of most jurors, were belied by their eyes.

Danny looked at a photo album and identified the picture Allen had given him so that the hit man would recognize Sheila. She was holding Daryl and a stuffed toy, with someone in a monkey costume looking over her shoulder. It was a happy picture.

"What did you do with that picture?" John Murphy asked.

"I took it to Sammy, along with $4000 in cash and the address for Sheila's house."

Danny said Allen nagged him to get the job done when he learned that Sheila might be preparing to leave Texas. "Allen told me about her court appearance and said she might be leaving. He said she might be at [her attorney] Ken Nunley's office and to tell Sammy and Joey to go there. They went back and forth to Sheila's house [in Boerne]. No one was there. They never found her."

But Allen wasn't willing to let it go. When he finally found Sheila's Sarasota address in October, he gave Danny more reasons she had to be stopped. "He said the abuse was going on in Florida," Danny testified. "He cared for one daughter much more than the other, and she was calling him. He said Sheila was beating the case by locking Daryl in a psych ward. He said Sheila has a lesbian lover in the D.A.'s office who got her off. He told me he'd pay $50,000 to get his daughters back."

At that point, Danny had asked how they should do it, and Allen said, "Use your imagination."

"What happens if she dies?" Danny said he'd asked.

"So be it," was Allen's answer. "The best way is if no one finds the body. Dump her in the ocean, or bury her in the woods."

"I told him I don't know if they'd be willing, but I'd let them know."

"You knew what he wanted?" Murphy pressed.

"He wanted Sheila murdered," Danny answered flatly.

John Murphy asked him how he got the address of the house in Sarasota.

"Allen Blackthorne had the address on a legal pad—across the bottom. He tore it off and gave it me. He said, 'Copy it.' " Allen wasn't about to have anyone see Sheila's address in his handwriting. Danny said he didn't know what happened to the original torn strip.

On November 4 Danny met Sammy Gonzales and Joey Del Toro at the Pan American Club, and Murphy asked him to recall that night, when the plan was activated. "Sammy called and said Joey was in town and ready to meet. I was giving a talk at the Hispanic Golf Association on recruiting new members—I saw that as critical," Danny testified. "I was a young member where the average age is near sixty. We needed young members."

And so they met. Danny's idea of what was "critical" jarred listening in the gallery. "I snuck out of the meeting and I told them, 'It's still on—she's in Florida. It's the same.'

"Joey said, 'How do I get my $10,000?' and I said, 'The easiest way is just to shoot her.' Joey asked for a gun, but I didn't have one. He asked Sammy, and Sammy didn't have one. I gave Joey $500 and the address in Sarasota. I told him to park at a strip mall nearby and walk to the house and to be sure and go in the daytime to avoid Jamie, her husband."

For some reason Allen showed up at Danny's house the next day wearing a tool belt that appeared new, with various tools falling out, as if he was unused to it. "He came over to help me with my fence," Danny said, still surprised. "I told Allen [Joey] was on [his] way, and he joked, 'It's been so long that I almost forgot about it.' "

Allen had assured Danny that if anything went wrong, he would take care of all legal expenses. "After we finished my fence, we played gin rummy."

And, of course, they played golf together on Friday, even as they both knew that Joey was stalking Sheila. Danny said he wanted to be sure Sheila was dead when Joey called. "He said he'd shot her and cut her in the neck."

That Friday evening, after Joey called to say the job was done, Danny recalled going to see Allen. Although Allen didn't have the extra money for Joey that night, he seemed unfazed. "Let's play it cool," he told Danny, "We have plenty of time before it's tracked back."

"We were supposed to meet on Monday at Denny's, but Allen didn't show up. I called and got Maureen, and she said reporters were outside, but Allen was doing fine. When he finally showed up, he told me he'd hired Roy Barrera, Junior, to be his attorney, and he gave me $10,000 for Joey. We went to the Silverhorn golf course to play, but it was too cold to golf. So we played gin instead.

"We talked on the putting green," Danny continued. "He asked about the artist's sketch on TV [of the man seen in Sheila's neighborhood]. Did it look like 'one of the guys'? I said, 'Yes,' and he got upset, but he still promised to hire lawyers for everybody who got in trouble."

Allen wanted to know how many men were in on the plot, and Danny told him, "One guy in San Antonio."

"Will he rat everyone out?" Allen asked.

"I don't know," Danny answered. "Would *I* rat him out? he wanted to know, and I said, 'Well, we'll see who our friends are.' "

IT was 3:42 P.M. on the second day of Allen Blackthorne's trial for murder when the prosecution ended its direct questioning of Danny Rocha. Richard Lubin leaped upon him like a hungry watchdog on a T-bone steak. Lubin was most adept at cross-examination, and he clearly enjoyed skewering the state's number one witness, anxious to reconstruct him as *the* killer. He was combative and sarcastic, teetering on the edge of appearing arrogant.

It went on for the rest of the afternoon and far into Wednesday. "How many meetings with the state, the feds, and the detectives?" Lubin asked.

"I don't know," Danny answered.

"Over fifty?"

"Don't know."

"Once every two weeks?"

"I'd have to do the math."

"You're good with numbers—you're a bookie," Lubin said derisively.

Lubin was trying to make the jury feel it was somehow unethical for the prosecution to spend a lot of time with a witness before he testified. It is not. It is standard defense procedure. It only makes sense.

"Maybe fifteen times—never to the FBI office, never to the state attorneys." Danny said he'd probably talked to the federal prosecuting team about three hours each time. After three years in solitary confinement, he had finally realized the ball was *not* in his court, and he was trying to find some way to see his wife and his boys, who were three, six, and nine. "I never gave a taped or a handwritten statement, though."

"No sworn statement?"

"No."

Yes, Danny agreed with Lubin, he *was* a hustler, although he preferred to think of himself as a handicapper. "Three types of people: one, a gambler, two, a good handicapper, and three, a hustler. I was more number two. The entire time I knew Allen, I thought I was hustling him on the golf course; the entire time, he was hustling *me*. I ended up being the pigeon."

The federal prosecutors had promised to "disclose to the state of Florida and Sarasota County: the nature, extent, and value of his testimony." Personnel from the U.S. Attorney's Office would fly to Florida to explain the value of his testimony, but Florida would still have the sole discretion to change his sentence.

For a "good handicapper," it wasn't much of a deal. The federal prosecutors promised to seek a waiver of the Department of Justice's petit policy and permit Rocha to plead guilty to an appropriate federal offense that carried a maximum punishment of life in prison. The sentence would not *exceed* any sentence ultimately imposed by the state of Florida.

Danny said he had no reason to believe his life sentence in Florida would be reduced. "I only want to go to a federal prison in California where my family is. Part of me doesn't want to hurt the Bellush family anymore. I've caused them so much pain."

Out of the thousands of words of Danny's testimony, the most salient were probably "Allen hired me. I hired Sam. Sam hired Del Toro. That's the basic truth. It *is* unthinkable. It goes against everything I thought I was."

Richard Lubin, whose cross-examination sometimes sounded

like final arguments, wanted to hammer into the jurors' consciousness that Danny was an admitted liar. If they believed that, it should
naturally follow that they would find Allen innocent. And yet, during
the dozen hours he was on the witness stand, Danny had said in so
many ways that *he* was the only link between Allen and the actual
killer, and he had no reason to want Sheila Bellush dead. If they believed Danny, they must find Allen guilty.

At 6:12 that long, long day, Judge Prado recessed court. Everyone was tired, and sick of Danny Rocha's terrible story. But he was
oddly believable on the essential details. Why on earth *would* he have
set out on an elaborate plot to kill a woman he never knew? He had
no motivation for her murder, nothing beyond greed. He'd said it
himself: "I can't understand [Lubin's] motive that I'd kill a woman I'd
never seen with some hope of a payoff down the road."

As John Murphy had said, "No matter how ugly the truth is,
that's what we have to work with."

The next morning, when Lubin announced that he was nearing
the end of Danny's cross-examination, Judge Prado lifted his eyes toward heaven and mouthed, "Thank you, God."

On redirect, Murphy asked Danny what he had gained from his
association with Allen Blackthorne.

"Ten thousand dollars and a life sentence," he replied.

Murphy asked him to say once more what Allen wanted.

"He wanted his [ex-wife] murdered. I told Del Toro that. I had
no personal interest in having Sheila Bellush killed."

"Who wanted her murdered, sir?"

"Allen Blackthorne."

Richard Lubin was sarcastic when he had referred to Sheila's
death as "just business" for Danny Rocha. "Do you think you deserve
to be in a nice prison after what you did to Sheila Bellush?" he asked.

"I try not to think of it," Danny said. "But I probably deserve
what I got. . . . My family has nothing now."

_____Chapter Forty-seven_____

SAN ANTONIO IS A RICH CITY, but 20 percent of its citizens
control 80 percent of the wealth. During Allen Blackthorne's trial, the
haves and the have-nots took their places on the witness stand as the
federal case progressed. Wealthy businessmen like Ray Barshick, who

built a chain of Souper Salad restaurants, and Ray Cevallos, who owned both florist and golf-equipment companies, told the jury about high-stakes golf and handicapping. They had played golf with Allen Blackthorne and with Danny Rocha, along with a number of others, and they described a world much different from the one the average weekend player knew.

Sheila's attorneys and friends spoke of her hellish marriage and her efforts in the legal system to get support for her daughters. They were women who had tried to help Sheila, and it was sparse territory for Richard Lubin to probe. He elicited only answers verifying that Sheila had paid her own way, working late into the night as she filled out the forms she needed to present her case again and again.

Even the men he had worked with at RS Medical recalled Allen's "battleground relationship" with Sheila. Mark McGraw, vice president of product development, testified that the company's 1999 sales totaled $26 million, but by that point, Allen was no longer active in the company except for his attendance at quarterly meetings. He had been virtually retired since 1993. However, in the fall of 1992, Mc-Graw once stayed at Allen's house, and his host had brought up his hatred for his ex-wife. "Allen said he had contacts to have Sheila taken to Mexico—and she wouldn't return," McGraw testified.

Murphy, Durbin, and Bernard had layered their case with meticulous care, with Danny Rocha only one segment of it. It was far from a "one witness case." This was the totality of Sheila's life—from the time she met Allen until her terrible death—and of Allen's life too. This approach became steadily more devastating to his defense.

District Judge Frank Montalvo recalled the day Allen had shocked him by giving up his parental rights. Montalvo had viewed the Blackthornes as a couple out to "even the score," forgetting the cost to their daughters. "Imagine a stampede," he said, "and the smaller animals get run over." Montalvo testified that he'd seen Allen cry as he gave up his daughters, but he hadn't believed a single tear.

No matter what anyone said on the witness stand, nothing seemed to upset Allen. In profile, he had an almost lizardlike appearance. When he smiled—always with half his face—his lids slid slowly over his eyes. His skin was dry and ashen as he turned to look for Maureen, ignoring the reporters who surrounded her. And she was always looking at him, like a smitten schoolgirl darting glances at a boy she had a crush on.

Rick and Kerry Bladorn were in San Antonio now, along with Daryl, waiting to testify. Rick was first. He recalled the Easter visit to Allen's house. Lubin produced an earlier statement in which Rick had said it was Easter, 1989, rather than the actual date, 1990. But Rick remembered dates by the vehicle he drove at the time; he thought in "car time."

"It was 1990," he said. "I bought a new van in October 1989, and I drove that on the trip to Mississippi."

Mike Appleby testified to the fruits of the FBI search warrant served at Allen's house. After nearly a quarter of a century as a special agent, he was unflappable. He had conducted over a hundred searches. They had found many bizarre things, and he read them into the record. Most damning, however, were the negatives of the birthday party with a set of prints—minus two.

So far, every witness had been, if not predictable, someone already associated with the case. But then a pretty dark-haired young woman walked tentatively into the courtroom. She looked frightened. When she took the witness stand, an interpreter stood beside her. Judge Prado put her somewhat at ease by speaking to her in his fluent Spanish.

Her name was Celia Blanco. She came from Nicaragua, and had been in the United States for seven years. For five of those years she was an illegal alien. Leaving her small son in her native country, Celia had come to America to make enough money to send for him and to pay the legal expenses of becoming a citizen.

From February 1997 to March 1998 Celia had worked in the Blackthornes' home at 223 Box Oak. Asked to describe her duties, she said, "Housekeeper, baby-sitter . . . and everything. I worked all hours and I lived there. I started at seven a.m. to eight thirty p.m. if they needed me. I was there on weekends too."

Celia said that there was only one baby when she began working for the Blackthornes, but Maureen had another baby in September 1997.

"Did Allen Blackthorne have a job?" Richard Durbin asked.

"No, he played golf. Maureen worked selling machines for medical work in a house office."

Celia knew the secretary too—Virginia L'Heureux—and she had met Danny Rocha in the summer of 1997 when he brought his children to swim in the pool. The witness had been only a background person to the Blackthornes, and they hadn't seemed to notice her much, so she had been privy to their comings and goings. She recalled Allen's trip to Oregon with Danny and his numerous court battles.

"Did it involve his children?"

"*Sí.*"

"Did he try to find Daryl?"

"*Si.*"

"When?"

"It was in October."

"Why do you remember?"

"I remember—after court—the girls disappeared. Allen was *crazy* trying to find the girls. I remember he said to Virginia, 'Call here! Call *there!*' Everywhere . . . for about a week." Celia had also seen Pat Aday, Sheila's former neighbor, "because she would come to the house to talk everything about Sheila."

Celia recalled the day of Sheila's murder very well. Just before Allen and Maureen went out to dinner to celebrate their "anniversary," the phone had rung, but someone picked it up before she got to it. She heard her employers talking secretly.

"I say, 'Is something happen, Maureen?' and she say, 'No, no. Nothing happened.' "

"Virginia came [to baby-sit] a little after they left and another call came. She say, '*What?* Do Maureen and Allen know that? How happened? When happened?' "

When Celia asked Virginia what was wrong, she told her that Sheila had died.

"That was why they were so weird. They *know.*"

Why, then, had Maureen told reporters that they learned of Sheila's death on the eleven-o'clock news hours later? Celia also remembered that Danny came to the house that night and met with Allen in the garage for about half an hour. But Allen hadn't seemed particularly upset, and he had gone golfing as usual on Monday.

On cross-examination, Kurt Volker asked Celia if the Blackthornes treated her pretty well, and she stared at him, perplexed. She looked at her translator and then at Judge Prado.

"Up until the end of 1997," Volker repeated, "things went very well?"

"*No-o-o-o.*" Celia's expression indicated that things had gone anything *but* well.

"You told Maureen your sister was having problems in Nicaragua?"

Celia turned to Judge Prado in alarm. She didn't understand about cross-examination. "Why do they have to question me?" she asked.

Judge Prado soothed her. "I'm here," he said in Spanish, and she seemed to relax.

"No—no problems," she answered.

"Your sister's husband lost his job, and he had no income and you hinted that Mrs. Blackthorne could offer your sister a job?"

Celia shook her head. She hadn't seen her family for seven years. Yes, her sister had come to America, but she didn't work for Maureen. She came to visit. Sometime later she had worked part-time for Maureen and part-time for Susan Glenny across the street.

Celia had gotten along well with Maureen as long as she was willing to be on duty seven days a week, night and day. Maureen frowned on her taking days off, and was very angry when she heard that a strange man had dropped Celia off at the Blackthornes' one night.

"Isn't that true?" Volker pressed.

"No."

"You weren't dating a man employed by IBM as an engineer?"

"No—he was a friend."

"Didn't [Maureen] tell you you should be in by eleven and no strange men dropping you off at their home?"

Celia denied that she had ever come home after 10:00 P.M. She got so few hours off as it was. But Maureen was angry with her. She didn't want strangers anywhere near her home.

"Didn't you remove property from their home and hide it?"

"*No!* Oh, my God." Celia looked stricken and confused.

"Did you *call?*" Prado asked, unable to resist the appeal to "God." The media row, getting his joke, smiled.

The defense had, perhaps, made a tactical error. What Celia had "stolen" was a picture of Brandon Blackthorne. She adored the three-year-old boy she had cared for, for over a year, but Maureen was jealous when he ran to her maid rather than to her.

Celia said she had saved up $1400 to pay an immigration lawyer to help her become a citizen. She explained that Maureen told her she knew someone who would represent her more capably, and she offered to hold on to Celia's savings to pay the attorney she recommended.

When nothing happened, and Celia asked for her money back, the Blackthornes summarily fired her. She had very little in the way of possessions—only a bed and television set. She had few friends in San Antonio, and the Blackthornes gave her no time to pack or find somewhere to go. Maureen was enraged when she found that Celia had slipped Brandon's photograph into her wallet. That early morning, the neighbors watched as Allen and Maureen threw Celia and all of her belongings out of their house. Her clothes and bedding blew around their yard, getting soaked by their automatic sprinkler system. Hysterically, Celia ran and threw herself on the hood of a neighbor's car as he prepared to drive to work, crying "Help me! Help me!"

But nearby residents chose not to be involved. The man told his wife to stay in the house, and he drove off. Eventually Celia found someone who let her call a cab, and she left with what little she could salvage.

"Are you a citizen now?" Richard Durbin asked as Celia finished her story of servitude to the Blackthornes—when she was afraid to speak up because she was an illegal alien.

"Yes," she said proudly, "I am."

MAUREEN Blackthorne had lost weight during her husband's trial, and there were dark half-moons carved beneath her eyes. After eight days of testimony she no longer appeared as confident as she had been in the beginning. She was alone in court, except for the defense team she and Allen had hired. At some point Richard Lubin's wife arrived from West Palm Beach, and she sat with Maureen, the two of them whispering and nodding as if they were longtime friends. Perhaps they were. Perhaps it was deemed better for the defense if the Blackthornes did not seem so lacking in support, a couple who apparently had no friends at all.

Maureen watched intensely as Virginia L'Heureux took the stand. If anyone knew the Blackthornes' private business, it was Virginia. She was familiar with all of their bank accounts and expenses; she had been part of their daily lives for years.

Virginia was terribly nervous, and she darted looks at Allen, but she was resolute as she told of contacting the Chuck Chambers agency in Sarasota. He was hired to find Sheila, and when they had Sheila's address, it was Virginia who had five copies made of the videotape of Sheila in court, although she didn't send them to Sheila's neighbors.

Allen had apparently been so sure that Virginia would never betray him, even after he fired her, that she had been privy to most aspects of his life. She knew that he kept some old pictures of his daughters in a blue file box in his office, but she didn't realize there were pictures of Sheila there too: the birthday-party photos from Jungle Jim's. "When Maureen and Allen got married," Virginia recalled, "all the pictures of the former women in his life were removed from the house." Maureen didn't want any reminders of the relationships Allen had had before she came along.

It had been Virginia who usually spoke to Sheila when she called.

The telephone-message books found in the FBI search five months before trial showed many, many calls from Pat Aday, Virginia said—but Allen didn't talk with Sheila in 1997.

"Why was that?" John Murphy asked.

"Because he hated her. He didn't want anything to do with her. It was a very volatile situation."

"Is Allen a controlling person?"

"Yes . . . very."

After the jury was dismissed, John Murphy turned to Virginia, who still sat in the witness chair.

"Are you afraid?" he asked.

"Yes," she answered softly. "I'm afraid of Allen."

SAMMY Gonzales testified—cheerfully, but endlessly. His story was the same rendition he had told Gary De Los Santos, the same testimony he had given in Danny Rocha's trial.

As everyone listened to him, he seemed to revel in his transitory celebrity. As always, Sammy told every single detail of every meeting. In an eerie way, being part of a murder plot was the most important thing that had ever happened to him. From the state's angle, he was a great witness because he was so precise. Given a laser pen to point out significant locations on golf courses and maps, Sammy enjoyed himself even more. Once he figured it out, he used the beam with almost every question.

Kurt Volker cross-examined Sammy, emulating his senior partner, Lubin, as he took a snarling head-on attack. "You're a murderer—just as if you slashed Sheila's throat. Don't you agree?"

"No, I don't," Sammy said in a thin, high voice, but he wouldn't fight back. Attacking him was like punching a paper bag in a high wind, and Volker was frustrated.

In the end, Sammy admitted that he netted only twenty dollars in the murder plot—and nineteen years in prison. At that, he had done better than Danny Rocha.

FBI special agent Mike Carlisle took the witness stand to read the long list of phone calls that connected Allen and Maureen's phones to Sarasota locations, Danny to Allen, Danny to Sammy, Sammy to Joey, Joey to Sammy, Joey and Sammy to Joey's girlfriends. The calls were an intricate mesh of connections, catching the plotters in a sticky spiderweb they could neither escape nor explain. Hadn't any of them realized that phone records existed?

With Allen and Maureen, it would be impossible to say *which* of them had placed the calls from their house phones or their cell phones. Their many phone lines were vital to them, and they prided themselves that they had only cordless sets. Their calls to and from Florida peaked in the period extending from the last week of September 1997 to the second week in October. Thereafter, there was apparently no more need for the frantic calls; Allen had located Sheila by then.

As for Joey Del Toro, in his panic—or perhaps with a searing guilty conscience—after the murder, he had left a map tracing his path to Sarasota and back and a trail of cell-phone calls. He was Sheila's killer, but who had paid him to do it?

_____Chapter Forty-eight_____

RUMORS ABOUNDED in the courthouse. Would Allen Blackthorne take the witness stand? Richard Lubin would not comment, and those familiar with homicide trials knew that defense attorneys pale at the thought of putting their clients on the stand in all but very unusual cases. Some in the press corps were betting Allen could not resist telling his story. Others thought he was much too clever for that.

June was winding down, and the heat outside the cool building was a shock to anyone but Texans and Floridians. This trial might well be over by the Fourth of July, but there was another one to come hard on its heels. Joey Del Toro was scheduled to go on trial in Sarasota immediately after Allen Blackthorne's verdict was read.

But first, the San Antonio jurors had to hear the prosecution case that had been presented in Danny Rocha's Florida trial. All of the precious physical evidence that Chris Iorio, Ron Albritton, and Gary De Los Santos had personally driven across the country, and all of the Sarasota detectives and technicians, the witnesses that Charlie Roberts and Henry Lee had questioned. The information might be familiar to investigators, but this jury didn't know about it: trace evidence, DNA, bloody clothes and blood transfers, photographs, ballistics, maps.

One compelling witness was the shy man whom John Murphy and Richard Durbin considered "a hero." Were it not for Jake Mast and his sixth sense that morning of November 7 that something was wrong, the investigators might never have identified the white car that "didn't belong in Gulf Gate."

Mast had reddish blond hair, glasses, a graying beard, and a soft

voice. In answer to Michael Bernard's questions, he said that he worked in Gulf Gate on Fridays. His white one-ton Dodge truck that said MAST'S LAWN CARE on the side, and the twenty-foot trailer full of mowers, weed-eaters, and edgers, were familiar to the residents. He explained that he parked his truck on Blue Water Street and mowed several lawns on both sides of the street that morning. "There was something unusual," he said.

"What was that?" Bernard urged.

"A white car going south on Blue Water toward Markridge with a driver with his hat pulled low. I wave to vehicles that go by. He didn't wave back. I never saw him before or since."

"But you saw him again that morning?"

"The car went by going north the next time. He parked the car here, on Goodwater." Mast gestured with the laser beam. "He got out of the car and walked toward Markridge. I was mowing 3063 Blue Water."

Jake Mast was very nervous, but he kept talking precisely in his soft voice. "I was very compelled to take the license plate. I was scared. I didn't want to look sideways at the car, so I mowed back and forth. I started memorizing on lot sixty, and I finished on lot fifty-four. I didn't look at the state, but I made a sentence, 'Yes, Bob runs sixty-two girls—YBR62G.' "

LISA Lanham, Sarasota County's criminalist, answered John Murphy's questions about the death investigation she was called to on November 7. "I was working the two to ten p.m. shift. I got the call at four thirty."

Once more, the petite criminalist, who looked more like a kindergarten teacher, recalled labeling hairs, fingerprints, and fibers, and photographing the entire house on Markridge. "There was blood on the floors and walls," she said quietly. "The door was open from outside to the garage. There were garbage cans along the outside yard. There was a chair overturned."

But Lisa had concentrated mostly on the kitchen and the utility room. "There's a blood trail and clots all through the kitchen—a drawer open. Clothes caught in the trail, and dropped blood and transferred stains on the kitchen counter just below the phone and on the phone."

Lisa's testimony, and the couple of dozen photographs that came into evidence as she testified, were very upsetting. The juror who could become ill reading the *National Geographic* gulped hard but kept going. It was late in the day, and Judge Prado asked the jurors if they wanted to quit, but they shook their heads. They wanted to go on.

Murphy passed the witness to Lubin.

"The lady was murdered? She was shot and stabbed?" Lubin asked.

"Yes."

"She had marks on her hands—[defense wounds]?"

"Yes."

It was clear that Richard Lubin wanted the jurors to doubt that Joey Del Toro could have attacked Sheila Bellush without getting a lot of blood on his camouflage fatigues. He was trying to establish that there was no blood—or very little—on his fatigues, but they had been washed. When Jody Williams, a criminalist with the Texas Department of Public Safety, took them from Carol Arreola's apartment, they smelled of fabric softener. Williams had observed them visually, but she hadn't tested them for blood. Jane Burgett, another DPS technician, and Williams had searched the Austin site and found two stains on Del Toro's combat boots, a swatch of transferred blood on the side of the driver's seat. But they had not done a presumptive test for blood on the "camo." The blood on the driver's seat later proved to be Del Toro's.

When Peter Tsingalles, the analyst in serology and DNA from the Florida Department of Law Enforcement's crime lab, testified, he recalled searching for body fluids in the samplers sent to him.

Richard Durbin asked him if he had enough blood for a "blueprint of life."

"Enough [to check for] forty-six volumes of life."

"Did you find Sheila's blood? Enough items for the presence of blood?"

"Plenty," Tsingalles said succinctly.

There were twenty swabs from each combat boot and the small stain found on the left bootlace. Several were positive for Sheila's blood. The camouflage pants had twelve stains, with one positive match on the back. There was no blood on the terrifying ski mask.

Richard Lubin kept hammering Tsingalles with questions about why he had failed to do more tests on the combat boots. If there had been prints in the blood around Sheila's body, why wasn't there more blood on the boots? Why hadn't he been more thorough?

The serologist didn't have an answer that suited Lubin, he had tested what was sent to him.

But Lubin had opened the door to some devastating testimony.

Durbin caught it and motioned to Ron Albritton and Chris Iorio. Where was Lisa Lanham, Durbin asked.

"She went to the Riverwalk," Iorio said. "She was dismissed."

"Well, you've got to find her. We need her back here."

Finding one pretty dark-haired woman among the tourists swarming over the Riverwalk was an almost impossible task, but Iorio and Albritton ran to their van and headed there. While they searched frantically for Lisa, Dr. Vincent Di Maio, Bexar County's chief medical examiner, was on the witness stand explaining to the jury what Dr. Broussard had found when he autopsied Sheila Bellush in Sarasota.

"We found Lisa," Chris Iorio recalled later, "and I don't know how. She had changed into shorts and was just getting ready to do some sightseeing. We had her court outfit in the van, and we grabbed her and threw her in the back of the van. We didn't have time to explain to her."

"Yeah," Albritton said, laughing. "If anyone had seen us, they would probably have called the police, because it must have looked as if we were abducting her."

No one in the courtroom had any idea how quickly Lisa Lanham had dressed in her court suit, smoothed down her hair, and taken a deep breath. As John Murphy said, "Recall Lisa Lanham," she walked in from the hallway, completely unruffled.

"Did you find footprints in the blood in Sheila Bellush's kitchen?" Murphy asked.

"Yes, I remember that I did."

"And why is that?"

"I took approximately five hundred photos in that house, and I saw footprints in the kitchen."

"Were they from shoes or boots?"

"No."

"What sort of footprints were they?" Murphy asked softly.

"They were the footprints of small children—children's bare feet. The little children there, the quadruplets, had blood on their feet and legs."

With that short redirect, Murphy had elicited a pathetic picture, an image of the four babies walking around their dead mother, leaving their prints in her blood. Had Lubin not been so aggressive in his cross-examination of the state's serologist, Lisa's testimony might not have been allowed in.

The courtroom was hushed. And then Lubin said briskly, "No questions."

Lisa Lanham was excused. This time she was able to stay on the Riverwalk.

Kerry Bladorn was next. Dressed in a pale lavender suit, with her long hair done like her sister's, she looked very much like Sheila. Kerry was on the witness stand for a very short time. Murphy asked her to remember a Christmas visit with Allen and Sheila in 1985.

Although the defense objected, Judge Prado overruled it.

"Allen said," Kerry recalled, " 'Sheila will never leave me. I'll take the children—or I'll kill *her*.' "

She also remembered the tense Easter visit to San Antonio in 1990, the morning she and Sheila sat at Allen's kitchen table discussing Sue Tuffiash's murder.

"Sheila said, 'Sue didn't deserve to die,' and Allen said, 'Sue pissed him off and she got what she deserved.' Then Allen said to Sheila, 'Don't you *ever* piss me off or the same thing will happen to you.' "

"What has Allen Blackthorne done to help raise Daryl?"

"Nothing," Kerry answered. "He has no contact at all."

Richard Lubin rose to cross-examine her. "When you visited Allen at Easter, 1990, Sheila came too? She moved into a house on that same block?"

"I never visited that house," Kerry said.

"She did move into a house on the same block with him?"

"To my understanding, that's correct."

Kerry left the stand frustrated. She hadn't had a chance to tell the jurors that Sheila had no choice but to move into that house so close to Allen. That was the *only* place he would help her finance, and she didn't have any money of her own at that point to buy a house. It had all been a disaster, with Sheila moving out in less than a year.

Kerry was upset all evening by the way the defense had stopped her from saying what she wanted to, twisting her words: There had been so much she meant to say so that Sheila's real killer would be punished. It seemed to her that she was only on the witness stand for a minute or two.

Daryl Leigh Bellush, a month short of fifteen, followed her aunt onto the witness stand. She was dressed in a plain cotton shift, and her blond hair was caught in a braid down her back. Like her sister Stevie, Daryl darted glances at her father, but he didn't look at her. He either whispered into his attorneys' ears or jotted down notes on the yellow pad in front of him.

While the jurors glanced from Daryl to Allen, John Murphy asked Daryl to tell them about her life since her mother married Jamie Bellush. She had chafed under Jamie's discipline, and been delighted when Allen had switched his affections from Stevie to her.

Allen was a laissez-faire parent. When eleven-year-old Daryl was at his house, there were no rules.

"Did your mother allow you to date?" Murphy asked.

"No, she didn't."

"Did you go to the movies with a boy?"

"Yes, I did."

"And who permitted you to do that?"

"My dad."

"Did your mom see you at the movies with a boy?"

"Yes, she did. She just said we'd talk about it when we got home."

"Did you figure you were in trouble?"

"Yeah."

Responding to Murphy's questions, Daryl explained that she went next door. "[Pat Aday] said that if I got in trouble, just go over there."

Sheila *was* mad, Daryl admitted, but she didn't spank her or strike her in any way. But Daryl had gone back to the Adays'. "I told them what had happened and that my mom was mad and yelling at me and that she was going to hit me."

"Even though she hadn't?"

"No, she hadn't yet."

"And what did the Adays do?"

"They called my dad and Maureen and then they called the police after that."

Daryl testified that after that incident, she was forbidden to go to the Adays' house. "She didn't feel that [Pat] was someone I needed to be around."

But Daryl had gone anyway without Sheila's knowledge; she had visited with Allen and Maureen and Brandon.

"This was after your father had given up his parental rights?" Murphy asked.

"Yes."

When Sheila and Jamie had gone to Florida looking for a house to rent, Daryl took advantage of their absence and went next door. "And so when your mom returned, did someone tell her that had happened?"

"Yes, the person who had been watching us at that time told her. She was really mad. She got her belt and spanked me with her belt and was yelling at me, and then I lied about what happened, and she called me a liar. She was extremely mad and yelling."

That was when Daryl had gone out and sat near the fence. Her mother had come to get her to help put the babies in the car so they could take their housekeeper to the bus station.

"What did you do?"

"I first went inside, and then I ran back outside and went over to the Adays' house. I told them what happened, and I'm not sure if they called my dad first or if they called the police first."

"And did you talk to your dad?"

"Yes. He was encouraging me to talk to the police and have my mom arrested. He said that it was time that she did, that that's what needed to happen."

"So when the police came, did you tell them what happened?"

"Yes, I did."

"Did you exaggerate?"

"Yes, I did, because it would sound more believable and I thought she would be arrested. And it didn't really sound all that bad if I didn't exaggerate it."

Daryl was taken to the Bridge, a youth shelter. "My mother and Jamie came to visit me," she said. "They brought me clothes and told me they were leaving for Florida. The Adays tried to get custody of me. But I didn't *want* to live with the Adays—I wanted to live with my mom."

Allen had clearly succeeded in disrupting Sheila's new family. Daryl recalled flying to Sarasota. "I went right into the YMCA shelter. I didn't know I was going there until I got to Florida."

Once, when her group was cleaning up at Lido beach, Daryl said, she had used Allen's 800 number to call him from a phone booth. "I don't recall telling him where I was." But later she had called him from the Y, which was against the rules. Counselors unplugged the phone from the wall. "They believed I was going to run away, and they called the police."

Daryl, only twelve at the time, recalled threatening to kill herself, and the officer who responded asked her to promise she wouldn't do that. "I said, 'Why don't you just give me your gun and I'll do it myself?' And they took me to an inpatient hospital for a week."

"Did you call Allen again?" Murphy asked.

"Yes, from the Baptist church and from other pay phones around our house. Once from the laundromat. I wouldn't give him the address, but I finally told him the street and described our house."

On cross-examination, Richard Lubin established that Daryl had come to dislike Jamie because of his belief that discipline should be done with belts and spoons. "You felt it was too much?"

"It was overboard," Daryl admitted.

The defense attorney asked her if it was true that, on September 22, 1997, she said she hated her mom, that her mom lied, and beat her, that she didn't want to live with her. "You told them at the shelter that your father would send you airfare?" Lubin read the Y counselor's evaluation aloud. "You were 'storming around . . . swearing,' making threats about yourself and others?"

"Yes."

"Have you spoken to Allen since you gave him the address on Markridge?" Murphy asked on redirect.

"No."

_____Chapter Forty-nine_____

THE JURORS HAD NEVER HEARD Allen Blackthorne speak; they had only seen him stand and smile as Richard Lubin introduced him. But now their client's voice, deep and smooth and charismatically seductive, boomed into the courtroom on tape as he told lie after lie.

Of the many calls emanating from a Blackthorne phone, there was one made at 5:23 A.M. on September 19, 1997. It went to a phone at A-1 Bail Bonds. With the superior sound system in Judge Prado's courtroom, it was easy for both the jury and the gallery to hear the two voices on the tape; one was that of Resa Kennedy, an A-1 employee, and the other was a man who gave his name as Al. His voice was deep but had the crackly sound of a longtime smoker.

September 19 would have been at the height of Allen's search for Sheila. Deputy Fred McDermott had told Allen that Sheila had posted bail and left San Antonio. Pretending to be "Al," to whom Sheila owed money, Allen now tried to pry information out of Resa Kennedy.

"Do you folks have a bond on a Sheila Bellush for $5000?" he began in a semi-official tone.

"Sir, I can't release that information. I don't know who you are," Resa Kennedy said.

"Well, I'm somebody they owe money to and they skipped out of state on me. I'm just trying to figure out where out of state they've run—if they have informed you of it."

"The best thing for you is to come down to the office in person. I couldn't tell you anything over the phone."

"I'm *thrilled* about coming down to the office," the male caller said with a chuckle.

"Yeah, I'm sure." Kennedy said, laughing. "I really can't tell you if we do have her or that we don't have her, see?"

"I know that you do have her because I informed you folks that she was talking about [it]. I had heard a rumor that they were fleeing to Florida."

"Al" tried to assure Kennedy that he had talked to someone in the bail-bonds company earlier, and that her boss knew all about the problem with Sheila. He was very calm and very good-natured about her hesitancy.

"I guess all I'm asking—I'm not asking you to release any information to me," he said earnestly. "I'll go talk to your boss on that. That's fine and I'm more than happy to do that. All I'm trying to find out is that—Have they registered their address with you, or are they in skip status with you?"

"We don't know if they're in Florida or not."

"Well, you know it was in the newspaper that they had gone to Florida."

"I don't read Sunday's paper."

"I got it here. I could fax it to you."

"What was she charged with?"

"Aggravated assault of a child."

"No wonder you got burned." Resa Kennedy was good. She had no intention of telling the caller anything about a client, but she strung him along, making him think she was about to capitulate. Allen said he'd lost $25,000 to Sheila Bellush, and a "colleague" was out $40,000.

"Where do you show for her last address?" Kennedy asked.

"On Boerne Glen."

"Well, I'm—Gosh, I don't know what to tell you, unless you just come down here and talk to them and see if they can find out anything, 'cause I'm sure that when she doesn't go to court, we're going to be looking right along with you."

"Well," Al said for the third or fourth time, "we're out $65,000 between the two of us."

Kennedy promised to make a note of that. "Who is it actually that you want—her or that husband of hers?"

"The husband."

"Okay, I'm making notes here," she fibbed.

Allen did persuade Kennedy to tell him that Sheila had checked in with her bail bondsmen on the September seventeenth, two days earlier, by phone. He, in turn, told her that the house on Boerne Glen was "totally closed up" but there was "stuff" in the house. "I found out that they paid $240,000 for the house, and they owe $228,000 mortgage on it."

"How the hell did they do that?" Kennedy asked.

"I do not know."

"On *your* money." She laughed.

"No, actually it wasn't our money. Our money came up about thirty days ago—twenty-five days exactly. We even got a little help from the sheriff's detective, McDermott. I think he was the arresting officer. I told him that there was some substantial debt and that we felt they were skipping out on it. His response was it wouldn't surprise him."

Allen was using a technique that had worked for him before. He was attempting to get Resa Kennedy on his side, trying to convince her that her company had been swindled along with him, that he had police helping him, and *now* he went for his never-fail story: his deep concern over the abuse of a child.

"[The police officer] shared a lot of information. He was so furious about it," he said. "The child was—when [Emergency Services] came out—I mean this child was bloody."

"Don't tell me they gave it back? How ignorant."

"Yeah," he said, laughing. "They took off with the child to Florida. According to the police officer, he was awful suspicious about things. And I asked him; 'Well, are you feeling pretty good that—that she'll be coming back?' And his response was he had serious doubts about it."

Convinced that he was making progress, Allen had a suggestion for Resa Kennedy, "Do something for yourself. It might help both of us. Do get a phone number [when she calls in], and I would put a note in the file that you guys should call back and verify the phone number."

"Okay," Kennedy said. "And who am I speaking with? Just by first name."

"My name's Al," Allen said. "What's your name—first name?"

"Oh, my name is Lee," she said—another fib.

Allen thanked her and hung up, but he called right back, asking questions about how to fax her the article on Sheila. He began again to try to learn Sheila's phone number and address in Florida. Speaking of McDermott's anger, he emphasized how evil Sheila was. "McDermott found out that she has five different identities."

"Well, that's too bad," Kennedy said. "It's going to be hard to track her."

"Something we found out recently," Allen added. "She's got an old warrant out in Hawaii. He was pretty open to share—they had a years-long history of problems with the family and evidence the caseworkers had collected. He actually shared quite a lot. There was some kind of relationship between her and the supervisor at DHS—Department of Human Services."

Allen seemed completely comfortable with "Lee" now, and he kept warning her that Sheila would probably never be back, that the bail-bonds company would be out $5000.

"You know," Kennedy said, "I appreciate the information. I'll pass it on."

"I'll be happy to keep you [informed]. There's two of us that are burning the midnight oil on this thing."

For all of his sly blandishments, Allen Blackthorne had found out exactly nothing from Resa Kennedy—not even *her* real name—but the tapes of those calls had survived to come back and bite him. If he had bothered to look up the number for A-1 Bail Bonds, a local call, Gary De Los Santos would never have known Allen made them. But Allen had called Information, and the charge went on his phone records.

And now a jury of his peers knew that Danny Rocha was not the only liar in the courtroom, and they had heard for themselves a master manipulator at work. They knew from Daryl how she had been played *until* she gave her father her mother's address. Now they had heard with their own ears how determined Allen was to find Sheila only six weeks before she was murdered.

And he had found her.

At 9:16 a.m. on June 23, 2000, Allen's trial was in its twelfth long day of testimony. Judge Prado still leaped into the room, carrying his omnipresent cup of coffee. Even though many of them had to get up long before dawn to drive to court, the jurors seemed to be doing well in the jury box, dimly lit so they could see their monitors better. The gallery, for the most part, was holding up. Only Maureen and Allen appeared diminished. Maureen no longer wore makeup and often wore the same clothing. Allen was like a parade-float character whose air was ever so slowly escaping. He looked tired and gray. His hair was greasy, and his ears stuck out more. It was hard to look back and picture the man who smiled so broadly on the first day of his trial. It was possible that it had never occurred to him before that he could lose. Although his attorneys still seemed supremely confident, they barely glanced anymore at the torrent of notes he handed to them.

The state rested its case that Monday morning. David Botsford, Allen's lawyer who was the expert on Texas law, rose to make a motion for a mistrial for the second time, arguing that Danny Rocha had promised Joey Del Toro future employment and *that* was what made him travel across state lines to commit what had become a federal crime. It wasn't at Allen's instigation at all; it was a "second conspiracy" begun by Rocha. Judge Prado denied the request, saying that the state had provided enough evidence to continue.

The opposing attorneys continued to argue the intricate points of the law out of the presence of the jury. The defense wanted count one dropped, removing the words "to kill" and leaving only count two: "to injure, harass, and annoy." Judge Prado denied that too.

The defense wanted the information that Danny Rocha had flunked a polygraph in Florida admitted. Judge Prado denied that motion.

The jury filed in, and at 10:12 A.M., the state rested its case once more.

The defense began. Richard Lubin hinted that they might be done with witnesses on Tuesday, the next day. Allen looked at him with some alarm.

Allen and Maureen had surrounded themselves with a buffer of attorneys for a long time, and the first defense witnesses *were* lawyers. Ray Perez was with Allen the morning he told Judge Montalvo that he was ready to sign away his parental rights. Lubin elicited the information that Allen had been on the steering committee to elect a man named Pennypacker who was running against Judge Montalvo, implying that Montalvo must have resented Allen.

Perez said he had tried to talk Allen out of giving up his daughters. "We went to the judge's chambers—Maureen was there. Allen kept crying and breaking down," unable to speak. Perez had had to say the actual words to Judge Montalvo. "He'd tried to stop the beatings," Perez testified, "but it didn't work. This was the only way he felt he could stop the beatings. He didn't want to drag his new family into the matter." Maureen and Allen had gone into a private room, and Perez said that he heard Allen "wailing. He had told me that with him out of the picture, there would be no reason to abuse Daryl anymore."

Richard Durbin rose to cross-examine Perez.

"How long did you represent Allen Blackthorne?"

"I never really did," Perez admitted. "I was going to in about three or four weeks, but I had no direct role."

Perez's wife, Lori Bendseil, was next on the witness stand. Allen had lived across the street from the Perez-Bendseils on Hunter's Lark. She testified that Allen "had some concerns" about his girls and asked her to take Daryl to lunch to see where she really wanted to live. She had agreed.

Bendseil said that she was the one who notified the Blackthorne residence that Sheila was dead; she had heard it from a lawyer friend, Jim Hill, in Ken Nunley's office. Since Nunley was Sheila's attorney, it had to be true and not just a rumor. She believed she had talked to Maureen about 4:30 or 5 that afternoon of November 7. Maureen had thought she was joking at first.

Lew Wood, who owned a burglar-alarm company and played golf with Allen three times a week, testified that Allen had asked him about the consequences of giving up his rights to Stevie and Daryl. "I told him that it had worked out well for me—that it was better for me, and the kids, of course." Wood's children had reunited with him when they were older.

The next defense witness was a little inbred. Jack Pytel, a member of their team, took the stand. He had been sent to talk to Judge Montalvo, and testified that Montalvo had not recalled that Allen was sobbing as he gave up his rights. Asked on cross about his retainer for this trial, Pytel said he was being paid $25,000. Courthouse habitués knew that it was Pytel who brought Allen his lunch every day so that he didn't have to eat jail food.

Wendy Parrish Cruz, a neighbor of Sheila and her girls in 1994, testified that Stevie and Daryl had no supervision after school, and that Stevie was at her house every day. Cruz testified that she had called their father and told him how "miserable" Stevie was.

A family lawyer testified that it was not unusual for parents to give up their rights. "This often happens before they are adopted by someone else." Allen could have talked to his daughters, she said. When they were eighteen and graduated from high school—or married—they could do what they wanted, but they wouldn't have a standing in inheritance.

Allen would never again have to pay for their support, the state pointed out in cross-examination. Nor would he have a chance at custody. He had told several people that he was going to regain custody of his two oldest children.

Patricia Aday took the witness stand in Allen's defense and detailed the numerous times she had helped out his frightened daughters. As the witness described the Bellushes' faults as neighbors and as parents, there was no way to describe her beyond the ultimate "nosy neighbor." She had called Allen frequently, and he'd rushed over to her house.

Lubin introduced photographs of Daryl and Stevie, showing their reddened thighs and cheeks. Aday said she had called the police, of course. And she had called Maureen to tell her that something was "going on over there" as the Bellushes packed to move on September 6. She was worried about Daryl and had offered to adopt her.

John Murphy questioned Pat Aday about her home-schooling of her own children. "You wanted to take care of your own children and not have others have an effect on them?"

"Ahhh, yes . . ." she answered slowly, and then acknowledged that she wouldn't want *her* eleven-year-old daughter to date without her permission.

FOR the defense's first day, there had been four attorneys, a golfing friend, and two neighbor women testifying for Allen; it was not a stellar opening. But rumor said that Allen was going to defy his own attorneys and might very well be on the witness stand after the weekend coming up. The courtroom was packed on Monday morning as attorneys from both sides huddled for a sidebar discussion with Judge Prado.

It was five minutes to ten when the clerk said, "Call Allen Blackthorne."

Dressed as any professional man, Allen sat easily in the witness stand, turning partially toward the jurors as he spoke mostly to them. His voice was deep and soft and devoid of any anger or anxiety. He recalled meeting Sheila in the fall of 1982, and marrying her in early 1983. "It started out good and went bad," he said.

Asked about his feelings for Stevie and Daryl, he replied to Richard Lubin, with a slight, sardonic smile, "I miss 'em—I love 'em."

Allen was convincing, for a man who had not even glanced up at his daughters as they testified. He hadn't seen them for almost three years. Would he not have been hungry for a chance to see his girls? He explained that he had changed his name from Van Houte to Blackthorne; he had no idea who his father really was. "I could never get a straight answer from my mom about whether she was married to my father."

"How did you come out after your divorce?"

"I was broke. A whole bunch of things hit at once. I sued my partners—they were family friends too. It turned into a long-drawn-out lawsuit. I had clothes, a lease car. No money. No bank account. I was wiped out—I lost everything."

Lubin led Allen through his struggle back up the ladder of success until he worked on the design to "launch RS Medical." Allen grew more voluble with each question, and his attorney reminded him to "give us a short version."

Allen was at his best describing his product, whose purpose was "to send waves to increase the blood flow," explaining that it worked on the diabetic foot and to repair the "anterior cruciate ligament. Most NFL teams have it. I started RS Medical. I brought Rick Terrell and his brother and their money into the company. We sold shares. The concept of the device is to market it to physicians as a prescription device, and they rent it to patients for a time."

He sounded brilliant despite the mere high school education he admitted to. Yes, he had to file for bankruptcy in 1992 because the debts from his marriage were too great. It was Sheila and her demands that had driven him to financial disaster by her preventing him from recouping what he had lost. Even so, Allen had managed to fully fund his girls' $28,000 trust fund.

"How'd you feel about Sheila at that time?" Lubin asked.

"I didn't like her. I *hated* what she did. She did a lot of things. . . ." It would become a familiar mantra.

Allen told the jurors that even though Sheila was awarded only 20 percent of his failing EMS business and he 80 percent, he *still* gave her the most money. "It was amicable," he said. "Sheila got $188,000 and I took $70,000."

Allen described his struggles to support his daughters, despite the court battles Sheila filed against him. "I was paying every month—what I could—on the $1250." Until her death, he said, he had paid child support, and he was fully paid off when she died.

"You have anything to do with her death?" Lubin asked almost casually.

"No," Allen said with an odd flatness. "I had nothing to do with it."

From his lips, the decade after his divorce from Sheila sounded so different. This was a man who said he fought desperately to protect his girls. "The nurse at Larkwood School called and said Stevie had a 'base-ball-sized bruise' and said to me, 'How can you sit by and do nothing?' "

"You weren't trying to get back at Sheila?"

"No," Allen said with surprise. "It was pretty smooth. I had the kids whenever I could. I had them a hundred extra days that year. If I filed something, she'd file in return. The 'baseball bruise' complaint went to [Child Protective Services]—there were a lot of complaints to CPS. They weren't responsive. I had real issues. I told them I was prepared to sue them. The trial was in January 1992? I didn't meet the burden. I couldn't show a substantial change in circumstances since the divorce."

"Your feelings about Sheila then?"

"I . . . I don't know. I didn't like Sheila. I *hated* her actions."

Allen had rational answers for every legal tussle with Sheila. He admitted that he asked RS Medical to stop support payments to the girls twice.

"You had a problem with names?" Lubin prompted.

"Sheila wanted to put them in the Boerne School with the Van Houte name. They never knew Van Houte." So he had shut off support payments to bring her into line. Ironically, Allen was confused about the names.

His demeanor wasn't slick or arrogant. He was very quiet and humble, a man brought down by a vindictive woman. He referred to Lubin as "Richard"; they were two colleagues trying to bring out the truth.

Allen was incredulous at Mike McGraw's testimony that he had bragged to him about taking Sheila to Mexico where she would never come back. "Everybody knew we did not like each other. I would *never* share anything with Mike."

As for remarks he allegedly made to Kerry Bladorn about killing Sheila, Allen was bewildered. They could not have visited him at Easter, 1990. He was sure he didn't have the girls then. And he had never discussed Sue Tuffiash's death with her and Sheila.

"Did you ever talk to Sheila about killing her?" Lubin asked.

"I dunno," Allen said, surprisingly. He recalled a party at Sheila's sister's before their divorce. "Sheila stood Daryl on a second-story window. She pushed the screen out and she fell. I was called. I *did* say, 'If anything happens to my kids, I will kill you!' I was mad—I never planned it."

"Did you ever threaten Sheila in Stevie's presence?"

"No— Well, let me back up. I might have. I think Stevie was there when Daryl fell out of the window. The time I took Stevie to

Oregon [when Sheila was knocked down by the car door]? That did *not* happen."

Allen was quite convincing. Was it possible that he would carry it off? The jurors knew only a fraction of his background, and he was both poised and chastened on the witness stand. But he had yet to face cross-examination. Those who knew him said he would never be able to control his rage if John Murphy pushed him too far.

Allen spoke with emotion about the excessive discipline in Sheila's marriage to Jamie. "*She* was very abusive after the divorce, but she stopped in 1992. Jamie was way too rough. Until Sheila's arrest in 1997, I hadn't heard anything about Sheila abusing the kids— there was no question that Jamie was. The counselors they went to said they'd talked to Jamie about his violence."

Lubin prompted Allen often, and he picked up the cues instantly. "Between 1992 and 1997, I didn't seek custody. I occasionally talked to Sheila on the phone, but I mostly put her on hold and gave the phone to Virginia. I thought it would be best if we didn't even have to see each other. I tried to avoid scenes with Sheila when I picked up the kids."

"In the beginning of 1997, what were your feelings about Sheila?" Lubin asked.

"Bad. I never stopped worrying about my kids."

"You have a family?" Lubin asked.

Allen smiled. "I met Maureen on November 7, 1992. [It was the wrong date, a Freudian slip? It was the day and the month that Sheila had died.] We have two children: Brandon Lee and Jacob Alexander." Allen faltered. He could not remember his sons' birth dates. "It's been crazy," he apologized.

"Did your family with Maureen influence your desire to be involved in controversy with Sheila?"

"Yes. Sheila could have her life; Maureen and I could have our life. The girls could come and visit."

"Were you happy in your life and in your marriage?"

"Very. *Very.*"

"Did it mean you loved Stevie and Daryl any less?"

"No," Allen answered with surprise. "I *always* loved Stevie and Daryl. I *still* love Stevie and Daryl."

Allen went into a very long explanation about his thought processes as, with Maureen's encouragement, he went about taking care of his girls. Stevie had pulled away from him, but Daryl wanted to live with him. Just to be sure, he'd asked Lori Bendseil to have lunch with Daryl to see what she really wanted.

"She took Daryl to lunch," he said quietly, "and she said, 'Allen, I don't think you can *not* do this.' I didn't think it out all the way—how it would work, separating the two girls."

"Did you talk to Maureen?" Lubin asked quickly, as if he was anxious to remind Allen of some script he'd moved away from.

"Extensively. It was a very, very, beginning process. For example, when do we begin?"

"On July 21, 1997, you came to court. Your thought processes?" Lubin asked. "How did you feel at the end of the day?"

"Boy," Allen said earnestly, turning to the jury. "The things I learned I didn't know. You get slapped in the face with things you've always known and didn't realize. How could this man split up these girls? All the turmoil. All they had was each other." His Adam's apple moved, and he choked as he stifled tears at the thought that he had almost torn his girls apart. "One allegation was raised again, after *ten years*. The same abuse. It wasn't true then and not this time either. It always had to do with me. I did this, I did that, without concern for the situation."

It was, of course, the *sexual* abuse allegations that had always driven Allen out of his court joustings with Sheila. Lubin had obviously chosen to bring it into the open and defuse it. Allen's choking tears were perfectly apt at this point. He was the innocent father, accused of the unthinkable.

Did the jurors believe his emotional agony?

The courtroom was enthralled—either with belief in his testimony or with admiration for his acting ability.

But it was time for lunch.

_____Chapter Fifty_____

AFTER LUNCH Richard Lubin continued to probe Allen's angst at giving his daughters away. Allen said he had realized that fighting Sheila over the girls wasn't in anyone's best interest. "There was no way to win. It was just enough to say 'no more.' These are *children*, not possessions. Her litigation would have carried on."

"What was your motivation?"

"Problems seemed to happen when they came to my house, when they left my house. Sunday evenings were 'hold your breath.' Friday evenings were 'hold your breath.' They only had a few years until they'd be on their own. All the little nasty things a parent can say to a child. That hurts a child."

"Did you think you were doing the best—"

"Yes," Allen said, crying openly.

"Was it hard?"

His voice trembled. "Very hard."

Allen cried through the next several questions, finally sobbing, "I sit here today and I don't know if I did the right thing. I can't tell you that I know—"

In the gallery Maureen started to cry too.

Lubin switched gears suddenly and began to ask about Danny Rocha and golf. Allen perked up considerably. He clearly enjoyed talking about golf, although he said he was hurt by Danny's testimony. "I knew he was a little bit of a hustler, but I never knew he laughed behind my back until I heard it in court. I didn't know he occasionally let me win."

Allen's version of the things his old golf partner had testified to was diametrically opposed to Danny's.

"You didn't talk a lot to Danny about the custody suit?" Lubin asked.

"No. He'd ask questions once in a while," Allen answered, perplexed. "I can't remember *ever* going into that much with Danny."

"It would help," Lubin said somewhat wryly.

"I know, Richard," Allen said earnestly. "But I just can't. I've sat down and thought about it. I can't recall saying much to Danny about the girls."

Allen rambled off-track and began to talk about people who had been supportive after Sheila's arrest, and Lubin hurried to reel him in, peppering him with questions about his asking Rocha to "take care of Sheila."

"I had nothing to do with it," Allen said firmly. "No. No. No. No."

"Did you get drunk on the plane?"

"No, Richard. And I never said I wanted her beat up, killed, harassed, annoyed."

Allen did admit that he had been pleased when Sheila was arrested, that he'd been a little vindictive. But mostly he was happy that his girls would be known to CPS and something would be done.

The thrust of the defense was that if Allen had erred and used poor judgment, it was only because he was a concerned father, desperate to save his daughters from the harsh punishment of their mother and new stepfather. Yes, he was thankful the Adays contacted him, but no, he wasn't behind their offer to adopt Daryl. "But I thought it was a good idea," he offered. He said it was just a coincidence that the Adays were represented by one of his attorneys. He didn't know why they never received a bill for legal services.

Whenever Allen had trouble "remembering," he apologized to Lubin, saying that certain memories were "fuzzy." Yes, Allen admitted calling the bail-bond company. "I didn't want her to run away from these charges. I *had* to lie [on the phone] because I wanted a warrant out on Sheila. I wanted probation watching her."

"You had a right, even though you weren't the legal dad?" Lubin asked.

"Absolutely."

His tears dried, Allen seemed very much at ease on the witness stand. He leaned back with his left foot perched on his right knee. Holding his left hand palm open, he tapped out important points with his right hand. He wanted A-1 to pull its bond on Sheila. "I *wanted* them to revoke her."

"What were you afraid of?"

"There was nothing in place to protect the girls. I fabricated a story. It was five thirty a.m.—I get up early sometimes—I just do. I lied. [If I didn't] they'd make me the issue. Nothing would get done. I had ten years of that. I made it up as I went along. Sheila and Jamie would *have* to face charges because bondsmen just care about their money."

"How about the Pensacola calls?" Lubin asked, referring to the calls made from the Blackthorne home to motels along the Bellushes' route to Sarasota.

"I can't explain that. I might kind of know, but I'm not a hundred percent sure."

That was an odd response. Allen was apparently bending over backward to give honest answers. But he was almost *too* earnest. Of course he'd searched for Daryl. What caring father wouldn't? He had hired McDermott, who came up empty, and Sarasota PI Chuck Chambers, who hadn't found her yet. Allen had to do the best he could to find her. Even Maureen made twenty-five calls to wilderness camps and shelters trying to find her stepdaughter.

"You gave no name [when you called Chambers]. Virginia hired the PI?"

"Again, I didn't want it to be an issue about *me*."

When Daryl called him from the Y shelter in Sarasota, Allen said he was immensely relieved to find his younger daughter. But then he heard her shouting, "Get away from me! Get away from me! Leave me alone! Stop it. Stop it!" As Allen repeated her cries, he mimicked her frantic fear.

"I felt terror," he said, his voice tremulous with emotion. "For *Daryl*. If you got a call like that and it was your child, you would know."

And then finally everything had come together. In their phone calls Daryl gave Allen enough clues to pass on to Chuck Chambers's operatives. So armed, they had easily located the Bellush address on Markridge on October 11.

Allen testified he then had several copies of the videotapes of Sheila's arrest, court appearance, and troubles with the law made to send to nearby neighbors and to Jamie's boss.

"I want to ask you something," Lubin began. "Did you learn a lesson from the fact of the Adays being neighbors and Wendy Cruz . . . about the value of neighbors being aware of the situation?"

Allen picked up the hint instantly and said, "And the Brookhollow neighbors and the Cedar Canyon neighbors—all of them."

"What lesson had you learned?"

"That the girls had always run to the neighbors for help—that they were outgoing girls. They made friends. And they would get to know the other neighbors around where they were living."

The videotapes "Quad Mom Arrested" and "Quad Mom on the Run" were a way for Allen to alert Sheila and Jamie's neighbors that the girls were in danger and that Sheila was a fugitive from justice. They *were* damning, slanted by the media at the time to suggest that Sheila, the once revered "Quad Mom" was actually a longtime child batterer.

"It wasn't mean-spirited," Allen testified about his reasons for Sheila's new neighbors to see the tapes. "I wanted every neighbor to know, to watch out, to pay a little more attention to the Bellush house. When they see the girls, don't just ignore them. Say hi to them. Ask them, 'Is everything okay?' "

But for some reason, Virginia had failed to send the tapes out, and Allen didn't either. He said he often had trouble getting around to office chores.

"Where were they sitting?"

"In a stack on my desk on the right-hand side, with the address on top."

And *that*, Allen suggested, must have been how Danny Rocha found Sheila's address. He could have easily read it there during one of his many visits to Allen's office—often when Allen was away. Why Danny got it into his head to hurt Sheila was a complete mystery to Allen.

When the reports that Sheila was dead came to him and Maureen in the late afternoon of November 7, Allen said he didn't believe it. "[Ken] Nunley's office had called Lori Bendseil and said that Sheila was dead or had an accident or whatever it was." Coming from that source, Allen negated it and went ahead with his plans to take Maureen to dinner. Later, when they just happened to run into Lori and her husband, Ray, they learned that it wasn't Nunley, but an associate named Jim Hill, who had told her about the rumor.

"We're taking it a little more seriously," Allen said. "I got home. Rocha is there at the house. He lost $1500 that day. He paid $900 and he owed $600. The deal was, you pay by the end of the day or there's no more golf, no more gambling, no more nothing. It's over."

But Danny had come over, Allen testified, to say he couldn't pay—promising he could pay in a day. "At that point, I don't care. I just say, 'That's fine.' "

After Danny left, Allen thought he'd either called Kim Hall in Sarasota or received a call from her.

"Okay, what happens with the TV?" Lubin asked.

"The ten-o'clock news—KENS-5—says Sarasota police say the ex-husband did it. 'Shocking news arriving out of Florida, quad mom Sheila Bellush has been murdered. Sarasota police say the ex-husband did it.' I was numb and shocked. It was disbelief. I mean, even though I saw it, it was still disbelief."

"What were you thinking about? Your first thought?"

"The girls."

"Well, what did you do about it? Did you know how to get in touch with them?"

"No," Allen said sadly, "I didn't know how to get in touch with them."

"What were *your* emotions?"

"I don't know. I mean it just— We hear earlier that she may be dead. You know as the evening goes on, we're finding out more information. We sit down. We turn on the news. We're right there watching, trying to find out what's happening. And, I mean, it's sad. It's shocking. And then, boom—the Sarasota police say I did it. It's just too much stuff. It's just too much. I can't tell you what my feelings were. I mean, I was angry. I was sad. I don't know what I was."

For many of those watching Allen testify, he was a revelation, a study in sociopathy. He clearly had no ability at all to understand or describe normal emotion. He was struck almost dumb when asked to do so, and he fumbled, searching for words that fit. He could talk about golf until the cows came home. He *knew* golf. He apparently did not know how grieving people were supposed to feel.

Allen said he retained attorney Roy Barrera, Jr., the next day. He said he had offered to move to Sarasota if state attorneys wanted to charge him there.

"Did you have any feelings," Lubin asked, "about contacting the girls the next day?"

"I *wanted* to find out if they were okay. I wanted to hear from them. I wanted to talk to them."

"And did you ask whether you could do that?"

"Yes. I asked Roy Barrera."

"And what advice did you receive?"

"He said no—under no circumstances."

"Have you wanted to do anything in terms of support or money for the girls?"

"Yes."

"And what have you been told?"

"That 'Allen, until this is over, you can't pay any money. It could be viewed as trying to buy testimony or a bribe or influence testimony.' And Richard, *you* said, 'You just have to be patient.' "

Now Allen asked Richard Lubin to back up a little. He wanted the jury to know that he was completely happy with his life and with Maureen and his little boys in November 1997 when Sheila died. He *was* unhappy about Daryl's situation, but he was worried and sad about Stevie too. All of his children mattered to him. He seemed like an actor who had suddenly remembered lines in a script that he'd forgotten to deliver, and wanted to get them in—if belatedly.

"I'm sorry about that," Lubin said. "I wasn't trying to overlook that."

"I know."

"Now, did you have anything whatsoever to do with setting this plan in motion with Rocha and these guys?"

"I didn't," Allen said firmly. "I had nothing to do with it."

"Did you suggest it to Rocha, hint it to Rocha, order him, request him—anything like that?"

"I didn't. I had nothing to do with it."

"Or with Gonzales or Del Toro or anyone else that may have been involved?"

"None of them."

"What do you want to tell this jury?"

Allen turned toward the jury box, his face a study of innocence and determination. "I wouldn't want to hurt her. I wouldn't want her killed. I mean, she was the mother of Stevie and Daryl. Who else did they have? Think about it. *Jamie?*" He made a deprecating sound. "What would have happened to these girls if Sheila were to be killed or die? Who would you believe they would go with?"

"*Jamie. . . .*" And that, Lubin wanted to show, was something Allen would have hated.

"Are you innocent of this crime?"

"I *am.*"

Direct examination was over, and Allen had conducted himself remarkably well. During more than five hours on the stand, he had never once shown anger, and he certainly cried at the appropriate times. Lubin had done a masterful job of asking him questions that would lessen the impact of the state's case. If Lubin couldn't convince the jurors that Allen loved Stevie and Daryl, he could not explain the dragnet search for Sheila that Allen mounted in the early fall of 1997.

THE benches were hard as stone, and yet no one waiting for the next act left the courtroom during the break, fearful that they might not get back in. Cross-examination began at five minutes to four on that hot Monday afternoon. This was the culmination of so many years of effort, John Murphy had waited a very long time to confront Allen Blackthorne.

"Mr. Blackthorne, this is a big day for you, isn't it?" he began.

"I'm sorry?" Allen seemed confused.

"This is a big day for you, isn't it?"

"Yes . . ." Allen said cautiously.

"Do you have to think about that?"

"Well, I think they have all been pretty big days."

"But this is a particularly big day, more important than any golf tournament you ever played in, isn't it?"

"Yes."

"Before playing in golf tournaments, you would practice, wouldn't you?"

"Yes."

"How many times have you practiced this?"

"Today?"

"Yeah."

Allen's eyes widened. "I *haven't.*"

"You haven't rehearsed this with Mr. Lubin. You weren't video-taped—ever?"

"Never."

Murphy pointed out that Allen's demeanor had changed markedly from the image he once presented on *48 Hours*.

Lubin objected, and Murphy moved on, asking Allen why he'd disliked his father so much that he'd changed his name.

"Well, okay," Allen said. "Would you like me to tell you the reasons? You tell me what you'd like, John."

"Go ahead. Tell us the reasons."

"Whether Guy is my father or not is something I'm unclear on. It's been a whole big controversy in my life."

Murphy suggested that Allen's name change had been about running away from the $300,000 debt he amassed in Hawaii. Gradually Murphy allowed the jurors to see the background of the man on the stand.

"You were divorced here, and you went through the divorce proceedings and there were all kinds of allegations and counter allegations: Is that correct?"

"Yes." Allen watched Murphy warily, while trying to maintain the same casually confident posture he had during Lubin's questioning.

"Some of those allegations were very hurtful, weren't they?"

"They were. They were ugly."

"Didn't make you happy, did they?"

"No," Allen said, squirming uncomfortably. "They were very disgusting stuff."

"There were two final decrees of divorce, weren't there?"

"John, I think there were like six—"

"My name is *Mr. Murphy*," the prosecutor boomed. "And you're Mr. Blackthorne." Murphy wasn't going to allow Allen to get away with the kind of buddy-to-buddy stance that he had with Lubin.

Allen got the message, but he didn't seem angry or embarrassed.

Murphy moved through the intricate money manipulations that accompanied Sheila's divorce from Allen. "You hid assets from your creditors in Hawaii, and then you hid assets from the divorce court when you got divorced from Sheila. Isn't that right?"

"Yes."

Allen admitted that, and the fact that he often refused to pay Sheila what she was awarded to care for Stevie and Daryl. Murphy submitted that he had failed to pay over $100,000 the courts had awarded to Sheila. Allen said that was correct. That sum had been reduced to $28,000, money that was to go into a trust for their girls. He said he'd paid that at the rate of $500 a month. Allen's voice grew softer as Murphy bored in. The timbre changed from the deeply confident "Al" of the bail-bonds tape to that of a man who sounded almost effeminate as he crumpled beneath the truth of his failure to provide for Stevie and Daryl.

"When did you finish paying into that trust?"

"In '97."

"Ninety-seven," Murphy said. "That's the same year you lost somewhere between $75,000 and $200,000 to Danny Rocha, golfing?"

"Yes."

"And you could *afford* only $500 a month to go into a trust for your children?"

"Yes."

"You lost more than that on a hole of golf, didn't you?"

"Yes."

"But you *loved* your daughters, isn't that right?"

"I do love my daughters."

When it came to the actual amount Allen had paid for the support of Stevie and Daryl over the preceding thirteen years, Murphy had him on the ropes. There was no way he could explain away the actual figures. Golf was clearly far more important to him.

Murphy moved on to the custody hearing in July 1997, asking about Allen's decision to give up rights to his daughters. Allen tensed ever so slightly. This was dangerous territory for him. He insisted he had given Stevie and Daryl up, both to protect his own young family and to keep the older girls from being separated from one another. It didn't matter how much *he* was hurt; he had to think of all of his children. But Murphy got too close to another reason—the "ugly, hurtful" allegations. The concept of sexual abuse concerning Stevie had never been confronted outright in this trial, and now it hovered over the defense like a vulture. Richard Lubin was poised to keep any mention of it from the jurors.

Allen was forced to agree that he had only sought custody of Daryl, and that Stevie caused too much dissension in his home. "So both of these girls were the subject of your motion seeking custody?" Murphy asked.

"No. Regardless of what that says, or means . . . it was clear from the transcript—there was no confusion. It was Daryl only."

"Because Stevie didn't want to live with you?"

"She did not."

"And she was causing conflict in your home?"

"Yeah. It created stress."

"Two witnesses testified [in the July 1997 hearing], and the same old ugly allegations came up again, didn't they?"

"Yes. One of them talked about it," Allen said. "The other also talked about it."

"And before another witness testified, you relinquished your parental rights?"

"Yes."

Allen's lies began to fall around him, piling up higher and higher. He admitted that he had never been on "the steering committee" to elect "Biff" Pennypacker judge—to replace Judge Montalvo, the judge who accepted his decision to give up Stevie and Daryl. Allen wasn't sure how his name got on a petition to disqualify Montalvo.

The Adays had never been billed for the legal services of Pat Guerra, one of Allen's attorneys, in their efforts to adopt Daryl in September 1997. Murphy produced records that showed Allen had paid him. His fine hand seemed to be controlling all the harassment of Sheila.

"You told us this morning," Murphy said, "that you loved your daughters very much. Isn't that right?"

"Yes," Allen said warily.

"And that they only had a few years until they would be out and about on their own? That hearing was in 1997. Your daughters were born in which years?"

"Daryl was born in 1985 and Stevie in . . . oh, boy . . . er, in 1984."

"So one of them was thirteen and the other—"

"Twelve."

"Was twelve?"

"Yes."

"How old do you think a child should be to be out and about on their own?"

"Like Sheila left home when she was sixteen and a half, almost seventeen, when she left." Allen said. "I left when I was younger. I would guess that probably by the time they were sixteen, seventeen years old, they were pretty well going to be making their own decisions on what they wanted."

"Did Stevie look to you like she was ready to be out and about and on her own?"

"No," Allen demurred. "I meant being able to leave her mother's home, if that's what she chose to do. I would prefer kids to stay, especially Stevie and Daryl, until they were twenty-one or twenty-two."

But *where* would Stevie and Daryl have stayed and who would care for them? Allen didn't want Jamie to have them, and Jamie and Sheila had already placed Daryl in a camp for incorrigibles. What were the girls supposed to do when they were "out and about"? Their mother was dead; their father had disowned them.

Allen's composure was slipping. When Murphy asked him to list his children, he left one out—the little girl he'd fathered out of wedlock with his former secretary. Lubin objected strenuously to the mention of that ten-year-old girl. Judge Prado overruled him.

Allen denied that he was the one who told Daryl he had given up all rights to her, violating a court order that a counselor should tell her.

"So Daryl was mistaken."

"She is mistaken."

"And all that stuff about abusing those children—that Jamie is the only one that did it, that isn't true is it?" Murphy asked.

"Since her and Jamie got together? I believe it is."

"Who is it that hit them with a shaft of a steel arrow?"

"In what year? I mean, I would have to know the years."

"Oh, maybe '93."

"I don't know," Allen said calmly.

"Who is it that banged Stevie's head into the wall about that period of time?"

"I don't know. I don't remember."

THE press row was making bets on just when Allen was going to break, but he held steady as Murphy pounded him. He appeared to be on tranquilizers or perhaps, he had programmed himself not to get angry, just as he had once programmed himself not to show pain when Tom Oliver pushed the pressure point on his hand.

Now Murphy asked Allen about his statement to *48 Hours*'s Peter Van Sant that "there is never a good reason to lie."

Oh, Allen wasn't talking about himself. He said that when he was speaking about Jamie Bellush. Someone had sent Van Sant a fax suggesting that Jamie was the killer.

"I had prepared a document—Richard Lubin had asked me to prepare a document—on not just Jamie, but on some other people, on some other theories."

"Including accusing Jamie of doing it."

"Well, I developed that theory, yes."

"But you do think there are times that you should lie?"

"Yes," Allen admitted. "I've lied. I don't think there's any question of that."

" 'The husband owes me $25,000' [from the A-1 tape]. Do you remember that lie?"

"Yes."

"He didn't owe you a dime, did he?"

"No."

"Did he owe your partner or associate or colleague $40,000?"

"No."

Allen admitted he had concocted that story just to find Sheila's address in Florida, making it up as he went along. He had been trying to get the bail bondsman to pull Sheila's bond.

Little by little, Murphy dragged more lies out of Allen. He had lied when he said Daryl was "beaten senseless and bloody"; she had only a scratch on her hand. He lied when he said there were warrants out for Sheila from Hawaii. He lied when he told Kim Hall that Sheila had stolen his kids. He lied when he told a Florida private investigator that he had custody of his children. He lied when he told Matt Hunt of the Chuck Chambers agency that Sheila had taken his daughters illegally. He lied when he told a Sarasota Y counselor that he would get custody of Daryl as soon as Sheila returned to Texas and signed certain papers.

Murphy asked Allen why, if he had been in so much "terror" after Daryl called him, screaming, from the Y shelter, he hadn't called the police. "Of course, you called the Sarasota police?"

"No. I talked to McDermott."

"Well, she wasn't in Bexar County. She was in Sarasota. And you're 'terrified' of what's happening to her."

"I know. McDermott told me *he* was calling the Sarasota police."

"You didn't have any trouble calling all those other people over in Sarasota: CPS, all kinds of people. But you couldn't find the number for the Sarasota police department?"

"I didn't know what to tell them."

"How about your daughter was screaming, you were terrified, she called from the Y shelter, said 'Leave me alone! Stay away from me'?"

"Well, that's why I called McDermott."

"Who was in San Antonio?"

"Yes, but he was on the case. He had a heart that was out to protect Daryl and the other kids—a real heart."

Matt Hunt, the Sarasota PI, had discovered early on that there was no warrant out for Sheila. The police wouldn't arrest her without a warrant. Allen said he'd reassured Hunt that it could sometimes take weeks for warrants to get into the NCIC computers (National Crime Information Center at the FBI in Quantico).

Maureen Blackthorne, usually sitting with Richard Lubin's wife in the second row of the gallery, was annoyed that Brigitte Woosley, the courtroom artist, sat in the only spot where she had room to draw—the end seat. Of late, Maureen had taken that seat, and now her foot kicked out, perhaps involuntarily, and knocked Woosley's container of colored pencils over. She made no effort to help pick them up as Woosley struggled to get them back in order.

John Murphy had done a brilliant job of wiping out Lubin's carefully constructed image of the kind and worried father. Allen's *real* persona had seeped through, although he maintained his composure throughout cross-examination.

Referring to Celia Blanco, the hapless maid/nanny who worked for the Blackthornes, Murphy asked, "You withheld those immigration papers from Celia Blanco, didn't you?"

"No. I could care less," Allen said, almost bored.

"You threw her out in the street with the sprinkler going—chook, chook, chook—didn't you?"

"If you knew our house, and you looked at where our sprinklers are—" Allen began.

"*Did* you throw her out or did you not throw her out of your house?"

"Yes."

"Including all the bag and baggage, TV, anything else that belonged to her?"

"Everything out. Outside the door on the driveway. She called a cab. They came and took her away. There was no sprinkler. The fact is our driveway is real wide, and our sprinklers don't cover our driveway. We have a *huge* driveway."

"And you withheld from Virginia the title to her car, didn't you?"

"I don't know— I've heard that, yes."

"She sent the last check and you didn't cash it and you never sent her the title?"

"I've heard that," Allen said again, as if he were somehow disconnected from his own actions.

"And that's all about control, isn't it?"

"All about *control?*" Allen sounded mystified.

"Control," Murphy repeated. "Controlling other people."

"I don't understand how that's about controlling someone." Allen seemed genuinely confused, as if Murphy were speaking another language.

"Like throwing out the illegal maid and threatening to call immigration. That's sort of a control thing, too, isn't it?"

"*I* didn't do that."

Suddenly Allen wasn't sure he knew that Daryl was in a wilderness camp. In a non sequitur, he repeated that he tried, always to avoid being "the focus." To assure that, he had other people handle tasks needed to reach his goals.

"Because every time you're the focus, you lose, don't you?" Murphy asked.

"I do, yes."

"And you were tired of losing to Sheila?"

"There was nothing more to lose," Allen insisted.

" 'That bitch thinks she can outsmart me, but I'm going to hire an investigator and find her.' Didn't you say that?"

"No, I didn't."

"But you *did* hire an investigator to find her, didn't you?"

"I did."

"You sat up there and you said you're not sure to this day if you didn't make a mistake. Is that right?"

"Yes."

"And your mistake was getting involved with someone as stupid as José Luis Del Toro—who will go over and put his fingerprint on the dryer while he is killing a woman in her own home. That was a mistake, wasn't it?"

"I wasn't involved with *anything* with José Luis Del Toro, *nothing.*"

"Well, Danny Rocha got Sammy Gonzales to get Joey Del Toro to go kill Sheila, and Danny Rocha never lost a single thing to Sheila, did he?"

"No—I don't believe they knew each other."

"*You're* the only one who ever lost to Sheila, aren't you?"

"Yes."

"And you got her address from your daughter by telling her that you wanted to visit her at Christmas. Is that right?"

"No, I got the address by just asking her. I told her that I was going to try to visit her by Christmas."

" '*Try?*' Christmas is very important to an eleven- or twelve-year-old, isn't it?"

"Definitely."

"And she wasn't telling you the address because her mother didn't want you to know, so you had to manipulate her, right?"

"That's not true. I told her I would even try to visit her *before*

Christmas. I told her we would see, that I was thinking about moving down to South Florida and I wouldn't be that far away—just a couple of hours away."

"You didn't visit her at Christmas, did you?"

"No, I didn't."

"You didn't visit her any Christmas since then, did you?"

"No."

"The next time you saw her was in that witness box, wasn't it?"

"It was."

"And when was the last time you saw Stevie before she testified?"

"Father's Day of 1997."

"When was the last time you called Stevie?"

"The Thursday following Father's Day, the twenty-sixth or twenty-seventh."

Three years ago.

"And you cared [so much] about those children that after their mother was murdered, you never did a thing for them, did you?" Murphy pressed.

"I haven't, no."

"And you cared [so much] about those children that you let your ego and your arrogance and your hatred for Sheila cause you to have her butchered, and you left those children without a mother or a legal father, didn't you?"

"I would *never* do that," Allen said. "There was no reason, and I would not do that. I did not do that. I had nothing to do with this."

"Nothing further, Your Honor."

MONDAY was another very long day in Judge Prado's courtroom, but still no one budged from the gallery seats. At 5:22 that Monday afternoon, Richard Lubin moved to patch up some of the grievous damage done during John Murphy's cross-examination. He elicited testimony from Allen that made him seem, perhaps, not as selfish about money. Allen said that when he had his child support reduced to $350 a month, he was only making $4000 a year. The jury didn't know that he was driving a brand-new Cadillac Alanti convertible at the time. Had they known, they would have had difficulty making the figures add up.

In an attempt to throw suspicion on Jamie Bellush, Lubin asked Allen to comment on the police reports he had reviewed.

"Was there information about life insurance?"

"Yes."

"Was there information about why the children were in life jackets?"

"Yes," Allen said. "And it even went beyond that. I was, 'How did the kids get life vests on when Jacob Mast saw Del Toro walking at nine fifteen a.m., and Fannie Mae Miller—the next-door neighbor—saw Sheila back up [the van] at nine thirty?' Jamie said he saw Sheila and the quads [go by]. Sheila comes home at nine thirty; Del Toro at nine-fifteen has entered the house—"

"Okay," Lubin interrupted, "I don't want to make a big issue of it." It was perilous to give Allen his head, because he tended to get himself in far too deep. Lubin wanted Allen to point his finger at Jamie as a suspect, but he didn't want him to go further.

"But we were just trying to figure out who did this at the time, weren't we?" Lubin asked pointedly.

"It wasn't just Jamie. It was all the pieces. It was just why did the kids have life vests on—naked, wearing life vests? Why did this . . . why did that [happen]? We've been trying to figure out lots of different things."

"But the [state's] implication was that somehow you were trying to blame [Jamie], rather than just investigate who did this thing?"

"Correct."

"Because we knew who *didn't* do it, didn't we?"

"Yes. *Absolutely.*"

"And who was that?"

"Me. I had nothing to do with it."

"I have no further questions, Your Honor."

REPORTERS and observers wandered out of the courthouse, bleary-eyed with callused, ink-stained fingers. The sun was still bright enough to hurt their eyes, and they realized it was still daylight. For the first time, many of them wondered if Allen might be acquitted. Murphy had forced him to admit lie after lie, but his bearing had remained so calm. He hadn't exploded into angry fragments after all. Everyone had expected that if he was foolish enough to testify, Allen Blackthorne's façade would have splintered and fallen away like the dried clay on a face mask.

Medication? Rehearsal? Or because he spoke the truth?

"Naw," a veteran male reporter scoffed. "He was so tranquilized he was right next door to a zombie."

_____*Chapter Fifty-one* _____

THE LIST OF DEFENSE WITNESSES was proving to be very short. Richard Lubin and Kurt Volker had started their case on Monday, June 26, and the last witness was called on Tuesday. It was Maureen Blackthorne, her husband's constant support, who followed him to the witness stand. She sent Allen an affectionate look as she prepared to be sworn in. She wore a navy-blue suit with a short skirt, like all of her skirts. Richard Lubin led her through her early life and her engagement and marriage to Allen, the birth of their sons, now four and a half and two and a half. He asked her to discuss her relationship with Stevie and Daryl.

"Stevie and I butted heads quite a few times."

But outside of that and Allen's penchant for gambling, their home had been very happy, Maureen said. Allen was a "great father."

"Now, when you first met Allen," Lubin asked, "did he need some training?"

"Absolutely." Maureen explained that Allen was allowed to play golf five days a week, but he needed to be home for dinner between 6:30 and 7:00 and on weekends.

Asked about her relationship with Daryl, Maureen instantly teared up, her voice choking. "It was very close."

"Did Daryl have a relationship with Brandon?"

"Brother and sister—"

"Are you okay for me to go on?" Lubin asked solicitously. And Maureen nodded her head, fighting for composure.

Asked about Danny Rocha, Maureen said she knew him. He and Allen played golf together, of course, and he had brought his little boys over to swim in the Blackthorne pool. "I made them ham sandwiches, but they wouldn't eat them with mayonnaise on them, and they wanted the crusts cut off."

She said that Rocha often came to their home when Allen wasn't there. "He would use the copier and hang around the office, talk to Virginia, use the phone at the office."

"Would you quarrel with Virginia's testimony that there were several occasions where he was in the office by himself?"

"That's correct."

No, Maureen had never had occasion to talk to Rocha about Sheila or the custody of the girls.

"Ever?" Lubin pressed.

"No, sir."

"Ever? Ever? Ever?"

"Ever, ever, ever. No, sir."

As she responded to Lubin's questions, Maureen's flat affect, her tone, her phrasing, was almost exactly like Allen's. She was an echo, except that she stuck to single-word answers and didn't wander off into long statements as Allen had. She broke into tears on cue, just as Allen had. Every time Daryl was brought up, she cried, blaming her sentimentality on "being a mom myself."

Maureen continually denied knowing anything about a plot and said she knew nothing about the term Black Cow. Yes, she had made numerous calls to wilderness camps in Florida, desperately trying to find Daryl. "I was frightened for her."

"Was there something about her voice that made you feel that way?" Lubin asked.

"Yes."

"And I don't want to go on and on ad nauseam with the same questions, but were you looking for her to track her mother down so you could have her killed?"

"No, sir."

"Or scared or threatened?"

"No, no."

"Intimidated?"

"No."

IN cross-examination, John Murphy asked Maureen probing questions about Allen's honesty, but she stonewalled him. One got the feeling that someone could have put sharpened bamboo under her fingernails and she still wouldn't say anything even vaguely incriminating about her husband.

"But Mr. Blackthorne didn't have any hatred or animosity for Mrs. Bellush—for Sheila, did he?" Murphy asked.

"He didn't like her," Maureen said.

"He especially didn't like her after you went and met her at the Water Street oyster bar, did he?"

Maureen would not give a straightforward answer. She denied that she had ever been worried about Allen's background, but admitted that her mother had hired a private investigator to explore his life before Maureen. That now made three versions of the PI story: her brother-in-law hired a private investigator, her mother hired one, and Maureen herself had hired one.

Lubin was on his feet. He didn't want any information about

Allen's background to come out, and he didn't want the jury to know what Sheila had warned Maureen about. He was obviously afraid that, just when he was on his last witness, a whole can of worms might be opened up.

Out of the jury's hearing, Murphy tried to persuade the judge to allow the PI's report—obtained by Maureen's own family in 1992—in. "The private investigator's report showed that he had bad debts," Murphy said. "And that he had been allegedly involved in sexual abuse, that he had been allegedly involved in abusing Sheila. I don't intend to get into the merits of it, but Sheila shared that [with Maureen] and *she* reported it to Allen. I'm sure that made Allen angry."

Judge Prado balanced one set of objections against the other. He overruled Lubin's and Botsford's objections, and allowed Murphy to continue cross-examining Maureen. Once more, she resolutely protected Allen, saying that he didn't get angry at all about Sheila's warnings.

"She said some pretty ugly things about him, didn't she?" Murphy asked.

"She said some things, yes," Maureen answered.

"Pretty *ugly* things, didn't she?" he persisted.

"Yes."

Maureen didn't attempt to deny the numerous phone calls she—or Allen—made to Florida. They were simply trying to find Daryl and be sure she was okay.

"You had had no interest in where *Sheila* was?"

"At that point, I was trying to locate Daryl."

"Later, I guess, the focus changed to Sheila rather than Daryl?"

"Well, there was a private investigator hired to do a 'locate' on Sheila, that's correct."

"That was done after the sixth?"

"That's correct."

"Okay. There was a call to Florida Power Corporation in St. Petersburg, Florida. Did you think that Daryl had subscribed to have power and light?"

"I would think not."

It was obvious that both the witness and Allen had spent the major part of September and twelve days in October looking for Sheila's address. Once they got it from Daryl on October 11, there was no need to call any longer. Whether Maureen knew why Allen was so anxious to pinpoint Sheila's location was debatable.

Murphy asked Maureen why she wasn't upset that Allen would share his birthday gift from her—the golf trip to Oregon—with

Danny Rocha, the man who had won $30,000 from him in one day.

"The thing that upset me was his gambling," Maureen answered. "It wasn't necessarily who he was doing it with."

She had no idea who paid Rocha's way. "I don't know," she said. "I'm sure it was paid from the bank account."

Maureen's entire testimony seemed designed to give Allen's credence, but she was so stingy with her answers and so resistant to Murphy that it was hard to believe she was totally in the dark about what Allen might or might not have done to Sheila. She was obviously a very strong personality, the first woman to have "trained" Allen, but she remembered so little.

She denied throwing Celia Blanco out of her house. She *had* held off on sending Virginia L'Heureux the title to the car she'd paid for because she was "advised" not to. She was not happy that Virginia had been let go by Allen. Maureen said she was "in and out" of the office during Allen's call to A-1 Bail Bonds, but she didn't know what had been said. She really didn't know who had called all the motels on the way to Florida on September 19.

"Was anybody else at home at that time, five twenty-two a.m.?"

"I would think everybody would be sleeping."

"Virginia wasn't there?"

"No, I don't believe so."

"Celia wasn't using the phone?"

"I believe not."

"So this was either you or Mr. Blackthorne?"

"I would be speculating, Mr. Murphy."

"Well, was it *Jacob*?" he asked, mentioning her baby son.

"Mr. Murphy," she said, looking down her nose, "I don't want to speculate."

As Murphy's cross-examination wound down, he recalled how concerned Maureen and Allen had been about his daughters. They had called numerous people in Florida, hired a private investigator there, called Deputy McDermott, had the Adays spying on Sheila. "What do you do when you find out their mother has been killed?" Murphy asked.

Maureen said that there were some "unfacts—or untruths" in his statements. He repeated them and added that their concern was so profound that they had even visited with Daryl at the Adays against Sheila's wishes.

"That's correct."

"And you're so concerned about them, what did you do about the girls the night of November seventh, 1997?"

"There was no way for us to be in contact with them on November seventh. We hired Roy Barrera the following day."

"To help you get in touch with the girls?"

"No, sir. He advised us not to communicate."

"*Both* of you? He advised both of you?"

"That's correct, yes."

Murphy asked Maureen why she hadn't gone through Ken Nunley, Sheila's attorney, to send some kind of message of condolence to Stevie and Daryl. "Or even some support for those girls?"

"Like I said, we had been advised that until the time is right not to do that."

"You have done absolutely nothing to help those girls from the time their mother was murdered, have you?"

"We have been advised not to do anything until after all of this is over, Mr. Murphy."

"Have you asked your lawyers to get ahold of them?"

"Yes. Roy Barrera."

"Have you given him any kind of funds to forward to them?"

"No, sir."

"Did you give him any kind of letter or card or sympathy card or *anything* to send to those girls?"

"No, sir."

"You've done nothing for those girls about whom you were so concerned, have you?"

"Like I said, with the advice of the attorneys we have done nothing. That's correct."

"Pass the witness," Murphy said, turning away in disgust.

With a few more questions from Richard Lubin, which failed to remove the sense that neither Maureen nor Allen gave Stevie or Daryl a thought after their mother's murder, witness testimony was over. There was no way of knowing what the jurors thought.

IT was 2:44 P.M. on Thursday, June 29, and not only was Judge Prado's courtroom packed, the overflow courtroom was full, too, with at least two hundred people anxious to hear final arguments. Each side had ninety minutes to present its summing-up of a case that had taken thirty-one months of investigation and more than three weeks of trial. The defense would have preferred to start all over again; Allen's lawyers had filed for mistrial several times, the latest instance only that morning when he was upset because he thought two jurors caught a glimpse of him in handcuffs. Judge Prado denied all those motions.

The jurors had heard more than fifty witnesses, many of them with dramatic and heartbreaking testimony. And yet, like all juries, they were inscrutable. Studying their faces, no one could detect which way they were leaning.

Richard Durbin rose to begin the state's closing arguments. Durbin's somewhat laid-back manner and soft brown eyes made him seem, initially, not as threatening to the defense as the more mercurial Murphy. That notion vanished as Durbin did a brilliant job of summing up the myriad facts in the case, laying out the key questions the jurors had to consider: "Was Allen Blackthorne a member of the conspiracy and was he a prime mover behind the crimes against Sheila?" And "Was Allen Blackthorne the man who *intentionally* orchestrated the murder of Sheila Blackthorne, or was he only a bystander?"

Durbin explained that the origin of the crimes lay in the turbulence of a terrible marriage that lasted three years, while the divorce lasted "ten years." Throughout his chronology of the events that led inexorably to Sheila's murder, the tall prosecutor used the defendant's own mantra, "*He didn't hate Sheila; he just hated the things she did.*"

Citing the court battles, the "ugly allegations" that always deterred Allen from pushing Sheila too far, Durbin said, "He could still wreak havoc in the Bellush household."

In September 1997, when Sheila and Jamie escaped to Florida, Allen still didn't hate Sheila, Durbin said sarcastically, "he just hated the thing she did."

And so "the hunt for Sheila is on. 'That bitch thinks she can outsmart me. I know she's gone to Florida and I'm going to find her.' He was a man lashing out. He's going to do whatever he can to Sheila:

"She was arrested and got out on bond."

"She was put in jail."

"She was put on probation."

"The press reported embarrassing stories."

"Her husband was humiliated before his employers."

"He was going to embarrass her before her new neighbors."

"And when none of those panned out, he had her killed."

Durbin attacked the defense position that Danny Rocha acted on his own. "[They say] he's a hustler, and he set out to hustle Allen Blackthorne by doing him the service of killing his ex-wife. Danny would either curry favor or extort Allen. Maybe he'd even prevent him from moving to Florida, and taking away Danny's main source of income."

But Durbin pointed out the almost endless flaws in this theory. "Danny, Sammy, and Joey Del Toro are idiots, but this would be the *dumbest* extortion scheme in history. Danny's a gambler, but he's not a risk-taker. He only took bets when the odds were in his favor. There was no defined payoff.

"In order for Danny to carry out the execution of Sheila Bellush, he had to know certain things, some of which he could not possibly have known without Allen:

"That Allen hated his ex-wife enough to want her dead."

"He had to know where she was."

"He had to know she lived in Boerne, the address there, and the directions to get there."

"He had to know that Sheila's photos were in the blue box in Allen's office, and be able to recognize Sheila in those photos."

"He had to know she was represented by Ken Nunley, and that she would be in court on September 15."

"He had to know where Nunley's office was."

"He had to know she had moved to Sarasota and that she was leaving for Florida right after her hearing."

"He had to be able to find out Sheila's address in Sarasota, without Allen's knowing about it—and know there was a strip mall near the house."

"He had to know that Daryl was in a youth shelter and then the hospital in Florida."

"How would he know that without Allen's telling him?" Durbin pointed out that Allen had the strongest motivation to lie. He had lied to the A-1 employee, to Kim Hall, to the Florida PI operatives, to Daryl, and about Jamie. "Even his *name* is a lie. Picked out of *Shogun.*"

Moreover, Durbin said, for Allen to be right, any number of other people had to be liars: Mike McGraw, Stevie, Daryl, Sheila, Kerry, Virginia, Celia, Danny, Jamie. "How is it that all these people managed to get together and lie at the same time? No—the liars in this case are Allen Blackthorne and Maureen Blackthorne. They've got more motive to do so than anyone else you've heard from."

"Allen Blackthorne *hated* Sheila Bellush," Durbin said. "He hated her when they were married. Over the years, his hatred became murderous."

Quotes flashed across the big screen opposite the jurors.

"Sheila would never leave because he [Allen Blackthorne] would take the children or kill her": Kerry Bladorn, Christmas, 1985.

"He's also threatened to have me killed. He's told me he would— he would kill me or have somebody do it, that he was in a position that he could have it taken care of": Sheila Blackthorne, October 15, 1987.

"And he repeated his threats to me. He said, 'You know what I've told you before?' and I said, 'About having me taken care of?' And he said, 'That's right.' And he goes, 'I'll make sure you never walk again, your face is maimed,' and he told me he was in position to have somebody else do it": Sheila Blackthorne, October 15, 1987.

"We would have conversations about her, and he would tell me that he hated her and that my mom lied about him and made up lies about him and got people to lie about him in court, and he wouldn't care if she was killed. He wanted her dead": Stevie Bellush's testimony.

And finally, *"Blackthorne said, 'Sue [Tuffiash] pissed me off and she got what she deserved. Don't ever piss me off because the same thing will happen to you' ": Kerry Bladorn, Easter 1990.*

"In 1997 Sheila Bellush did," Durbin ended quietly. "And in 1997 he did."

As Richard Durbin finished, Gene Smith put her hand over her eyes, Jamie Bellush stared straight ahead, and Daryl nervously twisted a yellow ball of Silly Putty in her fingers.

RICHARD Lubin's closing arguments were all about Danny Rocha's "psychopathic lying" and Allen's lack of motive. Without Rocha's "sinister spin," Lubin argued, all of the government's so-called evidence had an innocent explanation. Everything Allen had done was because he loved his daughters, not because he held any hatred in his heart for Sheila. Allen had no motive whatsoever, Lubin said, to harm Sheila. He had given up his parental rights.

"He owed no child support. Nor did he have a chance to regain custody if Sheila Bellush died. And the hatred? We've talked about it. It just wasn't there."

Ahhh, but Danny. "Danny Rocha is a pathological liar. His entire life is a hustle, a scam, a scheme. He's in a class of his own. The prosecution called him early so the jury would forget about him. It took him *three years* of manipulating to pull it off."

Condemning Danny Rocha seemed the defense's only hope of an acquittal. Danny most assuredly *was* a liar. He had admitted it himself several times. And it was Danny who sent a cokehead down to Florida to kill Sheila. Allen was the innocent victim who had no knowledge whatsoever of the conspiracy. "Allen had nothing to do with it," Lubin said fervently, "and the prosecution hasn't proved that he did. There is not one shred of evidence that Allen was involved."

Veteran court watchers knew that Lubin was reaching when he turned to patriotism, home, and family, and to complimenting the jurors. "The case isn't proven. We demand more in America! Smoke isn't enough. You said you could look him in the eye and presume him innocent. Think of the answers to what Mr. Murphy will say—because Allen Blackthorne is innocent! I've had Allen and Maureen and the family in my hands for two years now. Now I have to turn them over to you. Return the only just verdict: Not guilty on counts one and two."

At 5:36 P.M. John Murphy rose for the final, final argument. "Everybody lied but the defendant," he said sardonically. "Mr. Lubin's eloquent. I enjoyed listening to him. Yes, Danny Rocha lied and manipulated. He didn't want a life sentence—just like *that* man." He pointed to Allen, who refused to look up. "*That* man has manipulated the system from at least 1987. Life without parole *is* life without parole. What possible motivation does Danny Rocha have to fabricate now? *That* man has the eyes of a sociopath, and has the motivation to lie. Allen Blackthorne is the *only* person with a motive. The others' motivation was money, and the money came from *him*."

Murphy's outrage was genuine as he described Allen's "anger, arrogance, and manipulation. How many times did he go to court to mess with Sheila? This case is about hate. He used his children to get to her," Murphy said, his Irish complexion scarlet with fury.

The state was running out of time, and Judge Prado called out the minutes left to John Murphy, who pulled out photographs. He didn't show them to the jury. Instead, he spoke of Sheila's babies, covered with their mother's blood, waiting through what must have been an endless seven hours with her corpse for someone to come and find them. He addressed Allen. "If there's any justice, the fact that you lived in this house and have resources to get what you want. You threw your girls away."

"He could have sent a card to the church," Murphy told the court. "He never gave a damn about his lawyer's advice before. He didn't care about those girls. He hasn't sent them a dime, a card, or a call. He's abandoned them. He butchered their mother. The woman is dead, and he's still trashing her two and a half years after he had her butchered!"

And suddenly it was over.

Depending on the verdicts, in a few days Allen Blackthorne would either be home enjoying life with his family and playing golf— or in prison for the rest of his life.

_____Chapter Fifty-two_____

THE FEW SPECTATORS and reporters who lingered at the court-house in the hope that there would be a quick verdict were be disap-pointed. The jurors only deliberated long enough on Thursday evening to select a foreman: Brian D. Henry, a lanky retired rodeo clown. But on Friday morning there was optimism that a verdict *would* come in by the end of the day. The Fourth of July weekend was upon them. Some who sided with the defendant predicted gloomily that the jurors would probably hurry with their deliberations so they could enjoy the holiday.

The courtroom was locked now, and all the available chairs along the circular corridor on the third floor were filled with Sheila's family, reporters, investigators, and bystanders. Maureen, with her entourage, Pat Aday and Wendy Cruz, camped out on the first floor. Gene Smith and AP reporter Loydean Thomas rode the elevator down to the first floor once, and the door opened to reveal Maureen and Pat Aday. Gene said, "Come on in, ladies—I won't hurt you," but they stepped back and waited for another elevator.

Judge Prado gave the reporters a break when he told them they could use their cell phones *inside* the courthouse, and the hallway was soon alive with a cacophony of rings.

When the jurors went out to lunch, those who waited for their decision sighed with frustration. The air was electric with expectancy, especially when the jurors sent out a note with a question at 4:15: "We would like a statement made by Virginia, the secretary, about the address on the videotape. Who did the address belong to as said by the secretary?"

That might mean points for the defense, which claimed that Danny Rocha had found Sheila by reading her address off the video-tapes in Allen's office.

When the jurors sent out another note at 5:50 P.M., it seemed that surely they must have only a small point to straighten out before they had a verdict.

At 7:00 P.M. they adjourned and the people waiting straggled out. The jurors were back on Monday, and it didn't seem to matter to them that the Fourth of July was on Tuesday. It looked now as if it might be a long haul. As the days passed, they sent out a total of ten notes asking about the law and the evidence.

Judge Prado, unlike more austere jurists, stopped to talk with the media, who waited restlessly like greyhounds at the start of a race. Alternately teasing them gently and settling them down, Prado said the jurors were working "really hard," viewing photographs and studying evidence lists. The verdict would come when it came, and there was no hurrying it for the daily deadlines.

Maureen Blackthorne, book-ended by Pat Aday and Wendy Cruz, looked worried. Just as she came back from lunch on Monday, a bird flew into the windowed front of the courthouse and dropped like a stone, brushing her as it fell to earth. She was shaken, but her two friends told her that was a *good* omen. Perhaps.

KERRY Bladorn agonized over a decision she had never expected to face. Joey Del Toro, the last domino in the chain-reaction conspiracy, was scheduled to go on trial in Sarasota within a day or two. In her heart, she had promised Sheila she would be there, but she had also promised herself she would be in the courtroom when Allen Blackthorne was convicted, something she believed devoutly would happen. If she waited out the jurors in San Antonio, she would miss opening arguments in Del Toro's trial, but if she went to Florida, she risked the denouement of Allen's. After so long, it began to look as though the interweaving of all the strands of murder might come together in the same week.

There were rumors among law enforcement that Joey Del Toro was going to plead guilty to avoid a trial. Made aware of that, Kerry flew to Sarasota, while Gene Smith stayed in San Antonio. Jamie Bellush opted for Sarasota too. Whatever happened, someone from Sheila's family would be there.

Allen had expected to be home for the Fourth of July and undoubtedly on the golf course. Instead, he spent the day in his cell.

On Wednesday, July 5, the jurors failed to reach a verdict. The defense is always jubilant about extended jury deliberation; the sooner they come back, the more likely a conviction. The longer a jury takes, the more likely an acquittal or a mistrial. But Maureen commented that she wasn't getting her hopes up.

And then, on Thursday, July 6, it all came tumbling down, beginning in Sarasota, Florida. Joey Del Toro was ready to plead guilty to first-degree murder, fully aware that he faced a mandatory life sentence. As jurors continued to deliberate in San Antonio, Joey stood before Circuit Court Judge Paul Logan. In his blue shirt and khaki pants, he looked like a clean-cut young college student, his system long clear of the cocaine that helped drive him to a horrific act in 1997. Twenty members of his family had traveled from Texas to support him. This was not how they expected "our Joey" to end up.

After Joey's guilty plea, Jamie Bellush rose to face him. He held some 8" x 10" photographs in his hands; they were graphic and bloody closeups of Sheila's dead face and body, and he demanded that Del Toro look at what he had done to her. Then he turned toward Joey's family. "I'd like to show them to your family," Jamie shouted. "Does your family realize that when you stabbed her, the blade of the knife bent on her spinal column? Mr. Del Toro, you're a worthless coward. Cowards like you attack defenseless women who weigh 107 pounds. Cowards run from their crimes—like you did—like a scared child. It's unfortunate that I could not stand and watch you take your last breath with a needle in your arm."

Joey looked back at the husband of the woman he killed and spoke softly. "I do deserve to die," he said. He explained that he had found God's mercy in prison, and he apologized to Jamie Bellush and Kerry Bladorn. He spoke for thirty-five minutes, before breaking into a hymn. It was a bizarre a cappella performance and Jamie watched him, stony-faced.

Kerry Bladorn wanted to believe that Joey was sincere in his repentance. "I believe in the death penalty, Mr. Del Toro," she said. "But for some reason God chose to keep you on this earth."

"Sheila would have forgiven him," she said months later, "so I will try to believe that he means it when he says he believes in God."

Joey commented on Allen Blackthorne, a man he had never actually met. He said that even if Blackthorne should be acquitted, he would never find peace. "That man will always be in prison, whether inside or out. Anger, hate, resentment, unforgiveness put you in a prison you can't break. Only God can break it."

Outside the courtroom, Jamie told reporters he wasn't impressed by Joey's impassioned pleas for forgiveness. "It didn't change the fact that he killed my wife," he said.

While Jamie and Kerry prepared to fly back to San Antonio, the jurors there ended their thirty-three hours of deliberation at 11:29 A.M. It had all come to fruition on this Thursday, July 6. Word that there was a verdict raced around the courthouse like a prairie fire, and Judge Prado's courtroom filled up rapidly.

How odd that Del Toro and Blackthorne should be facing a sentencing judge within a few hours of one another. Joey knew he was going to prison for life, but Allen fully expected to be going home.

John Murphy reached out to clasp Gene Smith's hand. Richard Lubin watched him from across the room with his hands on his hips, his posture tense. And then he leaned over to grab Maureen Blackthorne's hand in an unconscious imitation of Murphy. "Whatever it is," he said tautly, "we'll keep fighting."

AT 12:15 P.M. Allen walked into the courtroom. He wore a blue blazer and khaki slacks, an outfit that he might have worn to have lunch at the Oak Hills Country Club. He smiled at Maureen and shook Richard Lubin's hand before he sat down. Maureen's mother bent her head in prayer in the front row of the gallery. Maureen herself fought to keep her chin from quivering as Lubin gave Allen a few perfunctory pats on the back.

Allen stood to face Edward Prado as the judge ripped open the envelope containing the verdict. It seemed for a moment that there was no air at all in the courtroom, and then Edward Prado read, "We, the jury, find the defendant, Allen Blackthorne, *guilty* as charged, on count one."

Allen stared straight ahead, his jaw set. Without changing expression, Gary De Los Santos inched his booted foot over to tap Michael Appleby's. It was a silent "Hooray!"

"We, the jury," Prado continued, "find the defendant, Allen Blackthorne, guilty as charged on count two."

"It's okay," Lubin whispered to Allen, who turned to repeat the same phrase to Maureen. Then he hugged his attorneys and shook their hands before the U.S. marshals hurried him out of the courtroom. Maureen broke into sobs as Lubin held her.

And although she didn't yet know about Joey Del Toro's hymn singing in a Sarasota courtroom only a few hours earlier, Gene Smith exited the courtroom and the courthouse saying "Thank you, Lord," and suddenly singing the Lord's Prayer in a high, pure voice. "I don't know why I did that," she said later. "I hadn't planned on it, and I haven't sung in years."

Interviewed after the verdict, the jurors said it had not been easy, and they had discussed everyone's reservations and questions. There was no one piece of evidence or one witness's testimony that convinced them. They were a diverse group. "There were logistics people, analytical people, salespeople, and creative people," juror Jesús De Hoyos said. "We even had a hard time agreeing on where to go for lunch."

Judge Prado had not wanted them to take notes; he wanted them to listen to the evidence and testimony, and they had. "What [Blackthorne] said and his actions were two different things," De Hoyos said. "Those were terrible threats [to Sheila]. When you look at the whole picture, you have to think that intent was much more than a simple beating."

De Hoyos credited foreman Brian Henry with the best summation of their decision. "He said that there are some pieces of the puzzle missing, but there is enough that the puzzle is together, and there is no reasonable doubt."

_____Chapter Fifty-three_____

ALLEN'S SENTENCING was set for November. In the meantime, he was being held in the Wackenhut detention center, the privately run jail in San Antonio. He had every intention of winning a new trial on appeal. And, unknown to his guards, he was still playing by his own rules. When the guards did an unscheduled check of the jail, they found contraband in Allen's cell. A cache of several cartons of cigarettes—with each cigarette worth two dollars in jail—was discovered near his bunk. Somehow he had managed to have them smuggled in, along with a cell phone. The phone had allowed him to work on his appeal, and for all anyone knew, to keep informed about the location of people who had "betrayed" him.

For breaking the rules yet again, Allen was first put in solitary and then transferred out of San Antonio to a jail with tighter security.

A few of the calls Allen made from his secret cell phone may well have been to someone in touch with Danny Rocha. The best guess was that he was calling an attorney working to protect him from a $32 million wrongful-death civil suit filed by Sheila's estate.

In early October, Danny Rocha filed a court document, dated September 22, 2000, saying that his testimony against Allen had all been a lie. He wrote, "In no way did Allen and Maureen know, encourage, help me, or ask me for any harm to happen to Sheila."

But who would believe him now? Danny Rocha had flip-flopped so many times that he had become the boy who cried wolf.

On October 2, Allen's motion for a new trial was rejected. But David Botsford felt that, since Danny had recanted his testimony and admitted to lying, Allen should have a new trial. Not likely.

It was hard to keep up with Danny's stories. FBI special agent Mike Appleby flew to California to interview Danny's mother and stepfather and his wife. Eva had moved there with their three boys. Appleby concluded that Danny had either been promised payment from Allen for recanting his testimony, or that he believed he could get money from Allen that would enable him to help his wife and sons, who were living in desperately poor circumstances. The trouble was that no one believed Danny any longer.

One of the conditions of Joey Del Toro's being allowed to plead guilty was that he would talk with Sarasota investigators and with Charlie Roberts, the Florida state attorney, and tell them what really happened in those terrible hours in the little white-and-yellow house on Markridge Road. He kept his promise, although he said he could not bring himself to speak of the moments when Sheila died; he would go up to that point and continue after it.

In the videotaping of that interview, Joey sat in one corner of the room as Chris Iorio questioned him. Captain Eggleston and Roberts watched and listened. Most of his story they already knew—the conspiracy, Joey's trip to Sarasota to attack a woman he had never met.

While Sheila was gone that morning of November 7, Joey said, he had crawled into the garage of the Bellush home through an unlocked window and stepped from there into the utility room. He had watched Sheila as she came home with the four babies and had been in the house with her for almost two hours, breathing shallowly as he observed her with the quadruplets.

She had no idea he was there, and she went about her morning routine, getting the toddlers ready for their swim by putting on their life jackets.

"I was going to leave," Joey said. "I watched her and saw that she wasn't a bad mother. She was very loving with the kids. I decided not to do it."

But as he turned to go back through the garage to the window, Joey said he either made a noise that alerted Sheila or she glanced toward the utility room and saw him. "We were facing each other—close."

He would not speak of what happened next, only that he had no way to get out of the house and back to his car. It was too easy for the other men in the room to picture the scene in their minds as Sheila turned her head and looked into the eyes of a stranger dressed in camouflage garb.

She has seen him, and now he cannot leave for fear she will call the police and he'll be trapped. He's still high on cocaine, and his mind

*is working ninety miles an hour, but not particularly well. He fires the
.45, using the white towel as a silencer, hitting her in the cheek and
breaking her jaw. But she is still on her feet. He cannot fire again, because the vacuum in the barrel has drawn the towel into it, making the
gun useless. Sheila turns to run toward her babies to protect them, but
he is right behind her. He grabs the knife from the magnetic holder on
the wall and slashes at her as she struggles across the kitchen, her feet
entangled in piles of clothing from the utility room—and probably
with one little boy holding on to her leg. He is doing horrendous damage to her, but a mother's instinct is so strong. Somehow she makes it
to the wall phone and reaches up to the rotary dial. And then she col-
lapses, unconscious. No help comes. No one calls and wonders why
the phone is constantly busy. The house is silent except for the babies,
who try to wake their mother up. . . .*

Even Sheila's killer was completely horrified by what he had
done. But it was too late.

ON November 2 many of those who had watched Allen's trial con-
vened once again in Judge Prado's courtroom for his formal sentencing. Except for the convicted man, everyone looked much the same as
they had in June and July. Allen, however, had visibly shrunk until he
was a cadaverous shadow of his former self. He had lost at least thirty
pounds. His eyes were sunken, shadowed holes, and his cheekbones
were sharply angled beneath yellowish taut skin. He no longer wore
street clothes; his baggy jail scrubs were the bright red of high-security
felony prisoners, and beneath the V-neck he wore what looked like a
white long-johns shirt.

Allen's expression was sullen, and he seemed angry. Rather than
pay much attention to the proceedings, he continually whispered to
one of his attorneys, Jack Pytel, who sat on his right. David Botsford,
suffering from the flu and laryngitis, was Allen's other attorney.
Richard Lubin and Kurt Volker had not come from Florida. They had
signed on, apparently, only for the original defense, and rumor had it
that Maureen was angry with them about their bill for per diem and
hotel expenses. Given the many attorneys on Allen's defense team, the
long hours and consecutive days they had worked in San Antonio,
their reported $80,000-plus tab was not exorbitant. The flat rate for
Allen's defense was rumored to be somewhere between $800,000 and
$1.2 million.

Botsford brought up some relatively minor items, then mentioned the matter of Danny Rocha's letter of recantation. Judge Prado

ruled that Rocha's courtroom testimony struck him as more credible than his letter saying none of it was true.

The state asked that Allen be made to pay for Sheila's funeral expenses and Jamie's child-care expenses during his trial, for the support Rick and Kerry Bladorn were providing for fifteen-year-old Daryl, and for mental health and psychologists' costs for all of Sheila's children. Allen was fighting that. It would be ruled upon later, Judge Prado said.

In the sentencing guidelines, Allen's crimes rated a "45," which meant he would serve two terms of life in prison—to run concurrently—pay the maximum fine, plus $2500 to the Crime Compensation Fund in Tallahassee, Florida, and $4500 to a similar fund in Austin, Texas, $10,600 to Jamie Bellush, and a $250,000 federal fine, all of which he was deemed capable of doing. Although it paled in comparison, there was also a special assessment of $100 on each count, something everyone convicted in the jurisdiction had to do.

There was no suspense. Prado's usually ebullient manner was subdued. He remarked that current statutory law precluded Allen Blackthorne from *ever* being released from prison, but he read probation clauses in case the law ever changed and he should walk the streets of Texas—or any other state.

There had been a score of letters to Judge Prado from people who loved Sheila and urged him to give Allen the maximum sentence in the guidelines. Two of them waited in person to speak. Botsford objected to more than one and said he felt there was really no need for anyone to speak before the sentence was imposed.

But Judge Prado allowed the two who sat nervously in the gallery to speak. Kerry Bladorn was first, even though Botsford said she didn't fall within the parameters of those allowed to speak. He insisted Kerry didn't qualify as a "victim." She was Sheila's *sister;* one wondered what the criteria were.

Kerry was nervous, and her voice was light and reedy as she began. But it was a defining point in her life—and in Sheila's.

"I've waited for the day to say how much Allen has impacted my family's lives," she said. "I cannot describe it in words, but I'll try. I've known Allen for many, many years, and he used to brag greatly about beating the system . . . but sooner or later if you break the rules, your house of cards is going to fall. And that time has come. And I appreciate that that has occurred and that Allen will finally be held accountable. I believe in the death penalty and I realize it will not be sought and I hope that he spends the rest of his life in jail, and comes to an understanding of the torment he has caused."

The second person was Daryl Bellush, Allen's younger daughter. She was fifteen now, a poised young woman wearing a pale blue sweater, her golden hair caught back in a barrette. But there was an edge of steel to her voice as she spoke. Allen, who had based his whole defense on how much he loved her—on how he had made scores of phone calls to find her and protect her from her mother—now made a pretense of ignoring her. He turned to whisper again to Jack Pytel. It was rude and most of all callous: It showed who he really was.

"This will help me come to a closing," Daryl began. "For the past three years, I've wanted to be able to say something that would hurt my dad as much as he has hurt me. Unfortunately, there's nothing I could ever say that would. First of all, I have no idea why you would do something to hurt my mom, but everyone who's been left behind is hurt: Stevie and Frankie and Joey and Timmy and Courtney and Jamie's family, and Rick and Kerry and Kelly and Ryan and Christopher and Patrick . . . and my grandma Gene and grandpa Don. There are so many other people. My dad cares about them as much as I do him—and that's not at all. He must sleep pretty good for messing up so many kids' lives. He's hurt Maureen too. He has a tendency not to care about people. He's hurt Brandon and Jacob now too. He must feel pretty good about that. He doesn't care about anybody but himself."

Daryl reminded her father of all the hate that was now directed toward him. She tried to imagine how her mother might have looked if she were still around. "I can look in the mirror and see her in my face, but I can't see her when she's cheering me on at a game I might be in, or how she'd look when I'm getting good grades—when I graduate from high school, from college, when I get married, when I would have given her a grandchild. Kerry will be there for me, but as much as I love her, my mom's not replaceable. Wherever she is, I hope she's happy.

"I don't consider Allen my dad or anyone I've ever had in my life. When he said he had nothing to do with my mom's murder, his eyes bugged out. That's exactly like mine do when I'm lying. Everyone knows he did it, but no one personally he'll talk to, except maybe Lucifer. I hope he rots in jail and dies there."

Daryl said Allen had given her only one thing, "the gift of hate."

Her biological father—for that was all the description Allen Blackthorne merited—stared into space, his face was totally empty of emotion.

Three muscular U.S. marshals handcuffed Allen and moved him quickly into the back corridors of the courthouse, where a van waited to take him back to jail and, soon, to prison. For ten minutes or so Judge Prado's courtroom resonated with happy voices and laughter. Effie Woods hugged Kerry and Daryl, and Gary De Los Santos, Mike Appleby, Richard Urbanek, Jesse Salazar, and Bill Blagg shook hands with John Murphy, Richard Durbin, and Michael Bernard. Chris Iorio and Ron Albritton grinned and shook hands with the Texans. It wasn't a wonderfully joyous occasion, but those who had worked together for so long seemed hesitant to leave the courtroom. This was the best ending there could be after three years minus five days of gargantuan efforts on the part of dozens of people who wanted to see that Sheila had justice. Slowly the hum of voices faded as the gallery shuffled out of the courtroom into the atrium area. Judge Prado pushed one of his console buttons, and the lights behind them faded to black.

Sheila wasn't in that courtroom, and yet, in a way, she was. She would have been so proud of Daryl, so proud of Kerry.

Afterword

WHENEVER I BEGIN to research a seemingly merciless killer, I am certainly curious about the "how?" of his (or her) crimes, the nuts and bolts of the way the crimes unfolded. But most of all, I am fascinated by the machinations that deftly hide all manner of destructive behavior behind their perfect masks. _Why_ do some human beings mature without conscience or empathy? Is there something genetically flawed in their makeup from the moment of conception? Could abuse in their early years have warped their personalities? Or is there actually some physiological "miswiring" in the brain that renders them unable to care about anyone beyond themselves? These questions are still impossible to answer definitively, just as they were when I began writing about true crime thirty years ago.

Of all the aberrant personalities I have written about, Allen Van Houte is perhaps the most complex. He was born with patently superior genes. He was brilliant and had the basic good health that allowed him to withstand neglect and abuse that would have killed weaker children. But even though gifted with the same intellect his father and his father's father before him shared, Allen was soon alienated from and competitive with his progenitors. The Van Houte men's tradition was estrangement. Guy Van Houte felt his father never really cared about him, and Allen was shunted aside by Guy even before he was born. His mother, Karen, soon handed Allen over to her parents. His grandmother loved him, but he had no allegiance to her. If ever a child was disconnected emotionally, it was Allen. Many would say he suffered from reactive attachment disorder. Aside from the nurturing he received from his maternal grandparents and his aunt Debbie, Allen was a throwaway child whose welfare usually came last in line behind his mother's and father's needs and wants, seven stepparents and myriad half siblings. He may well have been sexually abused by his grandfather, the traveling preacher. At some point long before he reached puberty, he appears to have trusted no one. Had he been of only average intelligence, his capability to do harm might well have been lessened. But he had almost all of the elements within him to be terribly dangerous.

Allen moved ahead as a single entity, a human being determined to survive despite the cost to anyone else. Everyone was expendable: parents, wives, children, friends. Never hampered by conscience, he rapidly learned to use charm and pitiable stories—which were often lies—to worm his way into people's lives. He was a self-made man in every sense of the term, and he was also a chameleon. He could easily mimic anything he perceived others wanted him to be—so that he could get what he wanted from them.

But so few people ever saw all the myriad facets of Allen Van Houte Blackthorne. While various factions of his relatives referred to each other as grifters, he was, perhaps, the biggest grifter of them all. What seems miraculous is that the poor boy from an isolated Oregon farm could, without any formal education, become wildly successful in business, not once but many times.

ALLEN's half brother Bruce, who had once been enthralled with him, came to see a much different persona when he grew up. "I see Allen as a little boy who was emotionally isolated and developed into a sociopathic personality," Bruce said. "Being in a repressed environment where he was never encouraged about anything he did—and he was smart and gifted—and getting pawned off on the relatives instead of being taken care of at home. And, finally, coming to our house, which would have been a very stimulating environment for him. And then basically being empowered by our family to develop in the direction he wanted, he could have succeeded. But he'd already developed a sociopathic personality, so it was too late."

But Allen wasn't a garden-variety sociopath. In a 1987 evaluation ordered in connection with his divorce from Sheila, a psychologist found him "challenging." It was perhaps an understatement, but the evaluation continued, "The word challenging appears to personify this individual, who may well view life in terms of overcoming obstacles and challenges, even if he has to create them artificially . . ."

Eventually Allen came to a point where he had to be fighting someone to believe that he had, indeed, survived. He was constitutionally unable to accept the fruits of his business successes. He systematically tore down what he had built and alienated friends and lovers. At the same time, he could not bear to lose even the smallest skirmish. His foes were often weaker than he was and his cruelty unbounded. It didn't matter—just as long as he won.

Somewhat surprisingly, Allen's test results did not indicate that he was an antisocial personality (a sociopath). He was far more complicated than that. His responses to standard tests showed that he could control or channel his feelings of aggression when he felt it necessary, and that he probably was often depressed. He did not, however, have more than a token ability to empathize with other people's feelings on any deep level, and he showed narcissistic traits. The world revolved around Allen. It always had. Given the true aspects of his bizarre and barren childhood, that wasn't surprising.

Allen isn't legally or medically insane. And he isn't even a typical antisocial personality, although that diagnosis comes closest to explaining the convoluted workings of his mind. More likely, his psyche is made up of many personality disorders, including borderline personality, narcissistic personality, and histrionic personality. For him to endure his early years, he pieced together a bizarre psyche. But he left out compassion and any sense of guilt.

Allen Blackthorne designed and manufactured himself just as he had modified the electromuscular stimulators that made him a multimillionaire. With his new image, he even created a new name so that he could finally move completely away from the family who he felt betrayed him. Until November 2000, Allen had always been able to slip away behind his façade when his life grew too uncomfortable. As he stood before Judge Prado to hear his life sentences, he must have realized that he could no longer do that.

He had lost. And he was trapped, his every moment controlled by someone else for the rest of his life. The man who had always been able to wear a mask of confidence and superiority stood in red jail scrubs as good as naked before those who had beaten him.

Shrunken as if some virulent cancer was eating him up from the inside out, he was a loser, the one thing he could never stand to be. For all his brilliance, it is quite probable that Allen does not have the insight to realize that it was not his enemies who brought him down. He did it himself when he tossed away his perfect life to pursue one small woman who had walked away from him.

Or possibly Allen was telling the truth when he said to his father in 1989, "You'll go to heaven, but I won't. I've sold my soul to the devil."

BEHIND bars in a federal prison in Beaumont, Texas, Allen Blackthorne continues to fight for a new trial. He has petitioned to be brought to a jail close to San Antonio so he can plan his defense for Jamie Bellush's civil suit against him, but his request has been denied.

Maureen and their two sons still live in the pink mansion on Box Oak, but her fortune is on hold. Although Allen signed his shares in RS Medical over to her, she cannot sell them. They are the one solid asset in the Blackthornes' estate, and a court order has frozen them. Jamie's civil suit for over $30 million against the Blackthornes has been delayed several times. It is currently set for late 2001. Maureen is caught in a vicious circle. Since she cannot sell the RS stock, she apparently cannot pay a lawyer to represent her in the civil suit, and she plans to defend herself. She says it is becoming difficult for her to support her two small sons. However, she is able to employ a Hispanic couple to take care of her estate, and recently she purchased a house for them to live in. Pat Aday and her mother are the only visitors Maureen has—beyond the process servers who periodically pound on her front door in vain and then leave papers tacked to it.

Jamie Bellush still lives in Newton, New Jersey, with Timmy, Joey, Frankie, and Courtney, who are now five years old.

Kerry and Rick Bladorn share their home with Daryl Bellush who is a junior in high school. Daryl hopes to go to medical school and has a straight-A 4.0 grad point average. She visited with Jamie and the quadruplets in the summer of 2000, and the trip washed away much of the bitterness between her and Jamie.

Stevie Bellush, seventeen, however, left Jamie Bellush's house and traveled to Oregon shortly before Christmas 2000. She wanted to be close to Rick and Kerry and is preparing to attend college in Oregon.

Gene and Don Smith are back in their Oregon home after too many years of travels to attend hearings and trials. Gene's health is not good, and it is still very difficult for her to deal with Sheila's murder.

Debbie and Tom Oliver are in business in Salem, Oregon, selling a medically accredited and updated version of the electromuscular stimulator. Of all Allen's relatives, they are the only two who worry about him. "I still love him," Debbie said wistfully, "the Allen I knew once." Nevertheless, Tom is inclined to believe that Allen has secreted millions of dollars in an offshore bank. Tom wonders about a mutual relative of Debbie and Allen and suspects the relative, a stockbroker, is helping Allen shelter the money.

Allen's mother, Karen, in her sixties, scarcely resembles the beautiful and wild young woman Guy Van Houte fell in love with. "She is grotesque now," Tom Oliver says quietly. "Her teeth are all worn down, her legs are locked in position, and she weighs about ninety pounds. She's had several surgeries at the Oregon Health Sciences Hospital, and a lot of dental work." At sixty-three, Karen moved into a nursing home in eastern Oregon, but they wouldn't let her keep her dog there and she left. Now one of her younger sons takes care of her. Karen has aged two decades beyond her years, twisted by arthritis, her self-inflicted injuries, and a hardscrabble life.

As much as she revised her life in her memory, any woman with only two children out of seven who have anything approaching a normal, serene life would have to question herself if, indeed, she could face the answers. Karen describes herself today as "really a pretty good mother."

When Guy Van Houte contacted me in May 2000, he began by saying, "I'm no fan of Allen's." Guy, sixty-four then, lived on the west coast of Florida with his pet poodle. He told me he was suffering from terminal testicular cancer. His sister Carol had died of cancer at the age of sixty-five in 1999. Although he did not appear at Allen's trial, Guy did manage to make one last trip to the Oregon coast to see his sons and to talk with me. He looked shockingly like Allen. Except that Guy's hair was snow-white, they were almost identical. He had Allen's "salesman's" charm and was voluble about his life and the financial ruin that fell upon him after Allen moved out of Hawaii and left him holding the bag. Although he managed to get certification for the electromuscular stimulator, Guy never regained financial stability. He was still struggling to work his way back when he died in May 2001.

Gary De Los Santos passed the Texas Rangers lieutenant's exam and is awaiting reassignment. Still at Company D in San Antonio, he hopes one day to work on a "cold case" squad if funding becomes available through the Texas state legislature.

Chris Iorio was named Deputy of the Year in Sarasota County for his work on solving Sheila's case.

Michael Appleby, Richard Urbanek, and Jesse Salazar are back at work as a team investigating allegations of police-department fraud.

John Murphy, Richard Durbin and Michael Bernard have new cases to prosecute.

Judge Edward Prado, "appointed forever," still presides over his federal courtroom in the John Wood Courthouse.